Czech American
Bibliography

Czech American Bibliography

A Comprehensive Listing with Focus on the US and with Appendices on Czechs in Canada and Latin America

Miloslav Rechcigl, Jr.
SVU Scholar in Residence

Under the Auspices of the Czechoslovak Society of Arts and Sciences (SVU)

2011

AuthorHouse™
1663 Liberty Drive
Bloomington, IN 47403
www.authorhouse.com
Phone: 1-800-839-8640

First published by AuthorHouse 10/07/2011

ISBN: 978-1-4670-2633-8 (sc)
ISBN: 978-1-4670-2632-1 (ebk)

Library of Congress Control Number: 2011916083

Printed in the United States of America

FOREWORD

The Czechoslovak Society of Arts and Sciences (SVU) is proud to introduce *Czech American Bibliography* by Miloslav Rechcígl, Jr. The author requires no introduction. For the last twenty-five years, he authored several titles which serve as a valuable resource to serious students of Czech Americana and he served for many years as President of SVU. This publication is a truly comprehensive bibliography. It is well organized and classified by subject and, above all, it is easy to follow.

Dr. Rechcígl devoted his time to assemble objective information on notable Americans with Czech or Czechoslovak roots and compiled several directories of scholars and cultural figures of Czech descent in America. At numerous meetings of the Society of Arts and Sciences we have been reminded of the contributions people of Czech heritage have made to America and world culture. This meritorious activity will help present and future scholars to develop this area of research and fill in the gaps that still exist.

The relevance of this bibliography is enhanced further by recent plans of the Czech government and Parliament to broaden and expand relations with their countrymen throughout the world.

Karel Raška, Jr.
President
Czechoslovak Society of Arts and Sciences

New Brunswick, NJ
8 August 2011

PREFACE

A few years ago this author published a brief tentative listing of selected English publications relating to Czechs in America. The present publication, which is generally based on this, has been updated and greatly expanded to make it a truly comprehensive bibliography. It also incorporates and updates the relevant publications in the classical Esther Jerabek's bibliography on *Czechs and Slovaks in North America* (1976). Since Silesia was an integral part of the Kingdom of Bohemia, for at least 400 hundred years, until 1742, when it was lost to Prussians, during the reign of the Empress Marie Theresa, the Silesian immigrants from that period have been included with the early immigrants from the Czech Lands.

Although emphasis is on English titles, including books, as well as articles, the relevant titles in Czech language have also been included, particularly in those areas where there is a paucity of English titles. Inasmuch as the now defunct Czech-American periodical *Amerikán, Národní kalendář* is such a splendid source of "Czech Americana," a special effort was made to list many of its articles in the relevant sections of this bibliography. English translations of the Czech titles were normally placed in parentheses. In a few cases, important titles in other languages were also included, as were a few significant websites.

In addition to individual books and articles, a number of relevant chapters from anthologies and other books have also been listed separately, to assure that all important subjects are covered. The criterion for selection was the usefulness for the study of Czech-American immigration and ethnic history and the overall quality of the publication.

To assure maximum utility, the bibliography has been organized and classified into specific sectors by subject. Under most major headings, general surveys are listed first, followed by more specific categories, which have, in turn, been subdivided into subcategories, etc. Individual entries in all sections are arranged chronologically. In cases where a given publication fits in more than one category, or subcategory, it was normally placed where it fitted most. However, in a few instances, when it seemed appropriate, it is listed it several places. It should be noted that under most subject areas separate biographical sections were added, comprising individuals of note in the respective fields. Considering the increased interest among Czech Americans in their ancestors was the basis for also including a separate section on genealogy.

Compared to the US, there is much less information available about Czechs in Canada and in Latin America and, in the latter case the preponderance of the existing publications is in Spanish. Inasmuch as this bibliography encompasses the entire America, the pertinent publications relating to these areas are listed in separate sections as Appendices.

I am indebted to the kindly counsel of a number scholars, who read parts of the bibliography, or the entire manuscript, including Ambassador Petr Kolář, Prof. Jaroslav Pánek, Prof. Vladimír Papoušek, Prof. Ivo Barteček, Dr. Zdeněk Uherek, Dr. Ivan Dubovický, Dr. Milena Secká, Dr. Stanislav Brouček, Dr. Oldřich Tůma, Dr. Zdeněk David, Prof. Clinton Machann and Prof. David Chroust. I would also like to express my appreciation to my wife Eva, who painstakingly proofread it page by page and to Jiří Eichler for his help with the index.

This bibliography is a must for every student and scholar, as well as interested layman of Czech American immigration and cultural history. Apart from providing information on just about every aspect of human endeavor that has bearing on the subject, it is hoped that it will induce serious researchers to do more work in areas that have not been adequately investigated, some information being located only in obscure or inaccessible magazines, while other areas as still in the phase of "terra incognita" or 'statu nascendi.'

CONTENTS

FOREWORD vii

PREFACE ix

Czechs in the United States

I. General Reference Aids 2
- A. Bibliographies 2
- B. Periodicals 3
- C. Archival Materials & Library Holdings 4
- D. Historiography 8
- E. Biographical Compendia 10
- F. Memoirs & Oral Histories 12
- G. Travels through America 17
- H. Czech-American Fiction 23
- I. Dissertations & Theses 26
- J. Directories 28
- K. Dictionaries & Textbooks 30
- L. Handbooks—Manuals—Guides 35
- M. Libraries—Museums—Archives 44

II. History 46
- A. Emigration & its Causes. Emigration Policy 46
- B. The New World 55
- C. Immigration and Settlement 61
- D. Historic Periods 67
- E. Regional & Local Histories 74
- F. Historic Places 91

III. The People ... 92
A. Anthropology ... 92
B. Demography ... 92
C. Language ... 94
D. Folklore ... 98
E. Ethnography ... 101

IV. Religion ... 102
A. General ... 102
B. Roman Catholics ... 103
C. Protestants ... 105
D. Jews ... 109
E. Freethinkers ... 111

V. The Society ... 114
A. Ethnic Identity ... 114
B. Assimilation & Acculturation ... 115
C. Social Organization ... 117
D. Family Organization ... 118
E. Health & Welfare ... 118
F. Women—Feminism ... 119
G. Labor Movement ... 121
H. Character ... 123
I. Attitude, Behavior, Communications ... 124
J. Cooperation ... 125
K. Image among Americans ... 125

VI. Economy ... 126
A. General ... 126
B. Living Conditions ... 127
C. Occupations ... 128
D. Labor ... 128
E. Farming ... 129
F. Commerce & Trade ... 131
G. Industry ... 132
H. Banking & Finance ... 134
I. Corporate Activities ... 135

VII. Public Life 135
A. Politics 135
B. Executive Branch 136
C. Legislative Branch 138
D. Judiciary Branch 139
E. Military 140
F. Community Leadership 144

VIII. Cultural Life 144
A. General 144
B. Education 145
C. Journalism & Publishing 149
D. Literature 153
E. Music 156
F. Visual Art 161
F. Drama and Dance 164
G. Sports 167

IX. Scholarship—Science—Technology 169
A. General 169
B. Humanities 171
C. Social Sciences 173
D. Biological & Medical Sciences 177
E. Physical Sciences 180
F. Engineering 182

X. Organizations 184
A. General Surveys 184
B. Fraternal & Benevolent 184
C. Religious 186
D. Heritage 186
E. Public Affairs and Political 187
F. Cultural—Scholarly—Scientific 188
G. Physical Education 188
H. Charitable & Relief 189

XI. Relations with the Old Homeland 189
A. Czech-US and US-Czech Relations and Contacts 189
B. Czech American Aid 192
C. Contacts & Attitudes of the Homeland to Czech-Americans & vice versa 201

XII. Genealogy 203
A. General References 203
B. Sources of Vital Data 206

Appendix A: Czechs in Canada

I. General References 221
A. Bibliographies 221
B. Biographies 221
C. Periodicals 221
D. Archival Material 222

II. History 222
A. General Surveys 222
B. Early Pioneers 224

III. Society 226

IV. Cultural & Other Contributions 226
A. General 226
B. Individuals 227

V. Organizations 230

Appendix B: Czechs in Latin America

I. General References 233
A. Bibliographies 233
B. Historiography 233
C. Biographies 235
D. Ethnography 235

II. History 235
A. General Surveys 235
B. Bohemian Jesuit Missionaries & Other Early Pioneers 237

III. Specific Countries 241
A. Argentina 241
B. Brazil 243
C. Chile 243
D. Cuba 244
E. Mexico 244
F. Paraguay 244
G. Venezuela 244

IV. Cultural and Other Contributions 245
A. General Surveys 245
B. Individuals 245

V. Organizations 246

VI. Relations with Czechoslovakia 246

Index 247

BIBLIOGRAPHY

Czechs in the United States

I. General Reference Aids

A. Bibliographies

1. Guides to Bibliographies

Rechcigl, Miloslav, Jr., "Czechoslovak American Bibliography: A State of the Art and Guide to Bibliographies," Kosmas 7 (1988), pp. 175-187.

Rechcigl, Miloslav Jr., "A Classified Guide to Bibliographies Relating to Czech, Slovak, and Ruthenian Immigrants in America," Kosmas 7 (1988), pp. 189-212.

2. Selected Bibliographies

Čapek, Thomas, Bohemian (Čech) Bibliography. A Finding List of Writings in English Relating to Bohemia and the Čechs. New York and Chicago: Fleming H. Revel Co., 1918. 256p.

Roucek, Joseph S., "Czechoslovak Bibliography," in: American Slavs: A Bibliography. New York: Bureau of Intercultural Education, 1944, pp. 11-24.

Kratochvíl, Antonín, Bibliografie krásné české literatury vydané v exilu—Únor 1948-Květen 1967, (Bibliography of Czech literature published in exile—February 1948-May 1967).Offprint from Studie Křesťanské akademie v Římě, No. 14 (1960) 24p.

Štědronský, F., "Bibliografický přehled prací k dějinám Čechů a Slováků v USA od počátku devadesátých let 19. století" (Bibliographical survey of publications relating to history of Czechs and Slovaks in US from the beginning of the nineties of the 19th century), in: Začiatky českej a slovenskej emigrácie do USA. Bratislava, Slovenská akadémia vied, 1970, pp. 314-329.

Jerabek, Esther, Czechs and Slovaks in North America: A Bibliography. New York: SVU, 1976. 448p.

Miller, Wayne Charles, "Czech Americans: A Guide to Czech-American Experience," in: A Comprehensive Bibliography for the Study of American Minorities. New York: New York University, 1975, pp. 631-636.

Rechcigl, Miloslav Jr., "Czechs, Slovaks and Ruthenians in the U.S.: A Selective Bibliography," Czechoslovak and Central European Journal 10, No. 1 (Summer 1991), pp. 83-132.

Kovtun, George J., Czech and Slovak History. An American Bibliography, Washington, DC: Library of Congress, 1996. 481p.

Kovtun, George J., "Czechs and Slovaks in the United States and Other Countries," in: Czech and Slovak History, An American Bibliography. Washington, DC: Library of Congress, 1996, pp. 345-367.

Rechcigl, Miloslav, Jr., "Czech Americans: A Selected Bibliography of Publications in English," in: Czech Americans in Transition. Edited by Clinton Machann. Austin, TX: Eakin Press, 1999, pp. 121-128.

Rechcigl, Miloslav, Jr., "Rechcigl's Writings Relating to Czechoslovak America," in: Czechs and Slovaks in America. By Miloslav Rechcigl, Jr. Boulder, CO: East European Monographs, 2005, pp. 307-314.

Rechcigl, Miloslav, Jr., "Publications of the Czechoslovak Society of Arts and Sciences (SVU): Formative Years and Bibliography," Kosmas 20, No. 1 (Fall 2006), pp. 83-102.

Jirásek, Zdeněk. Československá poúnorová emigrace a počátky exilu: Prameny a studie k dějinám československého exilu 1948-1889. Brno: Prius, 1999.

B. Periodicals

Čapek, Tomáš, "Soupis časopisů" (Survey of periodicals), in: Padesát let českého tisku v Americe. New York: Bank of Europe, 1911, pp. 81-186.

Štědronský, František, Zahraniční krajanské noviny, časopisy a kalendáře do roku 1938" (Newspapers, magazines and calendars abroad till 1938). Praha: Národní tiskárna, 1958. 166p.

Duben, Vojtěch, Czech and Slovak Periodicals outside Czechoslovakia as of September 1968. Prepared for the Fourth Congress of the Czechoslovak Society of Arts and Sciences in America, Inc., Georgetown University, Washington, DC, 1968. 28p.

Wynar, Lubomyr R., "Czech Press," in: Guide to the American Ethnic Press: Slavic and East European Newspapers and Periodicals. Kent, OH: Kent State University, 1986.

Jaklová, Alena, "Soupis čechoamerických periodik založených v 19. století" (Listing of Czech American periodicals established in 19th century), in: Čechoamerická periodika 19. století. Brno: Nadace Universitatis Masarykiana, 2006, 335p.

C. Archival Materials & Library Holdings

1. Archival Materials

Hamilton, Kenneth G., "The Resources of the Moravian Church Archives," Pennsylvania History, 27, No. 3 (July 1960).

Dwyer, Joseph D., Immigration History Research Center: Czech and Slovak American Collections. A Brief Description. Minneapolis: University of Minnesota, 1980.

Šisler, Stanislav, "Přehled archivních pramenů k problematice vystěhovalectví z českých zemí v letech 1848-1938 uložených ve Státním ústředním archivu v Praze (Survey of archival sources on emigration from the Czech Lands in the years 1848-1938 in the State Central Archives in Prague), in: Češi v cizině. Praha: Ústav pro etnografii a folkloristiku ČSAV, 1987, No. 2, pp. 281-334.

"Czech American Collection" in: The Immigration History Research Center: A Guide to Collections. Compiled and edited by Suzanna Moody and Joel Wurl. Westport, CT: Greenwood Press, 1991, pp. 53-64.

Hruban, Zdeněk, "Kde se ve Spojených státech nalézají archivní materiály o Češích a Slovácích v zahraničí" (Where in the US can be found archival materials about Czechs and Slovaks abroad). Práce ČSAV-A 1992, No. 4, pp. 214-219.

Babička, Vácslav, Prameny k dějinám zahraničních Čechů a Slováků ve Státním ústředním archivu v Praze: Vybrané dokumenty. Praha: Státní ústřední archiv, 1993. 54p.

Valášek, Hubert, Problematika moravského vystěhovalectví ve fondech Moravského zemského archivu v Brně" (Moravian immigration in the collections of the Moravian Regional Archive in Brno), in: Vystěhovalectví do Ameriky 1850-1914: Sborník příspěvků účastníků symposia v Lichnově 5. června 1999. Lichnov: Obecní úřad Lichnova, 1999, pp. 10-19.

Rechcigl, Miloslav, Jr., Czechoslovak American Archivalia. US-Based Archival Material Relating to Emigrés and Exiles from the Territory of the Former Czechoslovakia and Relevant Holdings Bearing on their Ancestral Land. A Tentative Listing. Rockville, MD: SVU, 2000. 294p.

Muhlena, David, "The NCSML Library Repository of Memoirs: Resource for Scholars," Slovo (Cedar Rapids), 4, No. 2 (Winter 2004), pp. 14-15.

Rechcigl, Miloslav, Jr., "Preserving Czech and Slovak American Archival Material," Kosmas 17, No. 2 (Spring 2004), pp. 95-96.

Czech and Slovak American Archival Materials and their Presentation. Proceedings of the Working Conference, held at the Czech and Slovak Embassies in Washington, DC on November 22-23, 2003. Edited by Miloslav Rechcigl, Jr. Prague: Prague Edition Ltd., 2004. 166p.

Fedor, Helen, "Czech—and Slovak-American Archival Material at the Library of Congress," in: Czech and Slovak American Archival Materials and their Preservation. Edited by Miloslav Rechcigl, Jr. Praha: Pražská edice, 2004, pp. 23-25.

Pasternak, Blanka, "Hoover Institution Archives Czech and Slovak Collections Online," in: Czech and Slovak American Archival Materials and their Preservation. Edited by Miloslav Rechcigl, Jr. Praha: Pražská edice, 2004, pp. 64-66.

Nečas, Daniel, "Immigration History Research Center at the University of Minnesota: Its Contribution to Preserving Czech and Slovak American Heritage," in: Czech and Slovak American Archival Materials and their Preservation. Edited by Miloslav Rechcigl, Jr. Praha: Pražská edice, 2004, pp. 67-72.

Rechcigl, Miloslav, Jr., "Konference o českých a slovenských archiválních materiálech ve Spojených státech amerických" (Conference about the Czech and Slovak archival materials in the US), in: Senát, 7, No. 1 (2004), p. 45.

Rechcigl, Miloslav, Jr., Czechoslovak American Archivalia. Part 1. Government Repositories. University-Based Collections. Collections Maintained by Public Museums and Libraries.

Collections of Ethnic and Related Organizations. Olomouc-Ostrava: Palacký University, 2004. 206p.

Rechcigl, Miloslav, Jr., Czechoslovak American Archivalia. Part 2. Personal Papers and Collections. Repositories Abroad Bearing on the Subject. Olomouc-Ostrava: Palacký University, 2004. 368p.

Křesťan, Jiří, "Spolupráce Státního ústředního archivu v Praze se zahraničními Čechy" (Cooperation of the State Central Archive in Prague with Czechs abroad), in: Archivy v mezinárodním kontextu. Praha: Státní ústřední archiv, 2004, pp. 185-191.

Ďurovič, Michal and Jiří Křesťan, "Archivy zahraničních Čechů: kam s nimi? Ze zkušeností Národního archivu" (Archives of Czechs abroad: What to do with them? From the experiences of the National Archives), in: Selected Papers of the 22nd World Congress of the Czechoslovak Society of Arts and Sciences, Palacký University, Olomouc, June 26 to July 4, 2004. Ostrava: Repronis, 2006, vol. 2, 393-398.

Motlíček, Tomáš and Jiří Šmeral, Průvodce po fondech a sbírkách Centra pro československá exilová studia při FF UP v Olomouci (Guide to Collections of the Center for the Czechoslovak Exile Studies at the Philosophical Faculty of Palacký University in Olomouc).Olomouc: Vydavatelství UP, 2007.

Figarová, Alena, Fond vystěhovalectví v muzeu ve Frenštátě pod Radhoštěm (Collection on Emigration at the Museum of Frenštát pod Radhoštěm). Diplomová práce, Masarykova Univerzita v Brně, 2008.

Farris, June Pachuta. "The Archives of Czechs and Slovaks Abroad (ACASA) at the University of Chicago," in: Czech Language News. Newsletter of the International Association of Teachers of Czech 31 (2009): 5-6. See also: http://idisk.mac.com/pes-Public/09spr.pdf

Vlha, Marek, "Nové prameny z amerických archivů k počátkům české komunity v USA" (New sources from American archives on the beginnings of the Czech community in the US), Časopis Matice moravské, 129, No. 1 (2010), pp.127-136.

2. Library Holdings

Osten, Margaret E., "The Oldest Czechoslovak Book Collection in America," in: Studies in Czechoslovak History. Edited by

Miloslav Rechcigl, Jr. Meerut: Sadhna Prakashan, 1976, Vol. 1, pp. 353-365.

Kovtun, George, The Czech and Slovak Collections at the Library of Congress. Washington, DC: Library of Congress, European Reading Room, n.d. See: http://www.loc.gov/rr/european/coll/czec.html

Zahradníček, Vladimír and Marcela Linková, Krajanská sbírka knihovny Náprstkova muzea: Soupis českých a slovenských krajanských tisků zahraničních a literatury o českém a slovenském vystěhovalectví. Díl 1. Knihy, brožury a separáty. Část 1 (Compatriot Collection of the Náprstek Museum Library: Listing of Czech and Slovak periodical press abroad and literature about Czech and Slovak emigration. Vol. 1. Books, pamphlets and reprints. Part 1). Praha: Národní muzeum, 1994. 169p.

Zahradníček, Vladimír and Marcela Linková, Krajanská sbírka knihovny Náprstkova muzea: Soupis českých a slovenských krajanských tisků zahraničních a literatury o českém a slovenském vystěhovalectví. Díl 1. Knihy, brožury a separáty. Část 2 (Compatriot Collection of the Náprstek Museum Library: Listing of Czech and Slovak periodical press Abroad and literature about Czech and Slovak emigration. Vol. 1. Books, pamphlets and reprints. Part 2). Praha: Národní muzeum, 1994. 220p.

Zahradníček, Vladimír and Marcela Linková, Krajanská sbírka knihovny Náprstkova muzea: Soupis českých a slovenských krajanských tisků zahraničních a literatury o českém a slovenském vystěhovalectví. Díl 2. Noviny, časopisy, kalendáře (Compatriot Collection of the Náprstek Museum Library: Listing of Czech and Slovak periodical press abroad and literature about Czech and Slovak emigration. Vol. 2. Newspapers, periodicals, calendars). Praha: Národní muzeum, 1994. 208p.

Zahradníček, Vladimír and Marcela Linková, Krajanská sbírka knihovny Náprstkova muzea: Soupis českých a slovenských krajanských tisků zahraničních a literatury o českém a slovenském vystěhovalectví. Díl 3. Rejstříky (Compatriot Collection of the Náprstek Museum Library: Listing of Czech and Slovak periodical press abroad and literature about Czech and Slovak emigration. Vol. 3. Indexes). Praha: Národní muzeum, 1994. 201p.

Secká, Milena, "American Czechs and the Collections of the Náprstek Library," Annals of the Náprstek Museum, Praha, 2000, pp. 22-28.

Secká, Milena, "Prameny k vystěhovalectví Čechů v 19. století ve sbírkách knihovny Náprstkova muzea" (Sources on Emigration of Czechs in the 19th century in the collections of the Náprstek Museum), in: Emigrace z českých zemí. Sborník referátů ze semináře v Mladé Boleslavi 2000. Mladá Boleslav: Okresní museum, 2001, pp. 115-117.

Siemaszkiewicz, Wojciech, "Czech and Slovak Collections in the New York Public Library," in: Czech and Slovak American Archival Materials and their Preservation. Edited by Miloslav Rechcigl, Jr. Praha: Pražská edice, 2004, pp. 46-54.

Muhlena, David, The Library and Archives of the National Czech & Slovak Museum & Library," in: Czech and Slovak American Archival Materials and their Preservation. Edited by Miloslav Rechcigl, Jr. Praha: Pražská edice, 2004, pp. 55-58.

Walter, Katherine L., "Czech and Slovak Collections in the University of Nebraska-Lincoln Libraries," in: Czech and Slovak American Archival Materials and their Preservation. Edited by Miloslav Rechcigl, Jr. Praha: Pražská edice, 2004, pp. 73-79.

Chroust, David Z., "Czech Collection in Texas A&M University," in: Czech and Slovak American Archival Materials and their Preservation. Edited by Miloslav Rechcigl, Jr. Praha: Pražská edice, 2004, pp. 80-83.

Ferris, June Pachuta, "Czech and Slovak Collections at the University of Chicago Library," in: Czech and Slovak American Archival Materials and their Preservation. Edited by Miloslav Rechcigl, Jr. Praha: Pražská edice, 2004, pp. 84-88.

A Guide to Czech Sources at the Nebraska State Historical Society. 9p. See: http://www.nebraskahistory.org/lib-arch/services/refrence/la_pubs/Czech_Reference_Guide_2010.pdf

D. Historiography

Kisch, Guido, "Czechoslovak Jews and America. I. Methodological and Bibliographical Remarks," Historia Judaica 6, No. 2 (October 1944), pp. 121-129.

Kutnar, František, "K pramenům a literatuře o počátcích hromadného vystěhovalectví z Čech do zámoří" (Sources and literature about the beginnings of mass emigration from Bohemia to abroad), Bulletin komise pro dějiny krajanů, Čechů a Slováků v zahraničí, 1 (1963), pp. 12-17.

Polišenský, Josef, Jan Staněk and František Štědronský, "Současný stav vědomostí k dějinám českého a slovenského vystěhovalectví" (The present state of knowledge about the Czech and Slovak emigration), in: Začiatky českej a slovenskej emigrácie do USA, Bratislava: Vydavateľstvo slovenskej akadémie vied, 1970, pp. 307-313.

Polišenský, Josef, "America's Western Coast in Czechoslovak Sources," Ibero-Americana Pragensia, 4 (1970), pp. 268-271.

Polišenský, Josef, "Problematika studia českého masového vystěhovalectví" (Problems in studying Czech mass emigration), in: Vysťahovalectvo a život krajanov vo svete. Martin: Matica slovenská, 1982, pp. 95-102.

Robek, Antonín, "K otázkám studia pramenů lidové provenience sociální emigrace do Spojených států amerických" (Issues concerning the study of the folk sources of social emigration to the US), in: Vysťahovalectvo a život krajanov vo svete. Martin: Matica slovenská, 1982, pp. 147-53.

Kašpar, Oldřich, Nový svět v české a evropské literatuře (New World in Czech and European literature). Praha: Karolinum, 1983. 120p.

Polišenský, Josef V., "Problems of Studying the History of Czech Mass Emigration to the Americas," in: Emigration from Northern, Central, and Southern Europe: Theoretical and Methodological Principles of Research. International Symposium. Krakow: Jagiellonian University, 1984, pp. 185-94.

Polišenský, Josef, "K otázkám českého vystěhovalectví do Ameriky (Issues concerning Czech emigration to America), in: Češi v cizině, 1, 1986, pp. 17-22.

Janak, Robert, "From the Historiography of Czech Texas," Czechoslovak and Central European Journal 9, No. 1 /2 (Summer/Winter 1990), pp. 134-143.

Bicha, Karel. D., "Czech-American Historiography: 1964-1987." Czechoslovak and Central European Journal, 9, No. 1 /2 (Summer/ Winter 1990), pp. 144-50.

Polišenský, Josef, "Prameny, metody a problémy" (Sources, methods and issues), in: Úvod do studia dějin vystěhovalctví do Ameriky. I. Obecné problémy dějin českého vystěhovalectví do Ameriky 1848-1914. Praha, Universita Karlova, 1992, pp. 47-56.
Opatrný, Josef, "Problems in the History of Czech Immigration to America in the Second Half of the Nineteenth Century." Nebraska History, 74, No. 3 and 4 (Fall /Winter 1993), pp. 120-29.
Luebke, Frederick C., Some Historiographical Observations," Nebraska History, 74, No. 3 & 4 (Fall/Winter 1993), pp. 218-222.
Nešpor, Zdeněk R., "Česká emigrace 19. a 20. století a jejich dosavadní studium (Czech emigration of the 19th and the 20th centuries and the status of their study), Soudobé dějiny, 2 (2002), pp. 245-284.
Rechcigl, Miloslav, Jr., "Dokumentace k dějinám zahraničních Čechů a Slováků s důrazem na Ameriku. Náhled ryze osobní" (Documentation relating to history of Czechs and Slovaks abroad with emphasis on America. A viewpoint, strictly personal), in: České archivy a pramneny k dějinám zahraničních Čechů. Edited by Milena Secká, Jiří Křesťan and Jan Kahuda. Praha: Národní archiv, 2007, pp. 81-102.
Rechcigl, Miloslav, Jr., "Czech and Slovak American Historiography," Kosmas, 24, No.1 (Fall 2010), pp. 83-124.

E. Biographical Compendia

Prantner, Emil F., These Help Build America. Chicago: Czechoslovak Review, 1922. 112p.
Reichel, William C., "Biographical Sketches of Moravian Emigrants to America," in: Memorials of the Moravian Church, vol. 1, p. 157ff.
"Americké dodatky" (American Additions), in: Album representantů všech oborů veřejného života československého. Ed. by. Fr. Sekanina. Praha: Umělecké nakladatelství, 1927, pp. 1199a-1206a.
Droba, Daniel D., Czech and Slovak Leaders in Metropolitan Chicago. Chicago: The Slavonic Club of the University of Chicago, 1934. 307p.

Reichman, John J., "Biographies of Czechs and Slovaks of Illinois," in: Czechoslovaks of Chicago. Chicago: The Czechoslovak Historical Society, 1937, pp. 67-107.

Čapek, Tomas, Návštevníci z Čech a Moravy v Americe v letech 1848-1939 (Visitors from Bohemia and Moravia in America in 1848-1939). Chicago: Tiskem Color Printing Co., 1940. 54p.

"Biographies," in: Panorama. Cicero, IL: Czechoslovak National Council of America, 1970, pp. 187-313.

Morkovsky, Alois J., Short Biographies of Czech and Other Priests in Texas. Hallettsville, TX: Author, 1982. 183p.

Pejskar, Jožka, Poslední pocta. Památník na zemřelé československé exulanty v lelech 1948-1981 (The last honor. Memorial to deceased Czech exiles in 1948-1981). Svazek 1. Curych: Konfrontace, 1982; Svazek 2. 1985; Svazek 3. 1989; Svazek 4. 1994.

Rechcigl, Miloslav, Jr., Postavy naší Ameriky (Personalities of our America). Praha: Pražská edice, 2000. 356p.

Pánek, Jaroslav, Svatava Raková and Václava Horčáková, eds., Scholars of Bohemian, Czech and Czechoslovak Studies. Prague: Institute of History, 2005. 3 vols.

Pacner, Karel, František Houdek and Libuše Koubská, Čeští vědci v exilu (Czech scientists in exile). Praha: Karolinum, 2007. 360p.

American People of Czech Descent. Anton Cermak, Jim Jarmush, John Zerzan, David Boreaunaz, Evan Lysacek, John G. Roberts, Clifford D. Simak. LLC Books, 2010. 618p.

Czech Emigrants: Czech Immigrants to Canada, Czech Immigrants to Israel, Czech Immigrants to the United Kingdom. Books LLC. General Books LLC, 2010. 208p.

Czech Expatriates: Tom Stoppard, Milos Forman, Milan Kundera, Anton Cermak, Ferdinand Peroutka, Bohuslav Martinu, Martina Navratilova. Books, LLC. General Books LLC, 2010. 350p.

Czech Immigrants to the United States: Milos Forman, Anton Cermak, Madeleine Albright, Mila Rechcigl, Jan Matulka, Charles Fried. Books, LLC. General Books LLC, 2010. 116p.

Czechoslovak Diaspora: Czechoslovak Emigrants, Czechoslovak Expatriates, Jan Kaplický, Oskar Morawetz, Julius Podlipny, Miloslav Rechcigl, Sr. Author Books LLC Editor Books LLC Publisher General Books LLC, 2010. 42p.

Czechoslovak Emigrants: Jan Kaplický, Oskar Morawetz, Miloslav Rechcigl, Sr., Fred Sersen. Books, LLC, General Books LLC. General Books, 2010. 34p.

Emigrants of Former Countries: Austro-Hungarian Emigrants, Czechoslovak Emigrants, Imperial Russian Emigrants, Soviet Emigrants. Books, LLC. Reviews. General Books, 2010. 76p.

"Sto českých vědců z exilu—Medailony" (One hundred scholars in exile—Biographies), in: Sto českých vědců v exilu. Encyklopedie významných vědců z řad pracovníků Československé akademie věd. K vydani pripravili Soňa Štrbáňová a Antonín Kostlán. Praha: Academia, 2011, pp. 210-583.

F. Memoirs & Oral Histories

1. General

Amerikán, Národní Kalendář. Chicago: A. Geringer, 1878-1958.

Kutnar. F., Dopisy českých vystěhovalců z padesátých let 19. století ze zámoří do vlasti (Letters of Czech emigrants in the fifties of the 19th century from abroad to their homeland), in: Začiatky českej a slovenskej emigrácie do USA. Edited by J. Polišenský. Bratislava: Vydavatel'stvo Slovenskej akadémie vied, 1970, pp. 211-306.

Šolle, Zdeněk, Prameny deníkové a memoárové povahy z let amerického pobytu Náprstkova a z doby po jeho návratu do vlasti (Sources in the form of a diary and memoirs concerning the years of Náprstek's stay in America and his return to his native land), Studie o rukopisech, 24 (1985), pp. 155-180.

Dluhošová, H., "Vzpominková vyprávění jako pramen k poznání etnické specifiky českých krajanů v Americe" (Memoirs as a source of knowledge of the ethnic specificity of ethnic Czechs in America). Praha: Ústav pro etnografii a folkloristiku ČSAV, 1986, No. 1, pp. 64-74.

Kašpar, O., Tam za mořem je Amerika. Dopisy a vzpomínky českých vystěhovalců do Ameriky v 19. století (Beyond the sea is America. Letters and reminiscences of Czech emigrants to America in the 19th century). Praha: Československý spisovatel, 1986. 235p.

Czech Voices. Stories from Texas in the Amerikán Národní Kalendář. Translated and edited by Clinton Machann and James W. Mendl, Jr. College Station: Texas A&M University, 1991. 149p.

Čelovský, Bořivoj, Ed., Emigranti. Dopisy politických uprchlíků z prvních let po 'Vítězném únoru' 1948 (Emigrants. Letters of political refugees from the first years after the 'Victorious February' 1948). Šenov u Ostravy: Tilia, 1998. 399p.

Secká, Milena, "Memoárové fondy v knihovně Náprstkova muzea" (Memorial collections in the Library of Náprstek Museum), 10. ročník odborné konference. Problematika historických a vzácných knižních fondů Čech, Moravy a Slezska, Olomouc 2001. Brno: Sdružení knihoven ČR, Vědecká knihovna v Olomouci, 2001, pp. 65-69.

Brouček, Stanislav, "Češi v cizině—K interpretaci autobiografických textů" (Czechs abroad—Interpretation of autobiographical texts), Acta Universitatis Palackianae Olomucensis, Facultas Philosophica. Historica 31, Olomouc, 2002, pp. 351-356.

Muhlena, David, "The NCSML Library Repository of Memoirs: Resource for Scholars," Slovo (Cedar Rapids), 4, No. 2 (Winter 2004), pp. 14-15.

Brouček, Stanislav, "Nad prameny subjektivní povahy o identitě zahraničních Čechů" (Sources of subjective character about the identity of Czechs abroad), in: Selected papers from the 22nd World Congress of the Czechoslovak Society of Arts and Sciences, Palacký University, Olomouc, June 26th to July 4th, 2004. Ostrava: Repronis, 2006, pp.389-392.

Pousta, Zdeněk, ed., Rozchod 1948. Rohovory s českými pounorovými exulanty (Separation. Discussions with Czech post-February exiles). Praha: Univerzita Karlova, 2006. 267p.

Novák, Jan, Za vodou (Beyond the water). Praha: Nakladatelstvi Franze Kafky, 2009. 192p.

New Oral History Project Underway, National Czech & Slovak Museum & Library, Cedar Rapids, IA, November 23, 2009. See: http://www.ncsml.org/Content/Oral-Histories.aspx

Vlha, Marek, Dopisy z války severu proti jihu (Letters from the War of North vs. South). Brno: Matice moravská, 2011. 136p.

2. Selected Memoirs

Heckewelder, John G. E., A Narrative of the Mission of the United Brethren among the Delaware and Mohegan Indians from its Commencement in the Year 1740 to the Close of the Year 1808.

Edited by Wiliiam Elsey Connelley, Philadelphia: M'Carty & Davis, 1820. 429p.

Maretzek, Max, Crotches and Quavers. Revelations of an opera manager in America. New York: S. French, 1855. 346p.

Dignowity, Anthony Michael, Bohemia under Austrian Despotism, Being an Autobiography. New York: Author, 1859. 236p.

Maretzek, Max, Sharps and Flats. A sequel to "Crotches and Quavers," New York: American Musician Publishing Co., 1890.

Zeisberger, David, Diary of David Zeisberger, a Moravian Missionary among the Indians of Ohio. Translated from German and edited by Eugene F. Bliss. Cincinnati, OH: Robert Clarke & Co., 1895.

Habenicht, Jan, Z paměti českého lékaře (From the memories of a Czech physician). Chicago: A. Geringer, 1897, 89p.

Wise, I. M., Reminiscences. Translated from the German and ed. by David Philipson, Cincinnati, 1901. 367p.

Pollak, Simon, The Autobiography and Reminiscences of S. Pollak, MD. St. Louis, MO. Edited by Frank J. Lutz. St. Louis: St. Louis Medical Review, 1904.

Iška, František, Z kněze svobodným myslitelem). Vlastní životopis (From priest to a freethinker). Autobiography). Chicago: Vesmír, 1907? 288p.

Bondi, August, Autobiography, 1833-1907. Galesburg, Ill.: Wagoner, 1910.

Zeisberger, David, The Moravian Records. The Diaries of Zeisberger relating to the first mission in the Ohio basin. Ohio Archeological and Historical Society Publications, Vol. 21 (January 1912), pp. 1-125.

Sadílek, F. F., Z mých vzpomínek na první doby ve Wilber (From my reminiscences of the first years in Wilber). Omaha: Národní tiskárna, 1914. 60p.

Haberman, Gustav, Z mého života. Vzpomínky z let 1867-1877-1884-1896 (From my life. Reminiscences from the years 1867-1877-1884-1896). Praha: Ústřední dělnické nakladatelství, 1914. 298p.

Jeritza, Maria, Sunlight and Life: A Singer's Life. New York: D. Appleton & Co., 1924. 261p.

Kraus, Adolf, Reminiscences and Comments. The immigrant, the citizen, a public office Jew. Chicago: Author, 1925. 244p.

Vlček, Frank, The Story of My Life. Edited by Winston Chrislock. Kent, OH: Kent State University Press, 2004. 392p; originally published in 1928.

Goldmark, Josephine Clara, Pilgrims of '48. New Haven: Yale University Press, 1930. 311p.

Welzl, Jan, Thirty Years in the Golden North. New York: Macmillan, 1932. 336p.

Čapek, Tomáš, Moje Amerika. Vzpomínky a úvahy. 1861-1934 (My America. Reminiscences and reflections. 1861-1934). Praha: Fr. Borový, 1935. 269p.

Gág, Wanda, Growing Pains. New York: Coward-McCann, 1940. 479p.

Flexner, Abraham, I Remember: The Autobiography of Abraham Flexner. New York: Simon and Schuster, 1940. 420p.

Voska, Emanuel Victor and Will Irwin, Spy and Counter-Spy: the Autobiography of a Master-Spy. Garden City: Doubleday & Co., 1940. 322p.

Natonek, Hans, In Search of Myself. New York: G. P. Putnam's Sons, 1943. 261p.

Brandeis, Frederika Dembitz, Reminiscences of Frederika Dembitz Brandeis: Written for her son, Louis, in 1880 to 1886. Privately printed, 1943. 48p.

Wechsberg, Joseph, Looking for a Bluebird. New York, Penguin, 1947. 197p.

Wechsberg, Joseph, Homecoming. New York: Alfred Knopf, 1946. 117p.

Zlámal, Oldřich, Povídka mého života (The story of my life). Chicago: Czech Benedictine Press, 1953. 246p.

Masaryk, Alice Garrigue, Dětství a mládí. Vzpomínky a myšlenky (Childhood and youth. Reminiscences and thoughts). Pittsburgh: Masaryk Publication Trust, 1960. 128p.

Hostovský, Egon, Literární dobrodružství českého spisovatele v cizině (Literary adventures of a Czech writer abroad). Toronto: Nový domov, 1966. 166p.

Schneider, Joseph, Some Recollections on my Fifty Professional Years. Berwyn, IL: American Engineering Society, 1967. 81p.

Yurka, Blanche, Bohemian Girl. Athens, OH: Ohio University Press, 1970. 306p.

Navrátilová, Martina with George Vecsey, Martina. New York: Alfred A. Knopf, 1975.

Schnabel, Artur, My Life and Music. New York: Dover, 1988. 288p.

Forman, Miloš and Jan Novák, Turnaround. A Memoir. Darby, PA: Diane Publishing Co., 1993.

Peroutka, Ferdinand, Deníky, dopisy, vzpomínky (Diaries, letters, reminiscences). Praha: Lidové noviny, 1995. 320p.

Čelovský, Bořivoj, Šel jsem svou cestou (I went my own way). Opava: Vade Mecum, 1996. 276p.

Zenkl, Petr, Mozaika vzpomínek (Mosaic of reminiscences). Olomouc: Centrum pro československá exilová studia, Filozofická fakulta Univerzity Palackého, 1998. 208p.

Filípek, Jan, Zpod šibenice do exilu (From gallows to exile). Praha: Author, 1998. 218p.

Filípek, Jan, Odlesky dějin československého exilu (Reflextions from the Czechoslovak exile). Praha: Author, 1999. 172p.

Hampl, Patricia, Romantic Education. New York: W. W. Norton & Company, 1999.

Povolný, Mojmír, Má cesta dvacátým stoletím (My journey through the 20th century). Brno: Šimon Ryšavý, 2001. 110p.

Odložilík, Otakar, Deníky z let 1924-1948 (Diaries from the years 1924-1948). Edited by Milada Sýkorková. Sv. 1. (1924-1939) 764p.; Sv. 2 (1939-1948). 656p. Praha: Výzkumné centrum pro dějiny vědy, 2002-2003.

Zeisberger, David, The Moravian Mission Diaries of David Zeisberger, 1772-1781. University Park, PA: Penn State Press, 2005. 666p.

Hašková-Coolidge, Eliška, Pět amerických prezidentů, česká babička a já (Five American Presidents, Czech grandmother and me). Autorčiny vzpomínky zaznamenala Marie Homolová. Praha: NLN, 2005. 229p.

Albright, Madeleine, Madam Secretary: A Memoir. Miramax, 2005. 736p.

Maretzek, Max, Further Revelations of an Opera Manager in the 19th Century America. The Third Book of Memoirs. Edited by Ruth Henderson. Sterling Heights, MI: Harmonie Park Press, 2006. 165p.

Urban, Joseph Jaroslav, Bohemus: Amazing Stories of His Life on Four Continents with History Attached to Places Visited or Lived. BookSurge Publishing, 2008. 542p.

Rechcigl, Miloslav, Jr. On Behalf of their Homeland: Fifty Year of SVU. An Eywitness Account of the History of the Czechoslovak Society of Arts and Sciences (SVU). Boulder, CO: East Europenan Monographs, 2008. 671p., 26 p. illustrations.

Demetz, Peter, Prague in Danger: The Years of German Occupation, 1939-1945: Memory and History, Terror and Resistance, Theater and Jazz, Film and Poetry, Politics and War. New York: Farrar, Straus & Giroux, 2008. 288p.

Slouka, Zdeněk, Jdi po skryté stopě. Lidské kroky politickou krajinou exilu (Follow a hidden trail. Human steps through a political landscape of exile). Praha: Academia, 2009. 805p.

Miller, Kenneth Dexter, Uncle from America. Minneapolis: Immigration History Research Center, University of Minnesota, 2010. 244p.

Rechcigl, Miloslav, Jr., Czechmate. From Bohemian Paradise to American Haven. A Personal Memoir. Bloomington, IN: AuthorHause, 2011. 771p.

G. Travels through America

Sealsfield, Charles, The Americans as They Are. Described in a Tour through the Valley of the Mississippi. London: Hurst, Chance and Co., 1828. 218p.

Sealsfield, Charles, The United States of North America as They Are. London: W. Simpkin and R. Marshall, 1828. 242p.

Grund, Francis J., The Americans in their Moral, Social, and Political Relations. London: Longman & Co., 1837. 423p.

Grund, Francis J., Aristocracy in America. From the Sketch-Book of a German Nobleman. London: Richard Bentley, 1839. 2 vols. 319p., 331p.

Grund, Francis J., Thoughts and Reflections on the Past Position of Europe and its Probable Consequence to the United Sates. Philadelphia: Childs and Peterson, 1860. 245p.

Štolba, Josef, V Severní Americe (In North America. Travel sketches). Praha, 1876. 181p.

Payer, Julius, New Lands within the Arctic Circle. Macmillan & Co., 1876. 2 vols.

Klutschak, Heinrich W., Als Eskimo der Erlebnisse der Schwatka'schen Franklin-Aufsuchungs-Expedition in den Jahren 1878-80. Wien: A. Hartleben, 1881. 247p.

Preiss, Eduard, "Po jižních státech. Z cestopisu kolem světa majora Eduarda Preisse" (Through southern states. From the travels of Eduard Preiss around the world), Amerikán, Národní Kalendář, 5 (1882), 159-177.

Preiss, Eduard, "Ze života a z cesty kolem světa maj. Eduarda Preisse" (From the life and travels around the world of major Eduard Preiss), Amerikán, Národní kalendář, 6 (1883), pp. 137-146.

Wagner, Jan, Čeští osadníci v Severní Americe (Czech settlers in the US). Praha, 1887.

Paclt, Čeněk, Čenka Paclta cesty po světě. Příhody a zkušenosti jeho na cestách po Americe, Austrálii, Novém Zélandě a Jižní Africe (Čeněk Paclt's travels around the world. Incidents and experiences during his travels in America, Australia, New Zealand and South Africa) .... vzdělal Jaroslav Svoboda. Mladá Boleslav: K. Vačlena, 1888. 423p.

Kroupa, Bohuslav, An Artist's Tour. Gleanings and Impressions of Travels in North and Central America and Sandwich Islands. London: Ward and Downey, 1890. 339p.

Wagner, Jan, Za Atlantským oceánem. Črty z cest po Severni Americe (Beyond the Atlantic Ocean. Sketches from travels throughout the US). Praha, 1890. 126p.

Pastor, J., Cesta do Spojených států severoamerických (Voyage to the US). Hamburg-New York, 1891. 96p.

Pastor, J., Cesta do Ameriky (Voyage to America). Hamburg: Author, 1892. 16p.

Pastor, J., Poučeni o jízdě do Spojených států severoamerických (Information about the travel to the US). Hamburg: Author, 1893. 16p.

Šmaha, Josef, Americké táčky. Dojmy ze zaoceánské cesty (American chats. Impressions from my trip beyond the ocean). Praha: J. B. Vilímek, 1894. 90p.

Kořenský, Josef, Cesta kolem světa, 1893-94 (Journey around the world, 1893-94). Praha: J. Otto, 1894. 2 vols.

Donato, A. Z., Kolem světa o jedné noze. Cesty a příběhy z dráhy umělecké (Around the world on one leg. Travels and incidents from a life of an artist). Chicago: A. Geringer, 1895. 176p.

Kořenský, Josef, Amerika (America). Praha: J. Otto, 1896. 224p.; 2nd ed., 1925. 302p.

Kořenský, Josef, Cesty po světě. Plavba do Nového Světa, Amerika (Travels around the world. Voyage to the New World). Praha: J. Otto, 1896. 224p.

Wagner, Jan, Zámořské klepy (Overseas talks). Praha, 1898-99.

Novák, Vladimír, Z cest po Spojených státech Severní Ameriky (From travels throught the USA). Praha: Tiskem České grafické 'Unie,' 1900. 51p.

Wagner, Jan, Král dollar a jeho ctitelé (Dollar Almighty and its admirers). Praha: Václav Řezníček, 1900. 192p.

Guth, Jiří, Na moři a za mořem (On the ocean and beyond the ocean). Kostelec nad Orlicí: Kunc a Hamerský, 1902. 214p.

Guth, Jiří, Moje prázdniny v Americe (My vacation in the US). Praha: Družstvo 'Máje', 1904. 137p.

Šnajdr, Václav, Výlet do Kalifornie. Cestopiosná črta (A trip to California. A travelogue. Cleveland: Dennice dávnověku, 1904. 214p.

Fiala, Anthony, Fighting the Polar Ice. New York: Doubleday, Page, 1906. 296p.

Havlasa, Jan, V kraji věčného jara. Jihokalifornské črty (In the land of eternal spring. South-Californian sketches). Praha: J. Rašín, 1909. 250p.

Sokol-Tůma, František, Z cest po Americe. Úvahy cestopisné, národnostní, sociální a výdělkové ze života amerického (From travels through America. Travel, national, social and economic reflections from American life). Moravská Ostrava: Fr. Tůma, 1910. 2 vols.

Havlasa, Jan, Listy ze San Franciska. Americké poznámky (Epistles from San Francisco. American notes). Král. Vinohrady: Parma, 1916. 152p.

Herites, František, Amerika a jiné črty z cest (America and other sketches from my travels). Praha: J. Otto, 1913. 252p.

Sokol-Tůma, František, Z cest po Americe (From travels through America). Moravská Ostrava: Fr. Tůma, 1910. 2 vols.; 2nd ed. Praha: Šrámek, 1925 2 vols; 3rd ed. Praha: J. Albert, 1934. 331p.

Kuděj, Zdenek Marian, Mezi dvěma oceány. Dobrodružství Čecha v dálné cizine (Between two oceans. Adventures of a Czech far abroad). Praha: Svěcený, 1917. 358p.

Vraz, Vlasta A., "Rozmanitosti z cest mého otce dalekými světy" (Episodes from the travels of my father through far away worlds). Amerikán, Národní kalendář, 41 (1918), pp. 209-222.

Kuděj, Zdeněk Marian, Z Nového světa. Americké obrázky (From the New World. American sketches). Praha: J. Otto, 1918. 275p.

Pelant, Karel, Amerika, jaká je v skutku (America, how it is in reality). Moravská Ostrava: A. Perout, 1919-20. 2 vols.

Červinka, Vincenc, Za oceán. Listy z Ameriky (Across the ocean. Letters from America). Praha: J. Otto, 1920. 180p.

Majerová, Marie, Dojmy z Ameriky (Impressions from America). Praha: Knihovna 'Holubice', 1920. 126p.

Čapek, Tomáš, Z New Yorku do Prahy a zpět (From New York to Prague and back). Praha: B. Kočí, 1922. 63p.

Dvořák, Ladislav, Vzpomínky na Ameriku a tužba po vlasti (Memories of America and yearning for home). Praha: V. Kotrba, 1923. 95p.

Krejčí, František Václav, Veliké dobrodružství. Dojmy a poznatky z cesty kolem světa (A great adventure. Impressions and knowledge from a trip around the world). Praha: A. Svěcený, 1924. 476p.

Špaček, Stanislav, Americké obrázky (American sketches). Praha: Jednota přátel Masarykovy akademie práce, 1927. 2 vols.

Vrázová, Vlasta: Život a cesty E. St. Vráze (Life and travels of E. St. Vraz). Praha: Československá grafická Unie, 1937. 337p.

Kořenský, Josef, Doma a za mořem (At home and beyond the ocean). Praha: F. Topič, 1925. 88p.

Hromádka, Josef Lukl, Cesty protestantského theologa (Travels of a Protestant theologian). Praha: V. Horák, 1927. 153p.

Foustková-Wattersonová, Zdenka, Listy z Ameriky (Letters from America). Praha: F. Topič, 1927. 211p.

Špaček, Stanislav, Americké obrázky (American sketches). Praha: Jednota přátel Masarykovy akademie práce, 1927. 2 vols.

Kolowrat-Krakovský, Jindřich. Amerika a my. Dojmy a úvahy (We and America. Impressions and reflections) Praha: Čin, 1928. 221p.

Peklo, Jaroslav, Z mých cest Spojenými státy severoamerickými (From my travels through the US). Praha: Nákladem odboru zemědělské rady, 1928. 46p.

Koudelka, Jaroslav, 10.000 mil Spojenými státy (10,000 miles through the US). Praha: A Svěcený, 1930. 235p.

Sobota, Emil, Amerika a evropský divák (America and an European observer). Praha: Merlantrich, 1930. 221p.

Forejt-Alan, Vladimír, Od Kordiller k Mississippi. Potulky českých novinářů-skautů po Americe (From Cordillera to Mississippi. Wanderings of Czech journalists-scouts through America). Praha: Šolc a Šimáček, 1930. 270p.

Mádl, Jan, Americké obrázky (American sketches). Praha: Author, 1932. 110p.

Welzl, Jan, The Quest for Polar Treasure. New York: Macmillan, 1933. 351p.

Pflanzer, Vilém, "Před Náprstkem do Ameriky" (To America before Náprstek), Amerikán, Národní kalendář, 59 (1936), pp. 147-151.

Rosenbaum, S. E., A Voyage to America Ninety Years Ago. The diary of a Bohemian Jew on his voyage from Hamburg to New York 1847. Edited by Guido Kisch. In: American Jewish Historical Society Publications, No. 35, 1939, pp. 65-113.

Nekola, Rudolf, Třináctý guverner. Výlet do dnešní Kalifornie a vyprávění z Kalifornie staré (The thirteenth governor. A trip to today's California and a narrative from the Old California). Praha: Toužimský a Moravec, 1939. 343p.

Hrdlička, Aleš, Alaska Diary, 1926-1931. Lancaster, PA: J. Cattell Press, 1943. 414p.

"Češi v první Byrdově výpravě k Jižnímu pólu" (Czechs in the First Byrd's expedition to the South Pole), Amerikán, Národní kalendář, 73 (1950), pp. 67-70.

Paclt, Čeněk, Zpívající digger. Podle dopisů, vzpomínek a zápisů Čeňka Paclta vypráví Donát Šainer (Singning digger. From letters, reminiscences and notes of Čeněk Paclt, narrated by Donát Šainer). Praha: Československý spisovatel, 1950. 208p.

Konečná, Elvira, Dojmy z cesty po ostrově Oahu" (Impressions from the trip on the Island Oahu), Amerikán, Národní kalendář, 74 (1951), pp. 89-97.

Konečná, Elvira, Sebrané vzpomínky a zkušenosti z Hawaii" (Reminiscences and experiences from Hawaii), 75 (1952), pp. 35-43.

Wallace, Paul A. W., "John Heckewelder's Travels," Now and Then, 10 (April 1952), pp. 105-119.

Heckewelder, John G. E., "A Canoe Journey from the Big Beraver to the Tuscawaras in 1773," Ohio Archeological and Historical Quarterly, 61 (1952), pp. 283-298.

Dubská, Irena, Americký rok (American year). Praha: Československý spisovatel, 1966. 456p.

Wallace, Paul A. W., "John Heckewelder's Travels," Now and Then, 10 (April 1952), pp. 105-119.

Jandáček, Antonín, U našinců v Texasu (With our countrymen in Texas). Granger, Tex.: 'Našinec' Pub. Co., 1955. 53p.

Dufek, George, Operation Deepfreeze. New York: Hartcourt, Brace, 1957. 243p.

Heckewelder, John, The Travels of John Heckewelder in Frontier America. Edited by Paul A. W. Wallace. Pittsburgh: University of Pittsburgh Press, 1958. 474p.

Holub, Miroslav, Anděl na kolečkách. Poloreportáž z USA (The angel on wheels. A half-reportage from the US). Praha: Československý spisovatel, 1963. 104p.; 2nd ed., 1964. 109p.

Polák, Josef, Americká cesta Josefa Václava Sládka (American trip of Josef Václav Sládek). Praha: Státní pedagogické nakladatelství, 1966. 108p.

Linck, Wenceslaus, Wenceslaus Linck's Reports and Letters, 1762-1778. Edited by Ernest J. Burrus. Los Angeles: Dawson's Book Shop, 1967.

Francl, Joseph, The Overland Journey of Joseph Francl: First Bohemian to cross the plains to the California gold field. Introduction by Richard Brautigan. San Francisco: W. P. Wrede., 1968 57p.

Holub, Miroslav, Žít v New Yorku (To live in New York). Praha: Melantrich, 1969. 169p.

Polišenský J. and J. Opatrný, "Václav Link a jeho Deník z cesty na sever Kalifornského poloostrova" (Vaclav Link and his diary from his trip north to Californian peninsula), Jižní Morava, 2 (1974), pp. 95-102.

Škvorecký, Josef, Velká povídka o Americe: 1969 (A tall tale about America). Toronto: 68 Publishers, 1980. 230p.

Šolle, Zdeněk, "Denik Viléma Pflanzera. Ke vzniku plánu Vojty Náprstka na cestu do Ameriky" (Vilém Pflanzer's diary. On the origins of Vojta Náprstek's plan for traveling to America), Studie o rukopisech, 20 (1981), pp. 119-160.

Šolle, Zdeněk. Přídpěvek k poznání Náprstkových příprav na cestu do Ameriky" (A contribution to the understanding of Náprstek's preparations for his voyage to America), Studie o rukopisech, 21 (1982), pp. 179-214.

Klutschak, Heinrich W., Overland to Starvation Cove: With the Inuit in search of Franklin, 1878-1880. Toronto: University of Toronto Press, 1987. 261p.

Kašpar, Oldřich, Tadeáš Haenke. Český účastník Malaspinovy výpravy (Tadeáš Haenke. Czech participants of Malaspin's expedition). Pardubice: Kora 1994. 39p.

Vaněk, Pavel, "Nedoceněný český cestovatel Vincenc-Čeněk Paclt" (Unappreciated Czech traveler Vincenc-Čeněk Paclt), in: Cesty a cestování v životě společnosti. Ústí nad Labem, Univerzita J.E. Purkyně, 1995, pp. 437-442.

H. Czech-American Fiction

Sealsfield, Charles, Life in the New World, or, Sketches of American Society. New York: J. Winchester, 1842. 349p.

Sealsfield, Charles, The Cabin Book, or, Sketches of Life in Texas. New York: J. Winchester, 1844. 155p.

Sealsfield, Charles, North and South, or, Scenes and Adventures in Mexico. New York: J. Winchester, 1944.

Sealsfield, Charles, Scenes and Adventures in Central America. Edinburgh: W. Blackwood & Sons, 1852. 298p.

Sealsfield, Charles, Frontier Life, or, Scenes and Adventures in the South West. New York: Auburn, Miller, Orton, & Mulligan, 1856. 376p.

Činoveský, J.F., Vystěhovalci v Americe. Obrazy ze žvota amerických usedlíků (Emigrants in America. Sketches from the life of American settlers). Tábor: J. K. Frank, 1868. 328p.

Štolba, Josef, Americké povídky (American stories), Praha: J. Otto, 1876. 838p.

Albieri, Pavel, Nevěsta za padesát dolarů. Česko-americký obrázek z Chicaga (Bride for fifty dollars. Czech-American portrait from Chicago). Praha: J. R. Vilímek, 1897. 226p.

Albieri, Pavel, Nová země. Příběhy českých vystěhovalců (New country. Episodes of Czech emigrants). Chicago: A. Geringer, 1897? 415p.

Albieri, Pavel, Z amerických toulek. Zaoceánské povídky a obrázky (From American wanderings. From stories and portraits beyond the ocean). Praha: J. Otto, 1898. 274p.

Albieri, Pavel, Dědička. Román z amerického života (Heiress. A novel from American life). Chicago, A. Geringer, 1900. 386p.

Albieri, Pavel, Dědička z hrobu (Heiress from the grave). Chicago: A. Geringer, 1903. 497p.

Jung, Václav Alois, Na prahu Nového světa. Ze zkušenosti českého novinářství v Americe (At doorstep of the New World. From the experiences of Czech journalism in America). Praha: 'Čas', 1903. 78p.

Škaloud, František J., U Kratinů. Roman ze života chicágských Čechů (At Kratinas.' A novel from life of Chicago Czechs). Chicago: A. Geringer, 1905. 99p.

Charvát, Otakar, Kresby a povídky. Drobná prosa (Drawings and stories. Short Prose). Omaha: Author, 1906. 189p.

Charvát, Otakar, Ztracené cesty (Lost travels). Omaha: Pokrok západu, 1907. 128p.

Škaloud, František J., Bordynkáři. Kousek českého života v Chicagu (Boarders. From a Czech life in Chicago). Chicago: A. Geringer, 1908. 170p.

Albieri, Pavel, Za krvavou stopu (After the bloody steps). Praha: J. Otto, 1907. 107p.

Miniberger, Václav, V mlhách. Z českoamerického života (In the Fog. From Czech-American life). Omaha: Bohemian American Pub. Co., 1909. 61p.

Folda, Folgin, Kupec a básník, anebo Politika a nehody pana Příhody. Českoamerická fraška (Merchant and a poet, or Politics and misfortunes of Mr. Příhoda. Czech-American farce). Omaha: Národní tiskárna, 1909. 115p.

Pšenka, Rudolf Jaromír, Washington Závora. Českoamerický román (Washington Závora. A Czech-American novel). Chicago: A. Geringer, 1910. 355p.

Miniberger, Václav, Sláva kazatelova. Román ze života českoamerického (The glory of a preacher. A novel from a Czech-American life). Praha: A. Reis, 1910. 170p.

Havlasa, Jan, Krajiny v oblacích (Lands in the sky). Praha: J. Rašín, 1910. 210p.

Sládek, Josef Václav, Americké obrázky a jiná próza (American sketches and other prose). Praha: J Otto, 1914. 2 vols.

Pšenka, Rudolf Jaromír, Mirva. Česko-americký románek z pohnutých dob všeevropské války (Mirva. A Czech-American novel from the eventful years of All-European War). Chicago: A. Geringer, 1916. 315p.

Havlasa, Jan, Půlnoční vítr. Americké novely: 1904-1910 (Midnight wind. American novels: 1904-1910). Praha: F. Topič, 1916. 263p.

Kuděj, Zdeněk Marian, Mezi dvěma oceány. Dobrodružství Čecha v dálné cizině (Between the two oceans. Adventure of a Czech in the far away land). Praha: Svěcený, 1917. 358p.

Cather, Willa S., My Antonia. Boston and New York: Houghton Mifflin Co., 1918. 418p.

Havlasa, Jan, Půlnoční vítr. Americké povídky (The midnight wind. American stories). 2nd ed. Praha: F. Topič, 1918. 263p.

Pšenka, Rudolf Jaromír, A přece Čech. Román ze života zámořských krajanů (A Czech after all. A novel from the life of our compatriots overseas). Chicago: A. Geringer, 1920. 144p.

Kárník, Jan, Americké obrazy a obrázky. Povídky ze života amerických Čechů (American sketches. Stories from the lives of American Czechs). Plzeň: Uniová tiskárna, 1922. 226p.

Pšenka, Rudolf Jaromír, Dolary a krev. Českoamerický román (Dollars and blood. A Czech-American novel). Blatná: V. Novotný, 1929. 282p.

Pšenka, Rudolf Jaromír, Na Novém světě. Obrázek ze života krajanů za mořem (In the New World. From the lives of our countrymen beyond the sea). Praha: Šolc a Šimáček, 1930. 170p.

Tůma, Vojtěch, Feuilletony česko-americké (Czech-American feuilletons). New York; New Yorské listy, 1933. 100p.

Miniberger, Václav, Lilie ve stínu mrakodrapů. Drama ze života chicágských Čechů o třech jednáních (Lily in the shadow of skyscrapers. A drama from the life of the Chicago Czechs in three acts). Chicago: The Challenge Pub. Co., 1937. 80p.

Miniberger, Václav, Jimův Homer Calvin. Z českoamerického života (Jim's Homer Calvin. From Czech-American life). Chicago: Challenge Pub. Co., 1939. 200p.

Kafka, Franz, Amerika. New York: New Directions, 1940. 299p.

Koudelka, Jaroslav, Pán na České řece (Lord on the Bohemia River) Praha: J. Salivar, 1946.

Král, Josef Jiří, Salt Water and Other Stories. Cleveland: Czech-American Labor News, 1946. 221p.

Němeček, Zdeněk, Tvrdá země. Román z exulantského prostředí v Kanadě (Harsh land. Novel from an exile environment in Canada). New York: C.S. Pub. Co., 1954. 238p.

Němeček, Zdeněk, Bloudění v exilu (Wanderings in exile). Lund: Sklizeň, 1958. 247p.

Machotka, Otakar, Povídky exulantovy (Stories of an exile). New York: SVU, 1968. 81p.

Němeček, Zdeněk, New York: zamlženo (New York: Overcast). 4th ed. Praha: Československý spisovatel, 1969. 329p.

Škvorecký, Josef, Scherzo capriccioso: Veselý sen o Dvořákovi (Scherzo capriccioso: A lively dream about Dvořák). Toronto: 68 Publishers, 1984. 555p.

Škvorecký, Josef, Nevěsta z Texasu. Romantický příběh ze skutečnosti (Bride from Texas. A romantic story from real life).Toronto: 68 Publishers, 1992. 636p.

I. Dissertations & Theses

1. Guide

Anderle, Josef "American Doctoral Dissertations on Czechoslovak History and Related Subjects, 1914-1974," Czechoslovak History Newsletter, 1 (1976), pp. 5-18. Ibid., 6, No. 1 (1983), pp. 3-4. Ibid., 11, No. 1 (1988), pp. 7-9.

2. Selected Dissertations

Horak, Jakub, The Assimilation of Czechs in Chicago. Ph.D. Dissertation. University of Chicago, 1920.

Kutak, Robert J., The Story of a Bohemian-American Village. Ph.D. Dissertation, Columbia University, 1933.

Jerabek, Milan Woodrow, Czechs in Minnesota. M.A. Thesis, University of Minnesota, 1939. 164p.

Kovacs, Sandor Bodonsky, Czechoslovaks in Virginia. Ph.D. Dissertation, University of Virginia, Charlottesville, 1939.

Lynch, Russell W., Czech Farmers in Oklahoma. Ph.D. Dissertation, Oklahoma Agricultural and Mechanical College, Stillwater, 1942. 112p.

Pazdral, Olga, Czech Folklore in Texas. M.A. Thesis, University of Texas, Austin, 1947.

Skrivanek, John, The Education of Czechs in Texas. M.A. Thesis. 1946. 139p.

Taggert, Glen L., Czechs in Wisconsin as a Culture Type. Ph.D. Dissertation, University of Wisconsin, Madison, 1948.

Šturm, Rudolf, Sojourn of the Czech Poet Josef Václav Sládek in the United States and the American Influences on his Writings. Ph.D. Dissertation, Harvard University, 1956.

Skrabanek, Robert L., Social Organization and Change in Czech-American Rural Community: A Sociological Study of Snook, Texas. Ph.D. Dissertation. Louisiana State University, 1949.

Hewitt, William P., The Czechs in Texas: A Study of the immigration and the development of Czech ethnicity 1850-1920. Ph.D. Dissertation, University of Texas at Austin, 1970.

Cink, Kenneth, Czech-American Radicalism in the United States, 1849-1924. Ph.D. Dissertation, University of Chicago, 1970.

Spllawn, Vlasta Margaret, Sociological Study of a Czech Community in Ellis County, Texas. M.A. Thesis. Texas Tech. University, 1972.

Henzl, Vera, Cultivation and Maintenance of Literary Czech by American Speakers. Ph.D. Dissertation, Stanford University, 1975.

Holick, Robert J., A Comparison of Reading Vocabulary and Reading Comprehension Skills. Between Bilingual and Monolingual

Czech-American Students. Ph.D. Dissertation, Texas A&M University, 1975.

Stasa, David M., A Comparative Study of the Detroit and St. Louis Sokol's Efforts to Preserve Czech Culture since World War II. Ph.D. Dissertation, St. Louis University, 1975.

Hewitt, William Philllip, The Czechs of Texas: A Study of the Immigration and of the Development of Czech Ethnicity., 1850-1920. Ph.D. Dissertation, University of Texas, Austin, 1978.

Johnson, Christopher G., An Oral History Study of Religiosity of Fifty Czech-American Elderly. Ph.D. Dissertation, Iowa State University, 1981.

McLaurin, Donald M., Life and Works of Karel Husa with Emphasis on the Significance of his Contributions to the Wind Band. Ph.D. Dissertation. Florida State University, 1985.

Walker, Rosie A. L., A History of the Rural Schools of the Czech Communities of Kolin and Libuse. Ph.D. Dissertation. Northwestern University of Louisiana, 1986.

Stone, G.M., Ethnicity: Class and Politics among Czechs in Cleveland, 1870-1940. Ph.D. Dissertation, Rutgers University, New Brunswick, 1993.

Dutkova-Cope, Lida, Texas Czech—An Ethnolinguistic Study. Ph.D. Dissertation, University of Arizona at Tucson, 1998.

Chroust, Daniel Zdeněk, Bohemian Voice: Contention, Brotherhood and Journalism among Czech People in America, 1860-1910. Ph.D. Dissertation, Texas A&M University, 2009.

J. Directories

Adresář amerických Čechů, sestavený v upomínku na Národopisnou výstavu československou v Praze r. 1895 (An address book of American Czechs, Compiled on the occasion of the Czecho-Slavonic Ethnographic Exhibit in Prague in 1895). Chicago: A. Geringer. 320p.

České Chicago. Adresář českých obchodníků, živnostníků a spolků (The Czech Chicago. An address book of Czech merchants, tradesmen and organizations). Chicago: Národní tiskárna, 1900. 251p.

Almanach československého lidu v New Yorku a okolí (An almanac of the Czechoslovak people in New York and the environs). New York: Česká tiskárna, 1904. 164p.

Adresář Čechů detroitských, obsahující správné adresy detroitských krajanů (Directory of Detroit Czechs, containing correct addresses of the Detroit compatriots). Detroit: Tel. Jed. Sokol Podlipný, 1908.

Španihel, Jaroslav. Adresář zahraničních Čechů (An address book of Czechs abroad). 4th ed. Praha: Národní rada česká, 1911. 106p.

Španihel, Jaroslav. Adresář Čechů ve Spojených státech severoamerických (An address book of Czechs in the USA). Praha: Národni rada česká, 1912. 84 p.; 1913. 104p.

Directory and Almanac of the Bohemian Population of Chicago. Chicago, 1915. 320p.

Index of Czechoslovak Organizations in the United States. Chicago: Exhibit Committee of the Czechoslovak Group, 1933. 115p.

Czech and Slovak American Private-Business Telephone Directory for Suburbs and Chicago, 1939-1940. Chicago: Czech Publishing Co., 1939.

American Czech and Slovak Telephone and Business Directory, 1941-1942 for Chicago and Suburbs. Chicago: Chicago Publishing Co., 1941. 140p.

Rechcigl, Eva and Miloslav Rechcigl, Jr., eds., Directory of the Czechoslovak Society of Arts and Sciences in America, Inc. New York: Society, 1966. 80p.; 2nd ed. 1968. 100p.; 3rd ed. 1972. 135p.; 4th ed. 1978. 137p.; 5th ed. 1983. 193p; 6th ed. 1988. 285p.; 7th ed. 1992. 390p.

Rechcigl, Miloslav, Jr., Eva Rechcigl and Jiří Eichler, SVU Directory. Organization, Activities and Biographies of Members. 8th ed. Washington, DC: SVU Press, 2003. 368p.

Rechcigl, Miloslav, Jr. Deceased Members of the Czechoslovak Society of Arts and Sciences (SVU). Washington, DC: SVU Press, 2009. 71p.

K. Dictionaries & Textbooks

1. Dictionaries

Jonáš, Karel, Slovník česko-anglický i anglicko-český. S doplňky všeobecnými i odbornými k dílu česko-anglickému, s úplnou výslovností a krátkou mluvnicí anglickou (Czech-English and English-Czech dictionary. With general and technical addenda, with complete pronunciation and a short English grammar). Racine, WI: Slavie, 1876. 30p., 520p., 626p.

Jonáš, Karel, Slovník česko-anglický s úplnou anglickou výslovností (Czech-English dictionary with complete English pronunciation). 2. vyd. zcela přepracované a doplněné. Racine, WI: Slavie, 1886. 608p.

Zdrůbek, František Boleslav, Kapesní slovnik anglické a české řeči s úplnou výslovností a přízvuky (A pocket dictionary of the English and Bohemian languages). Chicago: A. Geringer, 1888. 2 vols.; 288p., 390p.

Pastor, Josef, Kapesní slovník česko-anglický s úplnou výslovností pro samouky a hlavně pro americké vystěhovalce (Pocket Czech-English dictionary with complete pronunciation for the self-taught). Hamburg: Author, 1889. 116p.

Jonáš, Karel, Úplný slovník anglickočeský pro obecnou potřebu s dokonalou anglickou výslovností (Complete Czech-American dictionary for general use with complete English pronunciation). Racine, WI: Slavie, 1892. 723p.

Jonáš, Karel, Slovník česko-anglický s úplnou anglickou výslovností (Czech-English dictionary with complete English pronunciation). 4th ed. Racine: Slavie, 1896. 621p.

Soukup, Antonín M., Nový velký anglicko-český slovník (New English-Czech dictionary). Chicago: Author, 1900. 360p.

Soukup, Antonín M., Anglicko-český slovník (English-Czech dictionary). Chicago: Author, 1922. 360p.

2. "Tlumače" (Czech Interpreting Guides)

Jonáš, Karel, Českoanglický tlumač. Návod k naučení se angličtině pro české vystěhovalce v Americe (Czech-English 'tlumač.' Guide for learning English for Czech emigrants in America). Racine, WI: Slavie., 1865. 2 vols.

Jonáš, Karel, Nový tlumač americký ku snadnému a rychlému naučení se řeči anglické i pro jiné praktické potřeby vystěhovalců a osadníků české národnosti v Americe (New ‘tlumač’ for easy and quick learning of English and for other practical uses of emigrants and settlers of Czech nationality in America). Racine: Slavie, 1884. 251p.

Zdrůbek, František B., Bohemian and English interpreter. Česko-anglický tlumač pro Čechy americké. Chicago: A. Geringer, 1897. 255p; reprinted 1907.

Zdrůbek, František B., Cesko-anglický tlumač (Czech-American ‘tlumač.’ Chicago: A. Geringer, 1898. 258p.

Zdrůbek, František B., Česko-anglický tlumač pro Čechy americké se snadným mluvnickým návodem pro žáky i samouky (Czech-American ‘tlumač’ with easy speaking instructions for students and self-learners). Chicago: A. Geringer, 1907. 255p.

Jonáš, Karel, Nový tlumač americký ku snadnému a rychlému naučení se řeči anglické i pro jiné praktické potřeby vystěhovalců a osadníků české národnosti v Americe (New ‘tlumač’ for easy and quick learning of English and for other practical uses of emigrants and settlers of Czech nationality in America). 18th ed. Chicago: České ústřední knihkupectví, 1919. 267p.

3. Textbooks

Zdrůbek, František B., Anglická mluvnice, čili nový zkušený návod k naučení se čtení, psaní a mluvení v anglickém jazyku za tři měsíce (English grammar, or a newly tested guide to learn to read, write and speak English in three months). Cedar Rapids: Author, 1870. 206p.

Zdrůbek, František B., Nová anglická mluvnice anebo vůdce k nabytí zběhlosti v anglickém mluvení, čtení a psaní v čase nejkratším (New English grammar or guide to gain fluency in English speaking, reading and writing in shortest time). Chicago: A. Geringer. 1874. 269p.

Zdrůbek, František B., Postupná anglická mluvnice pro školy česko-anglické i samouky (Progressive English grammar for Czech-English schools and also for self-learners). 2nd ed. Chicago: A. Geringer, 1884. 204p.

Zdrůbek, František B., Základové českého pravopisu a mluvnice. Pro školy českoamerické (Fundamentals of Czech spelling and grammar. For Czech-American schools). Chicago: A. Geringer, 1882. 3rd ed. 95p.

Jonáš, Karel, Bohemian Made Easy. Učebnice češtiny pro anglicky mluvící národy. 2nd ed. Racine: Slavie, 1890.

Soukup, Antonín M., Praktická škola anglického jazyka (Practical school of English language). Chicago: Author, 1895. 283p.

Zdrůbek, František B., Anglický vyslovovatel. Navedení ku správnému vyslovování, hláskování, slabikování, čtení a psaní anglických slov s udáním výslovnosti a českých významů (English pronouncer. Guide to correct pronunciation, reading and writing of English words by providing pronunciation and Czech meanings). Chicago: A. Geringer, 1897. 213p.

Soukup, Antonín M., Znalec angličtiny. Nová anglická mluvnice (English expert. New English grammar). Chicago: Author, 1899. 196p.

Soukup, Antonín M., Čtenář novin anglických. Anglická mluvnice a pomůcka, jak se naučit číst noviny anglické (Reader of English newspapers. English grammar how to learn to read English newspapers). Chicago: Author, 1907. 192p.

Karník, Jan Jiří, Mluvnice jazyka českého. A Grammar of the Bohemian Language. New York: Česká svobodomyslná škola, 1912. 156p.; 2nd ed., 1917. 156p.

Francl, F., Učebnice jazyka anglického pro samouky (Textbook of English for self learners). New York: Bohemian Pub., and Importing Co., 1912-13. 248p.

Zmrhal, Jaroslav Josef, Anglicky snadno ve třiceti úlohách. Úplný kurs k naučení se mluvení jazyka anglického bez učitele (English easily learned in thirty lessons. A complete course to speak English without a teacher). Chicago: A Geringer, 1913. 112p.

Zmrhal, Jaroslav Josef, Methods for Bohemians to learn English. Milwaukee, WI: Caspar, 1913. 112p.

Nigrin, Jaroslav Victor, Bohemian Grammar (Bohemian Made easy). Improved edition. Chicago: Slavie Pub. Co., 1918. 192p.

Štěpánek, Orin, Simplified Czechoslovak Grammar and Conservation Book. Omaha: Historical Society of Nebraska, 1930. 320p.

Machek, A., Cvičebnice jazyka pro české školy v Americe (Czech textbook for Czech schools in America. Chicago: Sdružení českých svobodomyslných škol v Chicagu a okolí, 1932. 50p.

Machek, A., Druhá cvičebnice jazyka pro české školy v Americe (Second language textbook for Czech schools in America. Chicago: Sdružení českých svobodomyslných škol v Chicagu a okolí, 1933. 48p.

Machek, A., Mluvnice pro děti českých svobodomyslných škol (Textbook for children of Czech Free Thought schools). Chicago: Jednota ČSA, n.d. 94p.

Štěpánek, Orin, Czech (Bohemian) Grammar. Omaha: Czech Historical Society of Nebraska, 1933. 393p.

Našim dětem. Učebnice pro I. třídu českých svobodomyslných škol v Americe (For our children. Textbook for the 1st grade of Czech Free Thought schools in America). Chicago: Sdružení svobodomyslných škol v Chicagu, 1935. 124p.

Mikula, Bohumil E., Progressive Czech (Bohemian). Chicago: Czechoslovak National Council of America, 1936. 578p.; 5th rev. ed. 1965. 574p.

4. Readers

Jonáš, Karel, Slabikář a první čítanka. Počátky mluvnice a pravopisu pro československou mládež v Americe (Primer and reader. Fundamentals of grammar and spelling for Czechoslovak youth in America). Racine: Slavie, 1864. 64p.; 2nd ed., 1870.

Zdrůbek, František B., První čítanka česká pro školy česko-americké, od národního učitele (First Czech reader for Czech-American schools, by a native teacher). Chicago: A. Geringer, 1875. 116p.; 3rd ed. 1879; 5th ed. 1881.; 13th ed.

Zdrůbek, František B., Čítanka druhá pro školy česko-americké, od národního učitele (Second reader for Czech-American schools, by a native teacher). Chicago: A. Geringer, 1876. 140p.; 7th ed. 330p.

Koudelka, Josef Maria, První čítanka pro milou českou mládež. Pomocí několika přátel sestavil . . . (Reader for dear Czech youth). Chicago: Czech Benedictine Press, 1881. 82p.

Koudelka, Josef M., Druhá čítanka pro milou českou mládež. Pomocí několika přátel sestavil . . . (Second reader for dear Czech youth.

With the help of several friends compiled . . .). Chicago: Čeští Benediktini, 1881. 114p., 9p.

Koudelka, Josef M., Třetí čítanka pro milou českou mládež. Pomocí několika přátel sestavil . . . (Third reader for dear Czech youth. With the help of several friends compiled . . .). Chicago: Čeští Benediktini, 1882. 8p, 374p.

Zdrůbek, František B., Druhá čítanka pro školy českoamerické i pro domácnost (Third reader for Czech-American schools and also for home). 4th ed. Chicago: A. Geringer, 1895. 330p.

Zdrůbek, František B.,Třetí čítanka pro školy českoamerické i pro domácnost (Third reader for Czech-American schools and also for home). Chicago: A. Geringer, n.d. 292p.

Čítanka pro české děti v Americe (Reader for Czech schools in America). New York: Hlas lidu, 1903. 160p; Díl II. New Yorské listy, 1907. 114p; Díl III,. F. Lier, 1907. 152p.

Čítanka první (slabikář) s obrázky Mikuláše Alše a j. (First reader [primer] with pictures of Mikuláš Aleš and others). New York: New Yorské listy, 1907. 98p.

Nigrin, Jaroslav Victor, Čítanka první pro české svobodomyslné školy (First reader for Czech Free Thought schools). New York; New Yorské listy, 1910.

Beneš, Vojta, Česká čítanka československé mládeži v Americe (Czech reader for Czechoslovak youth in America). Praha: 'Právo lidu', 1912. 430p.

Beneš, Vojta, Druhá čítanka pro české děti v Americe (Second reader for Czech children in America). New York: Sbor zástupců České svobodomyslné školy, 1916. 166p.

Veverka, František, Třetí čítanka pro české svobodomyslné školy v Americe (Third reader for Czech Free Thought schools in America). Chicago: Sdružení českých svobodomyslných škol v Chicagu, 1917. 460p.

Vašků, Bedřich O., ed., Čítanka malých. První stupeň českoamerických škol (Reader for small children. First grade of Czech-American schools). New York: Sbor zástupců české svobodomyslné školy, 1918. 96p.

Mašek, Josef, Slabikář pro česko-americké svobodomyslné školy (Primer for Czech-American Free Thought schools). Cleveland: Sdružení svobodomyslných škol, 1919. 65p.

Zmrhal, Jaroslav J., Selected Readings in Czechoslovak for High Schools and Colleges. Chicago: A. Geringer, 1923. 2nd ed. 239p.
Vita, Sister M., comp., Druhá čítanka pro české katolické školy v Americe (Second reader for Czech Catholic schools in America). Chicago: Svaz českých katolíků, 1931. 284p.
Vita, Sister M., comp., Třetí čítanka pro české katolické školy v Americe (Third reader for Czech Catholic schools in America). Chicago: Svaz českých katolíků, 1934. 444p.

L. Handbooks—Manuals—Guides

1. Advising New Settlers

Příruční knížka o pozemcích dráhy Union Pacific ve státu Nebrasce (Pocket book about lands of the Union Pacific Railroad in Nebraska). Omaha: 'Pokrok západu,' 1873. 16p.
Popis Nebrasky a pozemků dráhy Union Pacific (Description of Nebraska and the lands of the Union Pacific Railroad). Omaha: 'Pokrok západu,' 1877.
Rosický, Jan, Jak je v Americe? Pro ponaučení nově do Ameriky přijetých krajanů ze své zkušenosti 45-letého pobytu v Americe a 30-letého působení žurnalistického (How is it in America? A guide for newly arrived countrymen in America from his experience of 45 years of stay in America and 30 years as a journalist). Omaha: Národní tiskárna, 1906. 48p.; 2nd ed., 1912.
Pokyny jak zabrati vládní pozemky a domoviny (Instructions how to take possession of government lands). Chicago: A. Geringer, 1913. 16p.
Janák, Jan, Nový osadník (The new settler). Omaha: Národní tiskárna, 1915.
Příručka Čechoslováků v cizině (A handbook for Czechoslovaks abroad). Praha: Vystěhovalec, 1927. 62p.

2. Advising Farmers

Juránek, Tomáš, Ovocná zahrada, čili, Nauka o pěstování ovocných stromů (Orchard, or, teaching about growing the fruit trees). Milwaukee: Author, 1878. 183p.
Jonáš, Karel, Zlatá kniha pro farmera. O vnitřních i zevnějších nemocech koní, skotu, dobytka skopového i vepřového, též drůbeže (Golden

book for a farmer. About internal and external diseases of horses, cattle, sheep, pigs and poultry). 3rd ed. Racine: Slavie, 1885. 364p.; 4th ed., 1893. 342p.

Ulčík, J., Včelaření (Bee Keeping). Omaha: Pokrok západu, n.d. 252p.

Breuer, Karel Hugo, Nemoce koňské (Diseases of horses). Omaha: Národní tiskárna, 1899. 520p.

Bašta, F. X., Drůbežnictví nové doby (Poultry production in new era). Omaha: Národní tiskárna, 1908. 181p.

Kašpar, Anton and J. Em. Kroupa, Praktický americký včelař (Practical American beekeeper). Omaha: Národní tiskárna, 1912. 64p.; 2nd ed., 1929.

Janák, Jan, Praktický farmářův rádce. Soubor důležitých údajů, návodů, předpisů, atd. (Practical farmer's guide. Collection of information, instructions, regulations, etc.). Omaha: Národní tiskárna, 1913. 138p.

Březáček, Josef, Hovorna zahradkářů. Dotazy a odpovědi zahradkářů (Discussions among gardeners. Inquiries and responses of gardeners). Chicago: L. Maly, n.d. 141p.

Janák, Jan, Choroby drůbež a jich léčení (Poultry diseases and their treatment). Omaha: Národní tiskárna, 1914. 156p.; 2nd ed., 1921.

Janák, Jan, Sadařství a štěpařství (Fruit growing and grafting). Omaha: Národní tiskárna, 1916. 116p.; 2nd ed., 1928.

Redakce 'Hospodáře,' Užitečná a praktická zařízení na farmě. Pro koně, dobytek, drůbež, zahradu, pole, domácnost a různé jiné (Useful and practical provisions on the farm. For horses, cattle, poultry, gardens, fields, household and various other). Omaha: Národní tiskárna, 1916. 201p.

Piskač, Antonín, Králikářství (Rabbit keeping). Omaha: Národní tiskárna, 1916. 72p.

Chládek, Vojta, Dbal a nedbal. Rozhovory dvou česko-amerických farmářů (One cares and the other doesn't. Conversations between a careful and careless farmer). Omaha: Národní tiskárna, 1917. 192p.

Heller, Richard, Zvěrolékař (Veterinarian). Omaha: Národní tiskárna, 1917. 202p.

Janák, Jan, Chov dobytka (Stock raising). Omaha: Národní tiskárna, 1917. 183p.

Musil, Ferdinand L., Praktické domácí zelinářství, k potřebě Čecho-Američanů (Practical vegetable gardening for the use of Czech-Americans). Chicago: Bratří Holanů, 1917. 158p.

Musil, Ferdinand L., Založení zelinářské zahrady a pařeniště (Establishing a vegetable garden and a hotbed). Chicago: Bratří Holanů, 1917. 52p.

Janák, Jan, Cement a beton na farmě (Cement and concrete on the farm). Omaha: Národní tiskána, 1917. 126p.

Musil, Ferdinad L., Rostliny kořenné, neboli koření kuchyňské (Herbaceous plants, or kitchen spices). Chicago: Bratří Holanů, 1918. 72p.

Janák, Jan, Americké drůbežnictví (American poultry production). Omaha: Národní tiskárna, 1918. 197p.

Horák, K. O., pseud., (Jan Em. Kroupa), Drobné ovoce a jeho pěstování (Small fruits and their production). Omaha: Národní tiskárna, 1918.

Kroupa, Jan Em., Domácí zelinářství (Vegetable gardening). Omaha: Národní tiskárna, 1920. 73p.

Čermak, Emil and Jan Em. Kroupa, Herbář, čili, Léčivé rostliny, jich popis, pěstování a upotřebení (Herbarium, or, Medicinal plants, their description, growing and use). Omaha: Národní tiskárna, 1922. 218p.

Rosická, Růžena, comp., Užitečná a praktická zařízení na farmě (Useful and practical contrivances for the farm). Omaha: Národní tiskárna, 1921. 224p.

Musil, Ferdinand L., Pro naše zahrady a zahrádky (For our gradens). Chicago: Denní hlasatel, 1937. 64p.

3. Advising Homes & Households

Klácel, Ladimír, Věčný kalendář, čili kniha svojanská, obsahující zajímavé a poučlivé čtení na všecky dny života (Eternal calendar, or 'Svojanov' book, containing interesting and instructive reading about every day of life), pts. 1-10. Milwaukee: A. Novák, 1877. 32p.

Tesař, František, Matka, vychovatelka dítek. Prospěšné rady rodičům (Mother, childrens' educator. Useful advice to parents). Praha: J. Kolář, 1877. 65p.

Klácel, Ladimír, Manželka a matka. Připomínky sebrané ze zkušeností pro založení a udržení blahého domova (Wife and mother. Suggestions collected from experiences for establishing and maintaining a happy home). Milwaukee: A. Novák, 1883. 44p.

Novák, Antonín, Spolehlivý domácí rádce. Hojná sbírka vyzkoušených a jednoduchých předpisů a rad k potřebě každé rodiny českoamerické a každého povolání lidského. Dle různých pramenů a vlastní zkušenosti sestavil (Reliable home advisor. A large collection of tested and simple advice and tips for the use of every Czech-American family and every occupation. According to various sources and one's own experience). Milwaukee: A. Novák, n.d.

Pokladnice, zlatá, domácí. Hojná sbírka nových předpisů pro rolníky, řemeslníky a živnostníky a jiná užitečná navedení pro hospodyně a kuchařky (Treasury, golden, home. A large collection of new regulations for farmers, artisans and tradesmen and other useful instructions for housewives and cooks). Milwaukee: A. Novák, 1889. 240p.

Domácí štěstí. Spolehlivý rádce v domácnosti a kuchyni. Pro českoamerické poměry upravil 'Starý Hospodář' (Happiness at home. A reliable guide for the household and the kitchen. For Czech-American conditions arranged by 'Starý Hospodář'). Milwaukee: A Novák, 1889. 300p.; 2nd ed., 1901.

Obcování s druhým pohlavím, aneb, Jak získá si jinoch lásku a přízeň díky (Association with the opposite sex, or, How does a young man gain love and favor of a girl). Chicago: A. Geringer, n.d. 53p.

Poučení jak může dívka v krátkém čase státi se nevěstou a mažlekou (Instructions how a girl in a short time can become a bride and a wife).Chicago: A. Geringer, n.d. 23p.

Umění jak v krátkem čase získati nevěstu dle přání s penězi neb bez nich. Praktický a bezpečný návod i věrný, potřebný rádce pro jinochy všech stavů, kteří se chtějí ženiti (The art of how to gain a bride in a short time with or without money. Practical and faithful instructions, a needy guide for young men who desire to get married). Chicago: A. Geringer, n.d. 46p.

Iška, František, Svobodomyslná výchova dítek. Rukověť pro rodiče a přátele mládeže (Free Thought education of children. Guide for parents and friends of young people). Chicago: A. Geringer, 1903. 80p.

Úplný Rychlý Počtář. Příruční knížka pro kupující a prodávající s tabulkami o ceně zboží v jakémkoli množství a jakékoliv hodnotě od 1 centu do 10 dolarů, at se váží nebo měří . . . (A complete rapid calculator. A pocket book for the buyers and sellers with tables of prices of merchandise in any amount and any value from 1 cent to 10 dollars, whether weighing or measuring). Chicago: A. Geringer, n.d. 249p.

4. Legal Matters

a. General Laws

Zdrůbek, František B., Vývoj práva, aneb Co jest hřích a co neni? (Development of law, or What is a sin and what isn't). Omaha: Author, 1874. 48p.

Jonáš, Karel, Zákony americké (American laws). Racine, WI: Slavie, 1879. 181p.; 2nd ed., 1886. 192p.

Král, Josef Jiří, Americké právo. Sbírka zákonův a výkladů právních pro osadníky česko-americké zvláště důležitých (American Law, Collection of laws and legal interpretations, especially important for Czech-American settlers). Vol. 1. Racine: Slavie, 1899. 381p.

Vojan, Jaroslav Egon Salaba, comp., Několik důležitých zákonů (Several important laws). Omaha: Národní tiskárna, 1909. 16p.

b. Naturalization & Citizenship

Král, Josef Jiří, Americké občanství (American citzenship). Cleveland: 'Americké dělnické listy,' n.d. 57p.

Pergler, Karel, Přistěhovalec v Americe. Stručný nárys přstěhovaleckých a naturalizačních zákonů Spojených Států (Immigrant in America. A brief outline of immigrant and naturalization laws of the US). Chicago: 'Spravedlnost,' 1907. 56p.

Geringer, Vladimír August, Jak dosáhnout naturalizace (How to gain naturalization). Chicago: A. Geringer, 1914. 40p.

c. Civics

Ústava Spojených Států amerických. Translated by F. B. Zdrůbek. Omaha: F. B. Zdrůbek, 1874. 32p.

Doležal, Karel, Naše republika, čili, Ústava Spojených Států severoamerických se zvláštním zřetelem o zastupování a právu lidu (Our Republic, or, Constitution of the US with special emphasis on representation and the rights of people). New York: J. S. Čada, 1887. 47p.

Pacák, Louis, Základy občanské nauky americké (Fundamentals of American civics). New York, 191? 232p.

Zmrhal, Jaroslav Joseph, První čítanka občanská (First civics reader). Chicago: Colonial Dames of Illinois, 1912. 64p.

Zmrhal, Jaroslav Joseph, Civic Primer. Designed for the guidance of the immigrant. Chicago: Colonial Dames of Illinois, 1915. 63p.

Občanský katechismus o právech a povinnostech amerických občanů (Civic catechism about the rights and responsibilities of American citizens). Chicago: Bohemian Benedictine Press, 1925. 72p.

Vašků, Bedřich, Co každý občan věděti má. Průvodce cizince do nauky občanské ve Spojených Státech severoamerických (What every citizen should know. Guide for foreigners to civics in the US). New York: New Yorské listy, 1928? 69p.

d. Parliamentary Rules

Pacák, Louis, Parlamentární řád, čili navedení pro předsedy, úředníky a údy všech spolků a při schůzích veřejných, jak udržeti pořádek a vésti jednání (Parliamentary procedures, or a guide for chairpersons, officers and members of all clubs and during public meetings, how to maintain order and conduct meetings). Chicago: A. Geringer, 1876. 18p.

Fischer, Edward A., Příruční kniha parlamentárních pravidel pro řízení uvažujících shromáždění (A pocket guide of parliamentary rules for conducting meetings). Chicago: A. Geringer, 1887. 284p.

Zdrůbek, František B., Parlamentární řád (Parliamentary rules). Chicago: A. Geringer, n.d. 86p.

5. Medical Matters

Pečírka, Josef, Domácí lékař a doplňky od Dra. J. Habenichta (Home physician, with Addenda from Dr. J. Habenicht). Chicago: A. Geringer, 1890. 402p.

Kneipp, Šebestián, Jak žíti. Rady a pokyny zdravým i nemocným, aby prostě, rozumně žili a přirozeně se léčili (How to live. Guidance and instructions to the healthy as well as to the ill, so that they could live rationally and naturally). Milwaukee: A. Novák, 1897. 324p.

Seznam léčebných prostředků (Inventory of therapeutic preparations). Chicago: Vyd. Společností 'České Herbarium,' n.d.

Zdravotní pokyny a rádce pro domácnost. Upravil 'Zkušeny odborník' (Health instructions and guide for a household. Arranged by an experienced professional). Chicago: Czech Benedictine Press, 1902. 45p.

Zima, Otakar, Nauka o pěstování krásy tělestné, čili, Kosmetika (Teaching about maintaining physical beauty, or, Cosmetics). Chicago: A Geringer, 1902. 119p.

Ježek, Jan P., Kneippovo léčení, neboli, Stručné poučení o jeho methodě o tom, po čem poznával nemoci a jak je léčil (Kneipp's treatment, or, Brief descriprion of his method, how he recognized diseases and how he treated them). Omaha: Národní tiskárna, 1902. 108p.

Breuer, K. H., Domácí léčení. Stručný popis jak léčit doma obyčejné nemoce a jak předejíti těžším nemocem a vyléčiti je v jich začátku. Pro americké krajany ze svých zkušeností napsal . . . (Home medical treatment. A brief description of how to treat ordinary diseases at home and how to prevent more serious diseases and cure them at their onset. For American countrymen written on the basis of his own experiences . . .). Omaha: Národní tiskárna, 1908. 202p.

Prokeš, Josef, Domáci léčení (Home medical treatment). Chicago: A. Geringer, n.d.

Kapr, V., Člověk a jeho poměr ku přírodě. Důležité poučení o manželství a jak léčit mnohé pohlavní choroby (Man and his relation to nature. Important information about marriage and how to treat many genital diseases). Chicago: A. Geringer, n.d. 169p.

Křížek, Čeněk, Základové porodnictví (Fudamentals of obstetrics). Omaha: Pokrok západu, n.d. 658p.

Warta, J. J., Poučné pojednání o očích, nose a hrtanu (Instructive discourse about eyes, nose and throat). Omaha: Author, 1919. 31p.

Breuer, Karel Hugo, Zdravověda (Hygiene). Chicago: A. Geringer, 1923. 631p.

Čermák, Emil, Domácí lékárna. Popis léků a jejich použití v domácím léčení . . . . Herbář, čili léčivé rostliny, jejich popis a upotřebení. (Home pharmacy. Description of medicines and their use at home. Herbarium, or medicinal plants, their description and use). Omaha: Národní tiskárna, 1939. 196p.

6. Etiquette

Dvorný společník. Pravidla slušného se chování, navedení i vzory k vyznání lásky, společenské hry, hádanky, přípitky, atd. (A courtly companion. Rules of proper behavior, a guide and illustrations of how to declare love, social games, riddles, toasts etc.). Chicago: A. Geringer, n. d. 238p.

Nejnovější tajemník lásky. Nepostradatelný návod pro mladé muže a dívky jak chovati se ve společnosti (Indispensable instructions for young men and women on how to behave socially). New York: Patria Pub. Co., n.d. 53p.

7. Letter Writing

Český gratulant. Sbírka přání k novému roku, k jmeninám a narozeninám (Czech congratulatory wisher. Collection of congratulatory messages on the occasion of New Year, name days and birthdays). Chicago, A. Geringer, 18?? 48p.

Gratulant. Hojná sbírka dětských přání, k novému roku, jmeninám a zrozeninám rodičů, přibuzných, přátel, a j. (Congratulator. Abundant collection of children's wishes for the New Year, names dates a birthdates of parents, relatives, friends etc.). Chicago: A. Geringer, 1887. 185p.

Dopisovatel českoamerický. Obsahuje návody ku správnému sestavení společenských dopisů, českých i anglických, různých obchodních a právních listin dle amerických zákonů (Czech-American correspondent. Contains instructions for formulation of social letters, Czech and English, various business and legal letters according to American laws). Chicago: A. Geringer, n.d. 122p.

Milostné dopisy, aneb, 'Tajemník lásky,' obsahující příklady a vzory dopisů všeho druhu, jaké jen vůbec zamilovaným psát se naskytuje (Love letters, or, 'Love Secretary,' containing examples and samples of letters of various kind for lovers). Chicago: A. Geringer, n.d. 96p.

Milostné dopisy. Sbírka různých dopisů pro zamilované (Love letters. A collection of various letters for lovers). New York: Patria Pub. Co., n.d.

Bohemian-American Letter Writing, or, Directions to compose correctly, letters, documents, etc., which occur in the social relations and business life in the United States. Chicago: A. Geringer, 1907. 122p.; also in Czech.

8. Speeches

Jurka, Anton, comp., Americký besedník. První sbírka proslovů a deklamací (American entertainer. The first collection of speeches and recitals). Chicago: A. Geringer, 1876. 482p.

Zdrůbek, František B., et al., Pohřební řeči nad rakví a u hrobu, pro veškeré dámské spolky (Funeral orations over the casket and by grave, for various women's clubs). Chicago: A. Geringer, n.d. 24p.

Zdrůbek, František B., et al., Pohřební řeči s přidáním řeči při pojmenování dítek, řeč kmotra, a poděkování otce (Funeral orations and speeches when naming infants, speech of a godfather and a thanking father). Chicago: A. Geringer, 1881. 24p.; 2nd ed., 1890. 56p.

Hájek, Josef J., comp., Úplná sbírka řečí a proslovů ke všem slavnostem spolkovým a národním (Complete collection of speeches and addresses for all club and national celebrations). Chicago: A. Geringer, n.d. 151p.

Kalda, Josef. Pohřební řeč pro různé stavy a věky (Funeral orations for various occasions and ages). Chicago: A. Geringer, 1886. 120p.

Besedník českoamerický. Sbírka proslovů, deklamací, sólových výstupů, blahopřání, atd. (Czech-American entertainer. Collection of addresses, recitals, solo performances, greetings, etc.) Racine: Slavie, 1898. 472p.

Janda, Alois, Kniha přípitků (A book of toasts). Omaha: Národní knihovna, 1902. 96p.

Janda, Alois, comp., Česko-americký besedník a deklamátor. Sbírka deklamací a veršovaných proslovů k rúzným slavnostem spolkovým a národním (Czech-American entertainer and declaimer. Collection of recitals and presentations in verses for various club and national celebrations). Omaha: Národní tiskárna, 1903-04. 3 vols.

Janda, Alois, Nový besedník českoamerické mládeže (New entertainer for Czech-American youth). Chicago: A. Geringer, 1910. 128p.

Janda, Alois, Proslovy a řeči ku slavnostem spolkovým. Stezkami dějin a k památce velkých duchů (Addresses and speeches at club celebrations. Through paths of history and in memory of great minds). Chicago: A. Geringer, 1910. 158p.

M. Libraries—Museums—Archives

1. General

Čapek, Tomáš, "Knihovny" (Libraries), in: Naše Amerika. Praha: Národní rada československá, 1926, pp. 445-446.

Wynar, Lubomyr R. and Lois Buttlar, "Czech-American Resources," in: Guide to Ethnic Museums, Libraries, and Archives in the United States. Kent, OH: School of Library Science, Kent State University, 1978, pp. 130-139.

Buttlar, Lois and Lubomyr R. Wynar, "Czech-American Resources," in: Guide to Information Resources in Ethnic Museum, Library, and Archival Collections in the United States. Westport, CT: Greenwood Press, 1996, pp. 72-76; "Czechoslovak Resources," Ibid., pp. 76-78.

Rechcigl, Miloslav, Jr., Czechoslovak American Archivalia. Part I (Government Repositories; University-Based Collections; Collections Maintained by Public Museums and Libraries; Collections of Ethnic and Other Related Organizations). Olomouc-Ostrava: Repronis, 2004. 206p.

Rechcigl, Miloslav, Jr., Czechoslovak American Archivalia. Part II (Personal Papers and Collections; Repositories abroad Bearing on the Subject; Virtual Archives on the Internet). Olomouc-Ostrava: Repronis, 2004. 368p.

České archivy a prameny k dějinám zahraničních Čechů (Czech archives and sources to history of Czechs abroad). K vydání připravili: Milena Secká, Jiří Křesťan a Jan Kahuda. Praha: Národní archiv, 2007. 226p.

2. Specific Institutions

Lifka, Bohumír, Národní knihovna Čechů a Slováků zahraničních (National Library of Czechs and Slovaks Abroad). Zvl. otisk z "Marginálií", Věstník Spolku českých bibliofilů, 9, No. 7-8 (1935). 11p.

Průvodce. Náprstkovo muzeum asijských, afrických a amerických kultůr (Guide. Naprstek Museum of Asian, African and American Cultures. Praha: Národní museum, 1999. 82p.

Secká, Milena, "Náprstkova krajanská knihovna" (Náprstek library on Czechs abroad), in: Česi za hranicemi na přelomu 20. a 21. století. Sympozium o českém vystěhovalectví, . . . Praha: Univerzita Karlova, 2000, pp. 243-246.

Blewitt, Paul and Simon Reynolds, "The Moravian Church Archives and Library," Journal of the Society of Archivists, 22 (2001): 193-203.

Nemecek, Paul M., "CSAGSI Library," Kořeny, 9, No. 3 (June 2005), pp. 5-6.

National Czech & Slovak Museum & Library. "30th Anniversary Commemorative Issue." Special issue, Slovo, 4, No. 2 (Winter 2004). 36p.

Křesťan, Jiří, The Central Czech Archives in Prague and the Czechs Abroad," in: Czech and Slovak American Archival Materials and their Preservation. Edited by Miloslav Rechcigl, Jr. Praha: Pražská edice, 2004, pp. 33-36.

Muhlena, David, "The Library and Archives of the National Czech and Slovak Museum & Library," in: Czech and Slovak American Archival Materials and their Preservation. Edited by Miloslav Rechcigl, Jr. Praha: Pražská edice, 2004, pp. 55-58.

Nečas, Daniel, "Immigration History Research Center at the University of Minnesota: Its Contribution to Preserving the Czech and Slovak American Heritage," in: Czech and Slovak American Archival Materials and their Preservation. Edited by Miloslav Rechcigl, Jr. Praha: Pražská edice, 2004, pp. 67-71.

Farris, June Pachuta, "Czech and Slovak Collections at the University of Chicago," in: Czech and Slovak American Archival Materials and their Preservation. Edited by Miloslav Rechcigl, Jr. Praha: Pražská edice, 2004, pp. 84-88.

Peuker, Paul, "The Unity Archives in Herrnhut," in: Czech and Slovak American Archival Materials and their Preservation. Edited by Miloslav Rechcigl, Jr. Praha: Pražská edice, 2004, pp. 135-138.

Rosene, Effie M., Czech Center Museum Houston, Welcome to the Czech Center Museum Houston. A Docent Historical Tour. Houston, TX, 2011.

II. History

A. Emigration & its Causes. Emigration Policy

1. General

Muller, K, Máme-li se stěhovat do Ameriky" (Should we emigarate to the US). Jindřichův Hradec, 1856.

Fořt, Josef, O stěhovaní se lidu našeho do ciziny (On the migration of our people abroad). Praha, 1876.

Jonáš, Karel, "Emigration from Bohemia," Reports from the Consuls of the US, 32 (1890), pp. 491-493.

Jonáš, Karel, "Bohemian and Hungarian Emigration to the United States," Reports from the Consuls of the United States, 32 (1890), pp. 493-494.

Auerhan, Jan, "České vystěhovalectví" (Czech emigration), Pokroková revue, 2 (1905-06), pp. 287-292, 366-373, 420-428, 483-486.

Balch, E.G., Slav Emigration and its Source: Bohemian Emigration," Charities and Commons, 15 (1906), 591-602.

Balch, Emily Greene, "Bohemian Emigration," in: Our Slavic Fellow Citizens. New York: Charities Publication Committee, 1910, pp. 63-84.

Miller, Kenneth D, "Emigration," in: The Czecho-Slovaks in America. New York: George H. Doran, 1922, pp. 42-46.

Šindelář, Bedřich, Několik poznámek k otázce vystěhovalectví v epoše kapitalismu (Some comments concerning the emigration question during capitalism), Sborník prací filosofické fakulty brněnské university, 3, Řada historická, č. 1 (Brno 1954), pp. 18-43.

Kutnar, F., "Počátky českého vystěhovalectví do zámoří" (Beginnings of the Czech emigration overseas), Dějepis a zeměpis ve škole, 4, No. 6 (1961-62), p. 184ff.

Kutnar, František, Počátky hromadného vystěhovalectví z Čech v období Bachova absolutismu (Beginnings of the mass emigration from Bohemia during Bach's absolutism), Rozpravy ČSAV, řada společenských věd, 74, No. 15 (1964).

Šatava, Leoš, "Evropská migrace na severoamerický kontinent v 19. století a její odraz v historii českého etnika" (European migration to the North American Continent in the 19th century and its reflection in the history of the Czech ethnic group), in: Migrační procesy a české vystěhovalectví 19. století do USA. Praha: Univerzita Karlova, 1989, pp. 44-71.

Polišenský, Josef. Úvod do studia dějin vystěhovalectví do Ameriky. I. Obecné problémy dějin českého vystěhovalectví do Ameriky 1848-1914 (Introduction to the study of history of emigration to America. I. General problems concerning the history of Czech emigration to America 1848-1914). Praha: Univerzita Karlova, 1992. 56p.

Korytová-Magstadt, Štěpánka, "Emigration in Bohemia and Moravia: A Closer Look," in: To Reap a Bountiful Harvest. Iowa City: Rudi Publishing, 1993, pp. 13-27.

Kořalka, Jiří and Květa Kořalková, "Základní tendence českého vystěhovalectví a české reemigrace do počátku 20. let 20. století" (Basic features of Czech emigration and reemigration until the 20s of the 20th century), Češi v zahraničí, 7 (1993), pp. 30-47.

Ulč, O., "Profil a motivace československých emigrantů v osmdesátých letech našeho století" (Profile and motivation of emigrants in the eighties of our century), Sociologický časopis, 31, No. 4 (1995), pp. 473-483.

Šatava, Leoš, "Vystěhovalectví do USA" (Emigration to the US), Češi v cizině, 9 (1996), pp. 155-171.

Vystěhovalectví do Ameriky 1850-1914. Sborník příspěvků účastníků sympozia v Lichnově 5. června 1999 (Emigration to America 1850-1914. Collection of papers from the Symposium in Lichnov, June 5, 1999). Lichnov: Obecní úřad Lichnov, 1999. 39p.

Hrubý, K. and S. Brouček, Eds., Češi za hranicemi na přelomu 20. a 21. století (Czechs abroad at the turn of the 20th and 21st centuries). Sympozium o českém vystěhovalectví, exulantsví a vztazích zahraničních Čechů k domovu, 29.-30. června, 1998. Praha, Karolinum ve spolupráci s Etnologickým ústavem AV ČR, 2000.

Brouček, Stanislav: Etapy českého vystěhovalectví (Periods of Czech emigration). Praha: Etnologický ústav akademie věd ČR, 2003.

Jaklová, Alena, "Česká emigrace" (Czech emigration), in: Čechoamerická periodika 19. století. Brno: Nadace Universitatis Masarykiana, 2004, 2006, pp. 26-37.

2. Reasons for Emigration

Šír, L., Vystěhovalecká otázka s hlediska národního a hospodářského (Emigration question from the national and economic points of view), Naše zahraničí, 3 (Praha, 1920), p. 170ff.

Československé vystěhovalectví, jeho příčiny, důsledky a vyhlídky (Czechoslovak emigration, its causes, consequences and prospects). Praha: Sociálni ústav, 1928.

Čapek, Thomas, "Sociological Factors in Czech Immigration," Slavonic Review, 22 (1944), pp. 93-98.

Mayer, Alfred M., R. Kocourek, V. Tlapák and J. Čech, Československé vystěhovalectví s hlediska potřeb naší doby (Czechoslovak emigration from the perspective of the needs of our time). Praha, 1934.

Kisch, Guido, "Jewish Emigration to America from Bohemia and its Causes," in: In Search of Freedom. London: Edward Goldston, 1948, pp. 19-69.

Šindelář, B., "Kořeny a povaha českého vystěhovalectví za kapitalismu" (The roots and characteristics of the Czech emigration during capitalism), in: Začiatky českej a slovenskej emigrácie do USA. Bratislava: SAV, 1970, pp. 13-48.

Chmelar, Johann, "The Austrian Emigration, 1900-1914," in: Dislocation and Emigration: The Social Background of American Immigration. Ed. Donald Fleming and Bernard Bailyn. Cambridge, MA, 1974, pp. 265-378.

Brouček, S., "K příčinám a důvodům vystěhovalectví Čechů a Slováků mezi dvěma válkami v dopisech adresovaných Emigračnímu ústavu v Praze" (Causes and reasons of Czech and Slovak emigration between the two Wars in letters addressed to the Emigration Institute), in: Češi v cizině. Praha: Ústav pro etnografii a folkloristiku ČSAV, 1987, Vol. 2, pp. 182-232.

Korytová-Magstadt, Štěpánka, "The Push to Leave, the Pull to Stay," in: To Reap a Bountiful Harvest. Iowa City: Rudi Publishing, 1993, pp. 29-43.

Jana Fornůsková, Factors that Drove Czechoslovaks to Emigrate to the U.S. Bachelor Thesis, Tomas Bata University, Zlin, 2009. 58p.

Hachová, Veronika, Slovinská a česká emigrace do US po roce 1945—příčiny a přijetí (Slovenian and Czech emigration to the US after 1945—Causes and acceptance). Bakalářská práce. Univerzita Pardubice, Fakulta filozofická, Pardubice, 2010. 61p.

3. Emigration from Specific Areas

Korčák, Jaromír, Vylidňování jižních Čech: Studie demografická (Depopulation of South Bohemia: A demographic study). Praha: Spolek péče o blaho venkova, 1929.

Barborová, Eva, "Vystěhovalectví do Ameriky v Táborském kraji v létech 1855-1862" (Emigration to America from Tábor Region in years 1855-1862), Jihočeský sborník historický, 35, No. 1-2 (1966), pp. 24-32.

Hoffmanová, J., Vystěhovalectví z Polné do Severní Ameriky ve druhé polovině XIX. století (Emigration from Polná to North America in the second half of the nineteenth century). Havlíčkův Brod, 1969.

Geršic, Miroslav, "Příspěvek k vystěhovalectví z Břeclavska na sklonku 19. století" (Emigration from Břeclav Region at the close of the 19th century), in: Jižní Morava,14 (1978), pp. 128-148.

Cironisová, Eva, "Vystěhovalectví v milevském okrese před první světovou válkou" (Emigration from the Milevsko District before World War I), Jihočeský sborník historický, 49, No. 3 (1980), pp. 147-561.

Cironisová, Eva, "Vystěhovalectví z Pelhřimovska v letech 1850-1914" (Emigration from the Pelhřimov Region in 1850-1914), Jihočeský sborník historický, 50 (1981), p. 178.

Strnadel, Drahomír, "Vystěhovalectví z Frenštátu do Texasu v druhé polovině minulého století na základě nových pramenů" (Emigration from Frenštát to Texas in the second half of the last century according to new sources), in: Vlastivědný sborník okresů Nový Jičín, 38 (1986), pp. 31-37.

Langer, Edward G., "Landskroner Emigration to the American Midwest," Friends Newsletter. Newsletter of the Friends of the Max Kade Institute, 7, No. 3 (Fall 1998). Also on Internet: http://mki.wisc.edu/Newsletter/newsf98.html

Šilar, František. Emigrants to Texas from Eastern Cechy. Houston, TX: Author, 1989. 67p.

Mikeska, Jan. Emigrants from Zádveřice to America 1850-1915. Beaumont, TX: Printed Privately, 1991. 18p.

Strnadel, Drahomír. Tam za mořem je Amerika: Vystěhovalectví z Frenštátska ve 2. polovině 19. století (Beyond the ocean is America. Emigration from Frenštát Region in the 2nd half of the 19th century). Frenštát p. R.: Muzeum města Frenštátu p. R., 1992. 48p., 34p.

Strnadel, Drahomír, "Vystěhovalectví v 19. století" (Emigration in the 19th century), in: 700 let Lichnova: Historie obce Lichnova 1293-1993. Lichnov: Obecní úřad Lichnov, 1993, pp. 91-95.

Brouček, Stanislav, "Stěhování obyvatelstva z jižních Čech v letech 1850-1938" (Emigration of population from southern Bohemia 1850-1938), Češi v cizině, 7 (1993), pp. 48-68.

Šimíček, Josef. The Hope Has its Name Texas. The Emigration to America from Villages Bordovice and Lichnov during 1856-1914. Veřovice, Czech.: SITEX, 1996. 180p.

Šimíček, Josef. The Pilgrims for Hope. The Emigration to America during 1855-1914 from Villages Mniší, Tichá and Vlčovice. Volume 1. Veřovice, Czech.: SITEX, 1996. 224p.

Strnadel, Drahomír. Emigration to Texas from the Místek District between 1855 and 1900. Victoria, TX: Victoria County Czech Heritage Society, 1996. 207p.

Strnadel, Drahomír. Texas. The Remote and Near Country. Země vzdálená i blízká. Trojanovice, CR: Obce Trojanovice, 1997. 80p.

Kysilka, Karel, Emigration to the USA from the Polička region in 1850-1890. The paper presented at the Genealogy Seminar of the Czech Heritage Society of Texas, Hillsboro, TX. July 31, 1999.

Cironisová, Eva, "Vystěhovalectví do Spojených států amerických z táborského politického okresu 1849-1914" (Emigration to the US from Tábor political district 1849-1914), Táborský archiv, 10 (2000-2001), pp. 365-390.

Kysilka, Karel, "Vystěhovalectví z Boleslavska do USA" (Emigration from the Boleslav Region to the US), in: Sborník materiálů ze semináře 'Historie emigrace z českých zemí', který se konal při příležitosti Setkání krajanů v Mladé Boleslavi 22.-25. 6. 2000. Mladá Boleslav: Okresní muzeum v Mladé Boleslavi, 2001, pp. 23-28.

Jermář, Jaromír, "Historie emigrace z Mladoboleslavska" (History of emigration from the Mladá Boleslav Region), in: Sborník referátů ze semináře 'Historie emigrace z českých zemí,' který se konal pri příiležitosti Setkání krajanů v Mladé Boleslavi 22.-25. 6. 2000. Mladá Boleslav: Okresní muzeum v Mladé Boleslavi, 2001, pp. 35-40.

Šimíček, Josef. The Pilgrims for Hope. The Emigration to America 1856-1914 from Frenštát and Trojanovice. Volume 2. Frenštát, p. R. Czech.: GEMROT, 2001. 537p.

Šimíček, Josef. West znamená Západ. Emigrace do Ameriky z obce Věřovice v letech 1867 až 1914 (West means west. Emigration to America from the village of Věřovice in 1867 to 1914). Věřovice: Zdeněk Halamík, 2003. 60p.

Mikeska, Jan. Emigrants from the Southeastern Moravia, Particularly from Zádveřice and its Surrounding Area to Texas 1850-1915. Database. Prague: Author, 2003. 262p.

Strnadel, Drahomír, Tam za mořem—vystěhovalectví z Frenštátska do Ameriky (Beyond the ocean—Emigration from Frenstat to America). 2004.

Klučka, Jiří, Strnadel, Drahomír, Šimíček, Josef. Tam za mořem: vystěhovalectví z Frenštátska do Ameriky v 2. polovině 19. století (Beyond the sea: Emigration from the Frenštát Region to America in the second half of the 19th century). In Libreto: Muzeum Novojičínska—Muzeum ve Frenštátě pod Radhoštěm. Frenštát p. R.: Muzeum Novojičínska—Muzeum ve Frenštátě pod Radhoštěm, 2005. pp. 82-88.

Strnadel, Drahomír, Tam za mořem je Amerika: Vystěhovalectví z Frenštátska ve 2. polovině 19. století (Beyond the sea: Emigration from the Frenštát Region to America in the second half of the 19th century). Katalog. Frenštát p. R.: Muzejní a vlastivědná společnost, 2006. 40p.

Šimíček, Josef, "Vystěhovalectví z Frenštátska do Ameriky v 2. pol. 19. století" (Emigration form the Frenštát Region to America in the 2nd half of the 19th century), in: Hlasy muzea a archivu ve Frenštátě pod Radhoštěm, 23, No. 1-4 (2006), pp. 56-67; Ibid. 24, No, 1-4 (2007), pp. 67-74.

"Vystěhovalectví z Kopřivnice do Ameriky do Texasu koncem 19. a na počátku 20. století" (Emigration from Kopřivnice to America to Texas at the end of the 19th and the beginning of the 20th century), Vlastivědný sborník okresu Nový Jičín.

Spěvák, Přemysl, Z Břeclavska do Argentiny. Vystěhovalectví v letech 1913-1938 (From Břeclav Region to Argentina. Emigration in 1913-1938). Bakalářská diplomová práce. Masarykova univerzita, Brno, 2008.

4. Emigration Policy

Hejret, Jan, Vystěhovalecká otazka: Příspěvek k české a slovenské otázce (The emigration question: A contribution to the Czech and Slovak question). Prague, 1909.

Pimper, Antonín, Vystěhovalecká otázka (The emigration question). Praha: Nakladatelství Alois Srdce, 1914).

Mézl, F., "Naše vystěhovalecká politika" (Our emigration policy), Sociální revue, 2 (1920/21).

Sum, A., "The Emigration Policy of Czecho-Slovakia," in: Proc. National Conference of Social Work, Milwaukee, June 22-29, 1921. Chicago: University of Chicago, 1921, pp. 453-459.

Boháč, A., Vystěhovalectví z Československé republiky. Sociální politika v Československé republice (Emigration from Czechoslovak Republic. Social policy in the Czechoslovak Republic). Praha, 1924.

Mézl, F., Výklad zákona o vystěhovalectví a prováděјícího nařízení k němu (Interpretation of the emigration law and its procedural regulation). Praha, 1924.

Boháč, A., "Naše vystěhovalecká politika" (Our emigration policy), Naše doba, 32 (1925).

Vystěhovalecká politika Československé republiky (Emigration policy of the Czechoslovak Republic). Praha: Ministerstvo sociální péče, 1927. 18p.

Brandejs, Stanislav, Naše vystěhovalectví a naše vystěhovalecká politika (Our emigration and our emigration policy). Praha: Orbis, 1926.

Vystěhovalecká politika Československé republiky. Výroční zprávy Komise pro vystěhovalectví a kolonizaci za roky 1926 az 1928 (Emigration policy of Czechoslovak Republic. Annual reports of the Commission for emigration and colonization for 1926 through 1928), Sociální revue, 8 (1927).

Chmelar, Hans, Höhepunkte der Őesterreichische Ausswanderung aus den im Reichsrat vertretenen Königsrechen und Ländern im den Jahren 1905-1914. Wien, 1974.

Dubovický, Ivan. Právní úprava vystěhovalectví z Čech od dob Josefa II do světové hospodářské krize 1933 (Legal regulation of emigration from Bohemia from the time of Josef II until the world economic crisis of 1933). Diplomová práce FF UK, Praha, 1984.

Brouček, Stanislav and Ivo Vasiljev, "K charakteristice československé vystěhovalecké politice mezi dvěma světovými válkami" (Characteristics of the Czechoslovak emigration policy between the two World Wars), Český lid, 72 (1985), pp. 71-80, 149-157.

Dubovický, Ivan, "Právo a vystěhovalectví. Pokus o historicko-antropologickou interpretaci práva" (Law and emigration. An attempt at historical and anthropological interpretation of law), Češi v cizině, 7 (1993), pp. 67-92.

Rychlík, Jan, Cestování do ciziny v Habsburské monarchii a v Československu: Pasová, vízová a vystěhovalecká politika, 1848-1989 (Traveling abroad in Habsburg Monarchy and in Czechoslovakia: Passport, visa and emigration policy, 1848-1989). Praha: Ústav pro soudobé dějiny AV ČR, 2007. 259p.

5. Reemigration

Vaculík, V., Vznik Československa a reemigrace zahraničních Čechů" (Birth of Czechoslovakia and reemigration of Czechs living abroad), Češi v cizině, 4 (1989), pp. 110-119.

Kořalka, Jiří and Květa Kořalková, "Základní tendence českého vystěhovalectví a české reemigrace do počatku dvacátých let 20. století (Basic features of the Czech emigration and the Czech reemigration until the early 1920s of the 20th century), Češi v cizině, 7 (1993), pp. 30-47.

Vaculík, Jaroslav, "Zahraniční Češi a Slováci a jejich reemigrace po první a druhé světové válce" (Czechs and Slovaks abroad and their reemigration after the First and Second World War), in: Československtví—součást Evropanství. Brno: Česko-slovenský výbor, 1996, pp. 185—190.

Valášková, Naďa, "Z Čech do Ameriky, z Ameriky do Ruska. Nerealizovaný projekt druhotné migrace" (From Bohemia to America, from America to Russia. An unrealized project of secondary migration), in: Češi za hranicemi na přelomu 20. a 21 století. Sympozium o českém vystěhovalectví. Praha: Etnologický ústav AV ČR v Praze, 2000, pp. 67-73.

Nešpor, Zdeněk R. Reemigranti a sociálně sdílené hodnoty. Prolegomena k sociologickému studiu českých emigračních procesů 20. století se zvláštním zřetelem k západní reemigrací 90. let. (Reemigrants and the socially held values. Prolegomena to sociological study of the Czech emigration processes of the 20th century with special emphasis on the Western reemigration of the nineties). Edice Sociologické texty/Sociological Papers SP 02:4. Praha: Sociologický ústav AV ČR, 2002.

Nešpor, Zdeněk R., "The Disappointed and Disgruntled. A Study of the Return in the 1990s of Czech Emigrants from the Communist Era," Sociologický časopis/Czech Sociological Review, 38, No. 6 (2002), pp. 789-808.

Mandelíčková, M., "Repatriace československých exulantů po roce 1948 a komunistická kampaň za návrat domů" (Repatriation of the Czechoslovak exiles after 1948 and the communist campaign for their return home), in: Studie z dějin emigrace: Sborník studentských prací. Olomouc: Univerzita Palackého, 2003, pp. 9-19.

Nešpor, Zdeněk R., "Reemigrace českých západních emigrantů v 90. letech 20. století z hlediska ekonomické sociologie" (Reemigration of Czech western emigrants in the 1990s of the 20th century from the perspective of economic sociology), Sociologický časopis, 1 (2005), pp. 31-35.

Hron, Madelaine, "The Emigré Experience of Return after 1989," Slavonic and East European Review, 85, No. 1 (January 2007), pp. 47-78.

6. Migration Prospects for the Future

Drbohlav, Dušan, "International Migration in the Czech Republic and Slovakia and the Outlook for East Central Europe," Czech Sociological Review, 2, No. 1 (1994), pp. 89-106.

Drbohlav, D., L. Lachmanová-Medová, Z., Čermák, E. Janská, D. Čermáková and D. Dzúrová, The Czech Republic: On its way from emigration to immigration country. IDEA Working paper, No. 11, 2009. http://www.idea6fp.uw.edu.pl/pliki/WP11_Czech_Republic.pdf

B. The New World

1. News of the Discovery of New World

Kramerius, Václav Matěj, Historické skize, kterak čtvrtý díl světa, Amerika, skrze Kolumbusa vynalezen byl (A Historical narrative about the discovery of America by Columbus). 1803.

Löher, Franz, Martin Behaim der Endecker Amerikas," Geschichte und Zustande der Deutschen in Amerika. Cincinnati, OH, 1847, pp. 1-8.

"Behaim Martin," in: Ottův slovník naučný. Praha: J. Otto, 1890, vol. 3, pp.618-619.

Löwenbach, Jan, Český objevitel Ameriky, Mikuláš Bakalář (Czech discoverer of America, Mikuláš Bakalář). New York: Čs. Kulturní kroužek, 1942. 50p.

Kisch, Guido, Czechoslovak Jews and America. II. News of the Discovery of America in the Ghetto of Prague, and the First Emigrants," Historia Juidaica 6, No. 2 (October 1944), pp. 129-138.

Polišenský, Josef and Peter Ratkoš, "Nové prameny k dejinám objavných cest" (New Sources to History of Voyages of Discovery)," Historický časopis, 10 (1962), pp. 563-568.

Šašek z Bířkova, Deník o jeho jízdě a putování pana Lva z Rožmitálu a Blatné z Čech az na konec světa (Šašek of Bířkov. Diary about his voyage and travels of Lord Lev of Rožmitál and Blatná). Translated from Latin by Bohumil Mathesius. Praha, 1974.

Hrubeš, Jiří, "Je 'Spis o nových zemích' jen informací o objevení Ameriky? Kritické poznámky k Mikuláši Bakaláři" (Is the "Writing about the New Lands' strictly a source of information about the discovery of America? Critical comments about Mikuláš Bakalář), Acta Universitatis Carolinae—Philosophica et Historica. Prague: Universita Karlova, 1974), pp. 51-65.

Polišenský, Josef and Peter Ratkoš, "'Codex bratislaviensis' a jeho zprávy o objevení Ameriky" (Codex bratislaviensis, as a source of information about the discovery of America), Historický časopis, 24 (1976), pp. 397-407.

Kneidl, P., "El Mundus Novus' de Américo Vespucio y el 'Escrito sobre las Nuevas Tierras' de Nicolás Bakalář," Ibero-Americana Pragensia, 13 (1970), pp. 99-129.

Kašpar, Oldřich, "Nová literatura ke Spisu o nových zemích a o Novém světě Mikuláše Bakaláře" (New literature about Mikuláš Bakalář' Spis o Nových zemích a o Novém světě), Studia Comeniana et Historica, 39 (1989), pp. 84-86.

Rechcigl, Miloslav, Jr., "Jak Češi objevili Ameriku" (How the Czechs discovered America), in: Postavy naší Ameriky. Praha: Pražská edice, 2000, pp. 19-21.

Rechcigl, Miloslav, Jr.," News about the Discovery of New World in Bohemia," in: Czechs and Slovaks in America. Boulder, CO: East European Monographs and New York: Columbia University Press, 2005, pp.34-35.

2. Early Perceptions & Early Contacts with the New World

Polišenský, Josef, "Styky Čechů a Slováků s koloniální Amerikou" (Contacts of Czechs and Slovaks with Colonial America), in: Bulletin Komise pro dějiny krajanů, Čechů a Slováků v zahraničí, 6 (1968-69), pp. 1-18.

Svejkovsky, František, "Three Centuries on Czech Literature, 1508-1808," in: East Central European Perceptions of Early America. Ed. Bela K. Kiraly and George Balany. Lisse: Peter de Ridder, 1977, 33-55.

Polišenský, Josef, "Česká touha po Novém světě" (Czech yearning for the New World), in: Úvod do studia dějin vystěhovalectví do Ameriky. II. Češi a Amerika, Praha: Univerzita Karlova, 1996, pp. 9-22.

Kašpar, Oldřich, "Nový svět jako exotická kuriozita v české literatuře 16. století" (New World as an exotic curiosity in Czech literature of the 16th century), in: Etnologie a kuriozity, Praha 2005, pp. 66-90.

Opatrný, Josef, "La imagen cambiante de América en la sociedad de Bohemia entre 1500 y 1848" (Chaging image of America in Bohemian society between 1500 and 1848), in: Latin America and the Atlantic World. El mundo atlántico y América Latina (1500-1850). Essays in Honor of Horst Pietschmann. Edited by Renate Pieper and Peer Schmidt. Lateinamerikanische Forschungen, 33 (2005), pp. 97-114.

3. Early Pioneers

a. General Surveys

Čapek, Tomáš, Památky českých emigrantů v Americe (Legacy of Czech emigrants in America). Omaha, NE: Pokrok západu, 1889. 104p.; 2nd ed., 1907.

Březáček, Josef, Čeští pionýři v Americe (Czech pioneers in America). Praha: Česká grafická unie, 1930. 173p.

Kisch, Guido, "The First Immigrants," in: In Search of Freedom. A History of American Jews from Czechoslovakia 1592-1948. London: Edward Goldston, 1948, pp. 13-17.

Čapek, Tomáš, "První Čechové američtí" (The First American Czechs), Amerikán, Národní kalendář, 76 (1953), pp. 27-32.

Fechtnerová, A. and O. Kašpar, "Češi, Moravané a Slezané v Novém světě v 17. a 18. století. Bio-bibliograficky přehled" (Czechs, Moravians, and Silesians in New World. A Bio-bibliographical overview), Folia Historica Bohemia, Praha, 13 (1990), pp. 289-325.

Rechcigl, Miloslav Jr., "In the Footprints of the First Czech Immigrants in America," Czechoslovak and Central European Journal, 9 (1990), pp. 75-90.

Rechcigl, Miloslav, Jr., "Moravian Brethren from Bohemia, Moravia and Silesia. Their Arrival and Settlement in America," Bohemia Zeitschrift, 32, No. 1 (1991), pp. 152-165.

Rechcigl, Miloslav Jr., "Early Jewish Immigrants in America from the Czech Historic Lands and Slovakia," Rev. Soc. Hist. Czechoslovak Jews, 3 (1990-91), pp. 157-79.

Sviták, Ivan, First Bohemians in America. Chico, CA: Author, 1993. 46p.

Rechcigl, Miloslav Jr., "Bohemian and Moravian Pioneers in Colonial America," in: Czech-Americans in Transition. Ed. by Clinton Machann. Austin, TX: Eakin Press, 1999, pp. 18-27.

Rechcigl, Miloslav, Jr., "První Češi v Americe" (First Czechs in America), in: Postavy naší Ameriky. Praha: Pražská edice, 2000, pp. 25-27.

Rechcigl, Miloslav, Jr., "První čeští přistěhovalci do Ameriky od nejzazších dob po revoluci roku 1848" (First Czech immigrants in America from the earliest times up to the Revolution of 1848), in: Emigrace z českých zemí. Mladá Boleslav: Okresní muzeum, 2001, pp. 13-21.

Rechcigl, Miloslav, Jr., "Bohemian and Moravian Pioneers in Colonial America," in: Czechs and Slovaks in America. Boulder: East European Monographs, 2005, pp. 35-46.

Rechcigl, Miloslav, Jr., "Pursuing the Bohemian Identity of Martinus Hermanzen Hoffman, an Early Settler in the 17th Century's New Amsterdam Century New Amsterdam: Fact, Legend or Hoax?" Kosmas, 22, No. 2 (Spring 2009), pp.89-97.

Rechcigl, Miloslav, Jr., "Arrival of First Czechs in America—by State. A Tentative Listing, Kořeny (Roots), 13, No. 2 (March 2009), pp. 5-6.

Mokotoff, Gary and Miloslav Rechcigl,Jr., "Who Were the First Jews in America?," Avotaynu, 27, No. 2 (Summer 2011), pp. 53-54.

b. Individuals

Jacobus Fabritius (1618-1693)

Evjen, John Oluf, "Jacobus Fabritius," in: Scandinavian Immigrants in New York, 1630-1674: with appendices on . . . Minneapolis, MN: K. C. Holter Co., 1914, pp.: 36, 230, 317, 364, 399-400, 418.

"Petition against Rev. J. Fabritius 24 February 1674," in: Documentary History of the State of New York. By Christopher Morgan. Albany, NY: Weed, Parsons & Co., 1850, pp. 242-243.

Acrelius, Israel, William Morton Reynolds, "Pastor Jacob Fabritius Blind," in: A History of New Sweden: or, The settlements on the River Delaware. Memoirs of Pennsylvania, vol. XI. Philadelphia: Historical Society of Pennsylvania, 1876, pp. 176-181.

Jurian Fradel (bf. 1625-aft. 1653)

Evjen, John Oluf, "Jurian Fradel," in: Scandinavian Immigrants in New York, 1630-1674: with appendices on . . . Minneapolis, MN: K. C. Holter Co., 1914, p. 409.

Joachim Gans (b. ca 1555)

Grassi, Gary C., "Joachim Gans of Prague. America's First Jewish Visitor," Review of the Society for the History of Czechoslovak Jews, 1 (1987), pp. 53-90.

Grassi, Gary C., "Joachim Gans of Prague: The First Jew in English America," American Jewish History, 86, No. 2 (June 1998), pp. 195-217.

Rechcigl, Miloslav, Jr., "První český kolonista v Severní Americe" (The first Czech colonist in America), in: Postavy naší Ameriky. Praha: Pražská edice, 2000, pp. 28-30.

Augustine Heřman (1621-1686)

Mallery, Charles Payson, Ancient Families of Bohemia Manor: Their Homes and their Graves. (Delaware Historical Society Papers, No.7). Wilmington, DE, 1888. 74p.

Glenn, Thomas Allen, "Bohemia Manor and the Herrmans," in: Colonial Mensions. Philadelphia, 1897, pp. 123-138.

Evjen, John Oluf, "Augustine Herrman," in: Scandinavian Immigrants in New York, 1630-1674: with appendices on . . . Minneapolis, MN: K. C. Holter Co., 1914, p. 414-416.

Čapek, Thomas, Augustine Herrman of Bohemia Manor. Prague: State Printing Office, 1930. 35p.

Heck, Earl L., Augustine Herman, Beginner of the Virginia Tobacco Trade, Merchant of New Amsterdam, and the First Lord of Bohemia Manor in Maryland. Richmond: William Byrd Press, 1941. 123p.

Rechcigl, Miloslav Jr., "Augustine Herman Bohemiensis," Kosmas. Journal of Czechoslovak and Central European Studies, 3, No. 1 (Summer 1984), pp. 139-48.

Rechcigl, Miloslav, Jr., The Descendants of Augustine Herman. The First Three Generations and Beyond," Maryland Geneaologacl Society Bulletin, 29, No. 3 (Summer 1988), pp. 276-299.

Rechcigl, Miloslav, Jr., "První opravdový Američan" (The first genuine American), in: Postavy naší Ameriky. Praha: Pražská edice, 2000, pp. 34-26.

Martinus Hermanzen Hoffman (1625-1713)

Evjen, John Oluf, "Martin Hoffman," in: Scandinavian Immigrants in New York, 1630-1674: with appendices on . . . Minneapolis, MN: K. C. Holter Co., 1914, pp. 314-318.

Max E. Hoffman, The Hoffmans of North Carolina. Asheville, NC: Author, 1938.

Rechcigl, Miloslav, Jr., Pursuing the Bohemian Identity of Martinus Hermanzen Hoffman. Early Settler in the 17th Century's New Amsterdam: Fact, Legend or Hoax?," Kosmas, 22, No. 2 (Spring 2009), pp. 89-97.

Joriszen Burger (1612-1671)

History of Queens County. New York: W. W. Munsell & Co., 1882.

Flint, Martha Bockée, "Burger," in: The Bockée Family (Boucquet). Poughkeepsie, NY, 1897, pp. 29-34.

Evjen, John Oluf, "Engeltje Mans," in: Scandinavian Immigrants in New York, 1630-1674: with appendices on . . . Minneapolis, MN: K. C. Holter Co., 1914, pp. 329-335.

Innes, John H., New Amsterdam and its People. New York: Charles Scribner's Sons, 1902, pp. 104-105, 128-130, 223-234.

Matthais Kreisler (Crisler) (1678-aft. 1759)

Crisler, William Neville, A Genealogy, History, and Chronology of the Kreisler-Crisler Family of the United States of America, or, more particularly, the descendants of Matthais Kreisler and Barbara Von Schellenberg Kreisler . . . Dallas?: Author, 1981. 567p.

.

Frederick Philipse (1625-1702)

Čapek, Thomas, Ancestry of Frederick Philipse, The First Lord and Founder of Philipse Manor at Yonkers, N Y. New York: Paebar, 1939.

Rechcigl, Miloslav, Jr., "Český 'Vanderbilt' v Americe" (The Czech 'Vanderbilt' in America), in: Postavy naší Ameriky. Praha: Pražská edice, 2000, pp. 37-39.

Juriaen Probasco (1627-1664)

Macy, Harry, Jr., "Juriaen Probasco's Place of Origin," The New York Genealogical and Biographical Record, 125, No. 4 (Oct. 1994), p. 204.

Hutchinson, Jack T., Leaves From the Tree An American Heritage. Decorah, IA: The Anundsen Publishing Co., 1989.

Kennedy, Alice H., Probasco Genealogy. Mohnton, PA: Author, 1954.

Jacob Varn (1650-1688)

Pricher, Jerry, Descendant Report for Jacob Varn. See: http://www.pricher.net/JVarnDescent/INDEX.HTM#CNTC

LaMartin, William, Descendants of Jacob Varn. See: http://www.lamartin.com/genealogy/varn.htm

C. Immigration and Settlement

1. Up to the Ocean and Across

Polišenský, Josef, "Cesta z domova k moři" (From home up to the sea), in: Úvod do studia dějin vystěhovalectví do Ameriky. I. Obecné problémy dějin českého vystěhovalectví do Ameriky 1848-1914. Praha: Univerzita Karlova, 1992, pp. 9-20.

Polišenský, Josef, "Druhá zkouška: cesta po moři" (The second challenge: Voyage across the sea), in: Úvod do studia dějin vystěhovalectví do Ameriky. I., op. cit., pp. 21-28.

Konecny, Lawrence H. and Clinton Machann, Perilous Voyages. Czech and English Immigrants to Texas in the 1870s. College Station, TX: Texas A&M University, 2004. 183p.

Jaklová, Alena, "Cesta přes Atlantic" (Voyage across the Atlantic), in: Čechoamerická periodika 19. století. Brno: Nadace Universitatis Masarykiana, 2006, pp. 38-40.

2. Before the Settlement. Ellis Island

Polišenský, Josef, "Třetí zkouška: Brána svobody nebo Ostrov zlomených srdcí" (The third challenge: The gate to freedom or island of broken hearts), in: Úvod do studia dějin vystěhovalectví do Ameriky. I., op. cit., pp. 29-34.

Trojacek, Mary Betik, Beyond Ellis Island: A Story About Czech Immigrants and Life on the Farm in the 1930's and 1940's. Trafford Publishing, 2006. 348p.

3. Settlement

Hellwald, Fr. and Jakub Malý, "Čechové v Americe" (Czechs in America), in: Země a objevitelé její. Praha, 1879, pp. 108-131.

Pastor, Josef, "Část 1. Popis amerických poměrů" (Description of American conditions), in: České osady v Americe, Roč. 2. Hamburk tiskem H. O. Potsiehl, 1886. 17p.

Wagner, Jan, Čeští osadníci v Severní Americe (Czech settlers in North America). Praha: Alois Hynek, 1887. 63p.

Šmaha, J., Americké táčky. Dojmy se zaokeánské cesty. (American chats. Impresions from the trip beyond the ocean). Praha, 1894.

"Čechové Američtí" (Czech Americans), in: Národopisná výstava českoslovanská 1885. See: http://www.zlate-mince.cz/Cechove_Americti.htm

Borecký, Jan, Kapitoly k dějepisu lidu česko-moravského ve Spojených státech (Chapters on the history of Bohemian and Moravian people in the United States). Cedar Rapids: Svlt, 1896. 42p.

Albieri, Pavel, "Čechové američtí" (American Czechs), in: Národopisná výstava českoslovanská v Praze 1895. Praha, 1897, pp. 289-304.

Humpal-Zeman, J., "Bohemian Settlements in the United States," U.S. Industrial Commission on Immigration and Education, 15 (1901), pp. 507-10.

Steiner, E. A., "The Bohemian in America," Outlook, 73 (April 25, 1903), pp. 968-72.

Kohlbeck, V, "Bohemians in the United States," The Champlain's Educator, 25 (January-March 1906), pp. 36-54.

Steiner, E.A., "The Bohemian Immigrant," in: On the Trail of the Immigrant. New York: 1906, pp. 225-237.

Habenicht, Jan, Dějiny Čechův Amerických (History of American Czechs). St. Louis, MO, 1910; Translated to English by Miroslav Koudelka and published as History of Czechs in America. St. Paul, MN: Czechoslovak Genealogical Society International, 1996. 581p.

Vojan, J. E. Salaba, Česko-americké epištoly (Czech-American epistles). Chicago: n. p., 1911.

Zíbrt, Čeněk, "Američtí Čechové ve světle nových spisů J. Salaby, T. Čapka a J. Habenichta" (American Czechs in the light of new works of J. Salaba, T. Čapek and J. Habenicht), Časopis Musea království Českého, 86 (1912), pp. 330-387.

Losa, Václav, The Bohemians in America. New York: Missionary Education Movement of the U.S. and Canada, 1913. 23p.

Balch, Emily G., "Bohemian Emigration," in: Our Slavic Fellow Citizens.1916, pp. 63-84.

Auerhan, Jan: Československé menšiny za hranicemi (Czechoslovak minorities abroad). Praha: Dr. A. Hajn, 1918.

Daniels, John, "A Bohemian Community," in: America via Neighborhood. New York and London: Harper & Brothers Publishers, 1920, pp. 28-39.

Čapek, Thomas, The Čechs (Bohemians) in America. Boston: Houghton Mifflin, 1920. 293p. Reprinted New York: Arno Press, 1969.

Hrbkova, S. B., "Americans of Czecho-Slovak Descent," Survey, 45 (June 1921), pp. 361-368.

Smetánka, Jaroslav, "Bohemians and Slovaks," Annals American Academy of Political and Social Sciences, 93 (1921), pp. 149-153.

Miller, Kenneth D., The Czecho-Slovaks in America. New York: George H. Doran, 1922. 192p.

Sears. Charles Hatch, "The Czechoslovaks in America. New York: Doran, 1922. 192p.

Hrbkova, S. B., The Czecho-Slovaks in America," Our World 4 (December 1923), pp. 88-91.

Klíma, Stanislav, Čechové a Slováci za hranicemi (Czechs and Slovaks Abroad). Praha, J. Otto, 1925. 302p.

Čapek, Tomáš, Naše Amerika (Our America). Praha: Národní rada československá, 1926. 686p.

Auerhan, J. and R. Turčin, Češi a Slováci za hranicemi" (Czechs and Slovaks abroad), in: Československá vlastivěda. Praha, 1931, Vol. 5, pp. 497-512.

Musil, Ferdinand L., Československá Amerika (Czechoslovak America). Chicago: Hlasatel, 1933. 40p.

World's Fair Memorial of the Czechoslovak Group (Czechs and Slovaks). International Exposition, Chicago, 1933. 184p.

Čapek, Tomáš, Moje Amerika. Vzpomínky a úvahy (1861-1934) (My America. Reminiscences and Reflections). Praha: F. Borový, 1935. 271p.

Folprechct, Josef: Naši krajané v cizině (Our countrymen abroad). Praha: Václav Petr, 1940.

Roucek, Joseph S., "Czechoslovak Americans," in: Our Racial and National Minorities. Their History, Contributions and Present Problems. Ed. by Francis J. Brown and Joseph S. Roucek. New York: Prentice-Hall, 1937, pp. 230-44; rev. ed., 1945, pp. 145-158.

Zemek, Bedřich, Češi a Slováci v Americe (Czechs and Slovaks in America). Praha: Ministerstvo informací, 1947. 47p.

Schermerhorn, R. A., "Czech and Slovak Americans," in: These Are Our People. Minorities in American Culture. Boston, 1949, pp. 292-319.

Dvornik, Francis, Czech Contributions to the Growth of the United States. Chicago: Benedictine Abbey Press, 1962. 120p.

Roucek, Joseph S. The Czechs and Slovaks in America. Minneapolis: Lerner Publications, 1967. 72p.

Panorama: A Historical Review of Czechs and Slovaks in the United States. Cicero, IL: Czechoslovak National Council of America, 1971. 328p.

Láska, Věra, The Czechs in America 1633-1977: A Chronology and Fact Book. Dobbs Ferry: Oceana Publications, 1978. 152p.

Freeze, Karen Johnson, "Czechs," Harvard Encyclopedia of American Ethnic Groups. Cambridge, MA: Belknap Press of Harvard University, 1980, pp. 261-72.

Saxon-Ford, Stephanie, The Czech Americans. New York: Chelsea House Publishers, 1989. 112p.

Chada, Joseph, The Czechs in the United States. New York: SVU Press, 1981. 292p.

Rippley, La Vern J. and Robert J. Paulson, German-Bohemians. The Quiet Immigrants. Northfield, MN: St. Olaf College Press, 1995. 278p.

Polišenský, Josef, Úvod do studia vystěhovalectví do Ameriky II. Češi a Amerika (Introduction to the study of emigration to America. II. The Czechs and America). Praha: Univerzita Karlova, 1996, 120p.

Czech-Americans in Transition. Edited by Clinton Machann. Austin, TX: Eakin Press, 1999. 136 p.

Rechcigl, Miloslav, Jr., "Czechs," in: Encyclopedia of Eastern Europe. Edited by Richard Frucht. New York-London: Goulard Publishing, 2000, pp. 184-185.

Molinari, C., "Czech Americans," in: Gale Encyclopedia of Multicultural America. Farrminton Hills, MI: Gale Publishing, 2000.

Daniels, Roger. Coming to America, A History of Immigration and Ethnicity in American Life. New York: Perennial, 2002.

Dubovický, Ivan, David Kraft and Milena Secká, Češi v Americe. České vystěhovalectví do Ameriky a česko-americké vztahy v průběhu pěti století (Czechs in America. Czech emigration to America and Czech-American relations during the course of five centuries). Praha: Pražská edice, 2003. 45p.

Dubovický, Ivan, Češi v Americe. Czechs in America. Praha: Comunicatio Humana, 2003. 64p.

Rechcigl, Miloslav, Jr. Czechs and Slovaks in America. Surveys, Essays, Reflections and Personal Insights Relating to the History and the Contributions of Czech and Slovak Immigrants in America and their Descendants. Boulder, CO: East European Monographs, 2005. Distributed by Columbia University Press, New York. 317p.

Tesařová, Lucie, Češi v Americe (Czechs in America). Diplomová práce, Ostravská Univerzita v Ostravě, 2005.

Chrislock, C. Winston, "Czechs," in: The American Midwest: An interpretative encyclopedia. Edited by Richard Sisson, Christian Zachar and Andrew Cayton. Bloomington, IN: Indiana University Press, 2007, pp. 234-236.

Stavařová, Ivana. The Czech-Americans. Diploma Thesis, Masaryk University, Faculty of Education, Brno, 2009. 128 p., 12p.

Rechcigl, Miloslav, Jr., Tam za tím mořem piva. Příspěvek k historii české a slovenské emigrace do Ameriky (Beyond the sea of beer. A contribution to the history of Czech and Slovak emigration to America) (in preparation).

4. New Bohemia

Čapek, Thomas, "New Bohemia in America," in: The Čechs (Bohemians) in America. Boston and New York: Houghton Mifflin Co., 1920, pp. 105-113.

Čapek, Tomáš, "Český stát" (Czech State), in: Naše Amerika. Praha: Nákladem Národní rady československé v Praze, 1926, pp.192-203.

Vasilijev, I., "K snahám české buržoasie o získání kolonií v době buržoazní ČSR" (Attempts by the Czech bourgeoisie to gain colonies during the bourgeois Czechoslovak Republic), Češi v cizině, 3 (1988), pp. 139-190.

5. Future of Czech-American Community. Preserving Czech Heritage
a. General

Vojan, J. E. Salaba, "Přítomnost a budoucnost českoamerické větve" (Current status and future of the Czech-American branch), Naše zahraničí, 2, No. 3 (1921), pp.133-139.

"K budoucnosti československé větve v Americe" (Future of Czechoslovak branch in America), Naše zahraničí, 7, (1926), pp. 5-7.

Chada, Joseph, "The Twilight of the Czech-American Community," in: The Czechs in the United States. SVU Press, 1981, pp. 215-234,

Polišenský, Josef, "Soumrak anebo svítaní české Ameriky" (Twilight or daybreak of the Czech America), in: Úvod do studia dějin vystěhovalectví do Ameriky. II. Češi a Amerika. Praha: Univerzita Karlova, 1996, pp.108-115.

Czechoslovak Society of Arts and Sciences, Czech-Americans in Transition: Challenges and Opportunities for the Future. The Bell County Exposition Center, Belton, Texas, July 12-13, 1997. 12p.

Czechoslovak Society of Arts and Sciences, Special Conference on 'Czech and Slovak America: Quo Vadis', University of Minnesota Medical School, Minneapolis, MN, April 24-26, 1999. 20p.

Czechoslovak Society of Arts and Sciences, SVU 2001 North American Conference, 'The Czech and Slovak Legacy in the Americas: Preservation of Heritage with the Accent on Youth'. University of Nebraska Lincoln, Nebraska, August 1-3, 2001. 66p.

Czechoslovak Society of Arts and Sciences, 2003 SVU North American Conference, 'The Czech and Slovak Presence in North America: A Retrospective Look and Future Perspectives,' Coe College, Cedar Rapids, Iowa, 26-2 June 2003. 40p.

Czechoslovak Society of Arts and Sciences, Special Conference and Festival on 'Czech and Slovak Cultural Heritage on Both Sides of the Atlantic,' American Czech-Slovak Cultural Club of North Miami, North Miami, FL, 17-20 March 2005. 50p.

b. **Preserving Czech-American Heritage**

"The Preservation of Czech-American Cultural Heritage: Proclamation by SVU," Zprávy SVU, 39, No. 5 (September-October 1997), pp. 1-2.

Rechcigl, Miloslav, Jr., "SVU New Initiative," Zprávy SVU, 40, No. 1 (January-February 1998), pp. 7-8.

"Resolution: The Preservation of Czech-American Cultural Heritage," Zprávy SVU, 40, No. 1 (January-February 1998), pp.8-9.

Rechcigl, Miloslav, Jr., "Preserving Czech Cultural Heritage," Zprávy SVU, 40, No. 6 (November-December 1998), pp. 6-8.

Rechcigl, Miloslav, "Survey of Czech and Slovak Historical Monuments in America," Zprávy SVU, 41, No. 6 (November-December 1999), 20-21.

Rechcigl, Miloslav, Jr., "Czechoslovak American Archivalia," Zprávy SVU, 43, No. 1 (January-February 2001), pp. 17-19.

Rechcigl, Miloslav, Jr., "Preserving Czech and Slovak American Archival Material," Kosmas, 17, No. 2 (Spring 2004), pp. 95-96.

Czech and Slovak American Archival Materials and their Preservation. Proc. of the Working Conference, held at the Czech and Slovak Embassies in Washington, DC on November 22-23, 2003. Edited by Miloslav Rechcigl, Jr. Praha: Prague Edition, 2004. 166p.

D. Historic Periods

1. General Chronology

Čapek, Tomáš, "Památné i významné dni a události z dějin amerických Čechů" (Memorial and important days and events from the history of American Czechs," in: Naše Amerika. Praha: Národní rada československá, 1928, pp. 481-515.

Láska, Věra, The Czechs in America. 1633-1977. A Chronology and Fact Book, Dobbs Ferry, NY: Oceana Publications, 1978. 152p.

Kovtun, George, "Chronology," in: The Czechs in America. Washington, DC: The Library of Congress, European Reading Room, Special Projects. See Internet: http://www.loc.gov/rr/european/imcz/ndl.html

2. Seventeenth Century Immigration

Čapek, Thomas, "Seventeenth-Century Immigration," in: The Čech (Bohemians) in America. Boston & New York: Houghton Mifflin Co., 1920, pp. 1-18.

Čapek, Tomáš, "17. století" (The 17th century), in: Naše Amerika. Praha: Národní rada československá, 1926, pp. 142-151.

Dvornik, Francis, "Czech Immigration in Colonial Days," in: Czech Contributions to the Growth of the United States. Chicago: Benedictine Abbey Press, 1962, pp. 7-18.

3. Eighteenth Century Immigration

Čapek, Thomas, "Eighteenth-Century Immigration, in: The Čech (Bohemians) in America. Boston & New York: Houghton Mifflin Co., 1920, pp. 19-24.

Čapek, Tomáš, "18. století" (The 18th century), in: Naše Amerika. Praha: Národní rada československá, 1926, pp. 151-152.

Dvornik, Francis, "Eighteenth Century," in: Czech Contributions to the Growth of the United States. Chicago: Benedictine Abbey Press, 1962, pp. 19-24.

Skalský, Gustav Adolf, Z dějin české emigrace osmnáctého století (History of Czech emigration in the 18th century). Chotěbor: Ev. Matice, 1911. 378p.

4. Nineteenth Century Immigration

Čapek, Thomas, "Nineteenth-Century Immigration," in: The Čech (Bohemians) in America. Boston & New York: Houghton Mifflin Co., 1920, pp. 25-58.

Čapek, Tomáš, "19. století" (The 19th century), in: Naše Amerika. Praha: Národní rada československá, 1926, pp. 152-163.

Goldmark, Josephine, Pilgrims of '48: One Man's Part in the Austrian Revolution of 1848 and Family Migration to America. New Haven, CT: Yale University Press, 1936. 311 p.

Kisch, Guido, "Before the Revolution of 1848," in: In Search of Freedom. History of American Jews from Czechoslovakia. London: Edward Goldston, 1948, pp. 21-25.

Dvornik, Francis, "The Great Migration," in: Czech Contributions to the Growth of the United States. Chicago: Benedictine Abbey Press, 1962, pp. 25-72.

Wittke, Carl, "The Czechs and Slovaks," in: We Who Built America. The Saga of the Immigrant. New York: Press of the Case Western Reserve University, 1939, pp. 407-418.

Kutnar, F., Počátky hromadného vystěhovalectví z Čech v období Bachova absolutismu (The beginnings of mass emigration from Bohemia in the time of Bach's absolutism. Praha, 1964.

Kašpar, O.: Tam za mořem je Amerika. Dopisy a vzpomínky českých vystěhovalců do Ameriky v 19. století (Beyond the sea is America. Letters and reminiscences of Czech emigrants to America in the 19th century). Praha: Československý spisovatel, 1986. 240 p.; also published in 1992 by Kora.

Šatava, Leoš, "České vystěhovalectví 19. století do USA" (Czech emigration of the 19th century to the US), in: Migrační procesy a české vystěhovalectví 19. století do USA. Praha: Universita Karlova, 1989, pp. 79-143.

Šolle, Zdeněk. "Czech Political Refugees in the United States during the Nineteenth Century," Nebraska History, 74, No. 3-4 (Fall/ Winter 1993), pp. 142-49.

Kašpar, O., "Tam za mořem je Amerika. Dopisy a vzpomínky českých vystěhovalců do Ameriky 19. stoleti" (Across the sea is America. Letters and reminiscences of Czech emigrants to America in the 19th century), Češi v cizině, 7 (1993), pp. 30-47.

Korytová-Magstadt, Štěpánka, To Reap a Bountiful Harvest: Czech Immigration beyond the Mississippi, 1850-1900. Iowa City: Rudi Publications, 1993. 179p.

Polišenský, Josef, "Revolučni intermezzo" (Revolutionary intermezzo), in: Úvod do studia dějin vystěhovalectví do Ameriky. II. Češi a Amerika. Praha: Univerzita Karlova, 1996, pp.23-28.

Šatava, Leoš, "České vystěhovalectví do USA" (Czech emigration to the US), Češi v cizině, 9, (1996), pp. 155-171.

Rechcigl, Miloslav, Jr., "Osudy našich osmačtyřicátníků v Americe" (The fate of our Forty-Eighters in America), Češi v cizině, 12 (2004), pp. 140-143,

5. Twentieth Century Immigration a. General

Češi za hranicemi na přelomu 20. a 21. století. Symposium o českém vystěhovalectví, exulantsví a vztazích zahraničních Čechů k domovu, 29.-30. června 1998 (Czechs abroad at the turn of the 20th and 21st centuries. Symposium about the Czech emigration, the exile and the relations between the Czechs abroad and the homeland, 29-30 June 1998). Ed. By Karel Hrubý a Stanislav Brouček. Praha: Etnologický ústav AV ČR, 2000. 340p.

Emigrace a exil jako způsob života. II. Sympozium o českém vystěhovalectví, exulantství a vztazích zahraničních Čechů k domovu (Emigration and exile as a means of life. II. Symposium about Czech emigration, exile and relations of Czechs abroad to their homeland). Praha: Etnologický ústav AV ČR, 2001.

Český a slovenský exil 20. století (Czech and Slovak exile of the 20th century). Uspořádal Jan Kratochvíl. Brno: Meadow Art, 2002. 159p.

Exil sám o sobě. 3. setkání nad českým vystěhovalectvím, exulantstvím a vztahy zahraničních Čechů k domovu (Exile for Itself. III. Meeting on Czech emigration, the exile and the relations of Czechs abroad to their homeland). Praha: Etnologický ústav AV ČR, 2006. 326p.

b. Before & through World War I

Chada, Joseph, "The Czech-American from 1880 to 1914," in: The Czechs in the United States. SVU Press, 1981, pp. 23-42,

Polišenský, Josef, "Vyvrcholení emigrace před první světovou válkou" (Peak of emigration before World War I), in: Úvod do studia dějin vystěhovalectví do Ameriky. II. Češi a Amerika. Praha: Univerzita Karlova, 1996, pp. 73-81.

Polišenský, Josef, "Panorama české Ameriky 1900-1914" (Panorama of Czech America 1900-1914), in: Úvod do studia dějin vystěhovalectví do Ameriky. II. Češi a Amerika. Praha: Univerzita Karlova, 1996, pp. 82-86.

Thompson-Raymová, Veronika, Čeští vystěhovalci ve Spojených státech amerických v průběhu první světové války (Czech emigrants in the US during World War I). Praha: FF UK, 2002, 79p.

c. **Between the Two World Wars**

Horak, Jacob, "Effects of the War upon Emigration from Czechoslovakia," The Social Service Review, 2, No. 1 (March 1928), pp. 76-81.

Chada, Joseph," Post-War Czech-America, 1919-1941," in: The Czechs in the United States. SVU Press, 1981, pp. 69-80.

Polišenský, Josef, "Američtí Češi mezi dvěma světovými válkami" (American Czechs between the two World Wars), in: Úvod do studia dějin vystěhovalectví do Ameriky. II. Češi a Amerika). Praha: Univerzita Karlova, 1996, pp. 94-99.

d. Refugees from Nazism

Křen, Jan, Do emigrace. Západní zahraniční odboj 1938-1939 (Toward emigration: The Western resistance abroad). 2nd ed. Praha: Naše vojsko, 1969. 712p.

Fermi, Laura, Illustrious Immigrants, the Intellectual Migration from Europe, 1930/41. 2nd ed. Chicago: University of Chicago Press, 1971. 431p.

Polišenský, Josef, "Období utrpení, nadějí a zklamání" (Period of suffering, hope and disappointment), in: Úvod do studia vystěhovalectví do Ameriky II. Češi a Amerika. Praha: Univerzita Karlova, 1996, pp. 100-106.

Sekyrková, Milada, "Druhý odboj z druhého břehu. Ze zkušeností a názorů Otakara Odložilíka na druhý odboj v USA v letech 1939-1943" (The second resistance from the second shore. From the experiences and thoughts of Otakar Odložilík in 1939-1943), Dějiny a skutečnost, 24, No. 3 (2002), pp. 46-51.

Čapková, Kateřina, Nejisté útočiště. Československo a uprchlíci před nacismem, 1933-1938 (The uncertain refuge. Czechoslovakia and fugitives from Nazism, 1933-1938). Praha: Paseka, 2008. 424p.

Rechcigl, Miloslav, "Czech Intellectual Immigrants in the US from Nazism," (in preparation).

e. Refugees from Communism—After February 1948

In Search of Haven: The Story of Czechoslovak Refugees. Washington, DC: Council of Free Czechoslovakia, 1950. 24p.

Kolaja, Jiří, "A Sociological Note on the Czechoslovak Anti-communist Refugees," Am. J. Sociology, 58, No. 3 (November 1952), pp. 289-.291.

Tigrid, Pavel, Politická emigrace v atomovém věku (Political Emigration in the Atomic Age). Paris: Svědectví, 1968. 100p.

Láska, Věra, "Refugee Students in the United States," in: Studies in Czechoslovak History. Ed. By Miloslav Rechcigl, Jr. Meerut: Sadhna Prakashan, 1970, vol. 1, pp. 366-373.

Pejskar, J., Útěky železnou oponou (Escapes through the Iron Curtain). Zűrich: Reporter, 1989. 127p.

Jirásek, Z. and M. Trapl, Exilová politika v letech 1948-1956 (Exile politics in 1948-1956). Olomouc: Univerzita Palackého, 1996. 120p.

Trapl, Miloš, Exil po únoru 1948: Počátky politické organizovanosti a činnosti poúnorové emigrace a vznik Rady svobodného Československa (Exile after February 1948: Beginnings of political organizing and the activity of the post-February emigration and the origin of the Council of Free Czechoslovakia). Olomouc: Univerzita Palackého, 1996. 66p.

Čelovský, Bořivoj, Emigranti. Dopisy politických uprchlíků z prvních let po 'Vítězném únoru' 1948 (The emigrants. Letters of political refugees from the first years after the 'Victorious February' 1948). Šenov u Ostravy: Tilia, 1998. 399p.

Jirásek, Z.: Československá poúnorová migrace a počátky exilu (Czechoslovak migration after February 1948 and the beginnings of the exile). Brno: Prius, 1999.

Paukertová, Libuše, "Několik základních údajů o odchodech z Československa, 1948-1991" (A few basic facts about departures from Czechoslovakia, 1948-1991), in: Češi za hranicemi na přelomu 20. a 21. století. Sympozium o českém vystěhovalectví, exulantství a vztazích zahraničních Čechů k domovu. Ed. By Karel Hrubý and Stanislav Brouček. Praha, 2000, pp. 25-31.

Lukeš, Igor, "Czechoslovak Political Exile in the Cold War: The Early Years," The Polish Review, XLVII, No. 3 (2002), pp. 332-343.

Čelovský, B., Seznam politických uprchlíků z roku 1948 (List of political refugees from 1948). Studijní materiály Ústavu pro soudobé dějiny AV ČR. Praha, 2003.

Kratochvíl, J., Český a slovenský exil. 20. století (Czech and Slovak exile of the 20th century). Brno: Meadow Art, 2004. 180p.

Igor Lukeš, "Československý politický exil za studené války" (Czechoslovak political exile during the Cold War), Střední Evropa, 2, 119 (2004), pp.:68-79.

Čelovský, Bořivoj, Uprchlíci po 'Vítězném únoru' (Refugees after 'Victorious February'). Šenov u Ostravy: Tilia, 2004. 272p.

Dvořáková, Zora, Politikové na útěku. Osudy změněné 25. únorem 1948 (Escaping politicians. Their fate being changed by February 25, 1948). Praha: Epocha, 2004. 248p.

Jeřábek, Vojtěch, Českoslovenští uprchlíci ve studené válce (Czechoslovak refugees after the Cold War). Stilus Press, 2005. 298p.

Pousta, Zdeněk, ed., Rozchod 1948. Rohovory s českými pounorovými exulanty (Separation. Discussions with Czech post-February exiles). Praha: Univerzita Karlova, 2006. 267p.

Kaplan, K., Poúnorový exil 1948-49 (Post-February Exile 1948-49). Liberec: Dialog, 2007. 200p.

Mandeličková, Monika, "Českoslovenští uprchlíci po roce 1948 a Spojené státy americké" (Czechoslovak refugees after 1948 and the US), in: Selected Papers from the 22nd World Congress of the Czechoslovak Society of Arts and Sciences, op. cit., pp. 399-403.

Rechcigl, Miloslav, Jr., "Exiloví vědci po roce 1948 a jejich organizování v zahraničí" (The exile scientists after 1948 and their organization abroad), Práce z dějin vědy, Sv. 21. Praha: Ústav pro soudobé dějiny AV ČR, 2009, pp. 165-186.

f. Refugees from Communism—After Soviet Invasion in 1968

Horna, Jarmila, Adjustment of Refugees: A Case Study. Czechoslovak Refugees of 1968-1969 in Edmonton, Alberta, Canada Discussion paper. Population Research Laboratory, 1973.

Ispa-Landa, Simone, "Bulgaria, Former Czechoslovakia, Hungary, Romania, Former Yugoslavia," in: The New Americans. A guide to Immigration since 1965. Cambridge: Harvard University Press, 2007, pp. 434-444.

Kostlán, Antonín, "Vědecký exil v období komunistického režimu: Emigrace z Československé akademie věd" (Exile scientists during the era of Communist regime: Emigration from Czechoslovak Academy of Sciences), Dějiny a technika, 43, No.3 (2010), pp. 153-181.

Pelikánová, Jitka, "Women in Exile after 1968 in the USA and Canada," in: Contributions of Czechs and Slovaks to Science and Technology in the 21st Century. Selected Papers from the Twenty-fifth Congress of the Czechoslovak Society of Arts and Sciences, Tábor, Czech Repuiblic, June 27-July 3, 2010. New York: Publishing House of the Czechoslovak Society of Arts and Sciences, 2011, pp. 183-193.

Sto českých vědců v exilu. Encykolpedie významných vědců z řad pracovníků Československé akademie věd (One Hundred Czech Scholars. K vydani pripravili Soňa Štrbáňová a Antonín Kostlán. Praha: Academia, 2011. 608p.

E. Regional & Local Histories

Alabama

"O české osadě Silver Hill, Ala." (Czech community Silver Hill, AL), Naše zahraničí 4 (1923), pp. 73-76.

California

"Czechoslovaks in San Diego," in: Slavs in California. By Stephen N. Sestanovich. Oakland, CA: 1937, p. 131-132; "Czechoslovaks in Metropolitan Los Angeles," Ibid., p. 135.

Austin, Leonard, Czechoslovaks," in: Around the World in San Francisco. Palo Alto: J. L. Delkin, 1940, pp. 34-35.

Colorado

Kutes, A., History of Czechs and Slovaks in the State of Colorado, 1876-1976. Denver, 1976.

Kedro, M. James, "Czechs and Slovaks in Colorado, 1860-1920," Colorado Magazine, 54, No. 2 (1977), pp. 92-125.

Santilli, Evelyn Hornak, "The Czechs in Louisville, Boulder County, Colorado," Naše Dějiny, 6, No. 4 (1987), pp. 4-5, 19.

Florida

Petrik, Robert, "Czechs and Slovaks in Florida". Paper delivered to the Czechoslovak Society of Arts and Sciences on June 27, 2003, at Coe College, Cedar Rapids, Iowa.

Idaho

Gentry, James R., "The Czechoslovakian Culture in the Buhl-Castleford Area," Idaho Yesterdays, 30, No.4 (Winter1987), pp. 2-14.

Illinois

"Národní život Čechů chicagských" (National life of Chicago Czechs), Amerikán, Národní kalendář, 1884, pp. 152-171.

Zdrůbek, František Boleslav, "Dějiny Chicaga a jeho Čechů" (History of Chicago and its Czechs), Amerikán, Národní kalendář, 7 (1884), pp. 139-151.

Zdrůbek, František Boleslav, "Osudy prvotních Českých osadníků chicágských" (History of the pioneer Czech settlers in Chicago), Amerikán, Národní kalendář, 7 (1884), pp. 185-204.

Jonas, Charles, "The Bohemians of Chicago," Chicago Sunday Times, January 24, 1892.

Zeman, Josefa Humpal, "The Bohemian People of Chicago," in: Hull House Maps and Papers. Edited by Jane Adams. New York: Thomas Y. Crowell, 1895; reprint, New York: Arno Press, 1970, pp. 115-128.

Fligl, L. J., "O Chicagu a Chicágčanech" (Chicago and Chicago people). Chicago: A. Geringer, 1896. 160p.

Masaryk Alice G., "The Bohemians in Chicago," Charities, 13, No.1 (December 3, 1904), pp. 206-210.

Beneš, A. E., "Před padesáti osmi lety" (Fifty-eight years ago), Amerikán, Národní kalendář, 47 (1924), pp. 288-299.

Vojan, Jaroslav E. S, "Začátky českého Chicaga" (Beginnings of the Czech Chicago). Chicago, 1925.

Pšenka, Rudolf Jaromír, Zlatá kniha československého Chicaga (Golden book of the Czechoslovak Chicago).Chicago: A. Geringer, 1926. 288p.

Pšenka, Rudolf Jaromír, Československé Chicago. Počátek českého vzrůstu metropole československé Ameriky" (The Czechoslovak Chicago. The beginnings and the growth of the Czechoslovak Metropolis of Czechoslovak America). Chicago: Svornost, 1933.

Reichman, John J., Czechoslovaks of Chicago. Chicago: Czechoslovak Historical Society of Chicago, 1937. 112p.

Bubeníček, Rudolf, Dějiny Čechů v Chicagu (History of Czechs in Chicago). Chicago: Author, 1939. 568p.

Novak, Frank, The History of Czech People in Edwardsville and Vicinity. A typescript. 1967.

Čada, Joseph, "Czechs of Chicago," in: Panorama. Cicero, IL: Czechoslovak National Council of America, 1970, pp. 30-34.

Rechcigl, Miloslav, Jr., "The First Czech in Chicago," Naše Rodina (Our Family), 8, No. 2 (June 1996), pp. 66-67.

Wilt, Vera A., "Czech Americans," in: The Ethnic Handbook: A Guide to the Cultures and Traditions of Chicago's Diverse Communities, ed. Cynthia Linton. Illinois: The Illinois Ethnic Coalition, 1996.

Sternstein, Malynne, Czechs of Chicagoland. Chicago: Arcadia Publishing, 2008. 128p.

Duzbábová, Lucie, Czech and Polish Migration in Chicago: A Land of Hope, A Land of Dispair? Bachelor's Thesis, Masaryk University, 2008.

Iowa

Merrill, Pauline Skorunka, "Pioneer Iowa Bohemians," Annals of Iowa, 26 (April 1845), pp. 261-274.

Peterka, Petr, "Waltham, Iowa," Amerikán, Národní kalendář, 5 (1882), pp. 149-151.

Kavalířová, Marie C. H., "Toledo, okres Tama, Iowa" (Toledo, Tama Co., IA), Amerikán, Národní kalendář, 5 (1882), pp. 151-153.

Lexa, Antonin, "Pleasant Ritch, okres Clayton, Iowa" (Pleasant Ritch, Clayton Co., IA), Amerikán, Národní kalendář, 5 (1882), pp. 153-154.

Luk, Vincent, "Z Oxford Junction, Iowa" (From Oxford Junction, IA), Amerikán, Národní kalendář, 9 (1886), pp. 154-155.

Hrbek, Sarah, "Bohemian Citizens Have Done Much for Cedar Rapids," The Cedar Rapids Sunday Republican, June 10, 1906.

Rudiš-Jičinský, Jan, "Bohemians in Linn County, Iowa, in: Atlas of Linn Co., Iowa. Iowa Publishing Co., 1907, pp. 209-224.

Shimek, Bohumil, "The Bohemians in Johnson County, Iowa. Iowa City, 1913. 10p.

Griffith, Martha Eleanor, Czech Settlement in Cedar Rapids, Iowa. Master's Thesis, University of Wyoming, 1942.

Griffith, Martha E., The History of Czechs in Cedar Rapids. Vol.1. 1852-1942. Reprinted from Iowa J. History and Politics, 42 (1944), pp. 115-161, 266-315. Cedar Rapids: Czech Heritage Foundation, 1972. 96p.; Vol. II 1942-1982. 1982. 111p.

Merrill, Pauline Skorunka, "Pioneer Bohemians," in: Annals of Iowa, 26 (1945), pp. 261-274.

Hlubůček, T. B., "Sláva českých Athen pohasíná" (Glory of the Czech Athens is dwindling), Amerikán, Národní kalendář, 75 (1952), pp. 52-56.

"The Czechs of Iowa," in: Panorama. Cicero, IL: Czechoslovak National Council of America, 1970, pp. 40-46.

Pecinovsky, Gerald G. Protivin: A Czech Settlement. Protivin, 1978. 44p.

Klimesh, Cyril A., They Came to this Place. A History of Spillville, Iowa and its Czech Settlers. Sebastopol, CA: Methodius Press, 1983. 239 p.

Klimesh, Michael F., "Beulah-Watson Czechs," in: Czech and Slovak Culture in International Context. Selected Papers from the 23rd SVU World Congress, University of South Bohemia, České Budějovice, June 24-July 2, 2006. Edited by Miloslav Rechcigl, Jr. České Budějovice, 2008, pp. 587-590.

Hunter, Mark Stoffer, "At Home on the River: A History of Bohemian Settlement in Cedar Rapids, Iowa," Slovo, 10, No. 1 (Summer 2009), pp. 4-9.

Kansas

Swehla, Francis J., "The Bohemians in Central Kansas," Kansas State Historical Society Collections, 13 (1913-14), pp.469-512.

King, Rebecca, J. H., "Bohemians," in: The Identification of Foreign Immigrant Groups in Kansas. M.S. Thesis, Kansas State University, Manhattan, 1948, pp. 45-57.

Nemcova, Bozena, People of Czech (Bohemian) Descent in Republic County, Kansas. Master's Thesis, University of Kansas, 1950.

Van Meter, Sandy, "Pilsen," in: Merion County, Kansas. Past and Present. Hillsboro, KS: M. B. Publishing House, 1972, pp. 295-303.

Shimmick, Lillian, "Early Czech Settlers of Decatur County, Kansas," in: Early Pioneer Families in Decatur County, Kansas. Hays, KS: Fort Hays State University, 1979.

Havel, Nelson, "The Czech Influence in Cuba, Kansas," Selected Papers from the 21st World Congress of the Czechoslovak Society of Arts and Sciences, University of West Bohemia, Plzeň, June 23-30, 2002. Ed. by Jan P. Skalny and Miloslav Rechcigl, Jr. Plzeň: Aleš Čeněk, 2004, pp. 576-579.

Louisiana

Marhefka, Blanche, "These My People," Common Ground, 1, No. 2 (Winter 1941), pp. 27-28.

Hlavac, James, Hidden Impact. The Czechs and Slovaks in Louisiana from the 1720s to Today. New York: iUniverse, Inc., 2006. 409p.

Maryland

Šimek, V. J., "Baltimore a jeho Čechové" (Baltimore and its Czechs), Amerikán, Národní kalendář, 2 (1879), pp. 145-148.

McCardell, Lee, "Baltimore's Czech Community Grew from Small Group Settling at Fells Point," Sun, October 10, 1943.

Kaessmann, Beta; Harold Randall Manakee and Joseph L. Wheeler, "Czechoslovakians or Bohemians," in: My Maryland. Baltimore: Maryland Historical Society, 1955, pp. 405-406.

"Baltimore's Prosperous Colony of Bohemians," Baltimore Sun, September 16, 1906, p. 16.

Slezak, Eva, "Czechs in Maryland before 1900," Maryland Genealogical Soc. Bull., 21, No. 1 (Winter 1980), pp. 18-26.

Slezak, Eva, "Baltimore's Czech Community: The Early Years," Czechoslovak and Central European Journal, 9, No. 1 & 2 (Summer-Winter 1990), pp.103-114.

Holzberg, James, "Czech-Slovak Heritage Preserved at Festival and Perry Hall Language School," Northeast Booster, September 23, 2010.

Rechcigl, Miloslav, Jr., "Czechs in Early Maryland and Old Baltimore," Maryland Genealogical Society Journal, 52, No. 2 (2011), pp. 293-306.

Michigan

Pospíšil, F., "Ze života prvního Čecha v Detroit (Life of the first Czech in Detroit), Amerikán, Národní kalendář, 1885, pp. 142-144.

"Oslava padsatiletého trvání první české kolonie v Michiganu" (Celebration of the 50th Anniversary of the first Czech colony in Michigan), Amerikán, Národní kalendář, 29 (1905), pp. 273-274.

Farský, Oldřich, "Traverse City a okolí a čeští pionýři" (Traverse City and the environs and Czech pioneers), Amerikán, Národní kalendář, 1908, pp. 244-264.

Benesh, Anton, "Michigan Czechs and Slovaks," in: Panorama. Cicero, IL: Czechoslovak National Council of America, 1970, pp. 54-57.

Minnesota

Breuer, Karel, "Česká osada v Minnesotě a její osadníci" (Czech community in Minnesota and its settlers), Amerikán, Národní kalendář, 4 (1881), pp. 166-176.

Fišer, Benjamin, "Ze zkušeností Čechů amerických. První osadníci poblíž Owatonna, Minn." (From experiences of Czech Americans. The first settlers near Owatonna, MN), Amerikán, Národní kalendář, 5 (1882), pp. 135-137.

Bažil, T., "Čechove v Lensburgu, okres Le Sueur, Minn." (Czechs in Lensburg, Le Sueur Co., MN), Amerikán, Národní kalendář, 6 (1883), pp. 181-182; Ibid., 21 (1898), p. 201.

Pavelka, Jan, "Popis městečka Chatfield, Fillmore Co., Minnesota" (Description of the Town Chatfield, Fillmore Co., MN), Amerikán, Národní kalendář, 9 (1886), pp. 153-154.

Breuer, Karel, "Česká osada Veselí v Minnesotě" (Czech community Veselí in Minnesota), Amerikán, Národní kalendář, 9 (1886), pp. 157-164.

Karták, Michael, "První počátky v Saint Paul, Minnesota" (Early beginnings in St. Paul, MN), Amerikán, Národní kalendář, 9 (1886), pp. 177-179.

New Prague, Minnesota. Brief Sketches of the History, Resources Advantages and Business Men. New Prague, MN: The New Prague Times, 1895. 72 p. Reprinted in 1984.

Breuer, Louis, "Městečko Lonsdale, Minnesota" (The City of Lonsdale, MN), 41 (1918), pp. 279-284.

Working, Win V., "Czechs Settle Garden Spot 'in big woods'," Southern Minnesotan, 2 (January 1932), pp. 13-14, 17-20.

Sršeň, Karel, "Sedmdesát pět let české osady v Minnesotě" (Seventy five years of Czech Settlement in Minnesota), Hospodář, 42, No. 1 (Feb. 5, 1932), pp. 74-75.

Kovář, Frantšek, "Dějiny Čechů v okrese Steele v Minnesotě" (History of Czechs in Steele Co., MN), Amerikán, Národní kalendář, 56 (1933), pp. 191-195.

Jerabek, Esther, "The Transition of a New World Bohemia," Minnesota History, 15 (1934), pp. 26-42.

Jerabek, Esther, "Little Bohemia in Western World in Early History of Silver Lake and McLeod County's Czech Settlement," Silver Lake Leader, Apr. 13-May 18, 1935.

Sršeň, Karel, Památník českých pionýrů v Minnesotě" (Memorial of Czech pioneers in Minnesota), Amerikán, Národní kalendář, 77 (1954), pp. 113-114.

New Prague Times, New Prague, MN. Centennial Edition 1846-1956. New Prague, MN, 1956. 36p.

Jerabek, Milan Woodrow, Czechs in Minnesota. M.A. Thesis, University of Minnesota, 1939. 164p.

Jerabek, Esther, "Czechs and Slovaks in Minnesota," in: Panorama. Cicero, IL: Czechoslovak National Council of America, 1970, pp. 47-50.

Wood, David, "Bohemian Flats is Long Gone but Memories Linger on," Minneapolis Tribune, August 25, 1974.

Writers' Program Minnesota, The Bohemian Flats. Minneapolis: University of Minnesota Press, 1941. 51 p.; Reprinted by Minnesota Historical Society Press, 1986.

Montgomery Bicentennial Committee, Montgomery. From the 'Big Woods' to the "Kolacky Capital' 1856-1976. Montgomery, MN, 1976.

Chrislock, C. Winston, "The Czechs," in: They Chose Minnesota: A Survey of the State's Ethnic Groups. Ed. by June Drenning Holmquist. St Paul: Minnesota Historical Society Press, 1981. pp. 331-51.

Hennepin County Historical Society, "Bohemian Flats," in: Hennepin County History, Special Issue, 1984.

Hopkins Centennial Committee, Hopkins Centennial Album, 1887-1987. Minneapolis: Kimm Co., 1987. 96p.

Missouri

Mikšička, A. V., "St. Louis a jeho Čechové" (St. Louis and its Czechs), Amerikán, Národní kalendář, 2 (1879), pp. 140-144.

Fuchs, Jan, "Owensville, okres Gasconade, Missouri" (Owensville, Gasconade Co., MO), Amerikán, Národní kalendář, 5 (1882), pp. 154-155.

Jícha, František, "St. Mary's, Missouri," Amerikán, Národní kalendář, 5 (1882), pp. 156-157.

Šulz, Joseph, Czech Contributions to St. Louis Community. 1965. 3p.

Soulard: The Ethnic Heritage of an Urban Neighborhood. St. Louis: Washington University Press, 1975.

Sullivan, Margaret LaPiccolo, "St. Louis Ethnic Neighborhoods, 1850-1930: An Introduction," Missouri Historical Society Bulletin, 33 (January 1977), pp. 64-76.

Corzine, Jay and Irene Dabrovski, "The Ethnic Factor and Neighborhood Stability: The Czechs in Soulard and St. Louis," Missouri Historical Soc. Bulletin, 33 (1955), pp. 77-93.
Jones, Patricia L.," What Ever Happened to Bohemian Hill?" Gateway Heritage, 5 (Winter 1984-85), pp. 22-31.
Sommer, June, ed., History of the Czechs in Missouri 1845 to 1904. St. Louis: St. Louis Genealogical Society, 1988. 71p.

Nebraska

Holeček, Josef V., "První dějiny okresu Knox" (The first history of Knox Co.), Amerikán, Národní kalendář, 1881, pp. 161-164.
Brázda, Dominik, "Cloudy, Cuming Co., Neb.", Amerikán, Národní kalendář, 5 (1882), pp. 137-142.
Lundák, J. F., "Spolkové počátky Pishelville, Neb." (Organizational beginnings in Pishelville, NE), Amerikán, Národní kalendář, 1886, p. 185.
Wilber v obrazech. Památné ilustrované číslo Přítele lidu. Dějiny města Wilber (Wilber in Pictures). Wilber: Přítel lidu, 1903. 40p.
Hrbková, Šárka, "Bohemians in Nebraska," Bohemian Review, 1, No. 6 (July 1917), pp. 10-14.
Hrbkova, Šárka, "Bohemians in Nebraska," Publications of the Nebraska Historical Society, 19 (1919), pp. 140-158.
Šedivý, Josef Pavel, "Vzpomínky z dob usazení Čechů v Knox okrese, Nebraska" (Recollections of the times of settlement of Czechs in Knox Co., NE), Pionýr, českoamerický kalendář, 5 (1920), pp. 95-105.
Holeček, Josef V., "První Čechové v Niobraře," (First Czechs in Niobrara), Amerikán, Národní kalendář, 45 (1922), pp. 227-256.
Rosicky, Rose, Pioneer Czechs in Colfax County, Nebraska. Omaha, 1926.
Sullenger, T. Earl, "The Czechoslovakian Population of Omaha," Journal of Applied Sociology, 11 (1927), pp. 561-564.
Rosicky, Rose, A History of Czechs (Bohemians) in Nebraska. Omaha: Czech Historical Society of Nebraska, 1929. 492 p. Reprinted by Whipporwill Publications (1987).
Prague Golden Jubilee Committee, The History of Prague. Saunders County, Nebraska, 1887-1937. Prague: Prague Herald, 1937. 52p.

Van Hoff, Joseph John, A History of the Czechs of Knox County, Nebraska. M.A. Thesis, University of Nebraska, 1938.

Kubicek, Clarence John, The Czechs of Butler County, 1870-1940. M.A. Thesis, University of Nebraska in Lincoln, 1938.

Kučera, Vladimír, ed. Czechs and Nebraska. Ord, NE: Quiz Graphic Arts, 1967. 424 p.

Svoboda, Joseph G., "The Czechs: The Love of Liberty," in Broken Hoops and Plains People. Edited by Paul A. Olson et al. Lincoln, NE: Nebraska Curriculum Development Center, 1976, pp. 153-191.

Kučera, Vladimír and Alfred Nováček, eds., Czech Contributions to the Progress of Nebraska. Ord, NE: Quiz Graphis Arts, 1976.

"The Czech-American Experience," Nebraska History, 74, No. 3&4 (Fall/Winter 1993), pp. 101-203.

New Jersey

Bartell, Frank W., "A Brief History of the Czechs in New Jersey," in: The New Jersey Ethnic Experience. Edited by Barbara Cunningham. Union City, NJ: W. H. Wise, 1977, pp. 158-166.

New York

Zdrůbek, František Boleslav, "Každý začátek je těžký. Pravdivé vyprávění ze života prvních českých vystěhovalců v New Yorku" (Every beginning is hard. True narrative from the lives of the first Czech emigrants in New York), Amerikán, Národní kalendář, 1(1878), pp. 54-65.

Tůma, Josef F., "Bohemia. Česká osada na Long Islandu, New York" (Bohemia. Czech community on Long Island, NY), Amerikán, Národní kalendář, 19 (1896), pp. 183-186.

Čapek, Jan Vratislav, Dějiny české Novoyorské a Národni jednoty Čechů amerických" (History of Czech New York and of National Unity of American Czechs). New York: Newyorské Listy, 1905. 93p.

Tůma, Josef J, Ku 50leté památce založení osady Bohemia, N.Y., odbyvané dne 4. července 1905 (the 50th memorial of the founding of the community Bohemia, NY, held July 4, 1905), Amerikán, Národní kalendář, 29 (1904), pp. 240-243.

Vojan, Jaroslav E. S., Velký New York. Dějiny New Yorku a české čvrti (Greater New York. History of New York and its Czech community). New York: New Yorské Listy, 1908. 244p.

Bittner, Bartoš, "Z doby zeleného mládí. Rozmarné vzpominky na starý New York (From the time of green youth. Humorous reminiscences of the old New York). Amerikán, Národní kalendář, 37 (1914), pp. 179-187.

Spurná, J., Osada Astorská, Long Island, N.Y. (The Astoria community, Long Island, NY), Amerikán, Národní kalendář, 39 (1916), pp. 257-251.

Čapek, Thomas, The Čech (Bohemian) Community of New York. New York: America's Making, 1921. 93p.

Tůma, Josef J., "Long Island a dějiny osady Bohemia" (Long Island and the history of Bohemia community), Amerikán, Národní kalendář, 1925, pp. 225-236.

Foxlee, Ludmila Kuchařová, "Češi v New Yorku (Czechs in New York), Amerikán, Národní kalendář, 75 (1952), pp. 37-51.

A History of Bohemia, Long Island. Sayville, Long Island, NY: Weeks & Reichel Printing, 1955. 80p.

Foxlee, Ludmila Kuchařová, "Češi v New Yorku" (Czechs in New York), Amerikán, Národní kalendář, 75 (1952), pp. 37-51.

Bušek, Vratislav and Jan Shintay, "The Czechs and Slovaks of New York," in: Panorama. Cicero, IL: Czechoslovak National Council of America, 1970, pp. 18-29.

Rechcigl, Miloslav, Jr., "Gateway to America," in: Czechs and Slovaks in America. Boulder, CO: East European Monographs, 2005, pp. 171-175.

North Dakota

Elznic, William H., Bohemians in Richland County," North Dakota Historical Bulletin, 4 (1915), pp. 62-80.

Schmirler, A. A. A., Wagon Migration. Veseleyville, D. T. 1880-1881. Grafton: Associated Printers, 1981. 242 p.

Pisek. The First Century: A History of Pisek, ND and Its People. Grafton: Associated Printers, 1982. 326 p.

A Century of Progress by the Czechs in New Hradec, North Dakota. New Hradec, ND: Ficek Family, 1989. 146p.

Ohio

Šnajdr, Václav, "Cleveland a jeho Čechové" (Cleveland and its Czechs), Amerikán, Národní kalendář, 1 (1878), pp. 92-97.

Česká osada a její spolkový život v Clevelandu, Ohio (Czech community and its social life in Cleveland, OH). Cleveland: 'Volnost' Press, 1895. 192p.

Chotek, Hugo, "Paměti prvních Čechů v Clevelandu" (Reminiscences of the first Czechs in Cleveland), Amerikán, Národní kalendář, 18 (1915), pp. 201-211, pp 211-217.

"Česká osada Toledo. Paměti kr. Ant. Škody a Fr. Pavlíčka" (Czech community Toledo. Reminiscences of Ant. Škoda and Fr. Pavlíček), Amerikán, Národní kalendář, 1915, pp. 293-296.

Ledbetter, Eleanor E., The Czechs of Cleveland. Cleveland: Mayor's Advisory War Committee, 1919. 40 p.

Pap, Michael S., "The Czech Community of Cleveland", in: Ethnic Communities of Cleveland. Cleveland: John Carroll University, 1973, pp. 75-101.

Zentos, N.J., Marley, W., "Czechs," in: The Encyclopedia of Cleveland History. Edited by D. D. Van Tassel and J. J. Grabowski. Bloomington: Indiana University Press, 1987, pp. 341-343.

Kukral, Michael A., "Czech Settlements in the 19th Century Cleveland, Oho," in: Moravians from World Perspective. Selected Papers from the 22nd World Congress of Czechoslovak Society of Arts and Sciences, Palacky University, Olomouc, June 26 to July 4, 2004. Edited by Miloslav, Rechcigl, Jr. Ostrava: Repronis, 2006, pp. 257-264.

Sabol, John T. and Lisa A. Alzo, Cleveland's Czechs. (Images of America). Mount Pleasant, SC: Arcadia Publishing, 2009. 128p.

Oklahoma

Hájek, J., "Čechové v Oklahomě a jejich postoj" (Czechs in Oklahoma and their stand, Amerikán, Národní kalendář, 29 (1906), pp. 227-232.

Buňata, Josef, "Praha v Oklahomě" (Prague in Oklahoma), Amerikán, Národní kalendář, 46 (1922), pp. 234-237.

Rabstejnek, Hermina, "A Tribute to Oklahoma and its Czech Pioneers," in: Panorama. Cicero, IL: Czechoslovak National Council of America, 1970, pp. 58-62.

Brown, Melvin L., Czech-Town U.S.A.: Prague (L Kolache-ville), Oklahoma. Prague, OK, 1977. 177 p.

Bicha, Karel D., The Czechs in Oklahoma. Norman: University of Oklahoma, 1980. 81p.

Naramore, Ronald, Ethnicity on the American Frontier: A Study of Czechs in Oklahoma. University of Oklahoma Dept. of Anthropology. Anthropology Club. Papers in Anthropology, 1973.

Oregon

Stastny, Matthew M., History of Bohemians in Oregon. Senior Thesis. June 1, 1912.

Good, Rachel Applegate. History of Klamath County, Oregon. Malin, OR: Klamath County Historical Society, 1941.

Kalina, Alois, "Z dějin české osady Malin v Oregonu" (From the history of Czech community Malin in Oregon), Amerikán, Národní kalendář, 65 (1942), pp. 151-158.

Petrik, Vlasta and Joseph Zumpfe. Settling of Southern Klamath Country by Czech Colonization Club. Merrill, OR: J. Zumpfe, 1985.

O'Donnell, Lida, "Czechs in Oregon: Scio, Scappoose and Malin," in: The Transformation of Czech and Slovak Societies on the Threshold of the New Millennium and their Role in the Global World. Selected Papers from the 21st World Congress, University of West Bohemia, Plzeň, June 23-30, 2002. Edited by Jan Skalny and Miloslav Rechcigl, Jr. Plzeň: Aleš Čeněk, 2004, pp. 611-614.

O'Donell, Lida, "Czech Footprints in Oregon," in: Moravians from World Perspective. Selected Papers from the 22nd World Congress of Czechoslovak Society of Arts and Sciences, Palacký University, Olomouc, June 26 to July 4, 2004. Edited by Miloslav Rechcigl, Jr. Ostrava: Repronis, 2006, vol. 2, pp. 271-275.

Pennsylvania

Kirchman, Max, "Allegheny—Pittsburgh," Amerikán, Národní kalendář, 1879, pp. 124-130.

Rechcigl, Miloslav, Jr., "The First Pennsylvania Settler from the Czechlands," Naše Rodina (Our Family), 9, No. 1 (March 1997), pp. 28-29.

Mohr, John McGuire, From Immigrant to Citizen: The Czechs of Allegheny City, 1873 to 1907. Ph.D. Dissertation, University of Pittsburgh, 2002.

South Dakota

Petrák, Anton, Popis krajanů u Kimball, Dakota Ty." (Our Compatriots near Kimball, Dakota Territory), Amerikán, Národní kalendář, 9 (1886), p. 157.

Dvořák, Josef A., ed. Dějiny Čechův ve statu South Dakota (History of Czechs in the State of South Dakota). Tabor, SD, 1920. 109p.

Chladek, Mrs. F. F. History of Bon Homme County: From Early Settlement Until 1921. Tyndall: n.p., [1921]. 47p.

Tůma, Emil, "Dějiny Čechů ve státě South Dakota," (History of Czechs in South Dakota), Naše zahraničí, 2, No. 1 (March 1921), pp. 18-23.

Vondracek, Paul F., History of the Early Czech Settlements in South Dakota. M.A. Thesis, University of South Dakota, 1963. 75p.

Dvořák, Joseph A., Memorial Book History of the Czechs in the State of South Dakota. Tabor, SD: The Czech Heritage Preservation Society, 1980. 189p.

Richards, Marilee. "Life anew for Czech Immigrants: The Letters of Mari and Vavrin Stritecky, 1913-1934," South Dakota History, 11, No. 4 (1981): 253-304.

Rau, John E., "Czechs in South Dakota" in: To Build a New Land: Ethnic Landscapes in North America. Ed. by Allen G. Noble. Baltimore, MD: Johns Hopkins University Press, 1992, pp. 185-306.

Tvaroh, Přemysl, Jak Češi v předminulém století osídlovali americkou prérii. Dějiny Čechů ve státu South Dakota (How Czechs settled American prarie two centuries ago. History of Czechs in the state of South Dakota). Růže, 2007. 56p.

Texas

Šiler, Josef, "Eagle Lake, okres Colorado, Texas" (Eagle Lake, Colorado Co., TX), Amerikán, Národní kalendář, 5 (1882), pp. 142-144.

Miller, Kenneth Dexter, "Bohemians in Texas," Bohemian Review, 11, No. 4 (1917), pp. 4-5.

Dongres, L. W., "Češi v Texasu" (Czechs in Texas), Amerikán, Národní kalendář, 1924, pp. 270-276.

Památník Čechoslováků v Texasu 1618-1918 (Czechoslovak memorial in Texas 1618-1918).

Maresh, H. B. and Estelle Hudson, Czech Pioneers of the Southwest. Dallas: South-West Press, 1934. 418 p. Reprinted Houston, TX: Western Lithograph, 1996.

Míček, Eduard, "How Czech Pioneers Helped to Make Texas History," Central European Observer, 13 (1935), pp. 341-342.

Wychopen, L.C., "Vzpomínky ze starých časů v Texasu" (Reminiscences from the old times in Texas), Věstník, 25, No. 3 (1937), p. 2; Ibid., 25, No. 4 (1937), p. 7.

Stastney, Mollie Emma, The Czechs in Texas. M.A. Thesis, The University of Texas, 1938.

Maresh, Henry R. "The Czechs in Texas," Southwestern Historical Quarterly, 50 (October 1946), pp. 236-240.

Hranicky, Roy, The History of the Czech Element in Texas. M.A. Thesis, Texas College of Arts and Industries, 1954.

Skrivanek, John M., "The Czech in Texas," in: The Czechoslovak Contribution to World Culture. Ed. by Miloslav Rechcigl, Jr. The Hague: Mouton & Co., 1964, pp. 510-515.

Mácha, Helen, "The Czechs in Texas from 1896 to 1900," Věstník, 53, No. 1 (January 6, 1965), pp. 4-5; Ibid., 53, No. 2 (Jan 13, 1965), pp. 5-6.

Malik, Joseph, "The Czechs in Texas," in: Panorama. Cicero, IL, 1970, pp. 35-39.

Bowmer, Martha, "Life as Loved by our Unique Czech Texans," Bell County This Month, Temple: Stillhouse Hollow Publishing Co., 1972, pp. 2-5.

Splawn, Vlasta Margaret, Sociological Study of a Czech Communuity in Ellis County, Texas. Master's Thesis, Texas Technical University, 1972.

Hejl, Edward H., Czech Footprints across Bluebonnet Fields. Fort Worth, 1979.

The Czechs in Texas. Papers from The Czechs in Texas: A Symposium. Edited by Clinton Machann. Temple, TX: Texas A&M University, 1979. 184p.

Machann, Clinton and James W. Mendl, Krásná Amerika. A Study of the Texas Czechs 1851-1939. Austin: Eakin Press, 1983. 280p.

Prochaska, Alvin J., "South Texas Czechs in Nueces County, Texas," Naše Dějiny, 8, No. 1 (1988), pp. 2-3.

Chotek, Hugo, Fom the Times of Hardship: Original historical story from the life of the first Czech immigrants to Texas. F.M. Duncan, 1988. 77p.

Czech Voices. Stories from Texas in the Amerikán, Národní kalendář. Translated and edited by Clinton Machann and James W. Mendl, Jr. College Station, TX: Texas A&M University Press, 1991. 147p.

Konecny, Lawrence H. and Clinton Machann, German and Czech Immigration to Texas: The Bremen to Galveston Route, 1880-1886," Nebraska History, 74, No. 3 & 4 (Fall/Winter 1993), pp. 136-141.

Zátopek, Jiří, "Historie osady Marak v Texasu" (History of the Marak community in Texas), in: Hlasy muzea a archivu ve Frenštátě pod Radhoštěm, 10, No. 1(1993), pp. 6-7.

Zátopek, Jiří, "Osada Frenštát v Texasu a její zakladatelé" (Frenštát community in Texas and its founders), in: Hlasy muzea a archivu ve Frenštátě pod Radhoštěm, 13, No. 1-2 (1996), pp. 17-20.

The Remote and Near Country. Trojanovice, Czech Republic: Obec Trojanovice, 1997. 80p.

Gallup, Sean N., Journeys into Czech-Moravian Texas. College Station, TX: Texas A&M University Press, 1998. 148p., 109 color photos.

Czech Heritage Society of Texas, Texas Veterans of Czech Ancestry. Austin: Eakin Press, 1999. 328 p.

Eckertová, Eva. "Svoboda a nový domov v Texasu" (Freedom and new home in Texas), in: Hlasy muzea a archivu ve Frenštátě pod Radhoštěm, 23, No. 1-4 (2006), pp. 68-80.

Konecny, Lawrence H. and Clinton Machann, Perilous Voyages: Czech and English Immigrants in Texas in the 1870s. College Station: Texas A&M University, 2004.183p.

Eckert., Eva, "From Moravia to Texas: The Story of Pioneer Immigrants," in: The Transformation of Czech and Slovak Societies on the Threshold of the New Millennium and their Role in the Global World. Selected Papers from the 21st SVU World Congress, University of West Bohemia, Plzen, June 23-30, 2002. Edited by Jan Skalny and Miloslav Rechcigl, Jr. Plzeň: Aleš Čeněk, 2004, pp. 543-551.

Eckertová, Eva, Kameny na prérii. Čeští vystěhovalci v Texasu (Czechs on the prarie. Czech emigrants in Texas). Praha: Nakladatelství Lidové noviny, 2004.

Chroust, David Z., "Jozef Ernst Bergmann: 'Father' of Czech-Speaking Immigration in Texas," Kosmas, 20, No. 1 (Fall 2006), pp. 48-64.

Eckertová, Eva, "Texas, divoký západ" (Texas, Wild West), in: Hlasy muzea a archivu ve Frenštátě pod Radhoštěm, 24, No. 1-4 (2006), pp. 59-67.

Stockbauer, Bette. "From Frenštat, Moravia, to Fayette County, Texas—A Chronicle of Two Brothers: Jan and Ferdinand Přibyl," Kosmas, 21, No. 1 (2007), pp. 90-110.

Hlavinka, Paul T., "Czech Immigration to Texas, 1900-1910. Causation and Characteristics," in: Czech and Slovak Culture in International and Global Context. Selected Papers from the 23rd SVU World Congress, University of South Bohemia, České Budějovice, June 24-July 2, 2006. Edited by Miloslav Rechcigl, Jr. České Budějovice, 2008, pp. 609-615.

Rechcigl, Miloslav, Jr.," The Lone Star State of 'Moravci" in the Formative Years," Kosmas, 23, No. 1 (Fall 2009), pp.42-63.

Wilson, Laurie J. and Peggy Holland Rankin, Ennis, TX. Mount Pleasant, SC: Ennis, TX, 2009. 128p.

Janak, Robert. "Kovar, Texas, in 1918: A Historical Snapshot of the Texas Czech Community." Kosmas, 23, No. 2 (2010), pp. 58-71.

Virginia

LaBaume, F. H., "Prosperous Settlements in Virginia. Slavonic Colony at New Bohemia," in: Norfolk and Western Guide, 1915. 51p.

Krupař, A. C., Dějiny Čechů v okolí Petersburg, Virginia (History of Czechs in the vicinity of Petersburg, VA). Petersburg, VA, 1915.

Carroll, R. G., "New Bohemia, Virginia. Colony of Alien Farmers," Country Gentleman, 18 (July 1, 1916), pp. 1290-91.

Hodges LeRoy, "Czechoslovaks in South Side Virginia," The Czechoslovak Review, 3, No. 5 (May 1919), pp. 115-118.

Anderson, Nels, Petersburg. A Study of a Colony of Czecho-Slovakian Farmers in Virginia." In: Immigrant Farmers and their Children. Ed. by Edmund de Schweinitz Brunner. Garden City, NY: Doubleday, 1929, pp. 183-21.

Kovacs, Sandra A., Czechoslovaks in Virginia. Ph.D. Dissertation, University of Virginia, 1939. 161p.

Baist, Stanley. "Old Czech Traditions Live on in Virginia." The Sunday Star Pictorial Magazine, December 28, 1947, p. 2.

Wells, John E., The Czech and Slovak Communities in Virginia. Richmond: VDOT Richmond District, September 19, 2007.

Pritchard, Joyce M., "Czechs of Southside Virginia. An international search of the landscape and the literature," in: Czech and Slovak Culture in International and Global Context. Selected Papers from the 23rd SVU World Congress, University of South Bohemia, České Budějovice, June 24-July 2, 2006. Edited by Miloslav Rechcigl, České Budějovice, 2008, pp. 577-583.

Wisconsin

Trousil, František, "První Češi v Carltoně, Wisconsin" (First Czechs in Carlton, WI), Amerikán, Národní kalendář, 5 (1882), pp. 144-146.

U. J., "Yuba, Wisconsin", Amerikán, Národní kalendář, 5 (1882), pp. 146-149.

Rezek, Jan, "Čechové v Kossuthtown, okres Manitowoc, Wisconsin" (Czechs in Kossuthtown, Manitowoc Co., WI), Amerikán, Národní kalendář, 5 (1882), pp. 155-156.

Zatočil, A, "Wauzeka, Wis.," Amerikán, Národní kalendář, 5 (1882), pp. 157-158.

Kolář, W., "Česká osada v Yuba, Wisconsin (Czech Community in Yuba, WI), Amerikán, Národní kalendář, 9 (1886), pp. 155-157.

Vlach, J. J., "Our Bohemian Population," in: Proc., State Historical Society of Wisconsin, at its 49th Annual Meeting and the State Historical Convention, 1901. Madison: Democrat Printing Co., 1902, pp. 159-162.

Novák, Anton, "Ze zašlých dob. Stručné dějiny osady v Milwaukee" (From the passed years. Brief history of the community in Milwaukee), in: Památník vydaný ke 14. sjezdu Jednoty ČSPS, konanému v Milwaukee od 30. srpna do 4. září 1909. 34p.

"Pioneer Czech Settlers of Langlade County," Antigo Journal, March 25, 1933.

Petura, J. L., Z dějin Caledonie, staré české osady ve státu Wisconsinu" (History of Caledonia, an old Czech community in the State of Wisconsin), Amerikán, Národní kalendář, 57 (1934), pp. 208-213.

Illichman, S. J., "Pionýrští čeští osadníci v okresu Langlade ve Wisconsinu" (Pioneer Czech settlers in Langlade Co., WI), Amerikán, Národní kalendář, 58 (1935), pp. 176-181.

Wojta, Joseph Frank, "The Town of Two Creeks, Manitowoc County," Wisconsin Magazine of History, 25 (1941), pp. 132-154.

Holmes, Frederick Lionel, "Czechs and Slovaks," in: Old World Wisconsin. Around Europe in the Badger State. Eau Claire, WI: E. M. Hale & Co., 1944, pp. 283-287.

Bicha, Karel D., "The Czechs in Wisconsin History," Wisconsin Magazine of History, 55, No. 3 (1972), pp. 194-203.

Beneš, Frank, Czechs in Manitowoc County, Wisconsin, 1847-1932. Manitowoc, WI: Manitowoc Historical Society, 1979. 43p.

Dushek, Camille, et al., Bohemians Prominent in Manitowoc County. History Accounts of Some of the Early Settlers, the History of Tisch Mills, etc. Manitowoc County Historical Society, Occupational Monograph 38, 1979 Series.

Rucker, Della G., History of Czech Settlements: Kewaunnee and Manitowoc Counties, Wisconsin, USA. Wisconsin's Ethnic Settlement Trail, Inc., 1995. 19p.

Rechcigl, Miloslav Jr., "Czech Pioneers in Wisconsin," Naše Rodina (Our Family), 9, No. 3 (September 1997), pp. 110-113.

Magstadt, Štěpánka, "The Czechs in Caledonia," in: Moravians from World Perspective. Selected Papers from the 22nd World Congress of Czechoslovak Society of Arts and Sciences, Palacký University, Olomouc, June 26 to July 4, 2001. Edited by Miloslav, Rechcigl, Jr. Ostrava: Repronis, 2006, pp. 265-270.

F. Historic Places

Pastor, Josef, "Seznam českých osad v Americe" (Listing of Czech communities in America), in: České osady v Americe. Ročník 2. Hamburk: H. O. Potsiehl, 1886. 12p. On Internet: http://www.genebaze.cz/cgi-bin/kn.cgi?k=JPCoA2

Čapek, Tomáš, "Slovanská osídlení" (Slavonic settlements), in: Naše Amerika. Praha: Národní rada československá, 1926, pp. 517-605.

Janak, Robert, Gazetteer of Czech Texas, 1939: Czech Communities in Texas in the year 1939. The Czech Heritage Society of Texas, 1995. 186p.

Rechcigl, Miloslav, Jr., Czech-American Historic Sites, Monuments, and Memorials. Rockville, MD: SVU, 1999. 112p.

Rechcigl, Miloslav, Jr., Czech-American Historic Sites, Monuments, and Memorials. Olomouc-Ostrava: Palacký University, 2004. 142p.

III. The People

A. Anthropology

Hrdlička, Aleš, "Bohemia and the Czechs," National Geographic Magazine, 31 (1917), pp. 163-189.

Miller, Kenneth D, "European Backgrounds," in: The Czecho-Slovaks in America. New York: George H. Doran, 1922, pp. 11-41.

Miller, Herbert Adolphus, "Czechoslovaks," in: Immigrant Backgrounds. Ed. by Henry Pratt Fairchild. New York: J. Wiley & Sons, 1927, pp. 143-199.

Malý, Jiří, "Čechoslováci v zahraničí, zvláště severoameričtí" (Czechoslovaks abroad, especially the North Americans), in: Československá vlastivěda. Sv. 2. Člověk. Praha: Sfinx, 1933, pp. 260-269.

Korytová-Magstadt, Štěpánka, "Background of Emigration in Bohemia," in: To Reap a Bountiful Harvest. Iowa City: Rudi Publishing, 1993, pp. 3-11.

B. Demography

Šembera, Alois Vojtěch, "Mnoho-li jest Čechů, Moravanů a Slováků a kde obývají. Příspěvek k etnografii Československé" (How many Czechs, Moravians and Slovaks are there and where they live. A contribution to the Czechoslovak Etnography). Časopis Musea království Českého, 50 (1876), pp. 393-418, 647-685.

Stručná statistika osad, míst, měst a okresů ve Spojených státech, Čechy obydlených" (Brief statistics concerning the communities, localities, towns and counties in the US, settled by the Czechs), Amerikán, Národní kalendář, 1 (1878), pp. 97-112.

"Stručná statistika osad, mist, měst a okresů ve Spojených státech, Čechy osídlených (Brief statistics concerning the communities, localities, towns and districts in the US, Settled by the Czechs). Amerikán, Národní kalendář, 3 (1880), pp. 143-161.

"Dodatek ku statistice české v Americe" (Supplement to the Czech statistics in America), Amerikán, Národní kalendář, 7 (1889), pp. 184-185.

Vojan, Jaroslav E. Salaba, "Kolik je nás?" (How many are we?), in: Českoamerické epištoly (Czech American Epistles). Chicago: Literární kroužek, 1911, pp. 57-70.

Boháč, Antonín, "Volné kapitoly ze statistiky slovanstva. Stěhovani Slovanů do Ameriky" (Random chapters from the Slavic statistics. Migration of Slavs to America), Slovanský přehled, 15 (1913), 433p.

Auerhan, Jan, Několik dat o Čechoslovácích ve Spojených státech severoamerických dle sčítání z roku 1910 (Some data about the Czechoslovaks in the U.S.A. based on the census of 1910). 1920.

Čapek, Thomas, "The Distribution of the Stock," in: The Čechs (Bohemians) in America. Boston & New York: Houghton Mifflin, 1920, pp. 59-68.

Miller, Kenneth D., "Distribution and Location," in: The Czecho-Slovaks in America. New York: George H. Doran, 1922, pp. 47-51.

Auerhan, Jan, Osoby československého původu v prvé a druhé generaci přistěhovalců ve Spojených státech severoamerických dle výsledku sčítání lidu z r. 1920" (Persons of Czechoslovak origin in the first and the second generations of immigrants to the USA, according to the Census of 1920), Naše zahraničí, 6 (1925), pp. 152-159.

Klíma, Stanislav, "Kolik je Čechů a Slováků ve Spojených státech" (How many Czechs and Slovaks are in the US), in: Češi a Slováci za hranicemi. Praha: J. Otto, 1925, pp. 183-185.

Varlez, L, Kontinentální vystěhovalecká statistika" (Continental emigration statistics). Praha: Ministerstvo sociální péče, 1925. 35p.

Čapek, Tomáš, "Statistika" (Statistics), in: Naše Amerika. Praha: Národní rada československá, 1926, pp. 607-637.

Barvínek, V. K., "Osoby československého původu v prvé a druhé generaci přistěhovalců ve Spojených státech severoamerických podle výsledku sčítání lidu z roku 1920" (Persons of Czechoslovak origin in the first and second generations of immigrants in the US according to the 1920 Census), Naše zahraničí, 9 (1928), pp. 101-104.

Auerhan, J. and R. Turčín, "Přehled čsl. zahraničních menšin a krajanských aglomerací" (Survey of Czechoslovak minorities abroad and their grouping), in: Ročenka Čs. ústavu zahraničního. Praha, 1930.

Auerhan. Jan, "Pokus o demografii zahraničních Čechů a Slováků" (Demography of Czechs and Slovaks abroad), in: Československá vlastivěda. Řada II. Národopis. Praha: Sfinx, 1936, pp. 97-139.

Čapek, Thomas, Czechs and Slovaks in the United States Census. New York: Paebar, 1939.

Čapek, Thomas, Slavs in the United States Census 1850-1940 with Specific Reference to Czechoslovakia.Chicago, 1943.

Mastný, V., "Statistika vystěhovalectvi českého proletariátu do Spojenýh států," Demografie, 4, No. 3 (1962), pp. 204-211.

Bušek, Vratislav, "Statistics on the Czechs and Slovaks in the United States," in: Panorama. A Historical Review of Czechs and Slovak in America. Cicero, IL: Czechoslovak National Council of America, 1970, pp. 13-14.

Williams, Jennifer D., Czechoslovak Population by State, 1980. Washington, DC: Library of Congress Congressional Research Service, Government Division, 1986. 3p.

C. Language

1. General

Dudek, J. B., "The Czech Language in America," American Mercury, 5 (1925), pp. 202-207.

Roucek, Joseph S., "Language Problems of American Minorities," V.O.C. Journal of Education, 4 (April 1964), pp. 18-32.

Mendl, James, Historical Czech and Moravian Dialects in the New World. M.A. Thesis, University of Texas, Austin, 1976.

Mendl, James, "Moravian Dialects in Texas," in: The Czechs in Texas. A symposium. Ed. by Clinton Machann. College Station: Texas A&M University, 1979, pp. 128-147.

Henzl, Vera, "Slavic Languages in the new environment," in: Language in the USA. Edited by Charles Albert Ferguson, Shirley Brick Heath and David Hwang. Cambridge: Cambridge University Press, 1981, pp. 293-319.

Eckert, Eva, "First-Generation American Czech: A Sociolinguistic Survey," Language Problems and Language Planning, 12 (1988), pp. 96-109.

Kučera, K., "Současné postavení českého jazyka v USA" (Present standing of the Czech language in USA), Naše řeč, 73 (1990), pp. 57-63.

Kučera, K. Český jazyk v USA (Czech language in the US). Praha, 1990.

Henzlová, V. M., "Kultivování češtiny v USA" (Promoting Czech in the US), in: Spisovná čeština a jazyková kultura 1993.Ed. by J. Jančáková, M. Komárek and O. Uličný. Praha, 1995, pp. 329-332.

Eckert, Eva, Language Change: The Testimony of Czech Tombstone Inscriptions," in Praha, Texas. Varieties of Czech. Edited by Eva Eckert. Atlanta, GA: Rodopi, 1993, pp. 189-215.

Hannan, Kevin, "Ethnic Identity among the Czechs and Moravians of Texas," American Ethnic History, 15, No. 4 (1996), pp. 3-31.

Hannan, Kevin, "Reflections on Assimilation and Language Death in Czech-Moravian Texas," Kosmas. Czechoslovak and Central European Journal, 16, No. 2 (2003), pp. 110-132.

Hannan, Kevin, "From One Monolingualism to Another Ethnic Assimilation as a Product of Language Displacement in Czech-Moravian Texas," Český lid, 91, No. 3 (2004), pp. 235-252.

Eckert, Eva, "Language and Identity: Reading Immigrant Press," in: Moravians from World Perspective. Selected Papers from the 22nd World Congress of Czechoslovak Society of Arts and Sciences, Palacký University, Olomouc, June 26 to July 4, 200l. Edited by Miloslav, Rechcigl, Jr. Ostrava: Repronis, 2006, pp. 345-353.

2. Americanization and Corruption of the Language

Čapek, Thomas, "Gamin Etymology—Pantáta—Corruption of the Language—Americanization of Names, in: The Čechs (Bohemians) in America. Boston & New York, Houghton Mifflin, 1920, pp. 114-118.

Hroch, Maximilián, "Mluva amerických Čechů v Chicagu. Ukázka od Pavla Albieriho 'Nevěsta za padesát dolarů' (Language of American Czechs in Chicago. llustration from Pavel Albieri's Nevěsta za padesát dolarů'), Český lid, 24 (1924), pp. 376-377.

Dudek, J.B., "The Americanization of Czech Given Names," American Speech, October 1925.

Čapek, Tomáš, "Kazimluvy' (Language corruption), in: Naše Amerika. Praha: Národní rada československá, 1926, pp. 419-425.

Kutac, Margaret May, English Loan Words in the Czech Literary Language of Texas. M.S.Thesis, University of Texas, Austin, 1967.

Perkowski, Jan, "Linguistic Change in Texas Czech," in: Studies in Czechoslovak History. Ed. by Miloslav Rechcigl, Jr. Meerut, India: Sadhna Prakashan, 1976, pp. 148-163.

Kochis, Bruce, "Czech in Nebraska," Languages in Conflict. Papers on Linguisticv Acculturation on the Great Plains. Ed. by Paul Schach. Lincoln: University of Nebraska Press, 1980, pp. 111-118.

Henzl, Věra M., "American Czech: A Comparative Study of Linguistic Modifications in Immigrant and Young Children Speech," Int. Rev. Slav. Ling., 6, No. 1-3 (1981), pp. 33-46.

Dutková-Cope, Lída, "The Language of Czech Moravians in Texas: Do You Know what '*Párknu káru* u hauza' Means" Southwest Journal of Linguistics, 20, No. 2 (2001), pp. 51-84.

Smith, C. S., "Texas Czech: A Study in Language Death," Kosmas, 14, No. 2 (2001), pp. 65-79.

Dutková-Cope, Lída, "Texas Czech: The Language of Texans Who Say they Speak a Different Type of Czech," Southwest Journal of Linguistics, 20, No. 1 (2001), pp. 29-69.

Jaklová, Alena, "Čechoamerická periodika z hlediska pragmaticko-lingvistického" (Czech American periodiacals from the pragmatic linguistic viewpoint), in: Sborník vybraných příspěvků 21. světového kongresu Společnosti pro vědy a umění v Plzni. Plzeň, Západočeská univerzita, 2002.

Hannan, Kevin, "Reflections on Assimilation and Language Death in Czech-Moravian Texas," Kosmas, 16, No. 2 (2003), pp. 110-132.

3. Maintenance and the Perspectives for Future

Malik, Joe, Efforts to Promote the Study of the Czech Language and Culture in Texas. M.Ed. Thesis, University of Texas, 1947. 92p.

Holick, Robert, A Comparison of Reading Vocabulary and Reading Comprehension Skills between Bilingual and Multulingual Czech-American Students. Ph.D. Dissertation, Texas A&M University, 1975.

Perkowski, Jan, "On Teaching the Texas Czechs and Germans their Ancestral Languages," CESAT Newsletter, 2 (December 1981), pp. 4-13.

Šašková-Pierce, Mila, "Czech Language Maintenance in Nebraska," Nebraska History, 74, No. 3-4 (Fall/Winter 1993), pp. 209-217.

Šašková-Pierce, Míla, "Rozklad a odolnost jazykových kategorií: Jazyk starousedlíků v Nebrasce" (Attrition and Resiliency of Language Categories and the Language of Settlers in Nebraska), Čestina doma i v zahraničí, 2 (1995), pp. 112-117,

Dutková, Lída, "Texas Czech of Texas Czechs: An Ethnolinguistic Perspective on Language Use in a Dying Language Community," in: Brown Slavic Contributions 11: Modern Czech Studies, 1999, pp. 2-10.

Šasková-Pierce, Míla, "Czech Language Instruction at the University of Nebraska-Lincoln," Czech Language News, Fall 2001, pp. 2-5.

Dutková-Cope, Lída, "The Future of Czech in Texas: How Can You Learn Something if it's not Offered to You?," Kosmas, 14, No. 2 (Spring 2001), pp. 80-104.

Cope, Lída, "Authentically Texas Czech: Preserving the Ethnocultural Community," in: Moravians from World Perspective. Selected Papers from the 22nd World Congress of Czechoslovak Society of Arts and Sciences, Palacký University, Olomouc, June 26 to July 4, 2004. Edited by Miloslav, Rechcigl, Jr. Ostrava: Repronis, 2006, pp. 330-344.

Eckert, Eva, "Reinventing Standard Czech in Texas," in: Czech and Slovak Culture in International and Global Context. Selected Papers from the 23rd SVU World Congress, University of South

Bohemia, České Budějovice, June 24-July 2, 2006. Edited by Miloslav Rechcigl, Jr. České Budějovice, 2008, pp. 289-297.

D. Folklore

1. General

McCabe, Lida Rose, "Peasant Art in New York's Bohemia," Art Work, 3 (1918), pp. 356-358.

Jakobson, Svatava Pírková. "The Study of Czechoslovak Folksong in the United States," American Folklife Center. Library of Congress, 1942.

Pazdral, Olga Julia, Czech Folklore in Texas, M.A. Thesis, University of Texas, 1943. 180p.

Babcock, C. Morton, "Czech Songs in Nebraska," Western Folklore, 8, No. 4 (October 1949), pp. 320-327.

Ryan, Lawrence, "Customs of the Czechs and in America," Catholic World, 174 (1951), pp. 188-193.

Ryan, Lawrence V., "Christmas Customs of the Czechs and in America," Catholic World, 174 (1951), pp. 188-193.

Pírková-Jakobson, Svatava, "Harvest Festivals among Czechs and Slovaks in America," J. American Folklore, 69 (July-September 1956), pp. 266-282.

Ryan, Lawrence, "Some Czech American Forms of Divination and Supplication," J. American Folklore, 69 (July-September 1956), pp. 281-285.

Reynish, Timothy, "Festivals of Czechs and Slovaks," Music and Musicians, 19 March, 1971, p. 18.

Machann, Clinton, "Czech Folk Music, Orchestras and Assimilation in Texas," Kosmas, 7 (1988), pp. 107-112.

Leary, James P., "Czech—and German-American 'Polka' Music," Journal of American Folklore, 101, No. 401 (July-Sept. 1988), pp. 339-348,

Greene, Victor, A Passion for Polka: Old Time Ethnic Music in America. Berkeley, CA: University of California Press, 1992. 355p.

Leary, James P., "Czech Polka Music in Wisconsin," in: Musics of Multicultural America. Edited by Kip Lornell and Anne Rasmussen. New York: Schirmer Books, 1997, pp. 25-47.

Gallup, Sean N., Journeys into Czech-Moravian Texas. College Station: Texas A&M University, 1998. 140p.

Rostinský, Joseph N., "The Moravian Folk Song: The Best Means of Preserving Czech Culture in Texas," in: Czech-Americans in Transition. Edited by Clinton Machann. Austin, TX: Eakin Press, 1999, pp. 44-49.

Dutková-Cope, Lida, "The Texas Czech Folk Music and Ethnic Identity," Pragmatics, 10, No. 1 (2000), pp 7-37.

Novak, John A., "The Czech Song in Texas: Style and Text," Kosmas, 17, No. 2 (Spring 2004), pp. 43-57.

Johnston, Jesse, "Performing 'Českost' (Czechness): Polka Music & Musical Ethnicity at Wisconsin Czech-American Festivals," in: Selected Papers from the 22nd World Congress of the Czechoslovak Society of Arts and Sciences, Palacký University, Olomouc, June 26th to July 4, 2004. Olomouc: Repronis, pp. 132-138.

Greene, Victor, A Singing Ambivalence: American Immigrants Between Old and New. Kent: Kent State University Press, 2004.

Greene, Victor, "Dealing with Diversity: Milwaukee's Multi-Ethnic Festivals and Urban Identity, 1840-1940," Journal of Urban History, September 2005.

Folkins, Gail and Andy Wilkinson, Texas Dance Halls: A Two-Step Circuit (Voice in the American West). Texas Tech University Press; 2007, 208p.

Vránová, Martina, "Texas-Czech Polka Dances: Through Negotiation in Autonomous Culture," in: Czech and Slovak Culture in International and Global Context. Selected Papers from the 23rd SVU World Congress, University of South Bohemia, České Budějovice, June 24-July 2, 2006. Edited by Miloslav Rechcigl, Jr. České Budějovice, 2008, pp. 616-618.

2. Food & Cuisine

a. General

Babcock, C. Merton, "Czech Soup in Nebraska," Western Folklore 8 (October 1949), pp. 320-327.

Dybala, Barbara and Helen Marik, Generation to Generation. Czech Foods, Customs and Traditions., Texas Style. Dallas, TX: Historical Society of the Czech Club, 1980.

Kittler, Pamela Goyan and Kathryn P. Sucher, "Central Europeans, People of the Former Soviet Union and Scandinavians," in: Food and Culture. 5th ed. Belmont, CA: Thompson Wadsworth, 2008.

Martin, Pat, The Czech Book Recipes and Traditions. Iowa City: Penifield Press, 1981. 60p.

Vintrová, Magdalena, "Devouring Ethnicity: Food as a Means of Ethnicity Initiation," in: Moravians from World Perspective. Selected Papers from the 22nd World Congress of Czechoslovak Society of Arts and Sciences, Palacký University, Olomouc, June 26 to July 4, 2004. Edited by Miloslav, Rechcigl, Jr. Ostrava: Repronis, 2006, pp. 361-372.

Wiggs, Augusta Chalabal, Recipes and Memoirs from a Czech-American Kitchen. Bloomington, IN: AuthorHause, 2009. 148p.

b. **Cookbooks**

Českoamerická kuchařka, aneb snadno pochopitelné a prozkoumané navedení ku připravování všelikých pokrmů, hodících se pro každou domácnost česko-americkou (Czech-American cookbook, or easily understood and tried directions for preparation of various foods, suitable for every Czech-American household). Milwaukee, WI: A. Novak, 1882. 120p.

Vzorná hospodyně. Zkušený rádce pro zavařovaní a nakládání ovoce a zelenin (Reliable manual for preserving and pickling fruits and vegetables). Milwaukee, WI: A. Novak, 1883. 65p.

Domácí štěstí. Spolehlivý rádce a průvodčí v domácnosti a kuchyni. Pro americké poměry upravil Starý Hospodář (Domestic happiness. A reliable manual and guide for housekeeping and the kitchen. Prepared for American conditions by Starý Hospodář). Milwaukee, WI: A. Novak, 1889. 300p.; ed. 1899. 540p.

Rosicky, Marie, Bohemian-American Cookbook. Omaha, NE: National Printing Co., 1915. 306p., 14p.

Rosická, Marie, Národní domácí kuchařka českoamerická (National Czech-American home cookbook). 3rd ed. Omaha: Národní tiskárna, 1909. 320p.

Rosická, Růžena, Domácí příprava ovocných nápojů, limonád, sladu, syrobu, octu a zmrzlin (Recipes for beverages, syrups, vinegars and ice cream). Omaha: Národní tiskárna, 1916. 46p.; 4th ed., 1920; ed., 1920. 75p.

Rosická, Růžena, Sbírka předpisů a rad pro domácnost (A collection of recipes and tips for the household). Omaha: Národní tiskárna, 1918.

Rosická, Růžena, Úsporná kuchařka (Economical cookbook). Omaha: Národní tiskárna, 1918.

Rosická, Růžena, Cukrář a perníkář (Cake, cookie and confectionery cookbook). Omaha: Národní tiskárna, 1918; 2nd ed., 1924; English edition, 1928.

Rosická, Růžena, Cake and confectionery book. Recipes for cakes, cookies, candies, Bohemian gingerbread, marchpane and honey cookery. Omaha: National Printing Co., 1926. 75p.

Jandáčková, Marie L., Česká národní kuchařka (Czech national cookbook). Chicago: A. Geringer, 1954. 448p.; English ed, 1956. 390p.; 2nd English ed., 1961. 416p.

Czechoslovak Day Prize Pastry Recipes. Chicago: Czechoslovak National Council of America, 1962. 67p.

The Czechoslovak Cookbook: Czechoslovakia's best-selling cookbook adapted for American kitchens. Includes recipes for authentic dishes like Goulash,... Pischinger Torte. Revised edition. Clarkson Potter, 1965. 288p.

Apfelback, Alma et al., Favorite Recipes of the Nebraska Czechs. Wilber, NE: Nebraska Czechs of Wilber, 1968. 223p.

Martin, Pat, Cherished Czech Recipes. Iowa City: Penfield Press, 1988. 160p.

Czech and Slovak Kolache Recipes and Sweet Treats. Iowa City: Penfield Press, 2001. 160p.

Louis, Carol, Czech Recipes (Cookbook—Czech This Out, Vol. 1)—State Fair Winning Yeast Bread Recipes. Morris Publishing, 2006. 108p.

Vanorny-Barcus, LaVina, My Czech Heritage Cookbook. CreateSpace, 2009. 160p.

E. Ethnography

Albieri, P., "Čechové američtí" (American Czechs), in: Národnostní výstava československá v Praze 1895 (Czech-Slavonic Ethnographic Exhibit in Prague 1895). Praha, 1897, pp. 289-304.

Heroldová, Iva, "Etnografická problematika českých národnostních menšin" (Ethographic problems of Czech national minorities), Český lid, 51: 366-378 (1964).

Heroldová, Iva, "České národnostní menšiny a národopis" (Czech national minorities and ethnography), Národopisné aktuality (Stážnice), 3, No. 3-4 (1966), pp. 12-20.

Robek, Antonín, "Ethnographic Questions of Czech Emigration to America," in: The Czechs in Texas. A Symposium. Ed. by Clinton Machann. Austin: Texas A&M University, 1979, pp. 32-42.

Kašpar, Oldřich and František Vrhel, Etnografie mimoevropských oblastí. Amerika. III. Severní Amerika (Etnography of Regions outside Europe. America. III. North America). Praha, SPN 1989. 173p.

Dluhošová, H., "Etnografie Čechů v Americe (Ethnography of Czechs in America). Diplomová práce, Univerzita Karlova, Filozofická fakulta—Katedra etnografie a folkloristiky, Praha, 1981.

Šatava, L., "K problematice formování a stabilizace českého etnika v USA: 1848-1914" (Concerning the formation and stabilization of the Czech ethnic group in the US: 1814-1914), in: Češi v cizině, 1 (1986), pp. 29-42.

Mohelská, Jana, Etnografické aspekty českého sociálního vystěhovalectví do Ameriky (Ethnographic aspects of Czech social emigration to America). Praha: FF UK, 1986, 101p., 17p. Addenda, 9p. pictures.

IV. Religion

A. General

1. Surveys

Miller, Kenneth D., "Religious Conditions," in: The Czecho-Slovaks in America. New York: George H. Doran Co., 1922, pp. 119-168.

Klíma, Stanislav, "Náboženský život Čechů v Americe" (Religious Life of Czechs in America), in: Čechové a Slováci za hranicemi. Praha: J. Otto, 1925, pp. 203-208.

Catlos, Edward, "The Religious Situation among the Czechoslovaks in America," in: New Americans Today. New York: Home Missions Council, 1935, pp. 19-21.

Barton, Josef J., "Religion and Cultural Change in Czech Immigrant Communities, 1850-1920," in Immigrants and Religion in Urban America. Eds. Randall M. Miller and Thomas D. Marzik. Philadelphia: Temple University Press, 1977, pp. 3-24.

Johnson, Christopher Jay, An Oral History Study of the Religiosity of Fifty Czech American Elderly. Ph.D. Dissertation, Iowa State University, 1981.

Perkins, Sharon, "Religious Pluralism among Czech Immigrants in Texas: Critiquing the Narrative of American Catholic History," Kosmas, 10, No. 2 (Spring 2006), pp.67-82.

2. Churches

Čapek, Thomas, "Churches," in: The Čechs (Bohemians) in America. Boston & New York: Houghton Mifflin, 1920, pp. 241—246-253.

Čapek, Tomáš, "Kostely," in: Naše Amerika. Praha: Národní rada československá, 1926, 441-445.

Kučera, Vladimír, Ed., Czech Churches in Nebraska. NE: Nebraska Czechs, Inc., 1976. 176p.

B. Roman Catholics

1. General

Houšť, Antonín, Krátké dějiny a seznam česko-katolických osad ve Spojených Státech amerických (Brief history and list of Czech Catholic communities in the U.S.A.). St. Louis, 1890. 551p.

Kohlbeck, Valentine, "The Bohemian Element. Short History of the Bohemian Catholic Congregations in Chicago," The New World, April 1900, pp. 136-140.

Kissner, J. G., "The Catholic Church and the Bohemian Immigrants," Charities, New York, 1904.

Kohlbeck, Valentine, "The Catholic Bohemians of the United States," Champlain Educator, 25 (January-March 1906), 35-54.

The First Czech Catholic Convention. Held in the St. John Nepomuk Church, St. Louis, September 24-26, 1907. 54p.

Liga českých kněží v arcidiecesi St. Paulské. Průvodce po českých katolických osadách v arcidiecesi St. Paulské (A Guide through the Czech Catholic communities in the Archdiocese of St. Paul, MN). Chicago: Tiskem Tiskárny Českých Benediktinů, 1910. 233p.

Rosicky, Rose, "Catholics," in: History of Czechs in Nebraska, Omaha: Czech Historical Society of Nebraska, 1929, pp. 291-337.

Národní Svaz Českých Katolíků v Texas. Naše Dějiny (Our History). Granger, TX: Našinec, 1939. 718p.

Centennial of St. John Nepomuk Church, St. Louis, Missouri: History of First Czech Catholic Church in the United States and the priests who served this Congregation. St. Louis: St. John Nepomuk Church, 1954.

Čada, Joseph, Czech-American Catholics 1850-1920. Lisle, IL: Benedictine Abbey Press, 1964. 124p.

Čada, Joseph, Czech Church Pioneers in America. Chicago: Czech Benedictine Abbey Press, 1964. 124p.

Mizera, Peter F., Czech Benedictines in America, 1877-1901. Lisle, IL: Benedictine Abbey Press, 1969. 124p.

A History of the Czech-Moravian Catholic Communities of Texas. Translated and edited by Rev. V. A. Svrcek. Waco, TX: Texian Press, 1974. 220 p.; 2nd printing 1983.

Švejda, George, "Czech Catholic Immigration to the United States of America," in: Czech Catholics in the 41st International Eucharistic Congress. Ed. Ludvík Němec. Philadelphia, 1977, pp. 88-93.

125th Jubliee of St. John Nepomuk Parish, St. Louis, Missouri. St. Louis: n. p., 1979.

Chada, Joseph, "Czech American Subculture: Catholicism," in: The Czechs in the United States. SVU Press, 1981, pp. 97-110.

Anderson, Timothy G., "Czech-Catholic Cemeteries in East-Central Texas: Material Culture and Ethnicity in Seven Rural Communities," Material Culture, 25, No. 3 (Fall 1993), pp. 1-18.

Harris, Eileen Nini, Bohemian Hill: An American Story. St. Louis: St. John Nepomuk Parish, 2004.

Klimesh, Steven A., "A History of the Oldest Standing Czech Catholic Church in the United States," in: Moravians from World Perspective. Selected Papers from the 22nd World Congress of Czechoslovak Society of Arts and Sciences, Palacký University,

Olomouc, June 26 to July 4, 2004. Edited by Miloslav, Rechcigl, Jr. Ostrava: Repronis, 2006, pp. 248-256.

2. Individuals

Joseph Hessoun (1830-1906)

V. T., "Hessoun, Joseph," in: Dictionary of American Biography 8, pp. 599-600.

Alois J. Klein (b. 1866)

Pastorek, John B., Brainard's Monsignor Klein, A Biography. Chicago: Bohemian Benedictine Press, 1932. 128 p.

Josef Maria Koudelka (1852-1921)

První biskup amerického Slovanstva" (First Bishop of American Slavs), in: Postavy naší Ameriky Praha: Pražská edice, 2000, pp. 68-70.

John Nepomucene Neumann (1811-1860)

Berger, John N., Life of Right Reverend John Neumann, D. D., Translated from German original by Rev. Eugene Grimm. New York: Benzinger Brothers, 1884

Curley, Michael Joseph, Venerable John Neumann, C.Ss.R., Fourth Bishop of Philadelphia. Washington, DC: Catholic University of America, 1952. 547p.

Neumann, J. N., The Autobiography of St. John Neumann, C.Ss.R. Fourth Bishop of Philadelphia. Boston: Daughters of St. Paul, 1977. 118p.

Starý, Václav, Prachatice a Jan Neumann (Prachatice and John Neumann). Prachatice, 1997. 232p.

Chotrpenning, Joseph F., He Spared Himself in Nothing: Essays on the Life and Thought of St. John Nepomucene Neumann, C.Ss.R. Philadelphia: St. Joseph University Press, 2008. 220p.

C. Protestants

1. General

Památník českých evangelických církví ve Spojených státech (Souvenir of Czech Protestant Churches in the U.S.). Eds. Vilém Šiller,

Václav Průcha and R. M. de Costello. Chicago: Křesťanský Posel, 1900. 290p.

Rosicky, Rose, "Protestants," in: History of Czechs in Nebraska, Omaha: Czech Historical Society of Nebraska, 1929, pp. 337-348.

Chada, Joseph, "Czech-American Subculture: Protestantism," in: The Czechs in the United States. SVU Press, 1981, pp. 111-127.

Kejř, Václav, České evangelické sbory v Americe (Czech Evangelic communities in America). Praha: Synodní rada československých církve evangelické, 1983. 81p.

Garver, Bruce M., "Czech-American Protestants: A Minority within a Minority," Nebraska History 74, No. 3&4 (Fall/Winter 1993), pp.150-67.

2. Bohemian Brethren

a. General

Chlumský, Adolf, History of the Evangelic Union of Bohemian-Moravian Brethren in Texas. Brenham, TX, 1907. 44p.

Christian Sisters Union, Unity of the Brethren in Texas 1855-1966. Taylor, TX: Unity of the Brethren, 1970. 178p.

Janak, Robert, "The Czech Heritage Society of Texas and Publications of Czech-Moravian Brethren Ministerial Records," in: Contributions of the Moravian Brethren to America. Selected Papers from the Conference of the Czechoslovak Society of Arts and Sciences at the Moravian College, Bethlehem, PA, June 8-10, 2007, pp. 21-32.

West, Theresie, "The Kingdom of God is in Texas," in: Selected Papers from the Conference of the Czechoslovak Society of Arts and Sciences, Moravian College, Bethlehem, PA, June 8-10, 2007. New York, NY: Publishing House of the Czechoslovak Society of Arts and Sciences, 2008, pp. 165-193.

b. Individuals

Josef Ernst Bergmann (1797-1877)

Klumpp, Dorothy and Albert J. Bláha, Sr., The Saga of Ernst Bergmann. Houston, 1981

Chroust, David, "Josef Ernst Bergmann: 'Father' of the Czech-Speaking Immigration in Texas," Kosmas, 20 (2006), pp. 48-64.

Adolf Chlumský (1842-1919)

Marek, Daniel J., "Adolf Chlumský—Father of the Unity of Brethren in Texas," The Brethren Journal, Brenham, TX (March 2000), pp. 13-16.

Henry Juren (1850-1921)

Marek, Daniel J., "The Rev. Henry Juren, Pastor and Educator: The Brethren Journal, March 1999, pp. 21-23.

Jan Zvolánek (1815-1890)

Sarris, K. E. Zwolanek and Elizabeth M. Zvolanek Semrad, The Zvolánek Clan of the Yesteryear and Today, 1610-1975. Privately printed, 1985.

3. Moravian Brethren

a. General

Čapek, Tomáš, "Moravané" (Moravians), in: Památky českých emigrantů v Americe. Omaha, NE: Nákladem Pokroku západu, 1889, pp. 65-79.

Hamilton, John Taylor, A History of the Church Known as the Moravian Church or Unitas Fratrum or the Unity of the Brethren during the 18th and the 19th Centuries. Bethlehem, PA: Times Publ. Co., 1900. 632p.

Rechcigl, Miloslav Jr., "The Renewal and the Formation of the Moravian Church in America," Czechoslovak and Central European Journal 9 (1990), pp. 12-26.

Schattschneider, David A., The Unitas Fratrum and the 'Renewed' Moravian Church: Continuity and Change," Czechoslovak and Central European Journal, 9 (1990), pp. 27-34.

Rechcigl, Miloslav Jr., "Moravian Brethren from the Czechlands," Naše rodina (Our Family), 12, No. 4 (December 2000), pp. 154-59.

Rechcigl, Miloslav, Jr. "The Moravian Brethren Heritage of the First Lady Barbara Pierce Bush," in: Contributions of the Moravian Brethren to America. Selected Papers from the Conference of the Czechoslovak Society of Arts and Sciences at the Moravian College, Bethlehem, PA, June 8-10, 2007, pp. 119-130.

West, Theresie M. "The Kingdom of God Is in Texas." Kosmas, 21, No.2 (2008), pp. 80-89.

Křížová, Markéta, Ideální město v divočině (Ideal city in the wilderness). Praha: Nakladatelství Lidové noviny, 2007. 264p.

b. **Individuals**

John Heckewelder (1743-1823)

Rondthaler, Edward, Life of John Heckewelder, Philadelphia: T. Ward, 1847.149 p.

Wallace, Paul A.W. Thirty Thousand Miles with John Heckewelder: The Travels of John Heckewelder in Frontier America. Pittsburgh, PA: University of Pittsburgh Press, 1985.

Rechcigl, Miloslav, Jr., "Misionář—badatel mezi americkými Indiány" (Missionary—Scholar among American Indians), in: Postavy naší Ameriky. Pražská edice, 2000, pp. 83-87.

Anna Nitschmann (1715-1760)

Grethe Goodman, Anna Nitschmann, 1715-1760. Founder of the Women Single Sisters' Choir (Keepers). Oaks Print. Co., 1985.

David Nitschmann (1696-1772)

De Schweinitz, Edmund, "David Nitschmann, First Bishop of the Renewed Brethren's Church," Transaction of the Moravian Historical Society, 2 (1986), pp. 149-167.

Rechcigl, Miloslav, Jr., "První biskup obnovené Jednoty" (The first Bishop of the renewed Unity of Brethren), in: Postavy naší Ameriky. Pražská edice, 2000, pp. 77-79.

David Zeisberger (1723-1808) de Schweinitz, Edmund. Life and Times of David Zeisberger. The Western Pioneer and Apostle of the Indians. Philadelphia: J. B. Lippincott & Co., 1870. 747p.

Rice, William H. David Zeisberger and his Brown Brethren. Bethlehem, PA: Moravian Publication Concern, 1908.

Zeisberger, David. Schoenbrunn Story: Excerpts from the Diary of the Reverend David Zeisberger, 1772-1777, at Schoenbrunn in the Ohio Country. Columbus: Ohio Historical Society, 1972.

4. Baptists

Vojta, Václav, Czechoslovak Baptists. Minneapolis: Czechoslovak Baptist Convention in America and Canada, 1941. 276p.

5. Presbyterians

a. General

Stalmach, Hilda Schiller, History of the Ministers and Churches of the Southwest Czech Presbytery. Smithville, TX: Synod of Texas United Presbyterian Church, 1962.

b. **Individuals**

Francis Kún (1825-1894)

Spinka, Matthew, "Francis Kún, a Czechoslovak Pioneer," Journal of the Presbyterian Historical Society, 12 (1924), pp. 115-121.

Rechcigl, Miloslav, Jr., "Prvni český evangelický kazatel: (First Czech Protestant preacher), in: Postavy naší Ameriky. Praha: Pražská edice, 2000, pp. 80-82.

D. Jews

1. General

Kisch, Guido, In Search of Freedom: A History of American Jews from Czechoslovakia 1740-1948. London: E. Goldstone, 1949. 373p.

Rechcigl, Miloslav Jr., "Early Jewish Immigrants in America from the Czech Historic Lands and Slovakia," Rev. Soc. Hist. Czechoslovak Jews 3 (1990-91), pp. 157-79.

Hahn, Fred, "Jews from the Bohemian Lands in the United States, 1848-1938" in: Great Britain, the United States, and the Bohemian Lands. Ed. by Eva Schmidt-Hartman and Stanley B. Winters. Munich: Collegium Carolinum, 1991, pp.31-45.

Wingfield, Nancy M., "Czechoslovak Jewish Immigration to the United States, 1938-1945," Czechoslovak and Central European Journal, 11, No. 2 (Winter 1993), pp.38-49.

Rosenbaum, S. E., Guido Kisch and Nathan Kravitz, A Voyage to America Ninety Years Ago. The Diary of a Bohemian Jew on his Historic Voyage from Hamburg to New York in 1847. San Bernardino, CA: Borgo Press, 1995. 120p.

Czech-American Jews: Madelaine Albright, Gerty Cori, Louis Brandeis, Alex Birns, Erich Wolfgang Korngold, Jaromir Weinberger, Freddy Perlmam. Books LLC. 180p.

Mokotoff, Gary and Miloslav Rechcigl,Jr., "Who Were the First Jews in America?," Avotaynu, 27, No. 2 (Summer 2011), pp. 53-54.

Rechcigl, Miloslav, Jr. Czech and Bohemian Jews in American History (in preparation).

2. Individuals

Max Heller (1860-1929)

Barbara S. Malone, Rabbi Max Heller: Reformer, Zionist, Southerner, 1860-1929.Tuscaloosa, AL: University of Alabama Press, 1997. 240p.

Dinnerstein, Leonard, "Rabbi Max Heller: Reformer, Zionist, Southerner, 1860-1929," The Mississippi Quarterly, Vol. 51, 1998.

Bernard Illowy (1812-1871)

Rabbi Bernard Illowy, Sefer Milchomot Elokim. PublishYourSefer.com, 2007. 244p.

Ellenson, David, A Jewish Legal Decision by Rabbi Bernard Illowy of New Orleans and its Discussion in Nineteenth Century Europe. American Jewish Historical Society, 1979.

Leo Jung (1892-1987)

Bader, Gershom, Moses Jung. "Meir Tsevi Jung." Jewish Leaders 1750-1940 Ed. Leo Jung. Jerusalem: Boys Town Jerusalem Publishers, 1964, pp. 295-316.

Jung, Leo, The Path of a Pioneer. Autobiography of Leo Jung. The Jewish Library, vol. 8. London, New York: Soncino Press, 1980.

Schacter, Jacob J., ed. Reverence Righteousness and Rachmanut: Essays in Memory of Rabbi Dr. Leo Jung. Northdale, New Jersey and London: Jason Aronson Inc., 1992.

Schacter, Jacob J., "Rabbi Dr. Leo Jung: Reflections on the Centennial of his Birth," Jewish Action, 53, No. 2 (Winter, 1992-1993): pp. 20-24.

Konvitz, Milton R., "Leo Jung-Rabbi for All Jews." Midstream 39.6 (Aug/Sept 1993).

Isaac Mayer Wise (1819-1900)

Wise, Isaac Maye, Reminiscences. Cincinnati: Leo Wise & Co., 1901. 361p.

May, Max B., Isaac Mayer Wise, The Founder of American Judaism: A Biography. New York: G. P. Putnam's Sons, 1916.

Heller, James G., M. Wise, His Life, Work and Thought. The Union of American Hebrew Congregations, 1965.

Stephen S. Wise (1874-1949)

Voss, Carl H., Rabbi and Minister: The Friendship of Stephen S. Wise and John Haynes Holmes New York: Prometheus, 1980.

Wise, Stephen S., The Challenging Years (New York: Putnam, 1949).

E. Freethinkers

1. General

Zdrůbek, František, B., Disputace, čili náboženské veřejné hádání mezi Fr. B. Zdrůbkem a V. Čokou o thési: Svatá víra hubí mravnost a blahobyt lidstva (Dispuation, or religious public polemics between Fr. B. Zdrůbek and V. Čoka). Chicago: Chicágský věstník, 1877. 31p.

Zdrůbek, František, B., Dvě veřejná náboženská hádání mezi . . . redaktorem 'Svornosti' a 'Amerikána' a . . . farářem u sv. Prokopa v Chicagu dne 17. a 19. dubna 1877 (Two public religious disputations between editor of 'Spravedlnost' and 'Amerikán' and . . . priest at St. Prokop's in Chicago on April 17th and 19th of April, 1877). 3rd ed. Chicago: A. Geringer, 1877. 63p.

Bittner, Bartoš, "Katechismus svobodomyslné mládeže" (Catechism of Freethinking youth). Chicago, 1898.

Palda, L. J., "O vývoji svobodomyslnosti Čechů amerických (On the evolution of Czech-American Freethinkers," Svojan, 12 (1905).

Palda, Lev, "Myšlenky o novém náboženství" (Thoughts about the new religion). Omaha, 1902.

Rudiš-Jičinský, Jan, Historical Sketch of Bohemian Free Thought in the United States. Cedar Rapids, IA: Free Thought Society, 1908. 20p.

Masaryk, T. G, "Svobodomyslní Čechové v Americe" (Czech Freethinkers in America), Naše doba (Prague), October 20, 1902, pp. 1-7.

Czech American Liberalism, 1907-11, or, Discussions, Deliberations and Resolutions passed at the Convention of Liberals. New York, 1911. 88p.

Vojan, J. E. Salaba, "Why Should We American Čechs Be Liberal-Minded?" in: Czech Reader. Ed. by Vojta Beneš. Prague, 1912, pp. 425-428.

Dočekalová, Kárník and Vašků, eds., Volná myšlenka česko-americká 1907-1911: čili jednání, usnesení a resoluce přijaté na druhém sjezdu svobodomyslných v Americe v zasedání, dne 3. a 4. září, roku 1911 v místnostech Národní budovy v New Yorku, N.Y. (Bohemian-American Freethought 1907-1911: or proceedings, decisions and resolutions adopted at the second Freethinkers' convention America in session on 3-4 September 1911). New York, 1913.

Čapek, Thomas, "Rationalism: A Transition from the Old to the New," in: The Čechs (Bohemians) in America. Boston & Houghton Mifflin Co., 1920, pp. 119-137.

Prantner, E. F., "Free Thinkers-American Czechoslovaks," in: The Czechoslovak Review, 6, No. 7 (1922), pp. 174-177.

Rosicky, Rose, "Liberals or Freethinkers," in: History of Czechs in Nebraska, Omaha: Czech Historical Society of Nebraska, 1929, pp. 287-291.

Vojan, J. E. S., "Racionalismus a jeho budoucnost" (Rationalism and its future), Svojan, 43, No. 12 (December 1937), pp. 177-180.

Čapek, Tomáš, "Čechoamerican reformátor: Racionalismus" (Czech-American Reformator: Rationalism), in: Naše Amerika. Praha: Národní rada československá, 1926, pp. 362-371.

"One Hundred Years of the Bohemian Freethinkers in Chicago," in: Panorama: A Historical Review of Czechs and Slovaks in the United States of America, 1970, pp. 82-84.

Bicha, Karel D., "Settling Accounts with an Old Adversary: The Decatholization of Czech Immigrants in America," Social History, 4 (November 1972), pp. 45-60.

Garver, Bruce M., "Czech-American Free Thinkers on the Great Plains, 1871-1914," in: Ethnicity on the Great Plains. Ed. Frederick Luebke. Lincoln: University of Nebraska Press, 1980, pp. 147-59.

Chada, Joseph, "Czech-American Subculture: Its Secularistic Phase," in: The Czechs in the United States. SVU Press, 1981, pp. 81-96.

Schneirov, Richard Samuel, Free Thought and Socialism in the Czech Community in Chicago, 1875-1887," in: Struggle a Hard Battle. Essay on Working Class Immigrants. Edited by Dirk Hoerder, DeKalb, IL: Northern Illinois University Press, 1986, pp.121-142.

2. Individuals

Ladimír Klácel (1826-1894)

Čapek, Tomáš, "Svobodomyslnost a Ladimír Klácel" (Free thought and Ladimír Klácel), in: Padesát let českého tisku v Americe. New York: Bank of Europe, 1911, pp. 33-42.

Dvořáková, Zora, František Matouš Klácel. Praha: Melantrich, 1976. 287p.

Peaslee, Margaret Heřmánek and Vítězslav Orel, "F. M. (Ladimír) Klácel: Teacher of Gregor Mendel," Kosmas: Czechoslovak and Central European Journal, 15, No. 1 (2001), pp. 31-54.

Peaslee. Margaret H. and Vítězslav Orel, "The Revolutionary Ideas of F. M. (Ladimír) Klácel. Teacher of Grergor Mendel," Biomed Pap Med Fac. Univ. Palacký Olomouc Czech Repub., 151, No. 1 (2007), pp. 151-156.

František Matouš Klácel—filosof, spisovatel a novinář. Sborník ze symposia konaného ve dnech 24.-26. září 2008 v České Třebové (František Matouš Klácel—philosopher, writer and journalist. Česká Třebová: Městské museum, 2008. 131p.

Frank B. Zdrůbek (1842-1911)

Habenicht, Jan, "Zdrůbek, František J," in: History of Czechs in America. Translated from Czech original by Miroslav Koudelka. (Dějiny Čechův Amerických, 1910). Minneapolis, 1996, p. 534.

V. The Society

A. Ethnic Identity

Čapek, Thomas, "New Bohemia in America," in The Čechs (Bohemians) in America. Boston & New York: Houghton Mifflin Co., 1920, pp. 105-113.

Pecival, Josef P. "K záchraně čs. větve ve Spojených Státech (Preserving Czechoslovak branch in the US), Naše zahraničí, 6 (1925), pp. 65-71.

"Jsou naši američtí krajané národnostní menšinou?" (Are our American cuntrymen a minority?), Naše zahraničí, 1931), pp. 150-151.

Kutak, Robert I., The Story of a Bohemian-American Village. Louisville, KY: Standard Printing Co., 1933. Reprinted New York: Arno Press, 1970. 156p.

Corzine, Jay and Irene Dabrowski, "The Ethnic Factor and the Neighborhood Stability: The Czechs in Soulard and South St. Louis." Bulletin Missouri Historical Society, 33 (January 1977), 87-93.

Roucek, Joseph S., "The American Czechs, Slovaks and Slavs in the Development of America's Climate of Opinion," in Czechoslovakia Past and Present. Vol. 1. Ed. by Miloslav Rechcigl Jr. The Hague: Mouton, 1968, pp. 815-43.

Bicha, Karel D., "The Survival of the Village in Urban America: A Note on Czech Immigrants in Chicago to 1914," International Migration Review, 8 (Spring 1971), pp. 72-74.

Naramore, Ronald, "Ethnicity on the American Frontier: A Study of Czechs in Oklahoma," Papers in Anthropology, 14 (Spring 1973), pp. 104-114.

Corzine, Jay, and Irene Dabrowski, "The Ethnic Factor and Neighborhood Stability: the Czechs in Soulard and South St. Louis," *Bulletin Missouri Historical Society,* 33 (January 1977), pp. 87-93.

Hewitt, William P., The Czechs in Texas: A Study of the Immigration and the Development of Czech Ethnicity, 1850-1920. Ph.D Dissertation, University of Texas, 1978.

Machalek, Richard," The Ambivalence of Ethnoreligion," in: The Czechs in Texas. Temple, TX, October 27-29, 1978. Ed. Clinton

Machann. College Station, TX: Texas A&M University, 1979, pp. 95-114.

Skrabanek, Robert L., We're Czechs. College Station: Texas A&M University Press, 1988. 240p.

Hannan, Kevin, "Ethnic Identity among the Czechs and Moravians of Texas," Journal of American Ethnic History, 15 (Summer 1996), pp. 3-31.

Screws, Raymond D., Retaining their Culture and Ethnic Identity: Assimilation among Czechs and Swedes in Saunders County, Nebraska, 1810-1910. Ph.D. Dissertation, University of Nebraska, Lincoln, 2003.

Hannan, Kevin, "Ethnic Identity among the Czechs and Moravians of Texas," American Ethnic History, 15, No. 4 (1996), pp. 3-31.

Dubovický, Ivan, "Češi v USA a otázka identity 1848-1938" (Czechs in the US and the question of their identity 1848-1938), Český lid, 83, No. 3 (1996), pp. 229-247.

Harris, Eileen Nini. Bohemian Hill: An American Story. St. Louis, Missouri: St. John Nepomuk Parish, 2004.

Korytová-Magstadt, Štěpánka, "From Immigrants to Ethnic Americans," in: Selected Papers from the 21st World Congress of the Czechoslovak Society of Arts and Sciences, University of West Bohemia, Plzeň, June 23-30, 2002. Edited by Jan P. Skalny and Milosav Rechcigl, Jr. Plzeň: Aleš Čeněk, 2004, pp. 597-604.

Biroczi, David, Czechs in America: The Maintenance of Czech Identity in Contemporary America. LAP Lambert Academic Publishing, 2010. 96p.

B. Assimilation & Acculturation

Balch, Emily Greene, "The Question of Assimilation," in: Our Slavic Fellow Citizens. New York: Charities Publication Committee, 1910, pp. 396-428.

Čapek, Thomas, "Through Intermarriages into the Melting Pot," in: The Čechs (Bohemians) in America. Boston & New York: Houghton Mifflin Co., 1920, pp. 96-99; "All Born in America belong to America," Ibid., pp. 100-104.

Horak, Joseph, The Assimilation of Czechs in Chicago. Ph.D. Dissertation, University of Chicago, 1920.

Hrbková, Šárka B., "O amerikanizaci" (About Americanization), Naše zahraničí, 2, No. 1 (1921), pp. 2-5.

Miller, Kenneth D., "Assimilation," in: The Czecho-Slovaks in America. New York: George H. Doran, 1922, pp. 104-118.

Bogardus, Emory Stephen, "The Slavic Immigrant," in Essentials of Americanization. Los Angeles: University of Southern California Press, 1920, pp. 175-190.

Dostál, Hynek, "Proč v Americe národnostně hyneme" (Why do we nationally perish in America), Naše zahraničí, 6 (1925) pp. 113-116.

Čapek, Tomáš, "Amerikanisace a děti" (Americanization and the children), in: Naše Amerika. Praha: Národní rada československá, 1926, pp. 406-439,

Roucek, Joseph S., "Problems of Assimilation: A Study of Czechoslovaks in the United States," Sociology and Social Research 17 (September/October 1931), pp. 62-71.

Kohnová, Marie J., "The Moravians and their Missionaries. A Problem in Americanization," The Mississippi Valley Historical Review 19, No. 3 (December 1932), pp. 348-361.

Kutak, Robert J., The Story of a Bohemian-American Village. Ph.D. Dissertation, Columbia University, 1933.

Roucek, Joseph S., "Problems of Becoming Americanized," in: Sociology and Social Research 17 (1933), pp. 243-250.

Duncan, H. G., "Czechoslovaks," in: Immigration and Assimilation. Boston: Heath, 1933, pp. 292-301.

Roucek, Joseph S., "Passing of American Czechoslovaks," American Journal of Sociology 39 (March 1934), pp. 611-625.

Jerabek, Esther, "Transition of a New World Bohemia," in: Minnesota History 15 (March 1934), 26-42.

Martin, William Earl, The Cultural Assimilation of the Czechoslovaks in Oklahoma City: A Study of Culture Contrasts. Thesis, Oklahoma University, 1935.

Šatava, Leoš, "Formování a stabilizace českého etnika v USA: 1848-1914," Český lid, 73, No.3. (1986), pp. 176-181.

Šatava, Leoš, K problematice formování a stabilizace českého etnika v USA (1848-1914)" (Problems of forming and stabilizing Czech ethnic group in the US).Češi v cizině. Praha: ÚEF ČSAV, 1986, No. 1, pp. 29-42.

Hejhal, John Stanley, The Czechs in the Melting Pot: Americanization in Colfax County, Nebraska, 1869-1959. Master's Thesis, University of Wyoming, Laramie, 1959.

Dubovický, Ivan, Czech-Americans: An Ethnic Dilemma," Nebraska History, 74, No. 3 & 4 (Fall/ Winter 1993), pp. 195-208.

Freund, J. L.: "Několik poznámek k otázkám a problematice emigrace" (A few comments regarding the emigration problems), Československá psychologie, 37, No. 1 (1993), pp. 68-75.

Diamant, J., Psychologické problémy emigrace (Psychological problems of emigration). Olomouc: Matice cyrilometodějská, 1995.

Kabala, Mirek, "Psychické problémy migrantů (Psychological problems of migrants), in: Češi za hranicemi ma přelomu 20. a 21. století. Symposium o českém vystěhovalectví, exulanství a vztazích zahraničních Čechů k domovu. Praha: Univerzita Karlova, 2000, pp.112-123.

Screws, Raymond D., "Not a Melting Pot: A Comparative Study of Swedes and Czechs in Saunders County, Nebraska, 1880-1910," Heritage of the Great Plains, 35, No. 1 (2002), pp. 4-22.

Eckert, Eva, Stones on the Prarie: Acculturation in America. Bloomington, IN: Slavica Publishers, 2007. 431p.

C. Social Organization

Hunter, Stanley Armstrong, A Sociological Study of Bohemians in New York. Master's Thesis, Columbia University, 1914.

Miller, Kenneth D., "Social Organization and Forces," in: The Czecho-Slovaks in America, New York: George H. Doran, 1922, pp. 82-85.

Johansen, J. O., "Bohemian Settlements and their Social Organization," in Immigrant Settlements and Social Organization in South Dakota. Brooking, SD: University of South Dakota, Department of Rural Sociology, 1937, pp. 23-29.

Žižka, Arnošt. "The Social Groups of Czech Immigrants in America," in: Czech Cultural Contributions. Chicago: Benedictine Abbey Press, 1942, pp. 28-78.

Clifford, Roy A., A Social and Economic Survey of Prague, Oklahoma and Vicinity. University of Oklahoma, 1947.

Tagggart, Glen, Czechs in Wisconsin as a Culture Type. Ph.D. Dissertation, University of Wisconsin, 1948.

Skrabanek, R. L. and V. J. Parenton, "Social Life in a Czech-American Rural Community," Rural Sociology 15, No. 3 (September 1950), pp. 221-231.

Skrabanek, Robert, Social Organization and Change in a Czech-American Rural Community. A Sociological Study of Snook, Texas. Ph.D. Dissertation, Louisiana State University and Agricultural and Mechanical College, 1951.

Kutak, Robert I., The Story of a Bohemian Village. Louisville, KY: Standard Ptg. Co., 1933; Reprinted in New York: Arno, 1970. 156p.

Splawn, Vlasta Margaret, Sociological Study of a Czech Community in Ellis County, Texas. Master's Thesis, Texas Technical University, 1972.

D. Family Organization

Tesař, František, Matka, vychovatelka dítek. Prospěšné rady rodičům (Mother, governess of her children. Useful advice to parents). Omaha: Pokrok západu, n.d. 66p.

Iška, František, Svobodomyslná výchova dítek. Rukověť pro rodiče a přátele mládeže (Free thought education of children. Guide for parents and friends of youth). Chicago: A. Geringer, 1903. 80p.

Miller, Kenneth D., "Moral Standards," in: The Czech-Slovaks in America. New York: George H. Doran, 1922, pp. 70-72; "Family Life," Ibid., pp. 72-73.

Martínek, Josef, Zachovejme si mládež (Preserve our youth). Cleveland: Nákladem 'Amerických dělnických listů', 1923. 23p.

Krestan, Jo-Ann, and Rita Mae Gazarik, "Czech and Slovak Families," in: Ethnicity and Family Therapy. 3rd ed. Ed. by Monica McGoldrick, Joe Giordano and Nydia Garcia-Preto. New York: Guilford Press, 2005, pp. 726-736.

E. Health & Welfare

Soukup, Antonín M., Matka a dítě. Lékařská kniha věnovaná česko-americkým ženám (Mother and child. A medical book addressed to Czech-American women). Chicago: Author, n.d. 234p.

Miller, June Eick, Politics and Care: A Study of Czech Americans within Leininger's Theory in Culture Care Diversity," J. Transcult. Nurs. 9, No. 1 (July 1997), pp. 3-13.

Krestan, Jo-Ann and Rita Mae Gazarik, "Czech and Slovak Families," in: Ethnicity and Family Therapy. Edited by Monica McGoldrick, Joe Giordano and Nydia Garcia-Preto. 3rd ed. New York: The Guilford Press, 2005, pp. 724-740.

F. Women—Feminism

1. General

Jonáš, Karel, Žena ve společnosti lidské, zvláště v Anglii a v Americe (Woman in human society, especially in England and in America). Praha: J. Otto, 1871.

Klácel, Ladislav, Manželka a matka (Wife and mother). Milwaukee: A. Novak, 1876. 44p.

Robbins, J. E., "Bohemian Women in New York," in: Charities and the Commons, 3 (December 1904), pp. 194-196.

Doležal, Karel, Žena ve společnosti lidské (Women in people's society). New York: J. S. Čada, 1888. 40p.

Robbins, Jane E., "The Bohemian Women in New York: Their Work as Cigar Makers. Home Work among Them," Charities (New York), 13, No. 1 (December 1904), pp. 194-196.

Butler, Elizabeth Beardsley, Women and the Trades. New York: Charities Pub. Co., 1909. 440p.

Balch, Emily Green, "Household Life," in: Our Slavic Fellow Citizens. New York: Charities Publication Committee, 1910, pp. 349-377.

Pehotsky, Bessie Olga, The Slavic Immigrant Women. Cincinnati, OH: Powell & White, 1925. 117p.

Abbott, Edith, "Bohemians in the Cigar-Making Industry," in: Women in Industry. A Study in American Economic History. New York: Appleton, 1910, pp. 196-200; reprinted in 1928.

Voska, Emanuel Viktor, Podíl americké ženy československé na revoluci a úkoly žen v nové naši republice (Role of Czechoslovak American women in the revolution and their mission in our new Republic).

Praha: Československé podniky tiskařské a vydavatelské, 1919. 16p.

Burnett, David W., "Ethnic Culture, Religion, and the Mental Health of Slavic-American Women," Journal of Religion and Health, 18, No. 4 (October 1979), pp. 298-307.

Zárasová, Alena, České ženy ve Spojených státech amerických: vliv doby a prostředí na rodinný a společenský život českých žen, žijících v USA v období od 2. poloviny 19. století do 20. let 20. století (Czech women in the US: The influence of the times and the environment on family and social life of Czech women living in the US from the 2nd half of the 19th century to the 20s of the 20th century). Diplomová práce. Praha: FF UK, 1997, 128p., 31 pictures.

Magstadtová, Štěpánka, "They Wished to Combine the Spirit of Bohemia and America: Czech Women's Clubs in Chicago, 1890-1940—the Liberal 'Progressive' Type," Kosmas, 19, No. 2 (Spring 2006), pp. 16-37.

Pelikánová, Jitka, "Women in Exile after 1968 in the USA and Canada," in: Contributions of Czechs and Slovaks to Science and Technology in the 21st Century. Selected Papers from the Twenty-fifth Congress of the Czechoslovak Society of Arts and Sciences, Tabor, Czech Repuiblic, June 27-July 3, 2010. New York: Publishing House of the Czechoslovak Society of Arts and Sciences, 2011, pp. 183-193.

Rechcigl, Miloslav, Jr., Czech (Bohemian) Women in US History (in preparation).

2. Individuals

Josefa Humpal-Zeman (1872-1906)

Schmelzer, Janet L, "Humpal-Zeman, Josefa (Josephine) (1872-1906)," in: European Immigrant Women in the United States: A Biographical Dictionary. Ed. by Judy Barrett Litoff and Judith McDonnell. New York: Routledge, 1994, pp. 146-147.

Noblitt, Julie A. with Alena Zárasová, "Josefa Veronika Humpal-Zeman," in: Women Building Chicago 1790-1990: A Biographical Dictionary, by Rima Lunin Schultz and Adele Hast. Bloomington & Indianapolis: Indiana University Press, 2001.

Anita Pollitzer (1894-1975)

Geboire, Clive, ed. Lovingly, Georgia: The Complete Correspondence of Georgia O'Keeffe and Anita Pollitzer. 1990.

Irwin, Inez Haynes. The Story of the Woman's Party. New York: Harcourt, Brace, and Co., 1921.

G. Labor Movement

1. General

Palda, Lev J., "Vzpomínky na první stávku českého dělnictva v Americe" (Recollections of the first strike of the Czech labor in America), in: Všedělnický kalendář 4 (1913), pp. 155-168.

Palda, Lev J, "Z bojů dělnických"(Labor struggles), Všedělnický kalendář 5 (1914), pp. 33-43.

Čapek, Thomas, "Socialism and Radicalism," in: The Čechs (Bohemians) in America. Boston & New York: Houghton Mifflin Co., 1920, pp.137-154.

Hlaváček, F. J., Zlomky českého počátečního hnutí dělnického v Americe" (Fragments about the Czech early labor movement in America), Ročenka amerických dělnických listů na rok 1924, s. 75.

Čapek, Tomáš, "Čechoameričan reformátor: Socialism a anarchism" (Czech-American reformator: Socialism and anarchism), in: Naše Amerika. Praha: Národní rada československá, 1926, pp. 372-403.

Polišenský, Josef, "Počátky českého a slovenského dělnického hnutí v Americe" (Beginnings of the Czech and Slovak labor movement in America), Slovanský přehled, 1954, pp. 109-111.

Cada, Joseph, A Survey of Radicalism in the Bohemian-American Community. Lisle, IL, 1957. 40p.

Greene, Victor, The Slavic Community on Strike. Notre Dame: Indiana University of Notre Dame Press, 1968.

Cink, Kenneth, Czech-American Radicalism in the United States, 1849-1924. Master's Thesis, University of Chicago, 1969.

Martínek, Josef. "One Hundred Years of the Czech Labor Movement in America, in: Panorama: A Historical Review of Czechs and Slovaks in the United States of America, 1970, pp. 85-89.

Dostálík, M., "České dělnické hnutí ve Spojených státech za hospodářské krize let 1875-1878" (Czech labor movement in the US during the economic crisis in 1875-1878), in: Začiatky českej a slovenskej emigrácie do USA. Bratislava: Slovenská akadémia vied, 1970, pp. 125-162.

Polišenský, Josef, "Český podíl na předhistorii 1. máje: Čeští dělníci a masakr v Chicagu roku 1886 (Czech part in the origin of the May Day: Czech workers and the 1886 Chicago massacre), In: Začiatky českej a slovenskej emigrácie do USA: Česká a slovenská robotnícka emigrácia v USA v období I. internacionály. Bratislava: Slovenská akadémia vied, 1970.

Čada, Joseph, A Survey of Radicalism in the Bohemian Community. Lisle, IL, 1957. 41 p.

Chada, Joseph, "Czech-American Subculture: Labor and Activism," in: The Czechs in the United States. SVU Press, 1981, pp. 159-170.

Schneirov, Richard Samuel, "Free Thought and Socialism in the Czech Community in Chicago, 1875-1887," in: Struggle a Hard Battle: Essays on Working-class Immigrants. Ed. by Dirk Hoerder. DeKalb,IL: Northern Illinois University, 1985, pp. 121-142.

2. Individuals

František Hlaváček (1853-1937)

Habenicht, Jan, "Hlaváček, František," in: Dějiny Čechův Amerických. St. Louis, MO: "Hlas," 1910, p. 745.

Čapek, Tomáš, Naše Amerika (Our America). Praha: Nákladem Národní rady československé, 1925, pp. 385-89.

Koukal, Pavel, "František Hlaváček," in: Regionalni knihovna Teplice—Osobnosti: http://www.knihovna-teplice.cz/index.php?scname=osobnosti&stranka%5B%5D=30&letter=H&person=578

Leopold Kochman (1847-1919)

Habenicht, Jan, "Kochman, Leo," in: Dějiny Čechův Amerických. St. Louis, MO: "Hlas," 1910, p. 753.

Čapek, Tomáš, Naše Amerika. Praha: Nákladem Národní rady československé, 1925, pp. 391-92.

Leo Meilbeck (1850-1883)
Čapek, Thomas, "Meilbek, Leo," in: American Czechs in Public Office. Omaha, NE: Czech Historical Society of Nebraska, 1940,

Anton 'Tony' Novotný (1886-1932)
Čapek, Tomáš, Naše Amerika. Praha: Nákladem Národní rady československé, 1925, p. 395.

Leo Palda (1847-1912)
"L. J. Palda," Květy americké 1, No. 11 (Aug. 15, 1885), pp. 322-325.
"Z minulých dob. Vzpomínky L.J. Paldy" (L. J. Palda's reminiscences), Osvěta americká (Omaha, NE) 11, No. 7 (Sept. 16, 1903), p. 6.

Josef Boleslav Pecka (1849-1897)
"Josef Boleslav Pecka," Všedělnický kalendář, 2 (1911), pp. 49-50.
Čapek, Tomáš, Naše Amerika. Praha: Nákladem Národní rady československé, 1925, pp. 397-98.

František Škarda (1848-1900)
"František Škarda mrtev" (František Škarda is dead), Dennice novověku, May 31, 1900.
Forman, Václav B., "František Škarda," Amerikán, národní kalendář, 24 (1901), pp. 245-46.
Čapek, Tomáš, Naše Amerika. Praha: Nákladem Národní rady československé, 1925, p. 401.

Valentin Wertheimer (1925-1978)
"Wertheimer, Valentin Jacob Thomas," in: Biographical Dictionary of Central European Emigrees, 1933-1945. Vol. 1. Politics, Economy and Public Life. Munchen . . . : K. G. Saur Verlag, 1983, pp. 814-815.

H. Character

Oliverius, J.A., Mravní hodnota českoamerického tisku a pojednání o tom, v jakém poměru stojíme k amerikanismu co Čechové (Moral value of Czech-American press and discussion about our stand as Czechs toward Americanism). Časová přednáška. Chicago, 1893.

Vlach, J. J., "Our Bohemian Population," in: 1901 Proc. of the State Historical Society of Wisconsin. Madison, WI: Democratic Printing Co., 1902, pp. 159-162.

Steiner, E. A., "Character of the Bohemians in the U.S.," Outlook (New York), 73 (April 25, 1903), pp. 968-72.

Cather, Willa S., My Antonia. Boston and New York: Houghton Mifflin Co., 1918. 418p.

Chalupný, Emanuel, Národní filosofie československá. Dil I. Národní povaha československá (The Czechoslovak national philosophy. Vol. 1 The Czechoslovak national character). Praha: Nákladem vlastním, 1935. 256p.

Folprecht, Josef, Studie o povaze zahraničních krajanů (Study of the nature of our countrymen abroad). Prague: Knihovna, Československý ústav zahraniční, 1947. Vol. 8.

Skrabanek, Robert L., We're Czechs. College Station: Texas A&M University Press, 1988. 240p.

Prchal, Tim, "The Bohemian Paradox: My Antonia and Popular Images of Czech Immigration. Critical Essay. Melus, vol. 29, No. 2 (Summer 2004), pp. 3-25.

Rechcigl, Miloslav, Jr., "The Czech Character," in: Czechs and Slovaks in America. Boulder, CO: East European Monographs, 2005, pp. 279-284

I. Attitude, Behavior, Communications

Sheldon, Carol L., "Political Attitude and Behavior of the Czechoslovak American Intellectuals," in: Studies in Czechoslovak History. Edited by Miloslav Rechcigl, Jr. Meerut: Sadhna Prakashan, 1976, vol. 1, pp.374-387.

Dubovicky, Ivan, "Czech-Americans: An Ethnic Dilemna," Nebraska History, 74, No. 3 & 4 (Fall/Winter 1993), pp. 95-208.

Nicholas, Sinclair, The AmeriCzech Dream: Cizinec v cizí zemi. Čelakovice: WD Publication, 2005. 293p.

Rabušic, L. and J. Hamanová, Hodnoty a postoje v ČR 1991-2008 (Values and Attitude in ČR 1991-1998). (European Values Study). Brno. Masarykova univerzita, 2009.

Englund, T. B., The Czechs in a Nutshell: A User's Manual for Foreigners. Praha: Práh, 2009.

Bočánková, M., Intercultural Communication: Typical Features of the Czech, British, American, Japanese, Chinese and Arab Cultures (2nd ed.). Praha: Vysoká škola ekonomická v Praze, Oeconomica, 2010.

Ficová, Klára, The Effect of Cultural Differences on Communication between Czechs and Americans. Bachelor Thesis. Masaryk University, Faculty of Education, 2011.

J. Cooperation

Čapek, Thomas, "Fraternal and Other Societies," in: The Čechs (Bohemians) in America. Boston & New York: Houghton Mifflin Co., 1920, pp. 254-264.

Klíma, S., Československá péče krajanská (The Czechoslovak policy towards Czechs abroad). Praha: Akademický dům, 1931.

Skrabanek, R. L., "Forms of Cooperation and Mutual Aid in a Czech-American Rural Community." Southwestern Social Science Quarterly 30, No. 3 (December 1949), pp. 83-88.

Skrabanek, Robert L., Working Together Makes Snook a Good Community," Progressive Farmer, 65, No. 3 (1950), pp. 86-87.

Bicha, Karel D., "Community or Cooperation? The Case of the Czech-Americans," in: Studies in Ethnicity: The East European Experience in America, Edited by C. A. Ward, P. Shashko, and D. E. Pienkos, Boulder: East European Monographs, 1980, pp. 93-102.

Chada, Joseph, "Czech-American Subculture: Fraternalism. SVU Press, 1981, pp. 137-146; "Czech-American Subculture: Fraternal and Social Life in Cultural Service," Ibid., pp. 147-158.

K. Image among Americans

Cather, Villa S., My Antonia. Boston and New York: Houghton Mifflin Co., 1918. 418p.

Čapek, Thomas, "The Immigrant as a Liability," in: The Čechs (Bohemians) in America. Boston and New York: Houghton Mifflin Co., 1920, pp. 94-95.

Miller, Kenneth D., "Moral Standards," in: The Czecho-Slovaks in America. New York: George H. Doran, 1922, pp.70-71.

Sheldon, Addison E., "Nebraska Czechs as I Have Known Them," in: A History of Czechs (Bohemians) in Nebraska. Compiled by Rose Rosicky. Omaha: Czech Historical Society of Nebraska, 1929, pp. 15-17.

Roucek, Joseph S., "The American Czechs, Slovaks, and Slavs in the Development of America's 'Climate of opinion,'" in: Czechoslovakia Past and Present. Edited by Miloslav Rechcigl, Jr. Mouton: The Hague—Paris, 1968, Vol.1, pp. 815-859.

Roucek, Joseph S., The Image of the Slavs in United States History and in Immigration Policy," American Journal of Economics Sociology, 28 (January, 1969), pp. 29-48.

Prchal, Tim, "The Bohemian Paradox: My Antonia and Popular Images of Czech Immigrants," Melus, 29, No. 2 (2004), pp. 3-25

VI. Economy

A. General

Balch, Emily Greene, "The Economic Situation of the Slavs in America," in: Our Slavic Fellow Citizens. New York: Charities Publication Committee, 1910, pp. 282-316.

Hospodářský stav českých venkovských obcí ve státech Nebraska, Iowa, Kansas, Minnesota a Dakota (Economic status of Czech rural communities in Nebraska, Iowa, Minnesota and Dakota). 1921.

Prantner, E. F., "What Czechoslovaks Contribute to American Economy and Culture," Czechoslovak Review 6 (1922), pp. 225-227.

Miller, Kenneth D., "The Immigrant in America. Part II. Economic Conditions. Occupations," in: The Czecho-Slovaks in America. New York: George H. Doran Co., 1922, pp. 55-64.

Čapek, Tomáš, "Práce, blahobyt a hospodářský stav"

(Work, prosperity and economic status), in: Naše Amerika. Praha: Národní rada československá, 1926, pp. 204-250.

Kisch, Guido, "Contributions to Secular Culture: Commerce and Industry," in: In Search for Freedom. A History of American Jews from Czechoslovakia 1592-1948. London: Edward Goldston, 1948, pp. 150-166.

Andic, Vojtech E., "Trends in Czech and Slovak Economic Enterprise in the New World," in: The Czechoslovak Contribution to World Culture. Ed. Miloslav Rechcigl, Jr. The Hague: Mouton, 1964, pp. 523-527.

Dvorník, Francis, "Czechs in the U.S. Economy," in: Czech Contributions to the Growth of the United States. Chicago. Benedictine Abbey, 1972, pp. 92-84.

Významní čeští podnikatelé v zahraničí. Čeští ekonomové v zahraničí (Significant Czech entrepreneurs abroad). Sborník konference. Ed. by Karel Kánský. Praha: Univerzita Karlova, 1999.

Bičík, M., "Ekonomice USA pomáhá i vlna přistěhovalců" (US economy is helped even by immigrants), Lidové noviny, February 24, 2000, p. 15, Rubrika: Ekonomika.

B. Living Conditions

1. General

Amerikán, Národní Kalendář, Chicago: A. Geringer, 1878-1957.

Miller, Kenneth D., "Housing Conditions," in: The Czecho-Slovaks in America. New York: George H. Doran Co., 1922, pp. 60-68.

Čapek, Tomáš, "Epopej českých začátečníků" (Epoch of Czech pioneers), in: Naše Amerika. Praha: Národní rada československá, 1926, pp. 180-187.

Dvornik, Francis, "Early Hardships," in: Czech Contributions to the Growth of the United States. Chicago: Benedictine Abbey Press, 1962, pp. 73-79.

Czech Voices. Stories from Texas in the Amerikán Národní Kalendář. Translated and edited by Clinton Machann and James W. Mendel. College Station, TX: Texas A&M University, 1991. 147p.

2. Rural Areas

Čapek, Tomáš, "Sídla na venkově" (Settlements in the rurual areas), in: Naše Amerika. Praha: Národní rada čskoslovenská, 1926, pp. 187-188.

3. Cities

Čapek, Tomáš, "Bydliště v městech" (Settlements in the cities), in: Naše Amerika. Praha: Národní rada československá, 1926, pp. 188-190.

C. Occupations

Čapek, Thomas, "Trades, Business, Professions," in: The Cechs (Bohemians) in America, Boston & New York: Houghton Mifflin Co., 1920, pp. 69-93.

Klíma, Stanislav, "Sídla a zaměstnání" (Settlements and employment), in: Čechové a Slováci za hranicemi. Praha: J. Otto, 1925, pp. 193-201.

Čapek, Tomáš, "Práce, blahobyt a hospodářský stav" (Work, Abundance and Economy), in: Naše Amerika. Praha: Národní rada československá, 1926, pp. 204-250.

Miller, Kenneth D., "Occupations," in: The Czecho-Slovaks in America. New York: George H. Doran Co., 1922, pp. 55-64.

Korytová-Magstadt, Štěpanka, "Endless Horizons: Settlement and Occupational Patterns of Early Czechs in America" in: To Reap a Bountiful Harvest. Iowa City: Rudi Publishing, 1993, pp. 47-59.

D. Labor

Riis, Jacob A, "The Bohemians: Tenement-House Cigar-Making," in: How the Other Half Lives: Studies among the Poor. New York: Scribner's 1890; reprinted in New York: Sagamore Press, 1957, pp. 100-110.

Woods, Robert et al., "Bohemians," in: The Poor in Great Cities: Their Problems and what is Doing to Solve them. London-New York: Kegan Publ., 1895, pp. 101-30.

Sheridan, Frank J., Italian, Slavic and Hungarian Unskilled Laborers in the United States," US Bureau of Labor Bulletin, 15, No. 72 (September 1907), pp. 403-486.

Buňata, Josef, "Doutnikáři" (Cigar makers), Amerikán, Národní kalendář, 47 (1924), pp.159-187.

Abbott, Edith, "Bohemians in the Cigar-Making Industry," in: Women in Industry. A Study in American Economic History. New York: Appleton, 1910, pp. 196-200.

Čapek, Tomáš, "Nádenictví" (Unskilled labor), in: Naše Amerika. Praha: Nákladem Národní rady československé, 1926, pp. 234-235.

Riis, Jacob A., "The Bohemian Tenement-House Cigar Making," in: How the Other Half Lives: Studies among the Poor. New York: Scribner's, 1890; Reprinted New York: Sagamore Press, 1957, pp. 100-110.

Dostálík, Milan, Česká dělnická emigrace v letech 1873-1878" (Czech labor emigration in 1873-1878), Slovanský přehled, 43, No. 2 (1957), pp. 37-40.

Začiatky českej a slovenskej emigrácie do USA: Česká a slovenská robotnická emigrácia v období I. Internacionály (The Beginnings of Czech and Slovak emigration to the US: Czech and Slovak labor emigration in the time of the I. Internationale). Bratislava: Vydavateľstvo Slovenskej akadémie vied, 1970. 335p.

E. Farming

Breuer, Hynek, "Rolník" (Farmer), Amerikán, Národní kalendář, 4, (1881), pp. 166-176.

Jonáš, Karel, Zlatá kniha pro farmera (A golden book for a farmer). Racine WI: Slavie, 1878. 160p; 4th ed. 1893. 342p.

Mashek, Nan, "Bohemian Farmers of Wisconsin," Charities, 13 (December 3, 1904), pp. 211-214.

Balch, Emily Greene, "Slavs as Farmers," in: Our Slavic Fellow Citizens. New York: Charities Publication Committee, 1910, pp. 317-348.

Balch, E. G., "Peasant Background of our Slavic Citizens," Survey, 24 (August 6, 1910), pp. 666-677.

Janák, Jan, Praktický farmářův rádce. Soubor důležitých údajů, návodů, předpisů, atd (Practical farmer's guide. Collection of important facts, instructions, rules, etc.) Omaha: Národní tiskárna, 1913. 138p.

Carroll, R. G., "New Bohemia, Virginia. Colony of Alien Farmers," Country Gentleman, 18 (July 1, 1916), pp. 1290-91.

Špaček, Stanislav, Zápisky z návštěvy amerických farem (Notes from a vist of American farms). Pardubice: Author, 1919. 37p.

Hodges, LeRoy, Slavs on the Southern Farms: An Account of Bohemian, Slovak and Polish Agricultural Settlements in Southern States. Washington, DC: Government Printing Office, 1914. 21p.

Beneš, Vojta, "Čeští farmáři ve Spojených státech" (Czech farmers in the US). Naše zahraničí, 5 (1924), pp. 65-73, 123-128, 184-186.

Doubrava, Ferdinand F. "Experiences of a Bohemian Emigrant Farmer," Wisconsin Magazine of History, 8 (March 1925), pp. 393-406.

Čapek, Tomáš, "Majetkový stav farmářů," in: Naše Amerika. Praha: Nákladem Národni rady československé, 1926, pp. 217-218.

Hodges, LeRoy, "The Bohemian Farmers in Texas," The Texas Magazine, 6, pp. 87-90.

Anderson, Nels, "Petersburg: A Study of the Colony of Czechoslovakia Farmers in Virginia," in: Immigrant Farmers and their Children. Edited by Edmund de Schweinitz Brunner. Garden City, NY: Doubleday, Doran & Co., 1929, pp. 183-212.

Lynch, Russell Ward, Czech Farmers in Oklahoma. Stillwater: Oklahoma Agricultural and Mechanical College, 1942. 119p.

Lynch, Russell, "Czech Farmers in Oklahoma," Economic Geography, 20 (January 1944), pp. 9-13.

Skrabanek, R. L., "The Influence of Cultural Backgrounds on Farming Practices in a Czech-American Rural Community," Southwestern Social Science Quarterly, 31, No. 4 (March 1951), pp. 258-267.

Nygrin, Rudy, Ze života domovináře a farmaření v Redlands na Floridě" (From the life of a cottager and the farming in Redlands, Florida), Amerikán, Národní kalendář, 78 (1956), pp. 126-131.

Kutak, Robert I., The Story of a Bohemian-American Village. Louisville, KY: Standard Printing Co., 1933. Reprinted New York: Arno Press, 1970. 156p.

Barton, Josef J., "Land, Labor, and Community in Nueces: Czech Farmers and Mexican Laborers in South Texas, 1880-1930," in: Ethnicity on the Great Plains. Edited by Frederick C. Luebke. Lincoln, NE: University of Nebraska Press, 1980, pp. 190-209.

Korytová-Magstadt, Štěpánka, A Dream Fulfilled: From Peasants to Farmers," in: To Reap a Bountiful Harvest. Iowa City: Rudi Publishinf, 1993, pp. 71-80.

Polišenský, Josef, "Z rolníků farmáři. Texas a Wisconsin" (From peasants to farmers. Texas and Wisconsin), in: Úvod do studia dějin vystěhovalectví do Ameriky II. Češi a Amerika. Praha: Univerzita Karlova, 1996, pp. 29-36.

Polišenský, Josef, "Druhá vlna přistěhovalecká: Nebraska a Kansas" (Second wave of immigrants: Nebraska and Kansas), in: Úvod do studia dějin vystěhovalectví do Ameriky II. Češi a Amerika, op. cit, pp. 48-52.

F. Commerce & Trade

1. General

Čapek, Tomáš, "Majetkový stav obchodníků a řemeslníků" (Financial status of merchants and tradesmen), in: Naše Amerika. Praha: Nákladem Národni rady československé, 1926, pp. 219-221; "Obchod, řemeslo, živnost" (Commerce, trade, business), in: Ibid., pp. 221-227.

Rechcigl, Miloslav, Jr., "Czech-American Tradesmen—Masters of their Profession," Naše Rodina (Our Family), 9, No. 4 (March 1997), pp. 20-23.

2. Individuals

David Adler (1821-1905)

Bruce, William George and Josiah Seymour Currey, "David Adler," in: History of Milwaukee, City and County. Chicago-Milwaukee: S. Clarke Publishing Co., 1922, Vol. 3, pp. 8-11.

Jonas Brandeis (1836-1903)

Watkins, Albert, "Brandeis, Jonas L.," in: History of Nebraska. Lincoln, 1913, vol. 3, pp. 555-559.

Biga, Leo Adam,The Brandeis Story. Omaha: Jewish Press.

Richard N. Cabela (1936-)

"Cabela, Richard N.," in: Wikipedia. See: http://en.wikipedia.org/wiki/Richard_N._Cabela

Col. Louis Fleischner (1827-1896)

Gaston, Joseph, Portland, Orgeon: Its History and Builders. Chicago-Portland: S. J. Clarke, 1911, vol. 2, pp. 258-262.

Henry Horner (1818-1878)

The First Czech in Chicago," Naše Rodina (Our Family), 8, No. 2 (June 1996), pp. 66-67.

Ray Kroc (1902-1984)

Boas, Max and Steve Chain. Big Mac: The Unauthorized Story of McDonald's. New York: Dutton, 1976. 212p.

Kroc, Ray and Robert Anderson, Growing it Out: The Making of McDonalds. New York: St. Martin, 1990.

Francis W. Lasak (1799-1889)

Lasak's Obituary, Chicago Tribune, February 28, 1889.

"Francis W. Lasak's Estate," New York Times, September 24, 1889.

Louis Taussig (1837-1896)

Heineman, Bret, "Louis Taussig & Co.," Antique Bottle and Glass Collector Magazine: http://www.glswrk-auction.com/021.htm

David Phillip Wohl (1886-1960)

Boxerman, Burton. "David P. Wohl—Shoe Merchant," Gateway Heritage, 9, No. 2 (Fall 1988), pp. 24-33.

G. Industry

1. General

Česká práce v Americe: Dějiny a popisy česko-amerických závodů průmyslových a obchodních (Czech work in America: History and description of Czech-American industrial and business plants). New York, 1898.

Čapek, Tomáš, "Průmysl" (Industry), in: Naše Amerika. Praha: Nákladem Národní rady československé, 1926, pp. 228-234.

2. Individuals

Arde Bulova (1869-1958)

"Bulova, Arde—Obituary," New York Times, March 24,1958, p. 27.

Ingham, John N., "Bulova, Arde," in Biographical Dictionary of American Business Leaders. Westport, CT: Greenwood Press, 1983, pp. 112-114.

Thomas J. Baťa (1914-2008)

Baťa, Thomas J. and Sonja Sinclair, Bata, Shoemaker to the World. Toronto: Stoddart Publishing, 1990. 341p.

Sigmund Eisner (1859-1925)

Scanell's First Citizens, 1917-1918. Paterson, NJ, vol. 1, pp. 157-158.

Charles Louis Fleischmann (1835-1897)

Klieger, P. Christian, Fleischmann Yeast Family, Arcadia Publishing, 2004. 124p.

Francis Korbel (1830-1920)

Seifert, Augustin, "Za starým osmačtyřicátnikem Fr. Korbelem" (Our old Forty-Eighter Fr. Korbel), Naše zahraničí, 1, No. 2 (1920), pp. 9-14.

Estée Lauder (1906-2004)

Lauder, Esté, Estée: A Success Story. New York: Random House, 1985.

Israel, Lee, Estée Lauder: Beyond the Magic: An Unauthorized Biography. New York: Macmillan, 1985.

Václav F. Severa (1853-1938)

Seifert, Augustin, "Československý mecenáš Václav F. Severa" (Czechoslovak philanthropist Václav F, Severa), Naše zahraničí, 1930, pp. 13-18.

Frank J. Vlchek (1871-1947)

Vlček, František J., Povídka mého života (Story of My Life). Praha: Družstevní práce, 1929. 365p.; Translated to English by Winston

Chrislock as The Story of My Life. Kent State University Press, 2005. 392p.

H. Banking & Finance

1. General

Čapek, Thomas and Thomas Čapek, Jr., The Czechs and Slovaks in American Banking. New York: Fleming H. Ravel Co., 1920. 60p.

2. Individuals

Henry W. Bloch (1922-)

Bloch, Thomas M., Many Happy Returns: The Story of Henry Bloch, America's Tax Man. Wiley. 2010. 256p.

Jacob Furth (1840-1918)

Speidel, Bill, Through the Eye of the Needle. Nettle Creek Pub., 1989. 149p.

Samuel Kohn (1782-1853)

Wolf, Lucien, "The Romance of a Bohemian Village," in Essays in Jewish History. London: The Jewish Historical Society of England, 1934, pp.55-59.

Rechcigl, Miloslav, Jr., "Český Kohn se neztratí ani v Americe aneb kdo uteče, ten vyhraje" (Czech Kohn doesn't get lost even in America or Who runs away wins), in: Postavy naší Ameriky, 2000, pp. 48-50.

Moritz O. Kopperl (1826-1883)

Hewitt, W. Phil, Moritz Kopperl," in: The Czech Texans. San Antonio: The University of Texas, Institute of Texan Cultures, 1972, pp. 8-10.

Joseph Charles Rovensky, (1886-1952)

Kernmeter, Donald L, "John E Rovensky, Industrialist and Banker." Presidential Address, 1977.

Burghard Steiner (1857-1923)
"Steiner, Burghard," in: History of Alabama and Dictionary of Alabama Biography. By Thomas McAdory Owen, Marie Bankhead Owen, vol.4, p. 619.

I. Corporate Activities

Michael Eisner (1942-)
Michael Eisner," in Newsmakers: The People behind Today's Headlines. Detroit: Gale Research, 1990, pp. 19-127.

VII. Public Life

A. Politics

1. General

Rosicky, Rose, "Political Activity," in: History of Czechs in Nebraska, Omaha: Czech Historical Society of Nebraska, 1929, pp. 444-455.

Odložilík, Otakar, "The Czechs," in: The Immigrants' Influence on Wilson's Peace Policies. Lewisburg, KY: University of Kentucky Press, 1967, pp. 204-223.

Kleinschmidt, John R., "The Political Behavior of the Bohemian and Swedish Ethnic Groups in Nebraska, 1889-1900. M.A. Thesis, University of Nebraska, 1968.

Láska, Věra, "Czechs and Slovaks," in: America's Ethnic Politics. Eds. Joseph S. Roucek and Bernard Eisenberg. Westport: Greenwood Press, 1982, pp. 133-53.

Stone, Gregory Martin, Ethnicity, Class and Politics among Czechs in Cleveland.1870-1940. Ph.D. Dissertation, Rutgers—State University of New Jersey, 1993. 304p.

2. Individuals

Charles Jonáš (1840-1896)
Bicha, Karel, "Karel Jonáš of Racine," Wisconsin Magazine of History, 63 (1979-1980), pp. 122-140.

Nesvadbík, Lumír and Josef Polišenský, "První Čech v Americe. Karel Jonáš, 1840-1896" (First Czech in America. Karel Jonáš, 1840-1896), Sborník Národního muzea v Praze 32, No.2 (1987), pp. 1-58.

Chrislock, C. Winston, Charles Jonáš 1840-1896: Czech National Liberal, Wisconsin Bourbon Democrat. Philadelphia: Balch IES Press, 1993. 216p.

Charles Pergler (1882-1994)

"Dr. Charles Pergler," in: I am an American: Famous Naturalized Americans. Edited by Richard Spiers Benjamin. New York: Alliance Book Corp., 1941, pp. 23-29.

Mildred Otenasek (1914-2004)

"Otenasek, Mildred M.," in: The American Catholic Who's Who 1960-61. Grosse Pointe, MI: Walter Romig, 1961, Vol. 14, p. 365.

Michael Peroutka (1952-)

Phillips, Howard, "Constitutionally Correct Peroutka," in: American Conservative; also on Internet:

Francis, Sam, "Peroutka for President: Wasting a Vote—or Sending A Message? **http://www.vdare.com/francis/peroutka.htm**

B. Executive Branch

Madeleine Albright (1937-)

Thomas Blood, Madam Secretary: Biography of Madeleine Albright. New York: St. Martin's Press, 1999. 289p.

Albright, Madeleine, Madam Secretary: A Memoir. New York: Miramax Books, 2003. 576p.

Anton Joseph Čermák (1873-1933)

Bernard, H. K., Anton the Mayor, Chicago: Marion Publishing Co., 1933. 93p.

Gottfried, Alex, Boss Cermak of Chicago: A Study of Political Leadership, Seattle, WA: University of Washington Press, 1962. 459p.

Drnec, Gustav and J. V. Welcl, Náš Čermák: Úžasná životní kariéra a mučednická smrt českoamerického přistěhovalce, starosty města Chicaga (Our Čermák. A remarkable career and. martyr's death of Czch-American immigrant, Mayor of Chicago).Chicago: Spravedlnost, 1933. 87p.

Julius Fleischmann (1871-1925)

"Fleischmann, Julius," in: National Cyclopedia of American Biography. 54 (1973), pp. 419-420.

Henry Horner (1878-1940)

Lewis, Lloyd, Henry Horner, Governor of Illinois: A Tribute. Chicago: Lakeside Press, 1949.

Littlewood, Thomas B., Horner of Illinois. Evanston, IL: Northwestern University Press, 1969, 273p.

Masters, Charles, Governor Henry Horner, Chicago Politics, and the Great Depression. Carbondale, IL: Southern Illinois University Press, 2007.

Fred Kohler (1864-1934)

Richardson, James F., "Kohler, Fred," in: Biographical Dictionary of American Mayors. Edited by Melving G. Holli and Peter A. Jones. Westport, CT: Greenwood Press, 1981, pp. 201-201.

Ralph J. Perk (1914-1999)

Campbell, Thomas, F., "Perk, Ralph J. (1914-)," in: Biographical Dictionary of American Mayors 1820-1980. Edited by Melvin G. Holli and Peter d'Alroy Jones. Santa Barbara, CA: Greenwood Press, 1981.

Harold E. Stassen (1907-2001)

"Stassen, Harold E., Current Biography 1948, pp. 597-600.

Caspar Willard Weinberger (1917-2006)

"Weinberger, Casper Willard," in: National Encyclopedia of American Biography 62 (1948), pp.37-38.

Reynolds, Paul, "Obituary: Caspar Weinberger," BBC News, March 28, 2006.

Casper Weinberger, In the Arena: A Memoir of the 20th Century. Washington, DC: Regnery Publishing Co., 2001.

C. Legislative Branch

1. General

"Životopisy českých zakonodárců v Americe za rok 1879" (Biographies of Czech legislators in America in 1879), Amerikán, Národní kalendář, 1880, pp. 137-139.

Čapek, Thomas, American Czechs in Public Office. Omaha: Czech Heritage Society of Nebraska, 1940. 9p.

Rechcigl, Miloslav Jr., U.S. Legislators with Czechoslovak Roots from Colonial Times to Present: With Genealogical Lineages. Washington, DC: SVU Press, 1987. 65p.

2. Individuals

George H. Bender (1896-1961)

May, Joseph, "George Harrison Bender," Dictionary of American Biography, Suppl. 7, pp. 49-50.

Roman Lee Hruska (1904-1999)

"Hruska, Roman Lee," in: National Cyclopedia of American Biography, Current Series, 1 (1953), pp. 262-263.

Honan, William H, "Roman L. Hruska Dies at 94; Leading Senate Conservative," New York Times, April 27, 1999.

John Forbes Kerry (1943-)

John Kerry—Bruce L. Brager, John Kerry: Senator from Massachusetts. Greensboro, NC: Morgan Reynolds Publishing, 2005. 125p.

William Langer (1886-1959)

William Langer: Late Senator from North Dakota. Washington, DC: Government Printing Office. 128p.

Adolph Sabath (1866-1952)

Adolph Sabath—Boxerman, Barton Alan, "Adolph Joachim Sabath in Congress," J. Illinois State Historical Society, 66 (1973), pp. 327-340, 428-443.

D. Judiciary Branch

Louis Dembitz Brandeis (1856-1941)

Mason, Alpheus Thomas, Brandeis: A Free Man's Life. New York: Viking Press, 1946. 713p.

Paper, Lewis J., Brandeis: An Intimate Biography of One of America's Truly Great Supreme Court Justices. Carol Publishing Corporation, 1987. 442p.

Urofsky, Melvin, Louis D. Brandeis: A Life. Pantheon, 2009. 976p.

Augustin Haidušek (1845-1929)

"Judge Augustine Haidusek, Pioneer Statesman and Jurist," in: Estelle Hudson and Henry R. Maresh, Czech Pioneers of the Southwest (Dallas: South-West, 1934), pp. 76-82.

Schovajsa, Henry J., "Augustin Haidušek and his Influence on Czech Culture in Texas," in: The Czechs in Texas. A symposium. Temple, TX, October 27-29, 1978. Ed. Clinton Machann. College Station, TX: Texas A&M University, 1979, pp. 83-87.

Jochec, Jesse, The Life and Career of Augustin Haidušek. M.A. Thesis, University of Texas, 1940.

Machann, Clinton, "Haidusek, Augustin (1845-1929," in: Handbook of Texas. Denton, TX: Texas State Historical Assn., 2000.

Otto Kerner (1908-1976)

"Kerner, Otto J.," in: National Cyclopedia of American Biography, Current Series, 12 (1964), pp. 71-72.

"Kerner, Otto—Obituary," Current Biography Yearbook 1976 (1977), p. 470.

Barnhart, William E., Eugene Schlickman and Bill Barnhart, Kerner: The Conflict of Intangible Rights. Urbana-Chicago: University of Illinois Press, 1999. 406p.

John G. Roberts (1955-).

Neubauer, David W. and Stephen S. Meinhold, Battle Supreme: The Confirmation of Chief Justice John Roberts and the Future of the Supreme Court. Belmont, CA: Wadsworth Publishing, 2005. 57p.

E. Military

1. Surveys

a. General

Čapek, Thomas, "The Čech as a Soldier," in: The Čechs (Bohemians) in America. Boston and New York: Houghton Mifflin Co., 1920, pp. 155-163.

Kisch, Guido, "Military Service," in: In Search of Freedom. London: Edward Goldston, 1948, pp. 103-113.

Sobotka, Margie, Czech Servicemen of Nebraska (Civil War, Spanish-American War, World War I) Hometown and Branch of Service. Elkhorn, NE: Author, 1976.

The Czech Heritage Society of Texas, Texas Veterans of Czech Ancestry. Austin, TX: Eakin Press, 1999. 328p.

Texas Czech Genealogical Society. Czechs in Uniform. A Tribute to Our Czech Veterans. 2 volumes. Texas Czech Genealogical Society, 2010. 1007p.

Rechcigl, Miloslav, Jr., Czechs in US Military (in preparation).

b. American Revolution

Harling, Frederick and Martin Kaufman, in: "Czechs and Slovaks," in: The Ethnic Contribution to the American Revolution. Westfield, MA: Westfield Biocentennial Committee, 1976, pp. 11-12.

Weinlick, John R., "Moravians and the Americn Revolution: an Overview," Trans. Moravian Hist. Soc., 23 (1977), pp. 1-16.

c. Mexican War

Sinkula, P., "Čeští dobrovolníci v Mexické válce 1864-1867" (Czech volunteers in the Mexican War 1864-1867), Sborník Národního muzea v Praze, Řada A-Historie, 25, No. 3 Praha, 1971), pp. 65-110.

d. Civil War

Čermák, Tomáš, "Čeští dobrovolníci v poslední občanské válce" (Czech volunteers in the last Civil War), Amerikán, Národní kalendář, 2 (1879), pp. 158-162.

Čermák, Josef, Dějiny občanské války s připojením zkušeností českých vojínů (History of Civil War with the addition of experiences of Czech soldiers). Chicago, 1889. 414p.

Bujarková, F. L., Proti srdci—proti vůli. Z utrpení texaských krajanů v době občanske války" (Against their heart—against their will. Suffering of Texas countrymen during the Civil War), Amerikán, Národní kalendář, 1929.

"Čeští dobrovolníci v poslední občanské válce" (Czech volunteers in the last civil war), Amerikán, Národní kalendář, 78 (1955), pp. 205-207.

Dvorník, Francis, "Czechs in the Civil War," in: Czech Contributions to the Growth of the United States. Chicago: Benedictine Abbey Press, 1962, pp. 80-91.

Wright, Judy Feldtman, Ed., Czechs in Gray—and Blue, too! San Antonio, TX: Judy Feldtman Wright, 1988. 243p.

Mácha, Z.: "Češi byli při tom" (Czechs were there), in: Americká občanská válka. By Leonid Křížek et al. Praha: X-Egem, 1994, pp. 120-132.

Vlha, Marek, "Czech Soldiers in the American Civil War: Previous Research and New Perspectives," Kosmas, 23, No. 2 (Spring 2010), pp. 43-57.

Vlha, Marek, Dopisy z války Severu proti Jihu (Letters from the War of North vs. South). Brno: Matice moravská, 2011. 136p.

e. Spanish-American War

Mašek, Matěj, Španělsko-americká válka r. 1898, se zvláštním zřetelem ku činnosti českých vojínů a s připojením zdařilých podobizen (Spanish-American War of 1898, with special attention to the activities of Czech soldiers with the attachment of pictures). Chicago: A Geringer, 1899.

Garcia, Angel and Josef Opatrný, "Čeští dobrovolníci na Kubě v roce 1898 a ohlasy americko-španělské války v českém krajanském tisku v USA" (Czech volunteers in Cuba in 1898 and the echoes from the Spanish-American War in Czech Ethnic Press in the US), Dějiny a současnost 9, No. 7 (1967), pp. 36-39.

Opatrný, J., "Češi a Slováci v Americe a španělsko-americká válka" (Czech and Slovaks in America and the Spanish-American War), Češi v cizině, 1 (1986), pp. 43-55.

f. World War I

Zecker, Robert, "The Activities of Czech and Slovak Immigrants during World War I," Ethnic Forum 15, No. 1-2 (Spring-Fall, 1995), p.35ff.

The Wartime Experiences of Cleveland Czechoslovak Legionnaire: The World War I Diary of Ladislav Křížek. By Stephen J. Sebesta. Bloomington, IN: Xlibris Corp., 2009. 144p.

g. World War II

Beneš, V., První vojáci nejzápadnější fronty (First soldiers of the most Western front). Praha, 1946.

Roucek, Joseph S., "American Czechoslovaks and World War II," World Affairs Interpreter, 17 (1946), pp. 85-90.

Lewis, M. White, ed., On All Fronts. Czechoslovaks in World War II. Boulder, CO: East European Series, 1991-2000.3 vols.

Farek, Florence Hertel. World War II Memoirs. A Collection of Stories from the Battle Front, the Home Front, and the Other Side. Schulenburg, TX: Author, 1998. 503p.

2. Individuals

Claude C. Bloch (1878-1967)

"Claude Charles Bloch," in: National Cyclopedia of American Biography 53 (1971), pp.519-520.

August Bondi (1833-1907)

Bondi, August, Autobiography, 1833-1907. Galesburg, Ill.: Wagoner, 1910.

Connelley, William E., "August Bondi," in: Standard History of Kansas and Kansans. Chicago: Lewis Publishing Company, 1918,

Stillman, Yanki, "August Bondi and the Abolitionist Movement," Jewish Currents, March 2004.

Solomon Bush (1753-1795)

Wolf, Simon, The American Jew as Patriot, Soldier, and Citizen, Philadelphia: The Levytype, 1895, pp. 45-47.

Brody, Seymour 'Sy', "Solomon Bush: Is Remembered as a Soldier and Citizen," in: Jewish Heroes and Heroines in America from Colonial Times to 1900. Hollywood, FL: Lifetime Books, Inc., 1996.

Leopold Karpeles (1838-1909)

Brody, Seymour 'Sy', "Sergeant Leopold Karpeles: Received the Congressional Medal of Honor," in: Jewish Heroes and Heroines in America from Colonial Times to 1900. Hollywood, FL: Lifetime Books, Inc., 1996.

Apollo Soucek (1897-1955)

"Soucek, Apollo," in Who Was Who in America, vol. 3.

"Honolulu Liners," Time, Monday, May 20, 1929.

Soucek, Apollo, "How I Broke the World's Altitude Record," Modern Mechanics, Sept. 1930, pp. 48-49, 180, 182.

Henry Delp Styer (1862-1944)

"Styer, Henry Delp," in: The National Cyclopedia of American Biography. New York: James T. White and Co., 1947, vol. 33, pp. 506-507.

Parshall, Ardis E., Henry D. Styer: A Sense of Fair Play," The Keepapitchin, October 13, 2008.

Wilhelm D. Styer (1893-1975)

"Gen. H. D. Styer at Milestone: Man Who Led American Troops into Siberia to Observe 80th Birthday," Los Angeles Times, September 21, 1942

"Wilhelm Styer, General, 81, Dies: West Pacific Commander Executed Yamashita," New York Times, February 28, 1975

"General Styer Dies at 81," Pacific Stars and Stripes, March 2, 1975.

Edward David Taussig (1847-1921)

Tucker, Spencer C., "Taussig, Edward David," in The Encyclopedia of the Spanish-American and Philippine-American Wars. Santa Barbara, CA: ABC-CLIO, LLC 2009, Volume 1, pp. 632-633.

"Rites for Admiral Taussig," Special to Washington Post. The Washington Post. Washington, D.C.: Feb 2, 1921.

Joseph Knefler Taussig (1877-1947)

Tucker, Spencer C., "Taussig, Joseph Knefler," in The Encyclopedia of the Spanish-American and Philippine-American Wars. Santa Barbara, CA: ABC-CLIO, LLC, 2009, Volume 1, p. 633.

F. Community Leadership

McClure, Archibald, "The Bohemians," in: Leadership of the New America. New York, George H. Doran, 1916, pp. 47-59.

Miller, Kenneth D., "Leadership," in: The Czecho-Slovaks in America. New York: George H. Doran Co., 1922, pp. 86-88.

VIII. Cultural Life

A. General

Matocha, B. F., "Work of Czechoslovaks in America," Current History 10 (May 1919), pp. 208-212.

Smetánka, J. F., "The Czechoslovak Contributions to America," Central European Observer, 13, No.1 (1935), pp. 389-391.

Padesát let kulturní práce. Na oslavu zlatého jubilea českých otců Benediktinů z opatství sv. Prokopa, Lisle, Ill (Fifty years of cultural work. Celebration of the golden jubilee of the Czech Fathers Benedictines from the St. Procopius Abbey, Lisle, Ill). Chicago, 1935. 64p.

Čapek, Thomas, "The Czechoslovaks: Their Contribution to America's Making," Interpreter Releases, 13 (1936), pp. 82-90.

Roucek, Joseph S., "Contribution of the Czechoslovak Immigrant to America," Slovak Sokol, 32 (1936), pp. 369-370, 371-372, 379-380, 384, 394-396.

Roucek, Joseph Slabey," The Cultural Contributions of American Czechoslovaks," Books Abroad, 11 (1937), pp. 413-415.

Žižka, Ernest J., Czech Cultural Contributions. Chicago: Benedictine Abbey Press, 1942. 145p.

Roucek, Joseph S., "Czechoslovak Americans," in: One America. The History, Contributions and Present Problems of Our Racial and National Minorities. Edited by Francis J. Brown and Joseph S. Roucek. 3rd ed. New York: Prentice Hall, 1952, pp. 57-68.

Dvornik, Francis, "Czech Cultural Achievements," in: Czech Contributions to the Growth of the United States. Chicago: Benedictine Abbey Press, 1962, pp. 95-106.

Šolle, Zdeněk, "Vojtěch Náprstek and his Era: Bohemia, the United States, and the Transmission of Cultures," East Central Europe, 17, No. 1 (Spring 1990), pp. 1-30.

Rechcigl, Miloslav Jr., "In Moravian Footprints in America," in: Ročenka. Yearbook of the Czechoslovak Genealogical Society International, 3 (1997-1998), pp. 35-43.

Rechcigl, Miloslav, Jr., "Contributions of Moravians to America," Kosmas 18, No. 2 (Spring 2005), pp. 94-105.

Machann, Clinton, "Czech-Moravian Heritage in Texas," in: Contributions of the Moravian Brethren to America. Selected Papers from the Conference of the Czechoslovak Society of Arts and Sciences at the Moravian College, Bethlehem, PA, June 8-10, 2007, pp. 55-62.

B. Education

1. General

Greenfield, John, "Moravian Educational Labors among the Indians," Pennsylvania Germans, 8 (1907), pp. 405-420.

Harden, Willam, "The Moravians of Georgia and Pennsylvania as Educators." Georgia Historical Qarterly, 2 (1918), pp. 47-56.

Beneš, Vojta, Je Čechům v Americe třeba české školy? (Do Czechs need a Czech school in America?). Cleveland: Sdružení českých svobodomyslných škol, 1914. 32p.

Beneš, Vojta, Contribution to the Reform of the Czech Schools in America. Cleveland, 1914. 88p.

Dostál, H., "Česko-katolické osady a jejich školství ve Spojených státech" (Czech-Catholic communities and their schools in the US), Naše zahraničí, 2 (1921), pp. 198-201.

Smetánka, Jaroslav F., "Čeština na amerických středních školách" (Czech language in American high schools), Naše zahraničí, 7 (1926), pp. 117-120.

Míček, Eduard, Amerika se učí (America is learning). Praha: Sfinx, Janda, 1932. 186p.

Skrivanek, J. M., The Education of Czechs in Texas. M.A. Thesis, University of Texas, 1946. 139p.

Kisch, Guido, "Contribution to Secular Culture: Education," in: In Search of Freedom. London: Goldston, 1948, pp. 145-150.

Plach, Maryrose, American Intergroup Education in a Czechoslovakian Neighberhood. Master's Thesis, DePaul University, Chicago, 1954.

Roucek, Joseph S., "Czech and Slovak Educational Heritage in the United States," Malaysian J. Education, 9 (1972), pp. 164-199.

Rechcigl, Miloslav, Jr., Educators with Czechoslovak Roots. Washington, DC: SVU Press, 1980. 122p.

Bodnar, John, "Schooling and the Slavic American Family," in American Education and the European Immigrant: 1840-1940. Urbana: University of Illinois Press, 1982.

Walker, Rosie Ann Locker, A History of the Rural Schools of the Czech Communities of Kolií and Libuše. Ph.D. Dissertation, Northwestern State University of Louisiana, Natchitoches, LA, 1986.

Kugler, John, A Study of Czechoslovak Immigration and their Contributions to Vocational Education in Chicago between 1875 and 1935. Dissertation, Chicago State University, 2003.

2. Schools

Zdrůbek, František B., "Sobotní a nedělní české školy v Amerce" (Saturday and Sunday Czech schools in America), Amerikán, Národní kalendář, 11 (1888), pp. 152-158.

Veleminský, Karel, Školy českoamerické (The Czech-American schools). Zábřeh, 1914.

Čapek, Thomas, "The Language Schools: Teaching of Čech" in: The Čechs (Bohemians) in America. Boston & New York: Houghton Mifflin Co., 1920, pp. 241-245.

Miller, Kenneth D., "Foreign Language Training Schools," in: The Czecho-Slovaks in America. New York: George H. Doran Co., 1922, pp. 178-183.

Klíma, Stanislav, "České a slovenské školy v Americe" (Czech and Slovak schools in America). in: Čechové a Slováci za hranicemi. Praha: J. Otto, 1925, pp. 222-223.

Čapek, Tomáš, "Školy" (Schools), in: Naše Amerika. Praha: Národní rada československá, 1926, pp. 442-445.

Nigrin, Jaroslav Victor, "Teaching of Bohemian in High Schools and colleges," Bohemian Review, 1. No. 5 (June 1917), pp. 11-12.

Smetanka, Jaroslav F., "Čeština na amerických středních školách" (Czech in American high schools), Naše zahraničí, 7 (1926), pp. 17-20.

Rosicky, Rose, "Schools," in: History of Czechs in Nebraska, Omaha: Czech Historical Society of Nebraska, 1929, pp. 412-430.

Machek, A., comp., Památník sdruženych svobodomyslných škol v Chicagu a okolí (Memorial book of the associated Freethinkers' schools in Greater Chicago). Chicago, 1930.

Jerabek, Esther, "Antonín Jurka. A Pioneer Czech Schoolmaster in Minnesota." Minneapolis History, 13 (1932), pp. 269-276.

Beneš, Anton, Dějiny české svobodomyslné školy v Detroit. Michigan, 1881-1941" (History of the Czech Freethinking School in Detroit, MI, 1881-1941). Detroit, 1942. 40p.

Beck, Herbert Huebener. The Beck Family School, "Transactions of the Moravian Historical Society, 14 (1949), p. 273ff.

Hummel, William W., "The Flowering of the 'Hidden Seed'.The Beck Family and the Moravian Tradition in Education," Transactions of the Moravian Historical Society. Nazareth: Whitefield House, 1969, Part 1, pp. 15-30.

Walker, Rosie, A History of the Rural Schools of the Czech Communities of Kolin and Libuse. Ph.D. Dissertation, Northwestern University of Louisiana, 1986. 324p.

Janecka, Ed. Dubina Schools. Weimar, TX: Author, 2002. 246p.

Klimesh, Michael F., Albert Bouska and Cyril M. Klimesh, "Oldest Czech-American Log Cabin School in America," in: Moravians from World Perspective. Selected Papers from the 22nd World Congress of Czechoslovak Society of Arts and Sciences, Palacký University, Olomouc, June 26 to July 4, 2001. Edited by Miloslav, Rechcigl, Jr. Ostrava: Repronis, 2006, pp. 299-312.

3. Individuals

Vojta Beneš (1878-1951)

"Beneš, Vojta," in: Český biografický slovník XX. století. Praha: Paseka, 1999, p. 82.

Abraham Flexner (1866-1959)

S. C. Wheatley, S. C., The Politics of Philanthropy: Abraham Flexner and Medical Education. Madison: University of Wisconsin Press, 1989.

Bonner, Thomas Neville, Iconoclast: Abraham Flexner and a Life in Learning. Baltimore: Johns Hopkins Univ. Press, 2002.

M. Karel Hrubý (1794-1882)

Čapek, Tomáš, "Prof. M. Karel Hrubý," in: Památky českých emigrantů v Americe (Memorials of Czech Emigrants in America). Omaha, NE: Nákladem Pokroku západu, pp. 91-95.

Habenicht, Jan, Dějiny Čechův Amerických (History of American Czechs). St. Louis, MO: 'Hlas', 1910, pp. 19-21.

Rechcigl, Miloslav, Jr., "Zapadlý vlastenec—Karel Hrubý," in: Postavy naší Ameriky. Praha: Pražská edice, 2000, pp. 121-123.

Antonín Jurka (1840-1917)

Jerabek, Esther, "Antonin Jurka, a Pioneer Czech Schoolmaster in Minnesota," Minnesota History, 13 (1932), pp. 269-276.

Louise Mannheimer (1845-1920)

Rogow, Faith, "Mannheimer, Louise Herschmann," in: Judy Barrett Litoff, Judith McDonnell, European Immigrant Women in the United States: a Biographical Dictionary. New York: Garland Publishing, 1994, pp. 185-186.

Julia Richman (1855-1912)

Brody, Seymour, "Julia Richman—Educator," in: Jewish Heroes & Heroines of America. Hollywood, FL: Frederick Fell Publishers, 2004, pp. 76-77.

Jaroslav J. Zmrhal (1878-1951)

"Zmrhal, Jaroslav Joseph," in: Czech and Slovak Leaders in Metropolitan Chicago. Chicago: University of Chicago Slavonic Club, 1934, p. 50.

C. Journalism & Publishing

1. General

Zdrůbek, F. B., První český časopis v Americe" (The first Czech periodical in America), Narodní noviny, 1 (1878), pp. 69-79.

"Životopisy českých redaktorů v Americe" (Biographies of Czech journalists in America), Amerikán, Národní kalendář, 1 (1878), pp. 118-27.

Redaktoři českoamerických časopisů. Tušové podobizny deviti žurnalistů z let 1877-1878 (Editors of Czech-American newspapers. Ink-drawn portraits of nine journalists from 1877-1878). Suppl. to Amerikán, Národní kalendář, vol. 2, 1878. Chicago: A. Geringer, 1878.

"České písemnictví v Americe" (Czech literature in America), Květy americké, 2 (1886), pp. 422-424.

Havlasa, J., "Z česko-amerického písemnictví" (Czech-American literature), Osvěta Americká, 16, No. 40 (28.4.1909), p.6.

Čapek, Tomáš, Padesát let českého tisku v Americe (Fifty years of Czech press in America). New York: The Language Press, 1911. 280p.

Čapek, Thomas, "Journalism and Literature," in: The Čechs (Bohemians) in America. Boston & New York: Houghton Mifflin Co., 1920, pp. 164-221.

Miller, Kenneth D., "Literature and the Press," in: The Czechoslovaks in America. New York: George H. Doran, 1922, pp. 93-104.

Čepička, K., Písemnictví československého zahraničí (Czechoslovak literature abroad), Naše zahraničí, 4 (1923), pp. 76-81.

Čapek, Tomáš, "Tisk" (Press), in: Naše Amerika. Praha: Národní rada československá, 1926, pp. 251-261.

Čapek, Thomas, "First Czech Book Printed in America," Central European Observer, 12 (1934), p. 104.

Duben, Vojtěch, "United States," in: Czech and Slovak Press Outside Czechoslovakia. Its History and Status as of January 1962. Washington, DC—New York, NY: Czechoslovak Society of Arts and Sciences in America, Inc., 1962, pp. 8-44.

Duben, Vojtěch N., Czech and Slovak Press Outside Czechoslovakia," in: The Czechoslovak Contribution to World Culture. Edited by Miloslav Rechcigl, Jr. The Hague—London—Paris: Mouton & Co., 1964, pp. 528-454.

Vráz, Vlasta, "Early Czech Journalism in the United States," in: The Czechoslovak Contribution to World Culture. Edited by Miloslav Rechcigl, Jr. The Hague—London—Paris: Mouton & Co., 1964, pp. 546-551.

Duben, Vojtěch, N., "The Journalistic Endeavors of Czech and Slovak Exile (1945-1964)," in: Czechoslovakia Past and Present. Edited by Miloslav Rechcigl, Jr. The Hague—Paris: Mouton, 1968, pp. 844-859.

Rostinský, Josef, "Two Functional Aspects of Czech Journalism in Texas," in: The Czechs in Texas. A Symposium, Temple, TX, October 27-29, 1978. College Station, Texas A&M University, 1979, pp. 75-81.

Chada, Joseph, "Czech-American Subculture: The Press," in: The Czechs in the United States. SVU Press, 1981, pp. 129-146.

Šatava, L., "Čeští vystěhovalci do USA v 19. století a jejich tisk" (Czech emigrants to the U.S. in the 19th century and their press), Sešity novináře, 19, No. 3 (1968), pp. 127-145.

Chroust, David, "Bohemian Voice: The Forgotten First Journal about the Czechs in English," Kosmas, 14, No. 2 (Spring 2001), pp. 1-27.

Jaklová, Alena, "Czech-American Periodicals," Kosmas 17, No. 2 (Spring 2004), pp. 33-42.

Eckert, Eva, "The Years of 'Svoboda' in the Texas Czech Community, 1880s-WWI," Kosmas, 16, No. 1 (2002), pp. 63-78.

2. Individuals

Meyer Berger (1898-1959)

Dillia, Irving, "Meyer Berger," in: Dictionary of American Biography, Suppl. 6, pp. 57-58.

Edward Bloch (1829-1906)

Singerman, Robert, "Bloch & Company: Pioneer Jewish Publishing House in the West", Jewish Book Annual, Vol. 52, pp. 110-30.

August Geringer (1842-1930)

"Geringer, August," in: National Cyclopaedia of American Biography, Current Series, Vol. B (1927), p. 336.

Rechcigl, Miloslav, Jr., "První český vydavatel v Americe" (First Czech publisher in America), in: Postavy naší Ameriky. Praha: Pražská edice, 2000, pp. 145-147.

Francis Joseph Grund (1798-1863)

Faust, Albert Bernhardt, "Grund, Francis Joseph," in: Dictionary of American Biography, Suppl. 1, pp. 362-364.

Harold Kleinert Guinzburg (1899-1961)

Bloomfield, Maxwell, "Guinzburg, Harold Kleinert," in: Dictionary of American Biography, Suppl. 7, pp. 306-307.

Vojta Náprstek (1826-1894)

Šolle, Zdeněk, Vojta Náprstek a jeho doba (Vojta Náprstek and his era). Praha: Felis, 1994. 256p.

Rechcigl, Miloslav, Jr., "Otec českého tisku v Americe" (Father of Czech press in America), in: Postavy naší Ameriky. Praha: Pražská edice, 2000, pp. 136-139.

Secká, Milena, "Milwaukee Flug-Blätter—první krajanský tisk" (Milwaukee Flug-Blätter—The first paper of our countrymen), in: Problematika historických a vzácných knižních fondů. Sborník z 19. odborné konference, Olomouc, 2010. Brno: Sdružení knihoven ČR . . . , 2011, pp. 163-167.

Oswald Ottendorfer (1826-1900)

Creswell, Barbara, "Oswald Ottendorfer," in: American Newspaper Journalists 1873-1900. Ed. Pery J. Ashby. Detroit, MI: Gale Res. Co., 1983, pp. 252-255.

Rechcigl, Miloslav, Jr., "Z revolucionáře na žurnalistu" (From a revolutionary to a journalist), in: Postavy naší Ameriky. Praha: Pražská edice, 2000, pp. 133-135.

Edward Rosewater (1841-1906)

J. D. H., "Rosewater, Edward," in: Dictionary of American Biography, 16, pp. 171-172.

Rechcigl, Miloslav, Jr., "Prvni úspěšný český novinář v Americe" (First successful Czech journalist in America), in: Postavy naší Ameriky. Praha: Pražská edice, 2000, pp. 143-144.

John Rosický (1845-1910)

Rosicky, Rose, "Rosický, John," in: History of Czechs (Bohemians) in Nebraska. Omaha, NE: Czech Historical Society of Nebraska, 1929, pp. 407-409.

Rechcigl, Miloslav, Jr., "Kulturní budovatel české Nebrasky" (Cultural builder of Czech Nebraska), in: Postavy naší Ameriky. Praha: Pražská edice, 2000, pp. 148-150.

Rosa Sonneschein (1847-1932)

Porter, Jack Nusan. "Rosa Sonneschein and The American Jewess: The First Independent English Language Jewish Women's Journal in the United States." American Jewish History, 67 (September 1978): 57-63.

Porter, Jack Nusan, "Rosa Sonneschein and The American Jewess Revisited: New Historical Information on an Early American Zionist and Jewish Feminist." American Jewish Archives, 32 (1980): 125-131

Arthur Ochs Sulzberger (1926-)

Diamond, Edwin, Behind the Times: Inside the New York Times. Chicago: University of Chicago Press, 1993. 450p.

Jones, Alex S. and Susan E. Tifft, The Trust: The Private and Powerful Family Behind The New York Times, Back Bay Books, 2000.

D. Literature

1. General

Sládek, J. V., Americké obrazky a jiná prósa (American sketches and other prose). Ed. by Ferdinand Strejček. Prague: J. Otto, 1907. 2 vols.

Čapek, Tomáš, "Soupis knih a tiskopisů" (Inventory of books and prints), in: Padesát let českého tisku v Americe. New York: Bank of Europe, 1911, pp. 187-243.

Den, Peter, "Czech Poets in Exile," in: Czechoslovakia Past and Present. Edited by Miloslav Rechcigl, Jr. The Hague—Paris, 1968, pp. 860-868.

Martínek, Josef. "One Hundred Years of Czech Poetry in America." In Panorama: A Historical Review of Czechs and Slovaks in the United States of America, 1970, pp. 78-81.

Šturm, Rudolf, "Czech Literature in America," in: Ethnic Literature since 1776. The Many Voices of America. Lubbock, TX: Tech. University Press, 1978, pp. 161-172.

Hora, Václav, "Česká a slovenská literatura mimo Československo, 1948-1987 (Czech and Slovak literature outside Czechoslovakia). Frankfurt: Dialog, 1987. 198p.

Kovtun, George J., Czech and Slovak Literature in English. Washington, DC: Library of Congress, 1988.

Hribal, C. J., Ed. The Boundaries of Twilight: Czecho-Slovak Writing from the New World. Minneapolis, MN: New Rivers Press, 1991.

Zach, Aleš, Kniha a český exil 1949-1990. (Book and Czech exile 1949-1990). Praha: Torst, 1995. 208p.

Knopp, František, Česká literatura v exilu (Czech literature in exile). Praha: Makropulos, 1996.

Papoušek, Vladimír, "Českoamerická poezie na počátku dvacátého století" (Czech-American poetry at the beginning of the 20th century), Estetika, 36, No. 1-3 (1999), pp.4-66.

Papoušek, Vladimír, Beletristická tvorba Čechoameričanů 1880-1914 (Czech-American fiction in the years 1880-1914). Praha: Edice Tvary, 2000. Sv. 16-17.

Papoušek, Vladimír, Česká literatura v Chicagu. Literární tvorba Čechoameričanů v letech 1880-1939 (Czech literature in Chicago.

Literary works of Czech-Americans in 1880-1939), Olomouc, 2001.

Papoušek, Vladimír, Trojí samota ve velké zemi. Česká literatura v americkém exilu v letech 1938-1968 (Tripple solitude in a big country. Czech literature in American exile in the years 1938-1968). Jihočany: H+H, 2001. 218p.

Papoušek, Vladimír, "Česká literatura v americkém kontextu a otázky literární historie" (Czech literature in American context and the literary history issues) in: Národní kontexty národní kultury. České Budějovice, 2004, pp. 75-89.

Sabatos, Charles, "Czech American Literature," in: The Greenwood Encyclopedia of Multiethnic American Literature. Edited by Emanuel S. Nelson. Westport, CT: Greenwood Press, 2005, pp. 536-541.

Machala, Lubomír, "Plody českého a slovenského literárního exilu po druhé světové válce" (Fruits of Czech and Slovak literary exile after the World War II), in: Sdružení knihoven České Republiky, Brno, 2010, pp. 8-12.

2. Individuals

Pavel Albieri (1861-1901)

Machann, Clinton, Evidence of Assimilation in Pavel Albieri's Nevěsta za padesát dolarů (Bride for Fifty Dollars)," Nebraska History, 74, No. 3 & 4 (Fall/ Winter 1993), pp. 183-188.

James T. Flexner (1908-2003)

"Flexner, James Thomas," in: World Authors 1970-1975. New York: H. W. Wilson, 1980, pp. 262-264.

Martin, Douglas, "James Thomas Flexner, Washington Biographer, 95, Dies," New York Times February 16, 2003.

Egon Hostovský (1908-1973)

"Hostovský, Egon—Obituary," New York Times, May 8, 1973, p. 46.

"Hostovský, Egon," in: World Authors 1950-1970.New York: H. W. Wilson, 1965.

Papoušek, Vladimír, Egon Hostovský. Člověk v uzavřeném prostoru. Praha: Nakladatelství H&H, 1996.188p.

Papoušek, Vladimír, "Egon Hostovský," in: Dictionary of Literary Biography. Vol. 215. Edited by Steven Serafin. Detroit, MI: Gale Research, 1999, pp. 120-128.

Arnošt Lustig (1926-2011)

"Arnošt Lustig 1925-," Contemporary Literary Criticism 56, pp. 181-190.

Haman, Aleš, "Man in a Violent World: The Fiction of Arnošt Lustig," Kosmas 11, No. 1 (Summer 1992), pp. 73-80.

Haman, Aleš, Arnošt Lustig. Praha: Nakladatelství H&H, 1995.104p.

Zdeněk Němeček (1894-1957)

Herben, Ivan, Zdeněk Němeček, spisovatel, básník, dramatik, legionář a diplomat (Zdeněk Němeček, writer, poet, legionnaire and diplomat). New York: Moravian Library, 1957. 34p.

Jan Novak (1953-)

Navara, Luděk, "Na obou stranách Atlantiku" (On Both Sides of the Atlantic), MF Dnes, 11. listopadu 2005.

Frederick Prokosch (1908-1989)

Squires, Radcliffe, Frederic Prokosch. New York: Twayne Publishers, 1964.

"Frederick Prokosch, 1908-", Contemporary Literary Criticism, 48, pp. 301-318.

Charles Sealsfield (1793-1864)

Uhlendorf, Bernhard Alexander, Charles Sealsfield. Ethnic Elements and National Problems in His Works. A Doctoral Thesis. Chicago: University of Illinois, 1922.

Jordan, E. L., America Glorious and Chaotic Land. Charles Sealsfield Discovers the Young United States. Upper Saddle, NJ: Prentice-Hall, 1969.

Schuchalter, Jerry, Frontier and Utopia in the Fiction of Charles Sealsfield. Frankfurt am Main—New York: Peter Lang, 1986. 337p.

Josef Václav Sládek (1845-1912)

Šturm, Rudolf, "America in the Life and Work of the Czech Poet Josef Sládek," Harvard Slavic Studies 2(1954), pp. 287-296.

Chroust, David Z., "Josef Václav Sládek (1845-1912) as an Interpreter and Example of the Czech American Experience," Kosmas, 15, No. 2 (Spring 2002), pp. 27-34.

Joseph Wechsberg (1907-1983)

"Joseph Wechsberg," in: Current Biography Yearbook, 1955, pp. 638-640.

Wechsberg, Joseph, Looking for a Bluebird. Westport, CT: Greenwood Press, 1974. 210p.

Franz Weiskopf (1900-1955)

"Weiskopf, Franz," in: Twentieth Century Authors, Suppl. 1, pp. 1059-1060.

Franz Werfel (1890-1945)

Franz Werfel, 1890-1945. Ed. Lore Barbara Foltin. Pittsburgh: University of Pittsburgh Press, 1961. 102p.

Fox, W. H., "Franz Werfel," in: German Men of Letters. Ed Alex Natan. Wolff, 1964, pp. 107-125.

Jungk, Peter Stephan, Franz Werfel. New York: Grove Weidenfeld, 1990. 318p.

E. Music

1. General

Fries, Adelaide Lisetta, Funeral Chorals of the Unitas Fratrum of Moravian Church. Raleigh, NC: Edwards & Broughton, 1905. 23p.

Nettl, Paul, "Czech Musicians at Home and Far Away," in: Modern Music, 17 (1940), pp. 160-163.

Löwenbach, Jan, "Czech Composers and Musicians in America," Musical Quarterly, 29 (1943), pp. 313-28.

Löwenbach, Jan, Hudba v Americe (Music in America). Praha: Hudební matice umělecké besedy, 1948. 120p.

Masaryk, Alice G., "Hudba ve Spillville" (Music in Spillville). New York: SVU Press, 1963. 15p.

Machann, Clinton, "Country-Western Music and the 'Now' Sound in Texas Czech Polka Music," JEMF Quarterly, 1969 (1983), pp. 3-7.

Karas, Joža, "Czechoslovak Musicians Abroad," in: Studies in Czechoslovak History. Ed. by Miloslav Rechcigl, Jr. Meerut: Sadhna Prakashan, 1976, Vol. 1, pp. 300-313.

Karas, Joža, "The Role of Czechs and Slovaks in the Development of American Music," Sci. Tech. Hum., 11, No.3 (Fall 1980), pp. 293-302.

Kučera, Vladimír, Czech Music in Nebraska. NE: Author, 1980.

Czech Music in Texas. Papers from Czech Music in Texas: A Sesquicentennial Symposium. Edited by Clinton Machann. College Station, TX: Komensky Press, 1988. 182p.

Sovík, Thomas, "Music of the American Moravians," Czechoslovak and Central European Journal, 9 (1990), pp. 35-46.

Keil, Charles, Angeliki V. Keil and Dick Blau, Polka Happiness. Philadelphia: Temple University Press, 1992.

Greene, Victor, A Passion for Polka: Old-Time Ethnic Music in America. Berkeley: University of Califiornia Press, 1992.

Leary, James P., Czech American Polka Music in Wisconsin" in: Music of Multicultural America: A Study of Twelve Musical Communities. Ed. by Kip Lornell and K. Rasmussen. New York: Schirmer, 1997, pp. 25-47.

Johnston, Jesse, "Performing 'Českost' (Czechness): Polka Music & Musical Ethnicity at Wisconsin Czech-American Festivals," in: Selected Papers from the 22nd World Congress of the Czechoslovak Society of Arts and Sciences, Palacký University, Olomouc, June 26th to July 4, 2004. Olomouc: Repronis, pp. 132-138.

Vičár, Jan, "Some Roots of the Music American Moravians," in: Contributions of the Moravian Brethren to America. Selected Papers from the Conference of the Czechoslovak Society of Arts and Sciences at the Moravian College, Bethlehem, PA, June 8-10, 2007, pp. 157-163.

Folkins, Gail, Texas Dance Halls: A Two-step Circuit. Lubbock, TX: Texas Technical University Press, 2007. 208p.

2. Individuals

Antonín Dvořák (1841-1904)

Arvey, Verna, Antonín Dvořák and American Music," Common Ground, 2 (Winter 1942), pp. 84-88.

Masaryk, Alice Garrigue, Hudba ve Spillville (Music in Spillville). New York, SVU Press, 1963.19p.

Ivanov, Miroslav, Novosvětská (The New World Symphony). Praha: Panorama 1984, 416p.

Tibbets, John C., Ed., Dvořák in America, 1892-1895. Pompton Plains, NJ: Amadeus Press, 1993. 452 p.

Beckerman, Michael B., New Worlds of Dvořák: Searching in America for the Composer's Inner Life. New York: W.W. Norton & Co., 1999. 200p.

Rudolf Firkušný (1912-1994)

Ewen, David, "Firkušný, Rudolf," in: Living Musicians. New York: H. W. Wilson, 1957, Suppl. 1, pp. 54-55.

"Firkušný, Rudolf," Current Biography (1979), pp.136-139.

Rudolf Friml (1879-1972)

Ewen, David, "Friml, Rudolf," in: Complete Book of the American Musical Theater. Holt, 1958, pp. 91-97.

Paris, Leonard Allen, "Friml, Rudolf," in: Man and Melodies. New York: Crowell, 1959, pp. 49-58.

Green, Stanley, "Rudolf Friml 1879-1972," in: World of Musical Comedy. 3rd ed. New York: Barnes, 1974, pp. 37-47.

Everett, William, Rudolf Friml. Champaign, IL: University of Illinois Press, 2008. 152p.

Anthony Philip Heinrich (1781-1861)

Upton, William Treat, Anthony Philip Heinrich. New York: Columbia University Press, 1939. 337p.

Howard, John Tasker, "Anton Philip Heinrich," in: Our American Music. New York: Crowell, 1965, pp. 226-238.

Marie Jeritza (1887-1982)

Wymetal, Wilhelm, Maria Jeritza. Wien-Leipzig, 1922. 51p.

Jeritza, Maria, Sunlight and Life: A Singer's Life. New York: D. Appleton & Co., 1924. 261p.

Rechcigl, Miloslav, Jr. "Sopranistka světové pověsti" (Sopranist of world fame), in: Postavy naší Ameriky. Praha: Pražská edice, 2000, pp. 221-223.

Jerome David Kern (1885-1945)

Fordin, Hugh. Jerome Kern: the Man and his Music Santa Monica, CA, 1975

Freedland, M. Jerome Kern: A Biography. London, 1978.

Bordman, Gerald. Jerome Kern: His Life and Music. New York, 1980.

Banfield, Stephen and Geoffrey Holden Block. Jerome Kern, New Haven, Connecticut, Yale University Press, 2006.

Erich Wolfgang Korngold (1897-1957)

Hoffmann, Rudolf Stephan, Erich Wolfgang Korngold. Wien: C. Stephenson, 1922. 129p.

Rechcigl, Miloslav, Jr, "Brňan, který zhudebnil Hollywood" (Brno native who brought music to Hollywood), in: Postavy naší Ameriky. Praha: Pražská edice, 2000, pp. 211-213.

Ernst Krenek (1900-1991)

Ewen, David, "Krenek, Ernst," in: Book of Modern Composers. 2nd ed. Knopf, 1950, pp. 353—362.

Krenek, Ernst, Exploring Music. New York: Riverrum, 1968. 248 p.

Phillips, A., A Salute to Ernst Krenek," Biogr. News., 2 (1975), pp. 370-371.

Max Maretzek (1821-1897)

Maretzek, Max, Crotchets and Quavers or Revelations of an Opera Manager in America. New York: S. French, 1855. 346 p. Reprinted—New York: De Capo Press, 1966.

Maretzek, Max, Sharps and Flats. New York: American Music Publishing Co., 1890. 87p.

Schonberg, Harold C., "The Don Quixote of Opera," American Heritage Magazine, 27, Issue 2 (February 1976).

Bohuslav Martinů (1890-1959)

Šafránek, Miloš, Bohuslav Martinů: His Life and Works. London: Wingate, 1962. 367p.

Clapham, John, Martinu's Instrumental Style," Music Review, 24 (1963), pp. 158-167.

Jarmila Novotná (1907-1994)

Matz, Mary Jane, "Novotná, Jarmila," in: Opera Stars in the Sun. New York: Farrar & Straus, 1955, pp. 22-27.

Rasponi, Lanfranco, The Last Prima Donnas. Alfred A Knopf, 1982

Artur Schnabel (1882-1951)

Searchinger, Cesar, Artur Schnabel. Westport, CT: Greenwood Press, 1973.

Wolff, Konrad, The Teaching of Artur Schnabel. New York: Prager, 1972. 189p.

Schnabel, Artur, My Life and Music. New York: Dover, 1988. 288p.

Arnold Schoenberg (1874-1951)

Rosen, Charles, Arnold Schoenberg. Chicago: University of Chicago Press, 1996. 128p.

Shawn, Allen, Arnold Schoenberg's Journey. New York: Farrar Straus and Giroux, 2002.

Ernestine Schumann-Heink (1861-1936)

Lawton, Mary, Schumann-Heink: The Last of the Titans. New York: Macmillan Co., 1928

Zwart, Ann Townsend, "Schumann-Heink, Ernestine," Notable Women, Vol. 3, pp. 240-242.

Rudolf Serkin (1903-1991)

"Serkin, Rudolf," Current Biography 1940 (1940), pp. 725-726.

Chasins, Abrams, "Rudolf Serkin," in: Speaking of Pianists. New York: Knopf, 1957, pp. 130-135.

Kolodin, I., "Complete Musician (Rudolf Serkin)," Horicon 4 (1961), pp. 82-87.

Lehman, Stephen and Marion Faber, Rudolf Serkin. A L ife. New York: Oxford University Press, 2002. 344p.

Jaromir Weinberger (1896-1967)

Ewen, David, "Weinberger, Jaromir," in: American Composers Today. New York: H. W. Wilson, 1949, pp. 258-260.

Rechcigl, Miloslav, Jr., "Skladatel, který zvěčnil Švandu dudáka" (Composer who immortalized Schwanda the Piper), in: Postavy naší Ameriky. Praha: Pražská edice, 2000, pp. 205-206.

F. Visual Art

1. General

Dvořáková, Jarmila, Umělec na útěku. Uprchlíci ve výtvarném umění (Artists on the Run. The visual art refugees). Toronto: Naše hlasy, 1960. 32p.

Šejnoha, Jaroslav, Svědectví a zkazky z umění výtvarného (Testimony and stories from visual art). Toronto: Nový domov, 1963. 13p.

Rechcigl, Miloslav, Jr., "První čeští umělci v Americe," in: Za tím mořem piva (in preparation).

2. Individuals

Oscar Berger (1901-1997)

Berger, Oscar, Famous Faces; Caricaturist's Scrapbook. London, Hutchinson. 1950,

Berger, Oscar, My Victims. How to Caricature. Harper & Bros. NY. 1952.

Charles Demuth (1883-1935)

Farnham, Emily, Charles Demuth. Norman: University of Oklahoma Press, 1971.

Haskell, Barbara, Charles Demuth. New York: Whitney Museum of American Art and H. N. Abrams, 1987. 240p.

Leopold Eidlitz (1823-1908)

Schuyler, Montgomery, "A Great American Architect: Leopold Eidlitz," The Architectural Record, 34 (1908), 163-179, 277-292, 364-378.

Holliday, Kathryn E., Leopold Eidlitz: Architecture and Idealism in the Gilded Age. New York, NY: W.W. Norton & Co., 2008. 200p.

Will Eisner (1917-2005)

Eisner, Will, The Will Eisner Sketchbook. Dark Horse, 2004. 200p.

Andelman, Bob, Will Eisner: A Spirited Life. An Authorized Biography, M Press, 2005.352p.

Eisner, Will, Life, in Pictures: Autobiographical Stories. W. W. Norton & Company, 2007. 496p.

Harrison Fisher (1877-1934

Fisher, Harrison and James Beebee Carrington, The Harrison Fisher Book: a Collection of Drawings in Colors and Back and White. C. Scribner's Sons, 1907.

Wanda Gág (1893-1946)

Gág, Wanda, Growing Pains: Diaries and Drawings for the Year 1908-1917. New York: Cowan-McCann, 1940. 479p.

Scott, Alma Olivia, Wanda Gág: The Story of the Artist, Minneapolis: University of Minnesota Press, 1949. 235p.

Hoyle, Karen Nelson, Wanda Gág. Minneapolis: University of Minnesota Press, 2009.

Victor Gruen (1903-1980)

Wall, Alex, Victor Gruen: From Urban Shop to New City. Barcelona-New York: Actar, 2006. 270p.

Hardwick, M. Jeffrey, Mall Maker: Victor Gruen, Architect of an American Dream. Philadelphia: University of Pennsylvania Press, 2010. 288p.

Frank L. Jirouch (1878-1970)

Prantner, E. F., "Frank L. Jirouch," These Help Build America. Chicago: The Czechoslovak Review, 1922, pp. 69-74.

Mario Korbel (1882-1954)

"Korbel, Mario—Obituary," New York Times, April 1, 1954.

Alois Lecoque Kohout (1891-1981)

Trnka, Jaroslav, Al. Lecoque. Paris: Recontres, 1955. 63p.

Probst, Vojtěch, "Lví život Kohouta," Litrerární noviny, January 25, 2011.

Alphonse Mucha (1860-1939)

Lees, Frederic, "A Great Decorative Artist, Alphonse Marie Mucha," Magazine of Art, 23 (1899), pp. 272-277.

Mucha, Jiří, Alphonse Mucha. His Life and Art. New York: Humanities Press, 1966. 391p.

Mucha, Jiří, Alphonse Mucha. The Master of Art Nouveau. Praha: Artia, 1966. 291p.

Chyle, Faith, "A Valuable Painting in a Modest North Dakota Church," Red River Valley Historian, 1, No. 4 (October 1967), pp. 16-22.

Richard Joseph Neutra (1892-1970)

Hines, Thomas, Richard Neutra and the Search for Modern Architecture. Oxford University Press, 1982.

Lamprecht, Barbara, Richard Neutra: Complete Works. Taschen, 2000.

Lamprecht, Barbara, Richard Neutra, 1892-1970: Survival through Design. Taschen, 2004.

Lavin, Sylvia, Form Follows Libido: Architecture and Richard Neutra in a Psychoanalytic Culture. Cambridge: MIT Press, 2005.

Albin Polášek (1879-1965)

"Věhlasný sochař Albin Polášek" (Renowned sculptor Albin Polášek). Amerikán, Národní kalendář, 74 (1951), pp. 21-24.

Sherwood, Ruth, Carving His Own Destiny: The Story of Albin Polášek, Chicago: Ralph Fletcher Seymour, Publisher, 1954. 466p.

Polasek, Emily, Albin Polášek. Winter Park, FL: 1960. 107p.

Vojtěch Preissig (1872-1944)

Vlček, Tomáš, Vojtěch Preissig—grafika a malba 1932-1938 (Vojtěch Preissig—graphics and paintings 1932-1938). Katalog výstavy, Galerie výtvarného umění v Roudnici nad Labem, 1983.

Rudolph Růžička (1883-1978)

Updyke, E. B., "Rudolph Ruzicka—an appreciation," Printing Art, 30 (1917), pp. 17-24.

The Engraved and Typographic Work of Rudolph Růžička. New York: Grolier Club, 1948. 36p.

Lathem, Edward Connery, Rudolph Růžička. Speaking Reminiscently. New York: Grolier Club, 1986. 150, 26p.

Paul Strand (1890-1976)
Stange, Maren, Ed., Paul Strand: Essays on his Life and Work. Aperture, 1991.320p.
Szegedy-Maszak, Andrew and Paul Strand, Toward a Deeper Understanding: Paul Strand at Work. Steidl/Aperture Foundation/ Pace/MacGill Gallery, 2007.

Ladislav Sutnar (1897-1976)
Heller, Steve, "The designer must think first, work later,' declared Ladislav Sutnar," Eye, 13 (1994).
Ladislav Sutnar—Obituary," Publishers Weekly, December 27, 1976.
Sutnar, Ladislav and Mildred Constantine, Ladislav Sutnar: Visual Design in Action. Brooklyn, NY: Five Ties Publishing, 2006. 196p.

F. Drama and Dance

1. General

Památník Ludvíkovy divadelní společnosti na oslavu desetiletého trvání divadla v Chicagu 1893-1901 (Memorial of Ludvík Theatrical Company on the occasion of the 10th anniversary of the Czech theater in Chicago). Chicago, ca 1903. 52p.
Kučera, Vladimír. Czech Dramas in Nebraska. Lincoln, NE: Author, 1979.
Murphy, David, "Dramatic Expressions: Czech Theatre Curtains in Nebraska," Nebraska History, 74, No. 3 and 4 (Fall / Winter 1993), pp. 168-82
Czechoslovak-American Puppetry. Edited by Vít Hořejš. New York: GOH Productions / Seven Loaves, 1994. 80p.
Srba, Bořivoj, Divadelní a kulturní aktivity českých politických emigrantů a zahraničních krajanů v letech druhé světové války" (Theatrical and cultural activities of Czech political emigrants and our countrymen abroad during World War II), Estetika, 36, No. 1-3 (1999), pp. 8-26.

Czech and Slovak Theatre Abroad. Věra Bořkovec, Ed. Boulder, CO: East European Monographs, 2006. 128p.

Rechcigl, Miloslav, Jr., "První čeští umělci v Americe," in: Za tím mořem piva (in preparation).

2. Individuals

Fred Astaire (1899-1987)

Freeland, Michael. Fred Astaire. An Illustrated Biography. Grosset & Dunlap, 1976.

Billman, Larry. Fred Astaire—A Bio-bibliography, Greenwood Press, 1997,

Boyer, G. Bruce. Fred Astaire Style, Assouline, 2005.

Epstein, Joseph, Fred Astaire. New Haven, CT: Yale University Press, 2009. 224p.

Garofalo, Alessandra, Austerlitz Sounded Too Much Like a Battle: The Roots of Fred Astaire Family in Europe. Editrice UNI Service, 2009.

Martin Beck (1867-1948)

Downer, Alan S., "Beck, Martin, in: Dictionary of American Biography, Suppl. 2, pp.32-33.

Miloš Forman (1932-)

"Forman, Miloš", Current Biography Yearbook, 1971 (1982), pp. 138-140.

Slater, Thomas J., Miloš Forman: A Bio-Bibliography. Westport, CT: Greenwood Press, 1987. 208p.

Oscar Homolka (1901-1978)

"Homolka, Oscar 1901-1978—Obituary," New York Times, January 29.1978.

Franziska Magdalena R. Janauschek (1830-1904)

McKay, Frederick E., and Charles E. Wingate, "Mme. Janauschek," in: Famous American Actors of Today. New York: Crowell, 1896, pp. 18-25.

Rechcigl, Miloslav, Jr., "Tragédka světové pověsti" (Tragedist of world fame), in: Postavy naší Ameriky. Praha: Pražská edice, 2000, pp. 231-233.

John Kříža (1919-1975)

"John Kříža of Ballet Theater, US Dance Pioneer Dies at 56," New York Tmes, August 29, 1976.

Kim Novak (1933-)

Fritch, Charles, E., Goddess of Love. Derby, CT: Monarch Books, 1962. 139p.

Brown, Peter H., Kim Novak. Reluctant Goddess. New York: St. Martin Press, 1986. 276p.

Rechcigl, Miloslav, Jr., "Česká Marilyn" (Czech Marilyn), in: Postavy naší Ameriky. Praha: Pražská edice, 2000, pp. 240-242.

Walter Slezak (1902-1983)

"Slezak, Walter," Current Biography, 1955 (1956), pp. 556-558.

Rechcigl, Miloslav, Jr., "Všestranný herec (Versatile actor), in: Postavy naší Ameriky. Praha: Pražská edice, 2000, pp. 234-236.

Sissy Spacek (1949-)

"Spacek, Sissy," Current Biography, 1978 (1979), pp.397-400.

Rechcigl, Miloslav, Jr., "Herečka s texaským přízvukem" (Actress with a Texas Accent), in: Postavy naší Ameriky. Praha: Pražská edice, 2000, pp. 243-245.

George Voskovec (1905-1981)

White, James T., "George Voskovec," in: Notable Names in the American Theatre. A Biographical Record of the Contemporary Stage. 16th ed. Pitman, 1977.

"George Voskovec—Obituary," New York Times, July 3, 1981.

Rechcigl, Miloslav, Jr., "Z Osvobozeného divadla na Broadway" (From 'Osvobozené divadlo' to Broadway), in: Postavy naší Ameriky. Praha: Pražská edice, 2000, pp. 237-239.

Blanche Yurka (1887-1974)

Yurka, Blanche, Bohemian Girl: Blanche's Yurka's Theatrical Life. Athens, GA: Ohio University Press, 1970. 306p.

Meserve, Walter J., Yurka, Blanche, June 19, 1887-June 6, 1974, Actress," in: Notable Women: The Modern Period, vol. 4, pp. 754-756.

G. Sports

1. General

Jičinský, J. R., Tracing the History of the American Sokols, 1865-1908. Chicago, 1908.

Jelínek, Jarka and Jaroslav Zmrhal, Sokol Educational and Physical Culture Association. Chicago: American Sokol Union, 1944. 112p.

Centennial of the Sokol in America, 1865-1965. Chicago: American Sokol Organization, 1965.

Nolte, Claire E., "Our Brothers across the Ocean: The Czech Sokol in America to 1914." Czechoslovak and Central European Journal, 11, No. 2 (Winter 1993), pp. 15-37.

Nerada, Zdeněk, Sparta Chicago 80. Chicago, 1996.

Rechcigl, Miloslav, Jr., "Czechs," in: Encyclopedia of Ethnicity and Sports in the United States. Edited by George E. Kirsch, Othello Harris, and Claire E. Nolte. Westport, CT—London: Greenwood Press, 2000, pp.122-127.

2. Individuals

Laddie Bakanic (1924-)

Bakanic, Ladislava 'Laddie,' in: Encyclopedia of Ethnicity and Sports in the United States. Ed. By George B. Kirsch, Othello Harris and Claire E. Nolte. Westport, CT: Greenwood Press, 2000, pp. 41-42.

George Blanda (1927-)

Twombly, Wells, Blanda, Alive and Kicking. The exclusive, authorized biography. Nash Pub, 1972. 305p.

George Halas (1895-1993)

Halas, George, Halas by Halas: The Autobiography of George Halas. New York: McGraw-Hill. 1979. 351p.

Davis, Jeff, Papa Bear: The Life and Legacy of George Halas. New York: McGraw-Hill, 2006. 544p.

McCaskey, Patrick, and Mike Sandrolini, Bear With Me: A Family History of George Halas and the Chicago Bears. Triumph Book, 2009. 224p.

Dominik Hašek (1965-)

Shultz, Randy, Dominik Hašek: The Dominator. Sports Publishing LLC, 2001. 128p.

John Havlíček (1940-)

"Havlíček, John," in: Encyclopedia of Ethnicity and Sports in the United States. Ed. George B. Kirsch, Othello Harris and Claire E. Nolte. Westport, CT: Greenwood Press, 2000, pp. 208-209.

Kent Hrbek (1960-)

Brackin, Dennis, Kent Hrbek's Tales from the Minnesota Twins Dugout. Sports Publishing, 2008. 192p.

Jaromír Jágr (1972-)

Jágr, Jaromír and, Jan Šmíd and Louis Charbonneau, Jágr: An Autobiography. Warwick Publishing Group, 1997. 285 p.

Frank Kříž (1893-1955)

"Kříž, Frank," in: Encyclopedia of Ethnicity and Sports in the United States. Ed. George B. Kirsch, Othello Harris and Claire E. Nolte. Westport, CT. Greenwood Press,2000, p. 275.

Ivan Lendl (1960-)

Eliot, Chip, Ivan Lendl. Mankato, MN: Crestwood House, 1988. 48p.

Czechoslovak Immigrants to the United States: Ivan Lendl. Books LLC, 2010. 34p.

Ivan Lendl. Eds. Frederic P. Miller, Agnes F. Vandome and John McBrewster. Alphascript Publishing, 2010. 120p.

Stanley Frank Musial (1920-)

Stewart, Wayne, Stan the Man: The Life and Times of Stan Musial. Triumph Books, 2010. 256p.

Martina Navrátilová (1956-)

Blue, Adrianne, The Lives and Times with Martina Navrátilová. New York: Carol Publishing Corporation 1995. 227p.

Howard, Johnette, The Rivals: Chris Evert vs. Martina Navrátilová Their Epic Duels and Extraordinary Friendship. Broadway, 2006. 304p.

IX. Scholarship—Science—Technology

A. General

Rechcigl, Miloslav Jr. and Jiří Nehněvajsa, "American Scholars and Scientists with Czechoslovak Roots—Some Key Characteristics," Journal of Washington Academy of Sciences, 58 (1968), pp. 213-22.

Rechcigl, Miloslav Jr., Educators with Czechoslovak Roots: U.S. and Canadian Faculty Roster. Washington: SVU Press, 1980. 122p.

Rechcigl, Miloslav Jr., "Czech Contributions to American Scientific and Technological Thought," Kosmas. Czechoslovak and Central European Journal, 12, No. 1 (Summer 1996), pp. 81-99.

Rechcigl, Miloslav, Jr., "Čeští a slovenští lékaři, přírodovědci a technici na americkém kontinentu" (Czechs and Slovak physicians, scientists and engineers on the American Continent), in: Acta Historiae Rerum Naturalium Necnon Technicarum—Prague Studies in the History of Science and Technology, Vol. 7. Prague: National Technical Museum, 2003, pp. 267-274.

Rechcigl, Miloslav, Jr., "NAS Members with Czech or Slovak Roots," in: Czechs and Slovaks in America. Boulder, CO: East European Monographs and New York: Columbia University Press, 2005, pp. 139-148.

Rechcigl, Miloslav, Jr.: "Czechoslovak Society of Arts and Sciences (SVU): Historical Milestones in its Development and Activities," in: Czechs and Slovaks in America. Boulder, CO: East European

Monographs and New York: Columbia University Press, 2005, pp. 149-160.

Pacner, Karel, František Houdek and Libuše Koubská, Čeští vědci v exilu (Czech scientists in exile). Praha: Univerzita Karlova, 2007. 360p.

Rechcigl, Miloslav, Jr. "SVU in the Formative Years," Kosmas, 22, No. 1 (Fall 3008), pp. 87-99.

Rechcigl, Miloslav, Jr., On Behalf of their Homeland: Fifty Years of SVU. An Eyewitness Account of the History of the Czechoslovak Society of Arts and Sciences (SVU). Boulder, CO: East European Monographs and New York: Columbia University Press, 2008. 668p. & illustrations.

Rechcigl, Miloslav, Jr., Exiloví vědci po roce 1948 a jejich organizování v zahraničí" (Exile scientists after 1948 and their organization abroad), in: Semináře a studie k dějinám vědy. Práce z dějin vědy, svazek 21. Praha: Kabinet dějin vědy, 2009, pp. 165-186.

Kostlán, Antonín, "Vědecký exil v období komunistického režimu: Emigrace z Československé akademie věd" (Exile scientists during the era of Communist regime: Emigration from Czechoslovak Academy of Sciences), Dějiny a technika, 43, No.3 (2010), pp. 153-181.

Mandelíčková, Monika, "Czech History in Exile," in: Contributions of Czechs and Slovaks to Science and Technology in the 21st Century. Selected Papers from the Twenty-fifth Congress of the Czechoslovak Society of Arts and Sciences, Tábor, Czech Republic, June 27-July 3, 2010. New York: Publishing House of the Czechoslovak Society of Arts and Sciences, 2011, pp. 131-136.

Rechcigl, Miloslav, Jr. "Czech and Slovak Recipients of the Highest Recognition the World Can Provide," in: Contributions of Czechs and Slovaks to Science and Technology in the 21st Century, op. cit., pp. 195-210.

Kostlán, Antonín, "Útěky do emigrace a Československá akademie věd" (Escapes to emigration and the Czechoslovak Academy of Sciences), in: Sto českých vědců v exilu. K vydání připravili Soňa Štrbáňová a Antonín Kostlán. Praha: Academia, 2011, pp. 19-207.

Rechcigl, Miloslav, Jr., "Accomplished Young American Professionals of Czech / Slovak Extraction," (in press).

B. Humanities

1. General

Kučera, Henry, "Czech Linguistics in the United States," in: Studies in Ethnicity: The East European Experience in America. Ed. by Charles A. Ward, Philip Shashko and Donald E. Pienkos. New York: Columbia University Press, 1981, pp. 27-37.

Luža, Radomír V., "Česká exilová historiografie a naše nedávná minulost v pohledu zblízka a z druhé strany Atlantiku" (Czech exile historiography and our recent past from a close look and from behind the second side of the Atlantic), in: Rozmluvy s historiky. Praha, 2005, pp. 85-102.

Mandelíčková, Monika, "Czech History in Exile," in: Contributions of Czechs and Slovaks to Science and Technology in the 21st Century. Selected Papers from the Twenty-fifth Congress of the Czechoslovak Society of Arts and Sciences, Tabor, Czech Republic, June 27-July 3, 2010. New York: Publishing House of the Czechoslovak Society of Arts and Sciences, 2011, pp. 131-136.

Rechcigl, Miloslav, Jr. "První čeští učenci a sociální vědci v Americe" (First Czech scholars and scientists in America), in: Za tím mořem piva (in preparation).

2. Individuals

Thomas Čapek (1861-1950)

Chroust, David Zdeněk, "Futile is the Work of the Father and Grandfather which the Son and Grandson Willfully Destroy: Thomas Čapek's Achievements in Preserving Czech-American Sources, Kosmas, 13, No. 1 (Fall 1998), pp. 169-184.

Chroust, David Zdeněk, "Toward a Biography of Thomas Čapek (1861-1950): Sources, Life Sketch and Biographical Models," in: Czech Americans in Transition. Ed. By Clinton Machann. Austin, TX: 1999, pp. 97-120,

Francis Dvornik (1893-1975)

Tribute to Francis Dvorník. Harvard Slavic Studies, Vol. II, Cambridge, MA: Harvard University Press, 1954, 390p.

Rechcigl, Miloslav, Jr., "Byzantolog světové pověsti" (Byzantologist of world fame), in: Postavy naší Ameriky. Praha: Pražská edice, 2000, pp. 253-255.

Herbert Feigl (1902-1988)

Savage, C. Wade, "Obituary for Herbert Feigl," Erkenntnis, 31, No. 1 (Jul., 1989), pp. v-ix

Erich Heller (1911-1990)

Flint, Peter B., "Dr. Erich Heller, Professor, 79; A Scholar of German Philosophy," New York Times, November 8, 1990.

Erich von Kahler (1885-1970)

"Kahler, Erich," in: International Encyclopedia of the Social Sciences. New York: Free Press, 1970, vol. 8, pp. 365-366.

Lauer, Gerhard, Die verspätete Revolution: Erich von Kahler. Wissenschaftsgeschichte zwischen konservativer Revolution und Exil, Berlin u. New York, de Gruyter, 1995 (Philosophie und Wissenschaft. Bd. 6),

Robert Joseph Kerner (1887-1958)

"Kerner, Robert Joseph," in: National Cyclopedia of American Biography, Current Series A, 1930, p. 293.

Rechcigl, Miloslav, Jr., "Wilsonův poradce pro evropské otázky" (Wilson's adviser on European issues), in: Postavy naší Ameriky. Praha: Pražská edice, 2000, pp. 247-249.

Hans Kohn (1891-1971)

Wolf, Ken, "Kohn, Hans," in: International Encyclopedia of the Social Sciences, vol. 18, pp.388-391.

Wolf, Ken, "Kohn's Liberal Nationalism: The Historian as Prophet," J. Hist. Ideas, 37 (1976), pp. 651-672.

Ernest Nagel (1901-1985)

Morgenbesser, Sydney, "Nagel, Ernest," in: International Encyclopedia of the Social Sciences. Biographical Supplement, 1979, pp. 78-84.

Otakar Odložilík (1899-1973)

Czech Renaissance of the Nineteenth Century: Essays presented to Otakar Odložilík in Honor of his Seventieth Birthday. Eds. Peter Brock and H. Gordon Skilling. Toronto: University of Toronto Press, 1970.

Němec, Ludvík, "Professor Otakar Odložilík. Czech Historian and Apostle of Czechoslovak National Tradition," East European Quarterly, 8, No. 1 (1974), pp. 5-28.

Rechcigl, Miloslav, Jr., "Český historik v Americe" (Czech historian in America), in: Postavy naší Ameriky. Praha: Pražská edice, 2000, pp. 256-258.

Matthew Spinka (1890-1972)

Battles, Ford Lo, "Matthew Spinka, Representative Christian Thinker," Bulletin of the Hartford Seminary Foundation, No. 24 (June 1958), pp. 49-51.

Rechcigl, Miloslav, Jr., "Americký komeniolog" (American Comeniologist), in: Postavy naší Ameriky. Praha: Pražská edice, 2000, pp. 250-252.

René Wellek (1903-1995)

Demetz, Peter," René Wellek: 22 August 1963," in: Essays on Czech Literature. By René Wellek.The Hague: Mouton & Co., 1963, pp. 7-16.

Martin Bucco, René Wellek. Boston, MA: Twayne Pub., 1982. 186p.

Rechcigl, Miloslav, Jr., "Světový expert na literární kritiku" (World expert on literary criticism), in: Postavy naší Ameriky. Praha: Pražská edice, 2000, pp. 262-264.

C. Social Sciences

1. General

Kosta, J., "O pracích českých a slovenských ekonomů v exilu: 1948-1990" (Works of Czech and Slovak economists in exile: 1948-1990), Politická ekonomie, 39, No. 9-10 (1991), pp. 825-837.

Rechcigl, Miloslav, Jr. "První čeští učenci a sociální vědci v Americe" (First Czech scholars and social scientists in America), in: Za tím mořem piva (in preparation).

2. Individuals

Alfred Adler (1870-1937)

The Individual Psychology of Alfred Adler. A Systematic Presentation in Selections from his Writings. Edited and annotated by Heinz L. Ansbacher and Rowena R. Ansbacher. New York: Harper & Row, 1965. 544p.

Hoffman, Edward, The Drive for Self: Alfred Adler and the Founding of Individual Psychology. New York: Perseus Books, 1997. 416p.

Edward L. Bernays (1891-1995)

Bernays, Edward, Biography of an Idea: Memoirs of Public Relations Counsel. New York: Simon & Schuster, 1965. 849p.

Rechcigl, Miloslav, Jr., "Muž, který ovlivnil americké veřejné minění" (Man who influenced American public opinion), in: Postavy naší Ameriky. Praha: Pražská edice, 2000, pp. 277-278.

Tye, Larry, The Father of Spin: Edward L. Bernays and the Birth of Public Relations. Picador, 2002, 320p.

Karl W. Deutsch (1912-1992)

From National Development to Global Community. Essays in Honor of Karl W. Deutsch. Ed. by. Richard I. Merritt and Bruce M. Russett. London: Allen & Unwin, 1981. 480p.

Rechcigl, Miloslav, Jr., "Inovačni politolog" (Inovative political scientist), in: Postavy naší Ameriky. Praha: Pražská edice, 2000, pp. 279-281.

Abraham Flexner (1866-1959)

Flexner, Abraham, I Remember: The Autobiography. New York: Simon and Schuster, 1940. 414p.

Parker Franklin, "Abraham Flexner 1866-1959," History of Education Quarterly 2 (1962), pp. 199-209.

Rechcigl, Miloslav, Jr., "Reformátor americké výchovy a vzdělání" (Reformer of American education and learning), in: Postavy naší Ameriky. Praha: Pražská edice, 2000, pp. 130-132.

Paul A. Freund (1908-1992)

Kurland, Philip B., "Paul A. Freund," in: International Encyclopedia of the Social Sciences, Biographical Supplement, Vol. 18, 202-205.

Cox, Archibald, "Paul A. Freund (16 February 1908-5 February 1992)," Proceedings of the American Philosophical Society, 138, No. 2 (June 1994), pp. 325-26.

Pace, Eric, "Paul A. Freund, Authority on Constitution, Dies at 83," New York Times, February 6, 1992.

Hans Kelsen (1881-1973)

"Kelsen Hans," Current Biography 1957 (1958), pp. 294-296.

Ebestein, William, "Kelsen, Hans," in: International Encyclopedia of the Social Sciences, Vol. 8, pp. 360-365.

Rechcigl, Miloslav, Jr., "Tvůrce normativní teorie práva" (Creator of normative theory of law), in: Postavy naší Ameriky. Praha: Pražská edice, 2000, pp. 271-273.

Paul Felix Lazarsfeld (1901-1976)

Qualitative and Quantitative Social Research: Papers in Honor of Paul F. Lazarsfeld. Ed. by Robert K. Merton, James S. Coleman, and Peter. H. Rossi. New York: Free Press, 1979.

Lazarsfeld, Patricia Kendall, The Varied Sociology of Paul F. Lazarsfeld. New York: Columbia University Press, 1982. 417p.

Realizing Social Science Knowledge: The Political Realization of Social Science Knowledge and Research: Toward New Scenario—A Symposium in Memoriam Paul F. Larzarsfeld. Ed. by Holzner, Knorr and Strasser. Physica-Verlag, 1983.(IHS-Studies No. 3). 336p.

Beardsley Ruml (1894-1960)

Mitchell, Broadus, "Ruml, Beardsley," in: Dictionary of American Biography, Supp. 6, pp. 558-560.

Reagan, Patrick D., Designing a New America: The Origins of New Deal Planning, 1890-1943 University of Massachusetts Press 2000.

Joseph Alois Schumpeter (1883-1950)

Harris, Seymour C., Schumpeter, Social Scientist. Cambridge, MA: Harvard University Press, 1951.

Schneider, Erich, Schumpeter, Life and Work of a Great Social Scientist. Bureau of Business Research, University of Nebraska, 1975.

Rechcigl, Miloslav, Jr., "Ekonomický myslitel z Třešti" (Economic scholar from Třesť), in: Postavy naší Ameriky. Praha: Pražská edice, 2000, pp. 268-270.

Alfred Schütz (1899-1959)

Wagner, H. R., Alfred Schütz: An Intellectual Biography. Chicago and London: The University of Chicago Press, 1983. 358p.

Barber, M., The Participating Citizen: A Biography of Alfred Schütz. New York: State University of New York Press, 2004. 322p.

Herbert A. Simon (1916-2001)

Models of a Man: Essays in Memory of Herbert A. Simon. Eds. Mie Augier and James G. March. MIT Press, 2004. 571p.

Frank William Taussig (1859-1940)

Opie, Redveras, "Frank William Taussig 1859-1940)," Economc Journal, 51 (1941), pp. 347-368.

Schumpeter, Joseph A., A. A. Cole and E. S. Mason, "Frank William Taussig," in: The Great Economists from Marx to Keynes. Ed. Joseph A. Schumpeter. New York: Oxford University Press, 1951, pp. 191-221.

Rechcigl, Miloslav, Jr., "Otec moderního ekonomického myšlení (Father of the new economic thought), in: Postavy naší Ameriky. Praha: Pražská edice, 2000, pp. 265-267.

Max Wertheimer (1880-1943)

Watson, Robert, "Wertheimer: Gestalt Psychology," in: The Great Psychologists. From Aristotle to Freud. Philadelphia: Lippincott, 1953, pp. 403-422.

Rechcigl, Miloslav, Jr., "Zakladatel pysychologie gestaltismu" (Founder of Gestalt psychology), in: Postavy naší Ameriky. Praha: Pražská edice, 2000, pp. 274-276.

King, D. and Michael Wertheimer, Max Wertheimer and Gestalt Theory. New Brunswick and London: Transaction Publishers, 2007. 438p.

D. Biological & Medical Sciences

1. General

Malý, Jindřich, "České lidové 'napravování' v Americe" (Czech folk chiropractic), Český lid, 18 (1909), pp. 408-410.

Navrátil, Michael, "Čeští lékaři v Americe" (Czech physicians in America), Věstník, Supplement to Časopis lékařův českých, 1914, No. 10-20.

Rechcigl, Miloslav, Jr. "První čeští přírodovědci a technici na americkém kontinentě" (First Czech natural scientists and engineers on American continent), in: Za tím mořem piva (in preparation).

2. Individuals

Carl F. Cori (1896-1984) and Gerty R. Cori (1896-1957)

"Carl F. Cori—Biography," in: Nobel Lectures, Physiology or Medicine 1942-1962, Elsevier Publishing Company, Amsterdam, 1964.

Brown, Barbara Illingworth, "Cori, Gerty Radnitz," in: Dictionary of American Biography. 1956-1960. Supp. 6. New York: Charles Scribner's Sons, 1980, pp. 126-127.

Rechcigl, Miloslav, Jr., "Manželská dvojice z Prahy—Laureáti Nobelovy ceny" (Husband and wife team from Prague—Laureates of Nobel Prize), in: Postavy naší Ameriky. Praha: Pražská edice, 2000, pp. 295-298.

Simon Flexner (1865-1946)

Flexner, James Thomas, An American Saga. The Story of Helen Thomas and Simon Flexner. Boston: Little Brown & Co., 1984. 494p.

Rechcigl, Miloslav, Jr., "Budovatel Rockefellerovy university" (Builder of Rockefeller University), in: Postavy naší Ameriky. Praha: Pražská edice, 2000, pp. 283-285.

Felix Haurowitz (1896-1987)

Frank W. Putnam, "Felix Haurowitz," National Academy of Sciences Biographical Memoirs, Vol. 64 (1994), pp. 135ff.

Aleš Hrdlička (1869-1943)

Anonymous, "Dr. Aleš Hrdlička: A Biographical Sketch," Anthropologie, 7, parts 1 & 2. (Dr. Aleš Hrdlička Anniversary Volume). Praha, 1929, pp. 6-49.

Jaffe, Bernard, "Aleš Hrdlička," in: Outputs of Science. New York: Simon, 1935, pp. 47-80.

Schultz, Adolph, Biographical Memoir of Aleš Hrdlička, 1869-1943," in: Biographical Memoirs of the National Academy of Sciences, 23 (1945), pp. 305-338.

Rechcigl, Miloslav, Jr., "Jak tyfus ovlivnil osud Aleše Hrdličky" (How typhus influenced the fate of Aleš Hrdlička), in: Postavy naší Ameriky. Praha: Pražská edice, 2000, pp. 289-291.

Carl Koller (1857-1944)

Rechcigl, Miloslav, Jr., "Objevitel lokální anestezie" (Discoverer of local anesthesia) in: Postavy naší Ameriky. Praha: Pražská edice, 2000, pp. 322-323.

Diamant, H., "Should they have got the Nobel Prize?" Adler Museum Bulletin (South Africa) 22, No. 3 (November 1996), pp, 18-20.

Karl Landsteiner (1868-1943)

Michael Heidelberger, Karl Landsteiner: June 14, 1868-June 26, 1943. Biographical Memoir. National Academy of Sciences. Columbia University Press, 1969.

Speiser, Paul and Ferdinand G. Smekal, Karl Landsteiner: The Discoverer of the Blood-groups and a Pioneer in the Field of Immunology. Biography of a Nobel Prize winner of the Vienna Medical School. Wien, Hollinek, 1975. 198p.

Frederick George Novy (1864-1957)

Fredrick George Novy. 1864-1957. A Biographical Memoir by Edmond R. Long. Washington, DC: National Academy of Sciences, 1959.

Rechcigl, Miloslav. Jr., "Průkopník americké mikrobiologie" (Pioneer of American microbiology), in: Postavy naší Ameriky. Praha: Pražská edice, 2000, pp. 286-288.

Simon Pollak (1814-1903)

Pollak, Simon, The Autobiography and Reminiscences of S. Pollak, Kessinger Publishing, 2009. 336p.

Rechcigl, Miloslav, Jr., "Průkopník oftalmologie" (Pioneer of ophthalmology), in: Postavy naší Ameriky. Praha: Pražská edice, 2000, pp. 318-319.

Hans Popper (1903-1988)

Gerber, Michael A. and Swan N. Thung, "Hans Popper, M.D., Ph.D.," Am. Pathology, 133, No. 1 (October 1986), pp. 13-14.

Schmid, Rudi, "Hans Popper, Nov. 4, 1903-May 6, 1988)," Biographical Memoirs of the National Academy of Sciences, 65 (1994), pp. 290-309.

Bohumil Shimek (1861-1937)

Lochwing, Walter F., Bohumil Shimek. Iowa City: University of Iowa Press, 1947. 36p.

Conard, Henry S., "Notes for a Biography of Bohumil Shimek". Iowa City, 1947. 76p.

Rechcigl, Miloslav, Jr., "Netipický vědec" (A nontypical scientist), in: Postavy naší Ameriky. Praha: Pražská edice, 2000, pp. 292-294.

Hellen Brooke Taussig (1898-1986)

Neill, C A and E. B. Clark, "The Paediatric Cardiology Hall of Fame: Helen Brooke Taussig MD. May 24, 1898 to May 21, 1986," Cardiology in the Young, 9, No. 1 (1999), pp. 104-108,

Rechcigl, Miloslav, Jr., "Žena, která zachránila na tisíce dětských životů" (Woman who saved thousands of children's lives), in: Postavy naší Ameriky. Praha: Pražská edice, 2000, pp. 332-333.

Paul C. Zamecnik (1912-2009)

Kresge, Nicole, Robert D. Simoni and Robert L. Hill, "The Discovery of tRNA by Paul C. Zamecnik," J. Biol. Chem., 280, October 7, 2005.

Stickgold, Emma, "Paul C. Zamecnik, at 96; discoveries helped revolutionize biochemistry," The Boston Globe, November 16, 2009.

E. Physical Sciences

1. General

Rechcigl, Miloslav, Jr. "První čeští přírodovědci a technici na americkém kontinentě" (First Czech natural scientists and engineers on American continent), in: Za tím mořem piva (in preparation).

2. Individuals

Felix Bloch (1905-1983)

Shampo, M. A. and R. A. Kyle, "Felix Bloch—Developer of Magnetic Resonance Imaging," Mayo Clin. Proc. 70, No. 9 (1995), p. 889ff.

Rechcigl, Miloslav, Jr., "Objevitel nukleární magnetické resonance" (Discoverer of nuclear magnetic resonance), in: Postavy naší Ameriky. Praha: Pražská edice, 2000, pp. 298-300.

Thomas Cech (1947-)

Radetsky, Peter, "Genetic Heretic," Discovery 11 (November 1990), pp. 78-82.

Rechcigl, Miloslav, Jr., "Chemik, který obrátil molekulární biologii vzhůru nohama" (Chemist who turned molecular biology upside down), in: Postavy naší Ameriky. Praha: Pražská edice, 2000, pp. 312-314.

Kurt Frederick Gödel (1906-1978)

Kreisel, C. "Kurt Gödel," Biographical Memoirs of Fellows of the Royal Society, 26 (1980), pp. 149-224

Rechcigl, Miloslav, Jr., "Největší logik po Aristotelesovi" (Greatest logician after Aristoteles), in: Postavy naší Ameriky. Praha: Pražská edice, 2000, pp. 305-308.

Arthur Haas (1884-1941)

"Arthur Erich Haas," in: Dictionary of Scientific Biography, 5 (1972), pp. 609-610.

Václav Hlavatý (1894-1969)

Perspectives in Geometry and Relativity. Essays in Honor of Václav Hlavatý. Ed. Banesh Hoffmann, Bloomington: Indiana University Press, 1966. 489p.

Rechcigl, Miloslav, Jr., "Čech, ktery potvrdil Einsteinovu teorii" (Czech who proved Einstein's theory), in: Postavy naší Ameriky. Praha: Pražská edice, 2000, pp. 301-304.

Walter Kohn (1923-)

"Walter Kohn," in: National Cyclopaedia of American Biography. James T. White & Co. 1984, Vol. 61, pp. 310-312.

Kohn, Walter, "Autobiography," in: Les Prix Nobel. The Nobel Prizes 1998, Editor Tore Frängsmyr, Stockholm: Nobel Foundation, 1999.

Wolfgang Pauli (1900-1958)

Lindorff, David, Pauli and Jung: The Meeting of Two Great Minds. Quest Books, 1994. 313p.

Enz, Charles P., No Time to be Brief, A Scientific Biography of Wolfgang Pauli. Oxford University Press, 2002. 584p.

Gieser, Suzanne, The Innermost Kernel. Depth Psychology and Quantum Physics. Wolfgang Pauli's Dialogue with C.G. Jung. Springer Verlag, 2005. 378p.

George Placzek (1905-1955)

Cassidy, David C., "Placzek, George," in: Dictionary of Scientific Biography, Suppl. 2, Vol. 18, pp. 714-715.

Van Hove, Leon, "George Placzek, 1905-1955," Nuclear Physics, 1 (1956), pp. 623-626.

Fisher, J., "George Placzek—An Unsung Hero of Physics," CERN Courier, 45 (2005), pp. 25-27.

Victor F. Weisskopf (1908-2002)

Physics and Society, Essays in Honor of Victor Frederick Weisskopf by the International Community of Physicists, Ed. by V. Stefan. New York: Springer Verlag, 1998. 236p.

"Weisskopf Dies at 93; was protégé of physicist Niels Bohr," MIT News, April 24, 2002,

Victor Frederick Weisskop 1908-2008. A Biographical Memoir by J. David Jackson and Kurt Gottfried, Washington, DC: National Academy of Sciences, 2003. (Biographical Memoirs of the National Academy of Sciences, Vol. 84). 27p.

F. Engineering

1. General

Rechcigl, Miloslav, Jr. "První čeští přírodovědci a technici na americkém kontinentě" (First Czech natural scientists and engineers on American continent), in: Za tím mořem piva (in preparation).

2. Individuals

Karl Arnstein (1887-1974)

When Giants Roared the Sky. Karl Arnstein and the Rise of Airships from Zeppelin to Goodyear. Edited by Eric Brothers. Akron, OH: Akron University Press, 2007. 276p.

Karl Jansky (1905-1950)

Greenstein, Jesse L., "Jansky, Karl Guthe," in: Dictionary of American Biography Suppl. 4, pp. 422-423.

W. T. Sullivan, ed., The Early Years of Radio Astronomy: Reflections Fifty Years After Jansky's Discovery. Cambridge University Press, 2005, 432p.; see especially Chap.1, "Karl Jansky and the discovery of extraterrestrial radio waves," pp. 3-42.

Rechcigl, Miloslav, Jr., "Zakladatel radioastronomie" (Founder of radioastronomy), in: Postavy naší Ameriky. Praha: Pražská edice, 2000, pp. 301-304.

Theodore v. Kármán (1881-1963)

Kármán, Theodore v. with L. Edson, The Wind and Beyond. Boston: Little, Brown, 1967. 376p.

Dryden, Hugh L., Theodore von Kármán. National Academy of Sciences. Biographical Memoir. Washington, DC: NAS, 1965, Vol. 38, pp. 345-384.

Gustav Lindenthal (1850-1935)

Cross, Hardy, "Lindenthal, Gustav," in: Dictionary of American Biography, 8, Suppl. 1, pp. 498-499.

Rechcigl, Miloslav, Jr., "Mistrný stavitel mostů v Americe" (Master builder of bridges in America), in: Postavy naší Ameriky. Praha: Pražská edice, 2000, pp.335-336.

Frank J. Malina (1912-1981)

Frank Popper, Frank Malina, Artist and Scientist. Works from 1936 to 1963. Paris, 1963.

Malina, F. J., "Reflections of an artist-engineer on the art-science interface," Impact of Science on Society, 24, No 1 (1974), p. 19ff.

Zibit, Benjamin, The Guggenheim Aeronautical Laboratory at Caltech and the Creation of the Modern Rocket Motor: How the Dynamics of Rocket Theory became Reality. Ph.D. Dissertation, City University of NY, 1999.

Karl Terzaghi (1883-1963)

Terzaghi, Karl, From theory to practice in soil mechanics. Selections from the Writings of Karl Terzaghi, with bibliography and contributions on his life and achievements. New York: Wiley, 1967. 425p.

Goodman, Richard E., Karl Terzaghi: The Engineer as Artist. ASCE Press, 1998. 355p.

Goodman, Richard E., "Karl Terzaghi's Legacy in Geotechnical Engineering," Geo-Strata Magazine of the ASCE, 3, No. 4 (October 2002), pp. 18-21.

X. Organizations

A. General Surveys

"Adresář českých spolků v Chicago" (Directory of Czech organizations in Chicago), in: České Chicago. Adresář českých obchodníků, živnostníků a spolků (Czech Chicago. A directory of Czech merchants, tradesmen and associations). Chicago: Národní tiskárna, 1900, pp. 229-251.

Balch, Emily Greene, "The Organized Life of Slavs in America," in: Our Slavic Fellow Citizens. New York: Charities Publication Committee, 1910, pp. 378-395.

Čapek, Thomas, "Fraternal and Other Societies," in: The Čechs (Bohemians in America. Boston and New York: Houghton Mifflin Co., 1920, pp. 254-65.

Index of Czechoslovak Organizations. Chicago: Exhibit Committee of Czechoslovak Group, 1933. 115p.

Musil, Ferdinand L., Československá Amerika. Ze spolkového a národního života Čechů a Slováků ve Spojených státech a v Kanadě roku 1932. (Czechoslovak America. Organizational and national life of Czechs and Slovaks in the US and Canada in 1932). Chicago: Denní Hlasatel, 1933. 40p.

McCarthy, E. R., The Bohemians in Chicago and their Benevolent Societies. M.A. Thesis, University of Chicago, 1950.

Exner, Petr. Historie kulturně-historických krajanských organizací v Texasu, USA (History of cultural-historical compatriot organizations in Texas, USA). Diplomová práce. Hradec Králové: Univerzita Hradec Králové, Pedagogická fakulta, 2004. 157p.

B. Fraternal & Benevolent

Rosický, Jan, Dějiny Česko-slovanského podporujícího spolku (History of Bohemian Slavonian Benevolent Society). Omaha: Věstník bratrský, 1881.

Pecka, Josef, Dějiny Česko-Slovanské bratrské podporující jednoty (History of Bohemian Slavic Benevolent Society). Chicago, 1894.

Chotek, Hugo, Dějiny Česko-Slovanské bratrské podporující jednoty v Spojených státech Severní Ameriky dle spolkových zápisků (History of Bohemian Slavic Benevolent Society in the US according to the Society's reports). 1895. 118p.

Machovsky, Anna, Dějiny českých dam ve Spojených státech Severní Ameriky (History of the Unity of Bohemian Ladies in the U.S.). New York, 1895. 420p.

Lojda, Václav, Dějiny československých podporujících spolků (History of Czech Slavic benevolent societies). St. Louis: V. J. Turecek, 1894. 103p.

Čapek, Thomas, The First Czech Society in America. Chicago: Czechoslovak National Council of America, 1950. 20p.

Janda, Rudolf, Sedmdesátipětileté jubileum Českého národního hřbitova v Chicagu, Il. (75 Years of the Czech National Cemetery in Chicago). Chicago: R. Mejdrich & Co., 1952. 571p.

Památník 15tiletého výročí slavnosti Ústředny moravských spolků (Souvenir of the 15th anniversary of the Federation of Moravian Societies). Chicago, 1953. 122p.

Martínek, Josef, Století Jednoty Č.S.A. 1854-1954 (One hundred years of the Č.S.A. 1854-1954). Cicero, IL: Č.S.A., 1955. 443p.

Slovacek, Marvin, A Sixty Year Insurance History of the Slavonic Benevolent Order of the State of Texas. M.A. Thesis, University of Texas in Austin, 1956.

Fifteenth National Convention of the Western Bohemian Fraternal Association, Program. Cedar Rapids, IA, 1963.

"Czechoslovak Society of America," in: Panorama. Cicero, IL: Czechoslovak National Council of America, 1970, pp. 158-167.

Valchar, Jerry E., History of the Farmers Mutual Protective Association of Texas (R.V.O.S.) Rolnický Vzájemně Ochranný Spolek Státu Texas. Temple, TX: RVOS, 1982. 131p.

Morris, Nick, A., History of the S.P.J.S.T. A Texas Chronicle 1897-1980. Temple, TX, 1984. 291p.

C. Religious

1. Catholic

Památník a dějiny České římsko-katolické ústřední jednoty žen amerických . . . . (Memorial and history of Bohemian Roman Catholic Central Union of American Women). Cleveland, 1930.

Kallus, Bohdan, Dějiny Katolické jednoty texaské (History of the Catholic Union of Texas). Taylor, TX: Našinec Publishing Co., 1927.

Čada, Joseph, The Catholic Central Union: Its Contribution to Fraternalism and American Cosmopolitan Civilization. Chicago, 1952. 54p.

Short History of K.J.T. La Grange, TX: Katolická Jednota Texaská, 1973.

Hannan, Kevin & John J. Karas. Czech Catholic Union of Texas. The K.J.T. Fraternal Benefit Society. La Grange, TX: Czech Catholic Union of Texas, 1989.

2. Protestant

Chlumský, Adolf, Unity of the Evangelic Union of Bohemian-Moravian Brethren in Texas. La Grange, TX, n.d. 44p.

Hegar, Joseph, Památník Podporující jednoty česko-moravských bratří (Memorial of the Benevolent Society of the Czech-Moravian Brethren Church in Texas. np., n.d.

Barton, Elsie. Fifty Years of Benevolence. A Golden Jubilee of the Mutual Aid Society of the Czech-Moravian Brethren 1905-1955. Taylor, TX: The Mutual Aid Society, 1958. 30p.

3. Jewish

Review of the Society for the History of Czechoslovak Jews. New York: Society for the History of Czechoslovak Jews, 1987-.

D. Heritage

Dějiny desetiletého trvání spolku starých českých osadníků v Chicagu (History of the 10th anniversary of the old Czech settlers in Chicago). Chicago: A. Geringer, 1908. 80p.

Janák, Robert. CHS at Fifteen. A History of the Czech Heritage Society of Texas from October 30, 1982 to December 31, 1997. Houston, TX: Czech Heritage Society of Texas, 2000. 160p.

E. Public Affairs and Political

Mašek, Josef, Památník Českého narodního sdružení v Clevelandě 1915-1920 (Memorial of the Bohemian National Alliance in Cleveland 1915-1920), ca 1921. 172p.

Beneš, Vojta, České národní sdružení. Vznik a historie revolučního hnutí osvobozeneckého mezi svobodomyslnými a evangelickými Čechy ve Spojených Státech amerických. (Bohemian National Alliance. Origin and history of the revolutionary liberation movement among the freethinking and evangelical Czechs in the USA). Chicago, 1925.

Poslání a úkoly Československé národní rady americké (Mission and goals of the Czechoslovak National Council of America). Chicago, n.d.

Třicet let plodné práce, 1910-1940. Památník Česko-americké jednoty (Thirty years of fruitful work, 1910-1940. Memorial of the Czech-American Union). Chicago: R. Mejdrich, 1940. 66p.

Martínek, Josef, Československá národní rada americká (Czechoslovak National Council of America). Chicago, 1962. 44p.

"Czechoslovak National Council of America," in: Panorama. Cicero, IL: Czechoslovak National Council of America, 1960, pp. 104-132.

Novotný, Jan, Slovanská lípa, 1848-1849: K dějinám prvního českého politického spolku (Slavonic Linden: A History of the first Czech political society) I-II. Acta Musei Pragensis, 75-76 (1975-76).

Bunža, Bohumír, ed., Rada svobodného Československa: Historie, program, činnost, dokumenty (Council of Free Czechoslovakia: history, program, activities, documents). Toronto, 1990.

Čelovský, Bořivoj, Politici bez moci. První léta exilové Rady svobodného Československa. (Politicians without power. The first years of the Council of Free Czechoslovakia). Šenov u Ostravy: Nakladatelství Tilia, 2000. 320p.

Raška, Francis D., Fighting Communism from Afar.The Council of Free Czechoslovakia. Boulder, CO: East European Monographs, 2008. 229p.

F. Cultural—Scholarly—Scientific

Přehled pětiletého působení Matice vyššího vzdělání, 1902-1908 (Overview of the five years activities of the Council of Higher Education). Milwaukee, WI: A. Novák, 1908. 72p.

Hrachovsky, Frank, 60 Years of the Council of Higher Education. Chicago: Council of Higher Education, 1962. 28p.

Hruska, John H. These Twenty Five Years, 1922-1947. Chicago: American Czechoslovak Engineers Society, 1947.

Rechcigl, Miloslav, Jr., Ten Years of the Czechoslovak Society of Arts and Sciences in America. Toronto: Nase Hlasy, 1966. 22p.

Rechcigl, Miloslav, Jr., Czechoslovak Society of Arts and Sciences, Inc. 1958-1988. Washington, DC: SVU Press, 1988. 73p.

Rechcigl, Miloslav, Jr., On Behalf of their Homeland: Fifty Years of SVU. Boulder, CO: East European Monographs and New York: Columbia University Press, 2008. 700p.

G. Physical Education

Rudiš-Jičinský, Jan, Památník Národní jednoty Sokolské ve Spojených státech. Na oslavu 25.letého trvání (Memorial of the American Sokol Union in the US. Commemoration of its 25th anniversary). New York, 1904. 224p.

Rudiš-Jičinský, Jan, Dějinami Sokolstva amerického 1865-1907 (Tracing the history of the American Sokol 1865-1908). Chicago: Národní tiskárna, 1908. 43p.

Čechoslováci a tělesná výchova. Stručný přehled sokolských a jiných tělocvičných organizací československých ve Spojených státech v letech 1865-1933" (Czechoslovaks and physical education. Brief overview of the Sokol and other physical educational Czechoslovak organizations in the US during 1865-1933), Denní Hlasatel, Chicago, August 20, 1933.

Jelínek, Jarka, Sokol, Educational and Physical Culturel Association. Chicago: American Sokol Union, 1944. 112p.

Hřebík, Antonín, Sokolstvo po únoru 1948 (Sokol after February 1948). Chicago: Denní Hlasatel, 1949. 38p.

Hřebík, Antonín, Čs. Sokolstvo v zahraničí, 1948-1958 (Czechoslovak Sokol abroad, 1948-1958). Chicago: Ústředí čs. sokolstva v zahraničí, 1958. 44p.

American Sokol Centennial, 1865-1965. St. Louis, MO: Sokol St. Louis, 1965.

Centennial of the Sokol in America, 1865-1965. Cleveland, 1965.

American Sokol Organization," in: Panorama. Cicero, IL: Czechoslovak National Council of America, 1970, pp. 133-144.

Czechoslovak Orel in Exile," in: Panorama. Cicero, IL: Czechoslovak National Council of America, 1970, pp. 156-157.

Jožák, Jiří, "Historie českého Sokola v USA 1865-1914" (History of Czech Sokol in the US 1865-1914), Paginae historiae. Sborník Státního ústředního archivu v Praze 6 (1998), pp. 151-188.

H. Charitable & Relief

"The American Fund for Czechoslovak Refugees," in: Panorama: Cicero, IL: Czechoslovak National Council in America, 1970, pp. 101-103.

American Fund for Czechoslovak Refugees, Inc., 1948-1980. New York, ca 1980. 20p.

Jeřábek, Vojtěch, Českoslovenští uprchlíci ve studené válce. Dějiny American Fund for Czechoslovak Refugees (Czechoslovak refugees in the Cold War. History of American Fund for Czechoslovak Refugees). Brno: V. Reitterová—Stilus, 2005. 296p.

XI. Relations with the Old Homeland

A. Czech-US and US-Czech Relations and Contacts

Sabath, Adolph J., "Speech in the U.S. House of Representatives Urging Recognition of Czechs and Slovaks as a Nation," Congressional Record, 56 (May 6, 1918), pp. 6136-38.

Tvrzický, Joseph, "Masaryk in America," Bohemian Review, 2 (1918), pp. 66-67.

Partl, Václav, "American Influence on Political Thought in Czechoslovakia," American Political Science Review, 17 (1923), pp. 448-452.

Beneš, Vojta, Masarykovo dílo v Americe (Masaryk's work in America). Praha: Svaz národního osvobození, 1925. 87p.

Pergler, Charles, Amerika a československá nezávislost (American and Czechoslovak independence). Praha: Český čtenář, 1926. 205p.

Mrázek, Jaroslav, "Wodrow Wilson a americké uznání Československé národní rady za vládu *de facto*" (Woodrow Wilson and American recognition of Ceskoslovenská národní rada as a *de facto* Government), Naše revoluce 9 (1933), pp. 129-247, 379-426.

Beneš, Eduard, An Appeal to the American People. Chicago: University of Chicago, 1939. 11p.

Štefánik, Milan, Activities of the United States in the Establishment of the Czecho-Slovak Republic, 1914-1919. M.A. Thesis, Kent State Univesity, 1942.

Kisch, Guido, "Woodrow Wilson and the Independence of Small Nations in Central Europe," Journal of Modern History, 19 (1947), pp. 235-238.

Selsam, J. Paul, The United States and the Funding of the Czechoslovak Republic," Social Studies, 40 (October 1949), pp. 259-263.

Mamatey, Victor S., "The United States and the Dissolution of Austria-Hungary," Journal of Central European Affairs, 10 (1950), pp. 256-270.

Mamatey, Victor S., "The United States Recognition of the Czechoslovak National Council of Paris, September 3, 1918," Journal of Central European Affairs, 13 (1953), pp. 47-60.

Hájek, J. S., Wilsonovská legenda v dějinách ČSR (Wilsonian legend in the history of the Czechoslovak Republic). Praha: Státní nakl. politické literatury, 1953. 217p.

Wechsberg, Joseph, "They're Losing Faith in America," Saturday Evening Post, 229 (July 28, 1956), p. 30, pp. 93-94.

Mamatey, Victor S., The United States and East Central Europe, 1914-1918: A Study in Wilsonian Diplomacy and Propaganda. Princeton: Princeton University, Press, 1957. 431p.

Pazourek, Vladimír, Demarkační čára (Demarcation line). Brno: Krajské nakladatelství, 1960. 311p.

Lubek, Sister M. Evangela, Foreign Relations between the United States and Czecho-Slovakia, 1920-1960. M.A. Thesis, De Paul University, Chicago, 1964. 150p.

Polišenský, Josef, "Styky Čechů a Slováků s koloniální Amerikou" (Contacts of Czechs and Slovaks with the Colonial America), Bulletin Komise pro dějiny krajanů, Čechů a Slováků v zahraničí 6 (1968-69), pp. 1-18.

Mamatey, Victor S., Building Czechoslovakia in America.1914-1918. Washington, DC: SVU, 1976. 17p.

Kovtun, Jiří, Masaryk and America: Testimony of a Relationship. Ann Arbor: University of Michigan Library, 1988. 100p.

Svoboda, George Josef, "Wilson and Masaryk: The Origin and Background of their Diplomacy," Czechoslovak and Central European Journal 8, No. 1 /2 (Summer/Winter 1989), pp. 54-67.

Mamatey, Victor S., "Masaryk and Wilson: A Contribution to the study of their Relations," in: T. G. Masaryk (1850-1937). New York: St. Martin's Press, 1989, Vol. 2, pp. 186-97.

Capron, Seth, "The View from the Czech Republic. The Status of Radio Free Europe Weighs Heavily on Czech-American Relations," TransAtlantic Perspectives, Vol. I, March 2002.

Calda, Miloš, "Česko-americké vztahy: Od vzdálené alternativy k blízkému spojenectví" (Czech-American relations: From a distant alternative to a close alliance)," in: Zahraniční politika České republiky 1993-2004: úspěchy, problémy a perspektivy. Edited by Otto Pick and Jiri Handl. Praha, 2004.

Unterberger, Betty Miller, "President Wilson, Professor Masaryk, and the Birth of Czechoslovakia," Kosmas, 17, No. 2 (Spring 2006), pp. 1-19.

"Address by H. E. William J. Cabaniss, US Ambassador to the Czech Republic," in: Selected Papers from the 22nd World SVU Congress, Palacký University, Olomouc, June 26 to July 4, 2004. Ostrava: Repronis, 2006, pp. 18-20.

"U.S.-Czech Bilateral Relations," Remarks by Ambassador Richard W. Graber. Association for International Affairs (AMO). Savoy Hotel, Prague, November 29, 2006.

Udell, Emily, "Czech-US Relations Dominated by Visa, Missile Defense Issues," Radio Praha, Talking Point 14: 53, May 12, 2006.

Klicperová-Baker, Martina, The Czech-American Relations. History, Current Viewpoints and Future Prospects. San Diego: Montezuma Publishing, 2007. 16p.

Kurfürst, Jaroslav, Deputy Chief of Mission, Czech Republic, Washington, D.C., "Czech-American Relations in the Context of the Euro-Atlantic Political Debate. Presented at the Acron Council on World Affairs, Global Scholars and Speaker Event, April 26, 2007.

Calda, Miloš, "Facing Centers and Peripheries, Old and New: the Czech-US Relations since 1993," in: Selected Papers from the Conference of the Czechoslovak Society of Arts and Sciences at the Moravian College, Bethlehem, PA, June 8-10, 2007, pp. 1-6.

Vlha, Marek, "Konference Česko-Americké vztahy mezi minulostí a současností" (Conference on Czech-American relations in the past and in the present), Časopis Matice moravské, 127, No. 2 (2008), pp. 580-581.

Kuksa, Milan. Zahraniční politika České republiky v letech 2002—2008 a její transatlantický rozměr. Kontinuita nebo diskontinuita? (Foreign policy of the Czech Republic in 2002-2008 and its transatlantic dimension. Continuity or discontinuity?) Bakalářská práce, Masarykova univerzita, Fakulta sociálních studií, Kateda mezinárodních vztahů a evropských studií, Brno, 2009. 49p.

B. Czech American Aid

1. Liberation from Austria and the Establishment of Czechoslovakia

Tvrzický, Joseph, "Masaryk in America," Bohemian Review 2, No. 5 (May 1918), pp. 66-67.

Československá Amerika pro osvobození vlasti (Czechoslovak American for the liberation of the homeland). Chicago: Český svět, 1919.

Beneš, Vojta, "Česko-slovenská Amerika v boji za samostatnost otčiny" (Czech-Slovak America in the struggle for the independence of their fatherland), Amerikán, Národní kalendář 43 (1920), pp. 253-262.

Čapek, Thomas, "The Part the American Cechs Took on the War of Liberation," in: The Čechs (Bohemians) in America. Boston & New York: Houghton Mifflin Co., 1920, pp. 265-278.

Buňata, Josef, Památník texasských Čechoslováků na práci vykonanou v letech 1914-1920 ve prospěch osvobození vlasti starých (Memorial of Texas Czechoslovaks for work carried out in 1914-1920 on behalf of their homeland). Ennis, TX: Krajský výbor ČNS pro Texas a Lousianu, 1921? 200p.

Beneš, Vojta, Revoluční hnutí v Severní Americe (Revolutionary movement in North America). Praha: Nákladem Památníku odboje, 1923. 97p.

Tůma, Emil, "Vděk československé Americe" (Obligation to Czechoslovak America), Naše zahraničí 4 (1923), pp. 55-59.

Sychrava, Lev and Jaroslav Werstadt, Československý odboj (Czechoslovak resistance). Státní nakladatelství, 1923. 200p.

Pergler, K., Za národní stát. Památník odboje (For national state. Memorial to Resistance). Praha, 1923. 202p.

Tůma, Emil, "Vděk československé Americe" (Appreciation to Czechoslovak America), Naše zahraničí, 4 (1923), pp. 197-229.

Šindelář, František, Z boje za svobodu otčiny (From the struggle for liberation of the fatherland). Chicago: Národní svaz českých katolíků, 1924. 328p.

Voska, Em. V., Československá Amerika v revoluci. (Czechoslovak America in revolution). Praha: Nákladem Památníku odboje, 1924, 64p.

Traub, Otto, "Českožidovské hnutí a jeho vliv při odboji České Ameriky proti Rakousku" (The Czech Jewish movement and its influence upon the struggle of American Czechs against Austria), Kalendář česko-židovský, 57 (Prague, 1925), p. 144ff.

Čapek, Tomáš, "Odboj" (Resistance), in: Naše Amerika. Praha: Národní rada československá, 1926, pp. 457-480.

Pergler, Charles, America in the Struggle for Czechoslovak Independence. Philadelphia: Dorrance & Co., 1926. 110p.

Šindelář, František, Z boje za svobodu otčiny (From the struggle for freedom of the homeland). Chicago: Národní svaz českých katolíků, 1924. 328p.

Beneš, Vojta, Československá Amerika v odboji (Czechoslovak America during resistance). Praha: Pokrok, 1931. 424p.

Getting, Milan, Americkí Slováci a vývin čs. myšlienky (American Slovaks and the development of the Czechoslovak Idea). Perth Amboy, NJ: Slovenská TJ Sokol v Amerike, 1933, 314p.

Martínek, Josef, Američtí svobodomyslní v boji za naši samostatnost (American Freethinkers in the struggle for our Independence). Praha, Volná myšlenka, 1936.

Jahelka, Joseph, "The Role of Chicago Czechs in the Struggle for Czechoslovak Independence," Journal of Illinois State Historical Society, 31, No. 4 (December) 1938), pp. 381-410.

Dérer, Ivan, The Unity of the Czechs and Slovaks. Has the Pittsburgh Declaration been Carried out? Prague: 'Orbis' Pub. Co., 1938. 78p.

Roucek, Joseph Slabey, "American Czechoslovaks and World War II," World Affairs Interpreter, 17 (1946), pp. 85-90.

Kisch, Guido, "Part in Czechoslovakia's Liberation," in: In Search of Freedom. London: Edward Goldston, 1948, pp. 127-135.

Mamatey, Victor S., The United States and East Central Europe, 1914-1918: A Study in Wilsonian Diplomacy and Propaganda. Princenton, NJ: Princeton University Press, 1957. 431p.

Stolarik, Mark, The Role of American Slovaks in the Creation of Czecho-Slovakia, 1914-1918. M.A. Thesis, University of Ottawa, Ottawa, 1967. 166p.

Ješina, Čestmír, Ed., The Birth of Czechoslovakia. Washington, DC: Czechoslovak National Council of America, Washington DC Chapter, 1968. 110p.

Pichlík, Karel, Zahraniční odboj, 1914-1918 bez legend (The resistance movement abroad, 1914-1918, without any legends). Praha: Svoboda, 1968. 504p.; republished in 1991.

Mamatey, Victor S., "The Establishment of the Republic," in: A History of the Czechoslovak Republic 1918-1948. Edited by Victor S. Mamatey and Radomír Luža. Princeton, NJ: Princeton University Press, 1973, pp. 3-38.

Chada, Joseph, "Czech-American Aid to Czechoslovak Freedom, July 1914-December 1917," in: The Czechs in the United Sates. SVU Press, 1981, pp. 43-53.

Chada, Joseph, "Czech-American Aid to Czechoslovak Freedom, 1917-1918," in: The Czechs in the United Sates. SVU Press, 1981, pp. 55-68.

Kalvoda, Josef, The Genesis of Czechoslovakia. Boulder, CO: East European Monographs, 1986. 673p.

Kovtun, Jiří, Masarykův triumf (Masaryk's triumph). Toronto: Sixty-Eight Publishers, 1987. 714p.

Hubenák, Ladislav, "Vznik Československa—Zahraničný odboj" (The Founding of Czechoslovakia—The resistance movement abroad), Slováci v zahraničí, 14 (1988), pp. 11-33.

Bielik, František, "Podiel krajanov v Spojených štátoch na vzniku spoločného štátu Čechov a Slovákov" (Participation of our compatriots in the US in the establishment of the common state of Czechs and Slovaks), Češi v cizině, 4 (1989), pp. 24-34.

Polišenský, Josef, "České a slovenské emigrace a nezávislost Československa" (Czech and Slovak emigration and the independence of Czechoslovakia), Češi v cizině, 4 (1989), pp. 35-39.

Galandauer, Jan et al., O samostatný československý stát 1914-1918 (For an independent Czechoslovak State 1914-1918). Praha: SPN, 1991. 117p.

Garver, Bruce, "Americans of Czech and Slovak Ancestry in the History of Czechoslovakia," Czechoslovak and Central European Journal, 11, No. 2 (Winter 1993), pp. 1-14.

Pichlík, Karel, "Relationships between Czechs and Slovaks during the First World War," Nebraska History, 74, No. 3 & 4 (Fall/Winter 1993), pp. 189-194.

Polišenský, Josef, "Američtí Češi a I. světová válka" (American Czechs and the World War I), in: Úvod do studia dějin vystěhovalectví do Ameriky. II. Češi a Amerika. Praha: Univerzita Karlova, 1996, pp.87-93.

Birth of Czechoslovakia. Seminar on the founding of independent Czechoslovakia in the Library of Congress, Washington, DC, October 8, 1998. Edited by Sharon L. Wolchik and Ivan Dubovický. Praha: Set Out, 1999. 111p.

Brož, Ivan, Masarykův vyzvědač (Masaryk's spy). Praha: Mladá fronta, 2004. 253p.

Rechcigl, Miloslav, Jr., "Czech America in the Struggle for Independent Czechoslovakia" in: Czechs and Slovaks in America. By Miloslav Rechcigl. Boulder, CO: East European Monographs, 2005, pp. 207-210.

Vondrášek, Václav and František Hanzlík, Krajané v USA a vznik ČSR v dokumentech a fotografiích. (Czech Americans and the establishment of the Czechoslovak Republic in documents and photographs). Praha: Ministersto obrany ČSR, 2008. 148p.

Majdová, Hana, Pomoc krajanů v Americe československé zahraniční akci v čele s T.G. Masarykem v období první světové války (Compatriots' aid in America for the Czechoslovak action headed by T. G. Masaryk during the First World War). Bakalářská práce, Masarykova univerzita, Pedagogická fakulta, Katedra historie, Brno, 2008.

Majdová, Hana, Úloha významných osobností československého zahraničního odboje působících v USA v letech 1914-1918 (Role of important personalities of the Czechoslovak resistance abroad in the US during 1914-1918). Diplomová práce. Masarykova univerzita, Pedagogická fakulta, Katedra historie, Brno, 2010.

Hájková, Dagmar, "Naše česká věc. Češi v Americe za první světové války (Our Czech cause. Czechs in America during the First World War). Praha: NLN, 2011. 162p.

a. Individuals

Vojta Beneš (1878-1951)

"Beneš, Vojta," in: Album representantů všech oborů veřejného života Československého. Ed. by Fr. Sekanina. Praha: Umělecké nakl. Josef Zeibrdlich, 1927, p. 897.

"Beneš, Vojta," in: Český biografický slovník XX. století. Praha: Paseka, 1999, I. díl, p. 82.

Václav František Jedlička (1887-?)

"Jedlička, Václav František," in: Album representantů všech oborů veřejného života Československého. Ed. by Fr. Sekanina. Praha: Umělecké nakl. Josef Zeibrdlich, 1927, p. 1201a.

"Jedlička, Francis W.," in: Czech and Slovak Leaders in Metropolitan Chicago. Ed. by Daniel D. Droba. Chicago: University of Chicago Slavonic Club, 1934, p. 90.

Thomas G. Masaryk (1850-1937)

Herben, J., T. G. Masaryk. Život a dílo presidenta Osvoboditele T. G. Masaryka (Life and work of president liberator T. G. Masaryk). Praha, 1926-27. 3 vols.

Kovtun, George J., Masarykův triumf v Americe: Příběh konce velké války (Masaryk's triumph in America: Incident of the end of the great war). Toronto: Sixty-Eight Publishers, 1987. 714p.

"Masaryk, Tomáš Garrigue," in: Český biografický slovník XX. stoleti. Praha: Paseka, 1999, II. díl, pp. 346-348.

Charles Pergler (1882-1954)

"Pergler, Karel," in: Album representantů všech oborů veřejného života Československého. Ed. by Fr. Sekanina. Praha: Umělecké nakl. Josef Zeibrdlich, 1927, p. 1079.

Charles Pergler Papers, Georgetown University, Washington, DC.

"Pergler, Karel," in: Český biografický slovník XX. století. Praha: Paseka, 1999, II. díl, p. 550.

Adolph J. Sabath (1866-1952)

Sabath, Adolph J., "Speech in the U.S. House of Representatives urging recognition of Czechs and Slovaks as a nation," Congressional Record, 56 (May 6, 1918), pp. 259-263.

"Sabath, Adolph J.," in: Album representantů všech oborů veřejného života Československého. Ed. by Fr. Sekanina. Praha: Umělecké nakl. Josef Zeibrdlich, 1927, p. 204a.

"Sabath, Adolph J.," in: Czech and Slovak Leaders in Metropolitan Chicago. Ed. by Daniel D. Droba. Chicago: University of Chicago Slavonic Club, 1934, p. 283.

Jaroslav F. Smetánka (1881-1937)

"Smetánka, Jaroslav František," in: Český biografický slovník XX. století. Praha: Paseka, 1999, III. díl, p. 155.

James F. Štěpina (1864-1923)

"James F. Štěpina," Amerikán, Národní kalendář, 1923, pp. 290-291.

"Štěpina, James, F.," in: Album representantů všech oborů veřejného života Československého. Ed. by Fr. Sekanina. Praha: Umělecké nakl. Josef Zeibrdlich, 1927, p.1150.

Jaroslav E. S. Vojan (1871-)

Vojan, Jaroslav," in: Album representantů všech oborů veřejného života Československého. Ed. by Fr. Sekanina. Praha: Umělecké nakl. Josef Zeibrdlich, 1927, p. 1206a.

"Vojan, Jaroslav E. S.," in: Czech and Slovak Leaders in Metropolitan Chicago. Ed. by Daniel D. Droba. Chicago: University of Chicago Slavonic Club, 1934, pp. 41-42.

Emanuel Viktor Voska (1875-1960)

"Voska, Emanuel Viktor," in: Album representantů všech oborů veřejného života Československého. Ed. by Fr. Sekanina. Praha: Umělecké nakl. Josef Zeibrdlich, 1927, p. 1181.

Červený, Jaroslav, Emanuel Viktor Voska. Kutnohorský rodák prvním spolupracovníkem prof. T. G. Masaryka v odboji proti Rakousku (Emanuel Viktor Voska. Kutná Hora native, the first collaborator of Prof. T. G. Masaryk in the resistance against Austria).Praha, 1928. 32p.

Voska, Emanuel V. and William H. Irwin, Spy and Counterspy. New York: Doubleday, Doran, 1940. 322p.

"Voska, Emanuel Viktor," in: Český biografický slovník XX. století. Praha: Paseka, 1999, III. díl, pp. 488-489.

Brož, Ivan, Masarykův vyzvědač (Masaryk's spy). Praha: Mladá fronta, 2004. 253p.

Oldřich Zlámal (1879-1955)

"Zlámal, Oldřich," in: Album representantů všech oborů veřejného života Československého. Ed. by Fr. Sekanina. Praha: Umělecké nakl. Josef Zeibrdlich, 1927, p. 1194.

Zlámal, Oldřich, Povídka mého života (Story of my life). Chicago: Czech Benedictine Presss, 1953. 246p.

2. Liberation from the Nazi Occupation

Beneš, Bohuš, Československá zahraniční akce (Czechoslovak resistance movement abroad). Chicago: Czechoslovak National Council of America, 1939. 110p.

Památník osvobozenecké akce Českého národního sdružení ve státu Michigan v historických letech 1939-1945 (Memorial of the liberation action of the Czech National Alliance in the State of

Michigan during the historic years, 1939-1945). Detroit, MI: Krajský výbor ČNS v Michigan, 1946. 147p.

Budín, Stanislav, Věrni zůstali. Druhý odboj amerických Čechů ve východních státech Unie, 1939-1945 (They remained faithful. The second resistance movement of American Czechs in the eastern states of the Union, 1939-1945). New York: Krajský výbor Českého národního sdružení, 1947. 303p.

Křen, Jan, Do emigrace. Západní zahraniční odboj, 1938-1939 (Toward Emigration. The Western resistance movement abroad, 1938-1939). Praha: Naše vojsko, 1967. 579p.

Papánek, Ján, "Organization in the United States of the Struggle for Czechoslovakia's Independence 1938 to 1941," in: Czechoslovak Past and Present. Ed. By Miloslav Rechcigl, Jr. Tha Hague-Paris: Mouton, 1968, vol. 1, pp. 214-223.

Křen, Jan, V emigraci. Západní zahraniční odboj 1939-1940 (In Emigration. Western resistance abroad). Praha: Naše vojsko, 1969. 615p.

Táborský, Edward, "Politics in Exile, 1939-1945," in: A History of the Czechoslovak Republic 1918-1948. Edited by Victor S. Mamatey and Radomír Luža. Princeton, NJ: Princeton University Press, 1973, pp. 322-342.

Duben, Vojtěch N., "The Information Media of the Czechoslovak Anti-Nazi Movement Abroad, 1939-1945," in: Studies in Czechoslovak History. Edited by Miloslav Rechcigl, Jr. Meerut: Sadhna Prakashan, 1976, Vol. 1, pp. 314-343.

Beneš, Bohuš. Amerika šla s námi (America went with us). Curych: Konfrontace, 1977. 188p.

Chada, Joseph, "Czech-American Aid to Czechoslovakia, September 1938-July 1942, in: The Czechs in the United Sates. SVU Press, 1981, pp. 171-185.

Chada, Joseph, "Czech-American Aid to Czechoslovakia, July 1942-January 1944," in: The Czechs in the United Sates. SVU Press, 1981, pp. 187-201.

Chada, Joseph, "Czech-American Aid to Czechoslovakia, 1944-1945," in: The Czechs in the United Sates. SVU Press, 1981, pp. 203-213.

Jožák, J., "Američtí krajané proti Mnichovu" (American compatriots against Munich), Češi v cizině, 3 (1988), pp. 21-43.

Jožák, Jiří, "Vztah amerického krajanského hnuti k pomnichovskému Československu" (The attitude of American Czechs to post-Munich Czechoslovakia), Češi v cizině, 4 (1989), pp. 590-62.

Jožák, Jiří, "K historii Čs. zahraniční akce v USA: 15.3-1.9.1939" (History of Czechoslovak campaign abroad in the US: March 15th—Sept. 1st, 1939), Historie a vojenství, 5 (1991), pp. 43-77.

Jožák, Jiří, "Američti krajané a čs. zahraniční odboj 1938-1945" (Our American compatriots and the Czechoslovak resistance abroad 1938-1945), Češi v cizině, 8 (1995,), pp. 12-25.

3. Liberation from the Communists

Beneš, Vojta, Poslání československých krajanů v Americe (Mission of Czechoslavak people in America). New York: New Yorské Listy, 1950. 53p.

Trapl, Miloš, Exil po únoru 1948. Počátky politické organizovanosti a činnosti poúnorové emigrace a vznik Rady svobodného Československa (Exile after February 1948. Beginnings of political organizing and activity of the post-February emigration and the origin of the Council of Free Czechoslovakia). Olomouc: Centrum pro československá exilová studia, Univerzita Palackého, 1996. 76p.

Jirásek, Zdeněk and Miloš Trapl, Exilová politika v letech 1948-1956 (Exile politics in 1948-1956). Olomouc, 1996. 120p.

Lukeš, Igor, "Czechoslovak Political Exile in the Cold War: The Early Years," The Polish Review, 47, No. 3 (2002), pp. 332-343.

Lukeš, Igor, Československý politický exil za studené války" (Czechoslovak political exile during the Cold War), Střední Evropa, 2, 119 (2004), pp. 68-79.

Raška, Francis D., "International Activities of the Council of Free Czechoslovakia," Kosmas, 21, No. 1 (Fall 2007), pp.45-69.

Tomek, Prokop, "The Highs and Lows of Czech and Slovak Émigré Action," in: Anti-Communist Minorities in the US. Political Action of Ethnic Refugees. Ed. Eva Zake. New York: Palgrave Macmillan, 2009, pp. 109-126.

C. Contacts & Attitudes of the Homeland to Czech-Americans & vice versa

Drtina, František, Kulturní styky amerických Čechů s domovinou (Cultural contacts of American Czechs with their homeland). Praha: Beaufort, 1918? 15p.

Československý ústav zahraniční, "Krajané v cizině a jejich styky s domovem" (Our compatriots abroad and their relations with the homeland) Ročenka 2. Praha, 1931. 53p.

Klíma, Stanislav, Československá péče krajanská (Czechoslovak care for their countrymen). Praha: Orbis, 1931. 34p.

Auerhan, Jan: Československé jazykové menšiny v evropském zahraničí: Národnostní poměry, v nichž žijí, a vztahy, které je poutají k staré vlasti (Czechoslovak language minorities in other European countries: Nationalistic conditions, under which they live, and which tie them to their old homeland). Praha: Orbis, 1935.

Brouček, Stanislav: Krajané a domov. Nástin dějin Československého ústavu zahraničního 1928-1939 (Our countrymen abroad and their homeland. Outline of history of the Czechoslovak Foreign Institute). Praha: Československý ústav zahraniční a Ústav pro etnografii a folkloristiku ČSAV, 1985.

Kašpar, Oldřich, Tam za mořem je Amerika: Dopisy a vzpomínky českých vystěhovalců do Ameriky v 19. století (Beyond the sea is America. Letters and reminiscences of Czech emigrants to America in the 19th century). Praha: Československý spisovatel 1986. 240p.

Brouček, S., Československý ústav zahraniční a kulturní podpora krajanským organizacím" (Czechoslovak Foreign Institute and cultural support of Czech organizations abroad), in: Zahraniční Slováci a národné kulturné dedičstvo. Martin, 1984.

Brouček, S., Krajané a domov. Nástin dějin Československého ústavu zahraničního 1928-1939 (Our compatriots and their homeland. Outline of history of the Czechoslovak Foreign institute 1928-1939), Praha, 1985.

Šolle, Zdeněk, "Vojtěch Náprstek and his Era: Bohemia, the United States, and the Transmission of Cultures," East Central Europe, 17, No. 1 (Spring 1990), pp. 1-30.

Češi za hranicemi na přelomu 20. a 21. století. Symposium o českém vystěhovalectví, exulantsví a vztazích zahraničních Čechů k domovu (Czechs abroad at the turn of the 20th and 21st centuries. A symposium about Czech emigration, the exile and relations of Czechs abroad with their homeland). Edited by Karel Hrubý and Stanislav Brouček. Praha: Univezita Karlova, 2000.

Bittmman, Ladislav, Mezinárodní dezinformace, černá propaganda, aktivní opatření a tajné akce (International misinformation, black propaganda, action procedures, and secret actions). Praha: Mladá fronta, 2000. 358p.

Emigrace a exil jako způsob života. II. Sympozium o českém vystěhovalectví, exulantství a vztazích zahraničních Čechů k domovu (Emigration and exile as a means of life. II. Symposium about Czech emigration, exile and relations of Czechs abroad to their homeland). Praha: Univerzita Karlova v Praze—Karolinum, ve spolupráci s Etnologickým ústavem AV ČR v Praze, 2001.

Nosková, Helena, "Československo a krajané 1918-1948" (Czechoslovakia and its compatriots), in: Emigrace z českých zemí. Sborník referátů ze semináře 'Historie emigrace z českých zemí,' Mladá Boleslav, 2000. Mladá Boleslav: Okresní museum, 2001, pp. 67-89.

Rosická, P., Česká emigrace v Severní Americe a její vztah k ČR (Czech emigration to America and its relation to the Czech Republic). Diplomová práce. Praha, Vysoká škola ekonomická, 2001.

Brouček, Stanislav: Exil sám o sobě (Exile about itself). Týden zahraničních Čechů: III. setkání nad českým vystěhovalectvím, exulantstvím a vztahy zahraničních Čechů k domovu: 28. září—4. října 2003. Praha: Etnologický ústav Akademie věd ČR v Praze, 2006

Brouček, Stanislav and Tomáš Grulich, Domácí postoje k zahraničním Čechům v novodobých dějinách (1918-2008) (Domestic attitudes toward Czechs abroad in contemporary history 1918-2008). Praha: Etnologický ústav AV ČR, 2009. 232p.

Brouček, Stanislav and Tomáš Grulich, Krajané a Česká republika. Hledání možnosti k nové otevřené spolupráci (Our Compatriots and the Czech Republic. Seeking possibilities for a new open cooperation). Praha: Etnologický ústav AV ČR, 2009. 88p.

XII. Genealogy

A. General References

1. Guides

Nelson, Vernon H., "Moravian Genealogical Research." Pennsylvania Genealogical Magazine, 29 (1975), pp. 41-50.

Rottenberg, Dan, "Czechoslovakia," in: Finding Our Fathers. New York: Random House, 1977, pp. 98-100.

Miller, Olga K., Genealogical Research for Czech and Slovak Americans. Detroit, ME: Gale Research Co., ca 1978. 187p.

Sobotka, Rudie, "Finding Your Czech Ancestors," Journal of Genealogy, 3, No. 7 (July 1978), pp. 14-23.

Wellauer, Marylyn A., Tracing Your Czech and Slovak Roots. Milwaukee, WI, 1980. 77p.

Blaha, Albert J., Czech Genealogists' Handbook for Tracing Your Czech Ancestors in the Lone Star State and Czechoslovakia. Houston, TX, 1984. 105p.; 4th ed., 1986.

Fast, Jane, Genealogical Research: Tracing Czech, Moravian, and Slovak Ancestry. Czech Fine Arts Foundation, Inc., 1984. 4p.

Schlyter, Daniel M., A Handbook of Czechoslovak Genealogical Research. Buffalo Grove, IL: Genealogy Unlimited, 1985. 131p.

Baxter, Angus, "Czechoslovakia," in: In Search of your European Roots. A complete guide to Tracing your ancestors in every country to Europe. Baltimore: Genealogical Publishing Co., Inc., 1986, pp. 53-64.

Milberger, Olivia and Doris Obsta, Checking your Czech Ancestors. Seventy-five (and Maybe More) Resources for Tracing your Czech Ancestors. Victoria, TX: Authors, 1990. 154p.

Rechcigl, Miloslav, Jr., Czech and Slovak Genealogy, A Bibliography of Publications in English and Guide to other Information Resources. Rockville, MD: Author, 1999.

Rechcigl, Miloslav, Jr., Czechoslovak Genealogy Sites on the Internet. Rockville, MD: SVU, 1999. 74p.

Ackman & Ziff Family Genealogy Institute, Czech and Slovak Republics: Jewish Family History Research Guide. New York: Ackman & Ziff Family Genealogy Institute • Center for Jewish History, 2007. 4p.

2. Archival Materials

A Guide to Czech Sources at the Nebraska State Historical Society, P.O. Box 82554, 1500 R Street, Lincoln, NE 6850. Also on Internet: http://www.nebraskahistory.org/lib-arch/services/refrence/la_pubs/Czech_Reference_Guide_2010.pdf

3. Periodicals

Naše Dějiny (Our History).The Magazine of Czech Genealogy and Culture. A bimonthly. Ed. by Doug Kubíček. Hallettsville, TX: The Old Homestead Publishing Co, 1982-89, Vol. 1-8.

Naše Rodina (Our Family). Newsletter of the Czechoslovak Genealogical Society. A quarterly. St. Paul, MN, 1989-. Vol. 1-.

Kořeny (Roots). Journal of the Czech & Slovak American Genealogical Society of Illinois. Quarterly. Chicago, IL, 1997-. Vol. 1-.

České stopy (Czech Foot Prints). Published by Texas Genealogical Society. Quarterly. 2001-.

Včera a dnes (Yesterday and Today). Journal published by Arizona Czechoslovak Genealogical Society. Quarterly, vol. 1-. 1997-.

The GBHS Heimatbrief Newsletter. Published by German-Bohemian Heritage Society (CBHS). Quarterly. New Ulm, MN, 1990-. Vol. 1-.

FEEFHS Newsletter. Published by Federation of East European Family History Societies (FEEFHS). Quarterly, vol. 1-. 1987-.

East European Genealogist. Published by East European Genealogical Society, Inc. (EEGS), Quarterly, vol. 1-, 1991-.

4. Gazetteers

Schlyter, Daniel M., "Czechoslovak Research and Use of Gazetteers," in: The Genealogical Helper, 33, No. 1 (January-February 1977), pp. 9-15.

Janak, Robert. Gazetteer of Czech Texas. Temple, TX: Czech Heritage Society of Texas, 1995. 186p.

Janak, Robert, Geographic Origin of Czech Texas. Beaumont, TX: Author, 1985. 40p.

Hejl, Edmond H., Villages of Origin (Protestant). Fort Worth, TX: Author, 1983. 112p.

Hejl, Edmond H., Villages of Origin Revisited. Beaumont, TX: Czech Heritage Society of Texas, 1993. 210p.

5. Genealogical Societies

Czechoslovak Genealogical Society International, Inc. (CGSI)
Address: P. O. Box 16225, St. Paul, MN 55116-0225
Publications: Naše Rodina (Our Family), Quarterly, vol. 1-, 1989-; Ročenka (Yearbook), Annually, vol. 1-5, 1992-2002.

Czech and Slovak American Genealogy Society of Illinois (CSAGSI)
Address: P.O. Box 313, Sugar Drove, IL 60554
Publication: Kořeny (Roots), Quarterly, vol. 1-, 1996-.

Czech and Slovak Genealogical Society of Arizona
Address: P.O. Box 82656, Phoenix, AZ 85071
Publication: Včera a dnes (Yesterday and Today), Quarterly, vol. 1-. 1997-.

East European Genealogical Society, Inc. (EEGS)
Address: P. O. Box 2536, Winnipeg, Manitoba R3C 4A7, Canada
Publication: East European Genealogist, Quarterly, vol. 1-. 1991-.

Federation of East European Family History Societies (FEEFHS)
Address: P.O. Box 4327, Salt Lake City, UT 84151-0898
Publication: FEEFHS Newsletter, Quarterly, vol. 1-, 1987-.

German-Bohemian Heritage Society (CBHS)
Address: P.O. Box 822, New Ulm, MN 56073-0822
Publication: The GBHS Heimatbrief Newsletter Quarterly, vol. 1-. 1990-.

Moravian Heritage Society
Address: 6N432 Oakwood Drive Saint Charles, IL 60174
Publication: Morava Krásná, Quarterly, vol. 1, 1994-.

Silesian American Genealogy Society (SAGS)
Address: 1910 East 5685 South, Salt Lake City, UT 84121-1343

Texas Czech Genealogical Society
Address: TCGS, 1231 CR 201A, Angleton, TX 77515-7629
Publication: České stopy (Czech Foot Prints), Quarterly, vol. 1-. 2001-.

B. Sources of Vital Data

1. Passenger Lists

Jordan, John W., Moravian Immigration to Pennsylvania, 1734-1767, with some account of the transport vessels, Transactions of the Moravian Historical Society, vol. 5, Part 2. Bethlehem, PA: 1896, pp. 51-**90.**

Jordan, John W., "Moravian Immigration to Pennsylvania 1734-1765," Pennsylvania Magazine of History and Biography, 33 (1909), pp. 228-246.

Sobotka, Margie, Czech Immigration Passenger Lists for Nebraska 1879. Abstracted from *Hospodář.* Elkhorn, NE: Author, 1982.

Mares, Claire, Ship Passenger Lists. Port of Baltimore, Maryland, 4 May through 30 December 1874, Freemont, NE: Eastern Nebraska Genealogical Society, 1984. 111p.

Hejl, Edmund, Galveston Passenger Lists. Post Civil War 1866-1871," Naše Dějiny 3, No. 1 (Jan.-Feb. 1984), pp. 12-13; Ibid. 3, No. 2 (March-April 1984), pp. 15-16; Ibid. 3, No. 3 (May-June 1984), pp. 16-18; Ibid. 3, No. 4 (July-Aug. 1984), 1984), pp. 15-17; Ibid. 3, No. 5 (Sept.-Oct. 1984), pp. 7-9; Ibid. 3, No. 6 (Nov.-Dec. 1984), pp. 16-17; Ibid. 4, No. 1 (Jan-Feb. 1985), pp. 9, 18-19; Ibid.4, No. 2 (Mar.-Apr. 1985), pp. 15-18.

Blaha, Albert J., Lists of Passenger Ships. Bremen and Hamburg to Indianola, Galveston, New Orleans and Charleston. Houston, TX: Author, 1984. 49p.

Blaha, Albert J., Passenger Lists for Galveston 1850-1855. Houston, TX: Author, 1985. 90p.

Blaha, Albert J., Passenger Lists of the Pioneer Czech Immigrants into Texas 1850-1870. Houston, TX: Author, 1986. 57p.

Baca, Leo, Czech Immigration Passenger Lists. Hallettsville, TX: Old Homestead Publishing Co., 1985-2000, Vol. 1-9.

Rechcigl, Miloslav, Jr., "Moravian Brethren from Bohemia, Moravia and Silesia: Their Arrival and Settlement in America," Bohemia Zeitschrtft, 32, No. 1 (1991), pp. 152-165.

2. Settler Lists

Iowa

Zaruba, Jerry, Jr., Family Records of the Bohemian Settlers in Ringgold County, Iowa. 1943.

Minnesota

Shepard, Karleen Chott, Earliest Czech Settlers in the West Seventh Street Area, St. Paul, Minnesota," Naše Dějiny, 5, No. 4 (1986), pp. 10-20.

Missouri

Sommer, June M., "Czech (Bohemian) Resources in St. Louis, Missouri, and the Surrounding Area, Part I," St. Louis Genealogical Society Quarterly, 39, No. 3 (Fall 2006), pp. 80-84.

Sommer, June M., "Czech (Bohemian) Resources in St. Louis, Missouri, and the Surrounding Area, Part II," St. Louis Genealocial Society Quarterly, 39, No. 4 (Winter 2006), pp. 115-120.

Nebraska

Sobotka, Margie, Index of Czech Settlers in Nebraska (Birthplace and County of Residence, 1864-1892). Elkhorn, NE: Author, 1976.

Sobotka, Margie. Nebraska-Kansas Czech Settlers 1891-1895. Omaha, NE: Eastern Nebraska Genealogical Society, n.d. 251p.

Pennsylvania

Neisser, George, A List of the Bohemian and Moravian Emigration to Saxony. Translated and edited by Albert C. Rau. Bethlehem,

PA: Times Publishing Co., 1913, in: Transactions of the Moravian Historical Society, 9 (1913), pp. 37-100.

Neisser, George, "Brief Treatise Concerning the Initial Spread of the Moravian and Bohemian Brethren in the North American Colonies and Missions from the year 1732 to 1741," in: A History of the Beginnings of Moravian Work in America, being a Translation of George Neisser's Manuscripts . . . begun by the late Rev. William N. Schwarze, archivist and completed by the Rt. Rev. Samuel H. F Gapp, archivist with extensive liturgical and historical notes by the Rt. Rev. S. H. Gapp. Bethlehem, PA: The Archives of the Moravian Church, 1955, pp. 5-26.

Texas

Blaha, Albert J., Settlements and Families in Texas before 1900. Houston, TX: Author, 1983.

Blaha, Albert J., ed. Czech Settlements and Families in Texas before 1900. Houston, TX: Author, 1983. 172p.

Fayette County History Book Committee, Fayette County, Texas, Heritage. Dallas, TX: Curtis Media, Inc., 1996. 2 vols., 1073p.

Gallup, Sean N., Journeys into Czech-Moravian Texas. College Station, TX: Texas A&M University Press, 1998. 140p.

Gillespie, Bettie, The History of Telico, Texas and Surrounding Communities. Dallas, TX: Curtis Media, Inc., 1995. 322p.

Janacek, John E., Czechs and Others at Eastgate, Liberty County, Texas. Yorktown, TX: DeWitt County View, 1993. 184p.

Juricek, Vlasta and Mary Ann Polansky, The History of the La Parita Community. Jourdanton, TX: Published Privately, 1990. 40p.

Kana, Sharon and Karen Phillipus, Centennial History of St. John the Baptist Parish, Ammannsville, Texas, 1890-1990. Ammannsville, TX: St. John the Baptist Parish, 1990. 207p.

Lee County Historical Survey Committee, History of Lee County, Texas. Austin, TX: Nortex Press, 2000. 389p.

Limmer, E. A., Jr., ed., Story of Bell County, Texas. Austin, TX: Eakin Press, 1988. 2 vols. 1056p.

Lee County Historical Survey Committee, History of Lee County. Quanah, TX: Nortex Press, 1974. 2 vols. 502p.

Mesecke, Anjanette, Proceedings of the Second Czech Symposium, Czech Footprints Across the Bluebonnet Fields of Texas, With a Focus on the Pioneer Czech Families of Texas. Temple, TX: Temple Junior College, 1983. 190p.

Texas Czech Genealogical Society, Czech Family Histories. 4 volumes. Texas Czech Genealogical Society, 2005, 2007. 984p.

White, Michael, ed., Rowena Centennial.Celebrating Rowena's First 100 Years, July 4th, 1998. Ballinger, TX: Ballinger Printing and Graphics, 1998. 100p.

Williams, Marjorie L., Fayette County Past & Present. La Grange, TX: Author, 1976. 473p.

3. Census Records

Blaha, Albert J., ed., Pioneer Czech Families in Texas before 1860. Houston, TX: Author, 1983. 106p.

Blaha, Albert J., ed., Czech Families of Fayette County. Houston, TX: Author, 1984. 2 vols. 778p.

Blaha, Albert J., Hranice: The Moravian Settlement on the Yegua. Houston, TX: Author, 1986. 327p.

Bujnoch, Dorothy & Anne Rhodes, Czech Footprints Across Lavaca County 1860-1900. Vol. 1. Hallettsville, TX: Authors, 1984. 470p.

Clowe, Grace Campbell, Austin County, Texas. Czech Census Extracts 1860, 1870, 1880 and 1900. Albuquerque, NM: By the Author, 1983. 358p.

Clowe, Grace Campbell, Colorado County, Texas. Czech Census Extracts 1860, 1870, 1880 and 1900. Albuquerque, NM: Author, 1983. 203p.

Clowe, Grace Campbell, Czech Extractions from McLennan County, Texas. Albuquerque, NM: Author, 1985. 70p.

Clowe, Grace Campbell, Czechs in Wesley and Latium, Washington County. Albuquerque, NM: Author, 1985. 104p.

Clowe, Grace Campbell, Declarations and Marriages of the Czechs in Colorado County. Albuquerque, NM: Author, 1985. 75p.

Gloeckner, Annie Mae, Czechs in Wharton County. Pierce, TX: Author, 1985. 93p.

Janak, Robert, Kovar, Texas, and its Czech Evangelical Community. Houston, TX: The Czech Heritage Society of Texas, 2009. 433p.

Layman, Helen, Czech Families in Fayette County, Texas in 1910. Extractions from the United States Census. Houston, TX: Czech Heritage Society of Texas, 2000. 396p.
Layman, Helen, Czech Families in Hill County, Texas in 1900 & 1910. Extractions from the United States Census. Houston, TX: Czech Heritage Society of Texas, 2001. 59p.
Layman, Helen, Czech Families in Milam County, Texas in 1880, 1900 & 1910. Extractions from the United States Census. Houston, TX: Czech Heritage Society of Texas, 2001. 154p.
Layman, Helen, Czech Families in Williamson County, Texas in 1910. Extractions from the United States Census. Houston, TX: Czech Heritage Society of Texas, 2000. 204p.
Layman, Helen, Czech Records of Burleson Co. Houston, TX: Czech Heritage Society of Texas, 1989. 149p.
Layman, Helen, Czech Records of Williamson Co. Houston, TX: Czech Heritage Society of Texas, 1990. 138p.
Layman, Helen and others, Brazos County 1900-1910 Czech Census Extractions. Texas Czech Genealogical Society, 2006. 147p.
Vrana, William, History of Moravia Community, Lavaca County, Texas, 1881-1996. Corpus Christi: By the Author, n.d.

4. Naturalization Records

Bujnoch, Dorothy & Anne Rhodes, Czech Footprints across Lavaca County 1860-1900. Vol. 2. Hallettsville, TX: Authors, 1986. 400p.
Ellis County Genealogical Society, Ellis County, Texas, Naturalization Records. Waxahachie, TX: Ellis County Genealogical Society, 1980. 72p.
Friemel, Nollie, Declarations of the Czechs in Fayette County. Fayetteville, TX: Author, 1982. 153p.
Clowe, Grace Cambell, Declarations and Marriages of the Czechs in Colorado County. Albuquerque, NM: The Author, 1985. 75 p. (Czech Footprints Across the Bluebonnet Fields of Texas).
Hejl, Edmond H., Czech Immigration and Naturalization Records in Texas. Beaumont, TX: Czech Heritage Society of Texas, 1997. 323p.

Leland, Anthony DeWitt, Declarations by the Czechs in Austin County. By the Author, 1983. 102p. Zavadil, John. Early Czechs in Gonzales County. Gonzales, TX: Author, 1986. 109p.

5. Church Membership Records

Reincke, Abraham, A Register of Members of the Moravian Church and Persons Attached to Said Church in this Country and Abroad between 1727 and 1754. Translated by W. C. Reichel. Transactions of the Moravian Historical Society, 1, No. 7-9 (1857-58), pp. 238-426.

Jordan, John W., "A Register of Members of the Moravian Church who Emigrated to Pennsylvania 1742-1767," in: Notes and Queries. Ed. By William H. Egle. Baltimore, MD: Genealogical Publishing Co., 1970, 4th ser., Vol. 1 (1893), pp. 162-163, 167-170, 174-175, 208-211, 303-304; Ibid., 4th series, vol. 2 (1894), pp. 1-3.

Jordan, John W., A Register of Members of the Moravian Church who Immigrated from Europe to America between 1734 and 1800. Salt Lake City: Genealogical Society of Utah, 1948.

6. Church Register Records

Barton, Rev. Josef, Taylor Czech-Moravian Brethren Church Records by Rev. Josef Barton. Vol. 1 (1910-1920). Houston: The Czech Heritage Society of Texas. 159p.

Blaha, Albert J. and Edmond H. Hejl, Register Records of the Czech-Moravian Brethren. Houston, TX.: Wesley 1980. 330 p.; Ross Prairie, 1982. 428 p.; Nelsonville, 1982. 161p.

Motycka, Anton, Register Records of the Czech-Moravian Brethren (Czech footprints across the bluebonnet fields of Texas). 1982.

Hejl, Edmond H., Czech-Moravian Brethren Register Records of Nelsonville, Texas, 1900-1921. Beaumont, TX: Czech Heritage Society of Texas, 1992. 337p.

Hejl, Edmond H., Czech-Moravian Brethren Register Records of Rev. Jindrich Juren, 1900-1921. Beaumont, TX: Czech Heritage Society of Texas, 1992. 136p.

Hejl, Edmond H., Rev. Adolf Chlumsky's Register Records of the Czech-Moravian Brethren in Texas. Fort Worth, TX: By the Author, 1986. 201p.

Hejl, James L., Rev. Frank J. Kostohryz's Baptismal Records. Ministerial Records Extracted from Monthly Copies of the Brethren Journal. Houston: The Czech Heritage Society of Texas, 2006. 221p.

Hejl, James L., Rev. Frank J. Kostohryz's Funeral Records. Ministerial Records Extracted from Monthly Copies of the Brethren Journal. Houston: The Czech Heritage Society of Texas, 2005. 266p.

Hejl, James L., Rev. Frank J. Kostohryz's Marriage Records. Ministerial Records Extracted from Monthly Copies of the Brethren Journal. Houston: The Czech Heritage Society of Texas, 2005. 117p.

Hrncir, Marilyn McGehearty, Czech Entries from the Register Records of the Holy Rosary Catholic Church, Bluff (Hostyn), Texas 1884-1900. Houston, TX: Published Privately, 1983. 132p. Republished in 1992 by the Czech Heritage Society of Texas.

Hrncir, Marilyn McGehearty, Extracts of Czech Entries from St. John the Baptist Catholic Church, Ammannsville, Fayette County, Texas. Houston, TX: Published Privately, 1983. 111p. Republished in 1992 by the Czech Heritage Society of Texas.

Hrncir, Marilyn McGehearty, Register Records of St. Mary's Catholic Church, Fayette County, Praha, Texas. Houston, TX: Published Privately, 1985. 80p. Republished in 1992 by the Czech Heritage Society of Texas.

Hrncir, Marilyn McGehearty, Sts. Peter and Paul Catholic Church, Frelsburg, Texas. Austin, TX: By the Author, 1988. 135p.

Janak, Robert, Rev. Frank Horak's Baptismal Records. Czech-Moravian Brethren Church Records of Caldwell, Texas, and Surrounding Congregations. Beaumont, TX: Czech Heritage Society of Texas, 1999. 251p.

Janak, Robert, Rev. Frank Horak's Confirmation Records. Czech-Moravian Brethren Church Records of Caldwell, Texas, and Surrounding Congregations. Houston: The Czech Heritage Society of Texas, 2006. 187p.

Janak, Robert, Rev. Frank Horak's Funeral Records. Czech-Moravian Brethren Church Records of Caldwell, Texas, and Surrounding Congregations. Beaumont, TX: Czech Heritage Society of Texas, 1998. 122p.

Janak, Robert, Rev. Frank Horak's Marriage Records. Czech-Moravian Brethren Church Records of Caldwell, Texas, and Surrounding

Congregations. Beaumont, TX: Czech Heritage Society of Texas, 2000. 94p.
Janak, Robert, Rev. Henry E. Beseda, Sr.'s Baptismal Records. Czech Moravian Brethren Church Records of Caldwell, Texas, and Other Congregations. Houston: The Czech Heritage Society of Texas, 2003. 209p.
Janak, Robert, Rev. Henry E. Beseda, Sr.'s Marriage Records. Czech Moravian Brethren Church Records of Caldwell, Texas, and Other Congregations. Houston: The Czech Heritage Society of Texas, 2002. 140p.
Janak, Robert, Rev. Josef Barton's Baptismal Records. Czech Moravian Brethren Church Records of Rev. Josef Barton and Other Ministers from Taylor, Texas, and Surrounding Congregations. Houston: The Czech Heritage Society of Texas, 2004. 349p.
Janak, Robert, Rev. Josef Barton's Funeral Records. Czech Moravian Brethren Church Records of Rev. Josef Barton and Other Ministers from Taylor, Texas, and Surrounding Congregations. Houston: The Czech Heritage Society of Texas, 2005. 168p.
Janak, Robert, Rev. Josef Barton's Marriage Records. Czech Moravian Brethren Church Records of Rev. Josef Barton and Other Ministers from Taylor, Texas, and Surrounding Congregations. Houston: The Czech Heritage Society of Texas, 2004. 175p.
Janak, Robert, Rev. Josef Hegar's Baptismal Records. Czech Moravian Brethren Church Records of Temple, Texas, and Surrounding Congregations. Houston: The Czech Heritage Society of Texas, 2002. 263p.
Janak, Robert, Rev. Josef Hegar's Confirmation Records. Czech Moravian Brethren Church Records of Temple, Texas, and Surrounding Congregations. Houston: The Czech Heritage Society of Texas, 2004. 169p.
Janak, Robert, Rev. Josef Hegar's Funeral Records. Czech-Moravian Brethren Church Records of Temple, Texas, and Surrounding Congregations. Beaumont, TX: Czech Heritage Society of Texas, 2000. 109p.
Janak, Robert, Rev. Josef Hegar's Marriage Records. Czech Moravian Brethren Church Records of Temple, Texas, and Surrounding Congregations. Houston: The Czech Heritage Society of Texas, 2001. 121p.

Janak, Robert, "The Czech Heritage Society of Texas and Publication of Czech-Moravian Brethren Ministerial Records," in: Selected Papers from the Conference of the Czechoslovak Society of Arts and Sciences at the Moravian College, Bethlehem, PA, June 8-10, 2007, pp. 121-32.

7. Civil Register Records

Barler, Beatrice Ripple, Marriage Licenses (Issued to Czechs) Austin County. Bellville, TX: By the Author, 1981. 86p. (Czech Footprints across the Bluebonnet Fields of Texas).

Cernosek, Donald & Grace Campbell Clowe, Czech Marriage Records of Fayette County 1850-1900. Houston, TX: Published Privately, 1984. 93p. (Czech Footprints across the Bluebonnet Fields of Texas).

Smith, E. F., Obituaries from May 1957 to May 1969: Lavaca County Tribune, Hallettsville, Texas. Conroe, TX: J. Valigura, 1984. 314p.

Hejl, Edmond H., Birth Records of the Nativity of Mary, Blessed Virgin, Catholic Church, High Hill (Fayette County), Texas 1875-1899. Beaumont, TX: Czech Heritage Society of Texas, 1992. 173p.

Hejl, Edmond H., Birth Records of the St. Michael's Catholic Church, Weimar (Colorado County), Texas 1889-1900. Beaumont, TX: Czech Heritage Society of Texas, 1992. 67p.

Sobotka, Margie, Marriages and Divorces. Nová Doba (New Era) Abstractions and Translations. By Margie Sobotka. Privately printed.

8. Cemetery Records

Schultze, Augustus, "The Old Moravian Cemetery of Bethlehem, PA 1742 1897," in: Transactions of the Moravian Historical Society, 5 (1897), pp. 97-218.

Beck, Abraham Reinke, "The Moravian Graveyards of Lititz, PA, 1744-1905." Transactions of the Moravian Historical Society 7 (1906), pp. 215-336.

Kluge, Edw. T., "The Moravian Graveyards at Nazareth, PA 1744-1904." Transactions of the Moravian Historical Society, 7 (1906), pp. 83-207.

Sobotka, Margie, Burials at Bohemian National Cemetery in Omaha, Jan. 1977—Dec. 1984. Omaha, NE: Author, 1985.

Janak, Robert, Old Bohemian Tombstones, Beaumont, TX, Vol. 1 (1983) 142p.; Vol. 2 (1985) 167p.; Vol. 3 (1987) 200p.

Janak, Robert. Czech Birthplaces on Texas Tombstones. Beaumont, TX: Author, 1999. 269p.

Janak, Robert, Czech Inscriptions on Texas Tombstones. Beaumont, TX: Author, 1997. 122p.

Bohemian National Cemetery, Chicago, Illinois. Transcribed, compiled, and edited by the Czech and Slovak Interest Group. Chicago: Chicago Genealogical Society, 1995-1998. Vol. 1. Burials, 1877-1887; Vol. 2. Burials, 1888-1892; Vol. 3. Burials, 1893-1895; Vol. 4. Burials, 1896-1899.

Janak, Robert, Old Czech Cemeteries at Granger, Texas. Houston, TX: The Czech Heritage Society of Texas, 2002. 127p.

Janak, Robert, Urbish Funeral Home Records. East Bernard, Wharton County, Texas, 1923-1965. Houston: The Czech Heritage Society of Texas, 2004. 364p.

Tise, Sammy, Lavaca County, Texas, Cemetery Records, vol. 1. Hallettsville, TX: Author, 1983. 177p.

Tise, Sammy, Lavaca County, Texas, Cemetery Records, vol. 2. Hallettsville, TX: Author, 1985. 286p.

Tise, Sammy, Lavaca County, Texas, Cemetery Records, vol. 3. Hallettsville, TX: Author, 1990. 180p.

Tise, Sammy, Lavaca County, Texas, Cemetery Records, vol. 4. Hallettsville, TX: Author, 1990. 188p.

Tise, Sammy, Lavaca County, Texas, Cemetery Records, vol. 5. Hallettsville, TX: Author, 1998. 266p.

Tise, Sammy, Lavaca County, Texas, Cemetery Records, vol. 6. Hallettsville, TX: Author, 1998. 209p.

Tise, Sammy, Wharton County Cemetery Survey. Hallettsville, TX: Author, 1998. 4 vols. 923p.

9. Newspaper Abstracts & other Sources

Sobotka, Margie, compiler. Fraternal Herald Obituaries & Index, Jan. 1975-Dec.1978. Omaha, NE: Sobotka, 1979.

Sobotka, Margie, compiler and Mayme S. Perina, translator. Nová Doba (New Era) Abstractions & Translations—Marriages & Divorces (1911-1914). Elkhorn, NE: Sobotka, 1981.

Sobotka, Margie, compiler, and Mayme S. Perina, translator. Nová Doba (New Era) Abstractions & Translations—Births (1911-1918). Elkhorn, NE: Sobotka, 1981.

The Denní Hlasatel Obituary Index 1891-1970. Chicago: CSAGSI, 1996.

Obituary Dates from the Denní Hlasatel (Gaily Herald): 1891-1899 By Joe Novak.

Obituary Dates from the Denní Hlasatel (Daily Herald): 1930-1939. By Joe Novak

Obituary Dates from the Denní Hlasatel (Daily Herald): 1940-1949. By Joe Novak.

Sobotka, Margie, compiler, and Mayme S. Perina, translator. Nová Doba (New Era),

Deaths & Obits (1911-1918). Elkhorn, NE: Sobotka, 1984. 97p.

Sobotka, Margie, Hlasatel Translations 1936-1937. Elkhorn, NE, June 1981. 30p.

Sobotka, Margie, Nová Doba (New Era). Abstractions and Translations, Deaths and Obituaries., Omaha, NE, 1984. 97p.

Smith, E. F., Obituaries from May 1957 to May 1969. Lavaca County Tribune, Hallettsville, Texas. Conroe, TX: Published Privately, 1984. 378p.

Labaj, Stacy Mikulencak, Obituaries of the Czech Moravian Brethren in Texas. (Taken primarily from the Brethren Journal). Houston, TX: Published Privately, 1986. 326p.

Sobotka, Margie, Hospodář 1935-1960 Deaths & Obits. Omaha, NE: By the Author, 1989. 249p.

Sobotka, Margie, compiler, Hospodář 1935-1960: Deaths & Obits. Elkhorn, NE: M. Sobotka, 1993.

Sobotka, Margie, compiler, Miscellaneous Obits from Denní Pokrok (Daily Progress), Nov. 1915. Elkhorn, NE: Sobotka, 1997.

Sobotka, Margie, compiler, Index of Names (1906-1930), Abstracted from Hospodář (Farmer). Elkhorn, NE: Sobotka, 1997.

Minnesota Deaths (1917-1927). Abstracted from Křesťanské Listy (Christian Journal). By Margie Sobotka and Karleen Chott Sheppard. 1997.

Sheppard, Karleen Chott & Margie Sobotka, Abstractions of Deaths and Miscellaneous Items (1916-1927), Křesťanské Listy, Christian Journal. Elkhorn, NE: Published Privately, 1998. 145p.

Pejskar, Jožka, Poslední pocta. Památník na zemřelé československé exulanty v letech 1948-1981 (The last honor. Memorial to deceased Czechoslovak exiles in 1948-1981). Svazek 1. Curych: Konfrontace, 1982. 323p.; Svazek 2 (1985). 368p.; Svazek 3 (1989). 317p.; Svazek 4 (1994). 247p.

10. Insurance Claims

Sobotka, Margie, Č.S.P.S. Lodge Death Claims, 1886-1896. Elkhorn, NE: By the Author, 1988.

11. Genealogical Surname Records

Czechoslovak Surname Index. Vol. 1. St. Paul, MN: CGS, May 1989. (946 surnames).

Czechoslovak Surname Index. Vol. 2. St. Paul, MN: CGS, Feb. 1990. (1250 surnames).

Czechoslovak Surname Index. Vol. 3. St. Paul, MN: CGS, June 1992). (1719 surnames).

Czechoslovak Surname Index. Vol. 4. St. Paul, MN: CGS, 1993. (1700 surnames).

Czechoslovak Surname Index. Vol. 5. St. Paul, MN: CGS, May 1994. (1509 surnames).

Czechoslovak Surname Index. Vol. 6. St. Paul, MN: CGS, March 1995. (1745 surnames).

Appendix A: Czechs in Canada

I. General References

A. Bibliographies

Czechs and Slovaks in Canada. A Reading List. Ottawa: Library of the Department of Citizenship and Immigration, 1965. 2p.

Gregorovich, Andrew, Czechs," in: A Bibliography of Canada's Peoples, Supplement 1: 1972-1979, Ed. By Gabriele Scar-dellato. Toronto, 1993, pp. 148-51,

Peprnik, Jaroslav, Perception of Canada in Czech Literature," in: Theory and Practice in English Studies 4 (2005): Proc. From the 8th Conference of British, American and Canadian Studies. Brno, Masarykova univerzita.

B. Biographies

"Contributions of Czechs and Slovaks to Canada," in: Naše Hlasy (Our Voices). Centennial issue. 1857-1967. Naše Hlasy, 13, No. 21-22 (May 27, 1967), pp. 23-61. Includes biographies.

Rechcigl, Miloslav, Jr., Eva Rechcigl and Jiří Eichler, "II. Biographical Section. Members' Directory," in: SVU Directory. Organization, Activities, and Biographies of Members. 8th ed. Washington, DC: SVU Press, 2003, pp. 33-358. Includes Czech Canadians.

Čermák, Josef, It all Started with Prince Rupert. The Story of Czechs and Slovaks in Canada. Luhačovice: Etelier IM Publishing Co., 2003. 367p. Includes biographies.

Zaoral, Roman, Osobnosti kanadského exilu. krajane.net March 4, 2008 11:06

Czech Immigrants to Canada: Vladimír Kulich, Petr Nedved, Alex Baumann, Lotta Hitschmanová, Rick Lanz, Václav Chvátal, Otto Jelinek, David Nykl. Memphis, TN: Books LLC, 2010. 78p.

C. Periodicals

Škvor, J. G. and Nikolai Žekulín, "Czech-Canadian Periodical Publishers. A Preliminary Checklist," Canada Ethnic Studies, vol. 1 (1969); vol. 5, No. 1-2 (1973), pp. 3-5, 31-33.

D. Archival Material

Zaoral, Roman, "Přehled archivních fondů k dějinám Čechů v Kanadě" (Overview of archival collections regarding the history of Czechs in Canada), in: České archivy a prameny k dějinám zahraničních Čechů. Ed. by Milena Secká, Jiří Křesťan and Jan Kahuda. Praha: Národní archiv, 2007, pp. 21-132.

II. History

A. General Surveys

Hájek, J., "Československá větev v Kanadě" (Czechoslovak branch in Canada), Naše zahraničí (1920).

Hájek, J, "Naši v Kanadě" (Our people in Canada), Amerikán, Národní kalendář, 45 (1922), pp. 213-220.

Ruda, V., "Čechoslováci v Kanadě" (Czechoslovaks in Canada), Naše zahraničí, 4 (1923), pp. 71-73.

Hájek, Josef, "Dějiny kanadských Čechoslováků" (History of Canadian Czechoslovaks), Naše zahraničí, 133, No. 5 (1931), pp. 211-214.

Buzek, Karel, L. Wauthierová, A. Haasová, eds., comp., Památník československé Kanady (Memorial of the Czechoslovak Canada). Toronto: Czechoslovak National Alliance in Canada, 1944. 207p.

Střížová, E., "Slované v Kanadě" (The Slavs in Canada), Slovanský přehled, Praha, 1954.

Hrubý, Jiří, Immigration des Tchèques et Slovaks au Canada. Ph.D. Dissertation, Universite de Montreal, Montreal, 1954.

Hikl, Mario, A Short History of the Czechoslovak People in Canada. Toronto: Across-Canada Press, 1955. 15p.

Čelovský, B., "People of Czech Origin," in: Encyclopedia Canadiana. Ottawa, 1958, vol. 1, pp 187-188.

Canadian Citizenship Branch, Czechs and Slovaks in Notes on the Canadian Family Tree. Ottawa, 1960, pp. 18-24.

Makon, K., "Československé vystěhovalectví do Kanady" (Czechoslovak emigration to Canada), in: Bulletin Komise pro dějiny krajanů, Čechů a Slováků v zahraničí, 5, (1967), pp. 3-10.

Naše Hlasy (Our Voices).Centennial Issue. 1867-1967, Vol. 13, No. 21-22, May 27, 1967. 100p.

Gellner, John and John Smerek, The Czechs and Slovaks in Canada. Toronto: University of Toronto Press, 1968. 172p.

Zemánek, Dita J., The Czech Emigrant Experience in Canada. Thesis.

Horna, Jarmila L. A., "The Entrance Status of Czech and Slovak Immigrant Women," in: Two Nations, Many Cultures: Ethnic Groups in Canada, edited by Jean L. Elliott. Scarborough, Ontario: Prentice-Hall of Canada, 1979, pp. 270-279.

Ivanov, M., Čech v Kanadě (A Czech in Canada). Praha 1994.

Jovanovich, Marek J., "Czechs," in: Encyclopedia of Canada's People. Ed. By Paul Robert Magocsi. Toronto: University of Toronto Press, 1999, pp. 397-405.

Vitula, M., "Z historie českých a slovenských krajanů v Kanadě do roku 1939" (History of Czechs and Slovaks in Canada until 1939), Časopis Matice moravské 118 (1999), pp. 97-110.

Čermák, J., Fragmenty ze života Čechů a Slováků v Kanadě (Fragments from the life of Czechs and Slovaks in Canada). Zlín, 2000.

Čermák, Josef, It all Started with Prince Rupert. The Story of Czechs and Slovaks in Canada. Luhačovice: Etelier IM Publishing Co., 2003. 367p.

Peterková, J., Historie a současnost české menšiny v Kanadě (History and the present status of Czech minority in Canada). Bakalářská práce. Pardubice, Fakulta humanitních studií, 2003.

Neviditelné oběti komunismu v zemi javorů. Sborník studentských prací (Invisible victims of communism in the land of maples. Collection of students' papers). Edited by Jakub Hodboď, Jan Goll and Václav Ulvr. Liberec: Gymnázium F.X. Šaldy v Liberci, 2006. 128p.

"Multikulturní kontrasty—kanadský experiment, Češi a svět" (Multicultural contrasts—A Canadian experiment, Czechs and the world), Revue Prostor 73/74, 2007.

Rosická, P., Česká emigrace v Severní Americe a její vztah k ČR (Czech emigration in North America and its relations to the Czech Republic). Diplomová prace. Praha, Vysoká škola ekonomická, 2001.

Zaoral, R., "Česká Kanada" (Czech Canada), Revue Prostor 73/74, 2007.

Zaoral, Roman, Češi ve světe—Kanada (Czechs in the world—Canada) Krajane.net 10 (March 4, 2008), p. 11.See: http://krajane.radio.cz/articleDetail.view?id=1236

B. Early Pioneers

1. General

La Trobe, Benjamin, With the Harmony to Labrador: Notes of a Visit to the Moravian Mission Stations on the North-East Coast of Labrador. London: Moravian Church and Mission Agency, 1888.

Hutton, J.E., History of Moravian Missions. London-Dublin: Moravian Publication Office, 1922. Gray, Elma E., Wilderness Christians: The Moravian Mission to the Delaware Indians. Toronto, 1956.

2. Individuals

Anthony Fiala (1869-1950)

"The Ziegler Polar Expedition," National Geographic Magazine, 16 (1905), pp. 439-440.

Fiala, Anthony, Fighting the Polar Ice. New York: Doubleday, Page, 1906. 296p.

"Finds a Base for Fiala," The New York Times, November 3, 1907.

Fiala, Anthony, "Polar Photography," National Geographic Magazine, 18 (1907), pp. 140-142.

Thaddeus Haenke (1761-1817)

"Haenke, Thaddeus Peregrinus Xaverius," in: Biographical Dictionary of American and Canadian Naturalists. Edited by Keir Brooks Sterling et al. Westport, CT: Greenwood Press, 1997, pp. 355-358.

Dictionary of Canadian Biography Online.

John Heckewelder (1743-1823)

Wallace, Paul A. W., "To Fairfield (Moraviantown) in Upper Canada: 1798)," in: The Travels of John Heckewelder in Frontier America. Pittsburgh: University of Pittsburgh Press, 1958, pp. 339-372.

Heinrich Klutschak (1814-1866)

Klutschak, Heinrich, Als Eskimo unter den Eskimos. Wien, 1881. 136p.

Klutschak, Heinrich, Overland to Starvation Cove: With the Inuit in Search of Franklin, 1878-1880. Edited by William Burr. Toronto: University of Toronto Press, 1993. 261p.

Bohuslav Kroupa (1838-1912)

Kroupa, Bohuslav, An Artist's Tour. Gleanings and Impressions of Travels in North and Central America and Sandwich Islands. London: Ward and Downey, 1890. 339p.

Wilhelm Labitsky (1829-1871)

Blatzell, W. J., "Labitsky, Joseph," in: Blatzells Dictionary of Musicians. Boston: Oliver Ditson Co., 1911.

Frank Xavier Richter (1837-1910)

Paterson, T. W., Encyclopedia of Ghost Towns and Mining Camps of British Columbia. Vol. 2, The Similkameen, Boundary and Okanagan. Langley B.C.: Sunfire Publications, 1981.

Jan Eskymo Welzl (1868-1948)

Těsnohlídek, Rudolf, Eskymo Welzl: Paměti českého polárního lovce a zlatokopa (Eskymo Welzl: Memoirs of a Czech Polar Hunter and Gold-digger). Praha: Fr. Borový, 1928. 255p.

Welzl, Jan, Thirty Years in the Golden North. Translated by Paul Selver. New York: Macmillan, 1932. 336p.

Welzl, Jan, The Quest for Polar Treasure. Translated by M. and R. Weatherall. New York: Macmillan, 1933. 351p.

David Zeisberger (1721-1808)

Zeisberger, David, David Zeisberger's Official Diary, Fairfield, 1791-1795 (Moravian Historical Society Transactions). Nazareth, PA: Whitefield House, 1963. 229p.

"Zeisberger, David," in: The Canadian Encyclopedia. Edited by James H. Marsh. Toronto: McClelland & Stewart, 1999.

III. Society

Tlapák, Václav, "Situace čsl. zemědělců a národní a kulturní život krajanů v Kanadě" (Conditions of Czechoslovak farmers and cultural life of our countrymen in Canada). Praha: Československý ústav zahraniční, 1931. 16p.

Cekota, Antonín, The Battle of Home. Some Problems of Industrial Community. Toronto: Macmillan Co. of Toronto, 1944. 373p.

Horna, Jarmila L. A., "The Entrance Status of Czech and Slovak Immigrant Women," in: Two Nations, Many Cultures: Ethnic Groups in Canada.Edited by Jean L. Elliott, Scarborough, Ontario: Prentice-Hall of Canada, 1979, pp. 270-279.

IV. Cultural & Other Contributions

A. General

Tlapák, Václav, "Národní a kulturní život krajanů v Kanadě" (National and cultural life of our compatriots in Canada), České zahraničí 2 (Praha, 1931), pp. 49-56.

Nekola, E. and E. Ash., eds., A Gem for the Canadian Mosaic: Pictures of Life and Work of Canadians of Czechoslovak Origin. Scarborough, Ont., 1957.

"Contributions of Czechs and Slovaks to Canada," in: Naše Hlasy (Our Voices). Centennial Issue. 1867-1967, Vol. 13, No. 21-22, May 27, 1967, pp. 23-61.

Nové divadlo Toronto, Canada 1970-1995 (New Theatre Toronto, Canada 1970-1995), Toronto, 1995.

Novotná, J., and V. Rollerová, Masaryktown—50 let českého a slovenského národního parku v Kanadě (Masaryktown—Fifty years of Czech and Slovak national park in Canada).Toronto, 1998.

Safertal, Frank, "It All Started with Adolf. Short History of the New Theatre in Toronto, Canada," in: Selected Papers of the 21st World Congress of the Czechoslovak Society of Arts and Sciences, University of West Bohemia, Plzeň, June 23-30, 2002. Edited by

Jan P. Skalny and Miloslav Rechcigl, Jr. Plzeň: Aleš Čeněk, 2004, pp. 129-137.

Skála, Josef P., "Czech Theatre on the Pacific Shores of Canada: 25 Years of Theatre around the Corner in Vancouver," Selected Papers of the 21st World Congress of the Czechoslovak Society of Arts and Sciences, Ibid., pp. 138-163.

Skála, J., "České krajanské divadlo na západním pobřeží Kanady" (Czech theatre on the western shore of Canada), Divadelní revue, 16 (2005), pp. 89-96.

Skála, J., "Impact of Fringe Festivals on the Development of the Theatrical Arts,", in: Morava viděna z vnějšku. Výběr přednášek z 22. světového kongresu Československé společnosti pro vědy a umění Olomouc 2004. Ostrava, 2006, pp. 208-210.

Čermák, Josef, "Czech & Slovak Theatre in Canada," in: Morava viděna z vnějšku. Výběr přednášek z 22. světového kongresu Československé společnosti pro vědy a umění Olomouc, 2004. Ostrava, 2006, pp. 166-169.

B. Individuals

Tomáš J. Baťa (1914-2008)

Baťa. Thomas J. with Sonja Sinclair, Bata. Shoemaker to the World. Toronto: Stoddart, 1990.341p.

Baťa, T., and S. Sinclairová, Tomáš J. Baťa, švec pro celý svět (Tomáš J. Baťa, Shoemaker for the whole world). Praha 1991.

Tomeš, Josef et. al., "Baťa, Tomáš Jan," in: Český biografický slovník XX. Století. Praha: Paseka, 1999, I dil, p. 57.

Obituary: "Thomas J Bata. Shoe magnate who moved the family business from Czechoslovakia to Canada to escape the Nazis," The Telegraph, Sept. 4, 2008.

Tomas Dusatko (1952-)

"Dusatko, Tomas," in: The Canadian Encyclopedia. Edited by James H. Marsh. Toronto: McClelland & Stewart, 2000.

Otto Jelínek (1940-)

Evolution . . . From Skater to Businessman," Skating magazine, Jun 1971.

Leon J. Koerner (1892-1972)
"Koerner, Leon J.," in: The Canadian Encyclopedia. Edited by James H. Marsh. Toronto: McClelland & Stewart, 2000.
"Koerner Foundation," in: The Canadian Encyclopedia. Edited by James H. Marsh. Toronto: McClelland & Stewart, 2000.

Vladimír Joseph Krajina (1905-1993)
Tomeš, Josef et al., "Krajina, Vladimír," in: Český biografický slovník XX. století. Paha: Paseka, 1999, II. díl, pp. 156-157.
"Krajina, Vladimir Joseph," in: The Canadian Encyclopedia. Edited by James H. Marsh. Toronto: McClelland & Stewart, 2000.

Antonín Kubálek (1935-2011)
"Kubalek, Antonin," in: the Candian Encyclopedia. Edited by James H. Marsh. Toronto: McClelland & Stewart, 2000.

Milan Kymlička (1936-2008)
Meredith, Joan. 'Milan Kymlicka's story: how to start again in a new country,' Canadian Composer, 55, Dec 1970.
"Kymlicka, Milan," in: The Canadian Encyclopedia. Edited by James H. Marsh. Toronto: McClelland & Stewart, 2000.

Stan Mikita (1940-)
Fischler, Stan, Stan Mikita. The turbulent career of a hockey superstar. Spokane, WA: Cowles Book Co., 1969. 213p.
"Mikita, Stan," in: The Canadian Encyclopedia. Edited by James H. Marsh. Toronto: McClelland & Stewart, 2000.

Oskar Morawetz (1917-2007)
Kaptainis, Arthur, "Oskar Morawetz: stability and integrity the hallmarks as a composer talks about "change," Canadian Composer, 169, Mar 1982.
Julien, David A., "Oskar Morawetz—music of the human experience," Centrenotes, 1, Nov-Dec 1983.
Schulman, Michael. "Oskar Morawetz: Canada's celebrated composer at 71 is as prolific as ever and still happy to be labelled a traditionalist," Canadian Composer, 226, Dec 1987.

"Morawetz, Oskar," in: The Canadian Encyclopedia. Edited by James H. Marsh. Toronto: McClelland & Stewart, 2000.
"Canadian composer Oskar Morawetz dies at 90," CBC News, June 16, 2007.

Peter Charles Newman (1929-)

"Newman, Peter Charles," in: The Canadian Encyclopedia. Edited by James H. Marsh. Toronto: McClelland & Stewart, 2000.

Jan Rubeš (1920-2009)

Kaptainis, Arthur, "Rubeš thrives on versatility," Toronto Globe and Mail, 5 Feb 1985.
Schabas, Ezra, Jan Rubeš: A Man of Many Talents. Toronto: Dundurn Press, 2007. 376p.
"Opera singer and actor Jan Rubes dies at 89," CBC News, June 30, 2009.
"Rubes, Jan," in: The Canadian Encyclopedia. Edited by James H. Marsh. Toronto: McClelland & Stewart, 2000.

Josef Škvorecký (1924-)

"Josef Škvorecký," Contemporary Authors: Autobiography Series 1 (1984), pp. 325-352.
"Josef Škvorecký," Contemporary Literary Criticism: Yearbook 1985, vol. 39, pp. 220-233.
Trenský, Paul I., The Fiction of Josef Škvorecký. London: Macmillan, 1991. 210p.
Tomeš, Josef et. al., "Škvorecký, Josef," in: Český biografický slovník XX. století. Praha: Paseka, 1999, III díl, p. 275.

Walter Susskind (1913-1980)

Kraglund, John. 'Walter Susskind Conducting,' Mayfair, Dec 1955.
Susskind, Walter," in: The Canadian Encyclopedia. Edited by James H. Marsh. Toronto: McClelland & Stewart, 2000.

Lubor J. Zink (1920-2003)

Tomeš, Josef et. al., "Zink, Lubor (Jan)," in: Český biografický slovník XX. století. Praha: Paseka, 1999, III díl, pp. 568-569.

Čelovský, Boris, Kopiník svobody: Život a dílo nevšedního novináře (Freedom lancer. Life and work of uncommon journalist). Praha: Tilia, 2001. 204p.

Ray, Randy, "Pugnacious expatriate Czech outlived the Union of Soviet Socialist Republics—Journalist fought first the Nazis and then the Red Menace, denouncing Soviet-style communism till its fall," The Globe and Mail, February 18, 2004, p. R5.

V. Organizations

Musil, Ferdinand L., Československá Amerika. Ze spolkového a národního života Čechů a Slováků ve Spojených Státech a v Kanadě roku 1932. (Czechoslovak America. Organizational and national life of Czechs and Slovaks in the US and Canada). Chicago: Denní Hlasatel, 1933. 40p.

Památník (A Memorial), Czechoslovak National Alliance in Canada Winnipeg, 1943.

Přístupa, G., "Stručná historie Čs. Národního sdružení v Kanadě" (Brief history of Čs. Národní sdružení v Kanadě), in: Kanadský Masaryktown. Toronto, 1952, pp. 11-19, 23-31.

A Gem for the Canadian Mosaic, Masaryk Memorial Institute, Inc. Toronto, 1957.

Bosley, E. M., M. Hamata, A. K. Wenzbauer, eds., Památník ČSPJ [Československé podpůrné jednoty] (Memorial of Československá podpurna jednota), 1913-1963. Winnipeg 1963. 116p.

Waldauf, Jan, "Sokol in Canada," in: Naše Hlasy (Our Voices). Centennial Issue. 1867-1967, Vol. 13, No. 21-22, May 27, 1967.

Dvacáté výročí Dámského odboru ČSNS Toronto. 1960-1970; II. 1970-1980. Toronto, 1980.

Zaoral, Roman, "Soupis českých krajanských a exilových spolků v Torontu po roce 1945" (Listing of Czech compatriot and exile organizations in Toronto after 1945), in: Sborník referátů ze semináře 'Historie emigrace z českých zemí,' který se konal při příležitosti Setkání krajanů v Mladé Boleslavi 22.-25. 6. 2000. Mladá Boleslav: Okresní museum v Mladé Boleslavi, 2001, pp. 125-154.

Appendix B: Czechs in Latin America

I. General References

A. Bibliographies

Kašpar, Oldřich, "Bibliografie českých a slovenských prací o dějinách Latinské Ameriky 16.-18. století" (Bibliography of Czech and Slovak works about history of Latin America of the 16th-18th centuries), in: Latinská Amerika—Dějiny a současnost. I. Praha, 1988, pp. 143-157.

Barteček, Ivo, "Výběrová bibliografie československé latinoamerikanistiky k dějinám 19. a 20. století za léta 1960-1987" (Selective bibliography of Czechoslovak Latino-Americana to history of the 19th and 20th centuries during 1960-1987), Ibid, pp. 189-202.

Kašpar, Oldřich and Anna Fechtnerová, "Češi, Moravané a Slezané v Novém světě v 17. století. Bio-bibliografický přehled (Czechs, Moravians and Silesians in the New World in 17th century. A bio-bibliographical survey), Folia Historica Bohemica, 13 (1990), pp. 289-326.

Barteček, Ivo, Vystěhovalectví do Latinské Ameriky" (Emigration to Latin America), Češi v cizině, 9 (1996), pp. 172-197. Includes extensive bibliography.

Kašpar, Oldřich, Ondřej Pokorný and Jana Vongreyová, Bibliografie k působení jezuitů z České provincie TJ ve španělském a portugalském zámoří v XVII. a XVIII. století (Bibliography on the work of Jesuits from the Czech Province in the Spanish and Portuguese Overseas Locations). Praha 2006. 26p.

B. Historiography

Jirečková, Olga and Milan Klášterský, "Nejstarší české zprávy o Latinské Americe" (The oldest news about Latin America), Dějiny a současnost, 4, No. 9 (1962), pp. 30-32.

Baďura, B., "Poznámky a organizace historického bádání o Mexiku" (Notes and organizations of historical research about Mexico), Československý časopis historický, 11 (1963), pp. 86-94.

Polišenský, Josef and Roman E. Roldan, "Prameny a problém československo-mexických vztahů" (Sources and problems in the study of Czechoslovak-Mexican relations), Československý časopis historický, (1964), pp. 365-374.

Polišenský, Josef, "America's Western Coast in Czechoslovak Sources, Ibero-Americana Pragensia 4 (1970), pp. 268-271.

Míšek, R., "Prameny k č. vystěhovalectví do Argentiny ve 20 letech" (Sources relating to Czechoslovak emigration to Argentina in the 20s), Bulletin Komise pro dějiny krajanů, Čechů a Slováků v zahraničí, 4 (1966), pp. 39-49.

Polišenský, Josef, "Prameny a problémy dějin českého a slovenského vystěhovalectvi do Latinské Ameriky" (Sources and problems of history of Czech and Slovak emigration to Latin America), Český lid, 68 (1981), pp. 3-9.

Polišenský, J. and S. Binková, "Prameny k dějinám portugalských objevných cest v ČSSR" (Sources to history of Portugal travels found in ČSSR), Sborník Národního muzea v Praze, Series C, 29, No. 4 (1984), pp. 227-234.

Barteček, Ivo, "Vystěhovalectví a studium vystěhovalectví—Občanský či národnostní princip? Příklad vystěhovalectví do Latinské Ameriky z Československa v letech 1918-1938"(Emigration and the study of emigration—Civil or national principle? An example of emigration to Latin America from Czechoslovakia during 1918-1938), Acta Universitatis Palackiamae Olomucensis—Facultas Philosophica Historica, 27 (1996), pp. 205-211.

Opatrný, Josef, "Tradice české iberoamerikanistiky" (Tradition of the Czech Latino-Americana),in: Kdo byl kdo. Čeští a slovenští orientalisté, afrikanisté a iberoamerikanisté. Praha: Nakladatelství Libri, 1999, pp. 48-54.

Opatrný, Josef, "Estudios iberoamerikanas en la Republic Checa en los anos 1990," Jahrbuch für Geschichte Lateinamerikas, Köln-Weimer-Wien: Bohlau Verlag, 2000, pp. 377-397.

Barteček, Ivo and Jaromír Pavlíček, "Česká komunita v Latinské Americe" (Czech community in Latin America), Acta Historica Acta Universitatis Palackianae Olomucensis—Facultas philosophica, 28 (1998), pp. 121-28.

Barteček, Ivo, "Česká krajanská komunita v Latinské Americe—Možnosti a meze výzkumu" (Czech emigrant community in Latin America—Possibilities and limits of research), Historica Acta

Universitatis Palackianae Olomucensis—Facultas philosophica, 31 (2002), pp. 377-382.

C. Biographies

Štěrba, F. C., Češi a Slováci v Latinské Americe (Czechs and Slovaks in Latin America) Washington, DC: Czechoslovak Society of Arts and Sciences in America, 1962. 61p.; reprinted by Palacký University, Olomouc in 2008.

Anna Fechtnerová and Oldřich Kašpar, "Češi, Moravané a Slezané v Novém světě v 17. a 18. století. Bio-bibliografický přehled (Czechs, Moravians and Silesians in the New World. Bio-Bibliographical Overview), Folia Historica Bohemica, 13 (1990), pp. 289-325.

D. Ethnography

Kašpar, Oldřich and František Vrhel, Etnografie mimoevropských oblastí. Amerika. I. Jižní Amerika. (Ethnography of Regions outside Europe. America. I. South America). Praha: SPN 1985. 166p.

Kašpar, Oldřich and František Vrhel, Etnografie mimoevropských oblastí. Amerika. II. Mezoamerika (Ethnography of Regions outside Europe. America. I. Central America). Praha: SPN 1986. 131p.

II. History

A. General Surveys

Kybal, Vlastimil, "Československé vystěhovalectví do Jižní Ameriky" (Czechoslovak emigration to South America), in: Jižní Amerika a Československo. Praha, 1928, pp. 133-144.

Kybal, Vlastimil, Po československých stopách v Latinské Americe (In the Czechoslovak Footsteps in Latin America). Praha: Česká akademie věd a umění, 1935 87p.; reprinted by Palacký University, Olomouc in 2003.

Polišenský, J. and J. Haubelt, "Přírodovědec Tadeáš Haenke a počátky českého novodobého zájmu o Latinskou Ameriku" (Naturalist Tadeáš Haenke and the beginnings of Czech modern interest in Latin America), Acta Universitatis Carolinae, Studia Historica, VI, 2 (1966), pp. 5-46.

Vasiljev, I., "Vystěhovalectvi Čechu a Slováků do Latinské Ameriky před druhou světovou válkou (Emigration of Czechs and Slovaks to Latin America before the World War II), Český lid, 73, No. 7 (1986), pp. 239-245.

Kašpar, O., "Přírodovědec Tadeas Haenke a počátky českého vystěhvalectví do Latinské Ameriky" (Naturalist Tadeas Haenke and the beginnings of Czech emigration to Latin America), Češi v cizině, 1 (1986), pp.165-178.

Barteček, I., "Vystěhovalectví z českých zemí a Československa do Latinské Ameriky. Bilance české latinoamerikanistiky (Emigration from the Czech Lands and Czechoslovakia to Latin America. The status of the Czech Latino-Americana)," Historie—Historica 3, Acta Facultatis Philosophicae, Universitas Ostraviensis, Ostrava 1995, pp. 143-160.

Polišenský, Josef, "Čeští lidé pod Jižním křížem" (Czechs under the Southern Cross), in: Úvod do studia dějin vystěhovalectví do Ameriky II. Češi a Amerika. Praha: Univerzita Karlova, 1996, pp. 53-57.

Barteček, Ivo, Cestovatelé z českých zemí v Latinské Americe (Travelers from the Czech Lands to Latin America). Ostrava 1996.

Barteček, Ivo, "Vystěhovalectví do Latinské Ameriky" (Emigration to Latin America), Češi v cizině, 9 (1996), pp. 172-197.

Opatrný, Josef, "Česká emigrace do Latinské Ameriky" (Czech emigration to Latin America), Historický obzor, 10, No. 9-10 (Sept.-Oct. 1999), pp. 214-221

Barteček, Ivo, "Cestovatelé z českých zemí v Latinské Americe v 19. století" (Travelers from the Czech Lands to Latin America in the 19th Century), in: Cesty a cestování v životě společnosti, Acta Universitatis Purkynianae, Philosophica et Historica III/1995, Studia historica II, Ústí nad Labem, 1997, pp. 421-428.

B. Bohemian Jesuit Missionaries & Other Early Pioneers

1. General Surveys

Kalista, Zdeněk, Cesty ve znamení kříže: Dopisy a zprávy českých misionářů XVII.-XVIII. věku ze zámořských krajů (Travels in the sign of the Cross. Letters and reports of Czech missionaries of 17th and 18th centuries from abroad). Praha: Evropský literární klub, 1941, 240p.; 2nd ed, Praha 1947. 320p.

Odložilík, Otakar, "Čeští misionáři v Mexiku" (Czech missionaries in Mexico), Obzor (Londýn), No. 1 (1944), pp. 53-60.

Odložilík, Otakar, "Misioneros Checos en México," Boletín de la Sociedad Mexicana de Geografía y Estadística (México) 60, No. 5 (May-June 1945), pp.423-436.

Odložilík, Otakar, "Czech Missionaries in New Spain," The Hispanic American Historical Review (Durham), 25 (1945), pp. 428-454.

Ryneš, Václav, "Los jesuitas bohémicos trabajando en las misiones de América Latina después de 1620," Ibero-Americana Pragensia, 5 (Praha 1971), pp. 193-202.

Bielik, F., "Zo života Slovákov a Čechov v Patagonii" (From the life of Slovaks and Czechs in Patagonia), in: Slováci v zahraničí. Martin, 1985, Vol. 11, pp. 148-152.

Svátek, Josef, Česká provincie Tovaryšstva Ježíšova a iberská Amerika (Czech Province of the Jesuit Order and Latin America), ZM Kroměříž 1991, No.1, pp. 1-10.

Fechtnerová, A. and O. Kašpar, "Češi, Moravané a Slezané v Novém světě v 17. A 18. stoleti. Bio-bibliograficky přehled" (Czechs, Moravians, and Silesians in New World. A Bio-bibliographical overview), Folia Historica Bohemia, Praha, 13 (1990), pp. 289-325.

Kašpar, Oldřich, Los jesuitas checos en la Nueva España, 1678-1767 (México 1991).

Kašpar, Oldřich, "Jezuité z české provincie v Novém světě 1-2" (Jesuits from the Czech Province in the New World 1-2), Historický obzor, 2, (1992), pp. 56-60; Ibid. 3 (1992), pp. 79-83.

Kašpar, Oldřich, "Několik osudů moravských jezuitů v Novém světě" (Fate of a few Moravian Jesuits in the New World), Severní Morava, 67 (1994), pp. 11-22.

Barteček, Ivo, Jezuité zemí Koruny české v Latinské Americe (Jezuits of the Bohemian Crown in Latin America). Ostrava: Scholaforum, 1997. 21p.

Rychlík, Martin, Stručný nástin přínosu českých jezuitů etnologii (Brief survey of the contribution of the Czech Jesuits to ethnology). Praha: Ústav etnologie, Filozofická fakulta UK, 1998. 27p.

Kašpar, Oldřich, Jezuité z české provincie v Mexiku. Olomouc: Danal, 1999. 147p.

Kašpar, Oldřich: Kamenné misie českých jezuitů v Dolní Kalifornii (Stone missions of Czech Jesuits in Lower California), Kámen, 8, No. 1, (2002), pp. 83-87.

Novotná, Eva (ed.). Katalog výstavy 'Čeští jezuité, cestovatelé a objevitelé: k 450. výročí příchodu jezuitů do Prahy' (Catalogue of exhibitio: 'Czech Jesuits, travelers and discoverers: on 450th anniversary of the arrival of the Jesuits in Prague'). Praha, 26. 6. 2006—22. 9. 2006. 1. vyd. Praha: Geografická knihovna PřF UK, 2006. 48p.

Kašpar, Oldřich and Ondřej Pokorný, Jezuité z české provincie a jejich díla ze 17. a 18. století veŠpanělsku, v Mexiku a na Filipínách (Jesuits from the Bohemian Province and their works from 17th and 18th centuries in Spain, Mexico and Philipines). Praha, 2006. 62p.

Kulhánek, Jiří, Čeští jezuitští misionáři v Jižní Americe v XVII. a XVIII. století (Czech Jesuit missionaries in South America in 17th and 18th centuries). Bakalářská diplomová práce. Masarykova univerzita v Brně, Filozofická fakulta, Historický ústav, 2006.

Kašpar, Oldřich, Ondřej Pokorný and Jana Vongreyová, Bibliografie k působení jezuitů z České provincie TJ ve španělském a portugalském zámoří v XVII. a XVIII. století (Bibliography on the work of Jesuits from the Czech Province in the Spanish and Portuguese Overseas Locations). Praha 2006. 26p.

Kašpar, Oldřich and Jan Baťa, "Jezuité na obou březích Atlantiku" (Jesuits on both sides of the Atlantic Ocean), in: Svatováclavské slavnosti. Praha, 2006, pp. 16-81.

Křížová, Markéta, Ideální město v divočině (Ideal city in the wilderness). Praha: Nakladatelství Lidové noviny, 2007. 264p.

"První rodák z českých zemi v Americe dobýval s Cortesem říši Azteků" (First Czech native helped to conquer the Aztec Empire), iDnes, November 2, 2009. See: http://zpravy.idnes.cz/prvni-rodak-z-ceskych-zemi-v-americe-dobyval-s-cortesem-risi-azteku-1f5-/zahranicni.aspx?c=A091102_144115_vedatech_jw

2. Individuals

Wenceslao Christmann (1647-1723)

Binková, Simona, "El P. Wenceslao Christmann, S. J., primer bohemio en el Paraguay," Ibero-Americana Pragensia, 23, No. 9 (Praha 1999), pp. 143-152.

Samuel Fritz (1654-1725)

Journal of the Travels and Labours of Father Samuel Fritz in the River of Amazons between 1686 and 1723, London 1922.

Šilhan, F., "P. Samuel Fritz T.J., misionář, cestovatel a první kartograf v údolí amazonském" (Father Fritz T. J., missionary, traveler and the first cartographer of the Amazon Valley), Zprávy z české provincie T. J. (1928), pp. 44-53.

Šimek Vladimír and Kamila Broulová Šimková, Samuel Fritz—České stopy na březích Amazonky (Czech footprints on the shores of the Amazon river). Příbram: Kant, 2002. 128p.

Adam Gilg (1650/3-aft. 1753)

Binková, Simona, "Výzkumné cesty a činnost Adama Gilga a Ignáce Xavera Kellera v Sonoře a Horní Pimeríi" (Exploratoy travels and activities of Adam Gilg and Ignác Xaver Keller in Sonora and Pimeria alta), Český lid, 82, No. 4 (1995), pp. 273-292.

Ignaz Xaver Keller (1702-1759)

Hanáková, Markéta, "Otázky kolem života a smrti českého misionáře Ignáce Xavera Kellera" (Questions about the life and death of the Czech missionary Ignác Xaver Keller), Český lid, 82, No. 4 (1995), pp. 293-306.

Václav Link (1736-1797)

Linck, Wenceslaus, Wenceslaus Linck's Diary of His 1766 Expedition to Northern Baja California. Edited by Ernest J. Burrus. Los Angeles: Dawson's Book Shop, 1966.

Linck, Wenceslaus, Wenceslaus Linck's Reports and Letters, 1762-1778. Edited by Ernest J. Burrus. Los Angeles: Dawson's Book Shop, 1967.

Polišenský J. and J. Opatrný, "Václav Link a jeho Deník z cesty na sever Kalifornského poloostrova" (Vaclav Link and his diary from his trip north to Californian peninsula), in: Jižní Morava 1974-II, pp. 95-102.

Binková, Simona, "Wenceslao Link y su actividad en Baja California en 1763," Ibero-Americana Pragensia XXIV (Praha 1990), pp. 243-153.

Jan Neumann (1659-1704)

Roedl, Bohumír, "José Neumann y su historia de las rebeliones indias en zona Tarahumara," Ibero-Americana Pragensia 7 (Praga 1974), pp. 175-178.

Rodríguez, Luis Gonzales, "Joseph Neumann, 1648-1732: Historiador y etnógrafo de la Tarahumara," Ibero-Americana Pragensia 20 (Praga 1986), pp.141-158.

Roedl, Bohumir, "La crónica de Joseph Neumann comofuente histórica", pp. 11-86: Joseph Neumann, "Historia de las Sublevaciones Indias en la Tarahumara": Ibero-Americana Pragensia Supplementum 6 (Praha 1994), 189p.

Binková, Simona, "La problemática de la etnicidad en el noroeste novohispano y la actitud de los misioneros jesuitas de Bohemia, siglos XVII y XVIII," Ibero-Americana Pragensia 25 (Praha 1991), pp. 171-176.

Václav Richter (1653-1696)

Fechtnerová, A., "Prostějovský rodák Jindřich Václav Richter a Latinská Amerika 17. století" (Jindřich Václav Richter from Prostějov and Latin America), Zpravodaj muzea Prostějovského, Prostějov 1983, pp. 18-21.

Augustin Strobach (1646-1684)

Procházka, Matěj, Misie jesuitská vůbec a P. Augustina Strobacha T. J. zvlášť (The Jesuit mission in general and that of Father Strobach T.J. in particular). Brno: Dědictví sv. Cyrilla a Methoděje, 1886.

Valentin Stansel (1621-1705)

Casanovas, J. Keenan, "The Observations of Valentine Stansel, a Seventeenth Century Missionary in Brazil," Archivum Historicum Societatis Iesu, 62 (1993), pp. 319-330.

Tadeáš Haenke (1761-1816)

Kašpar, Oldřich, "Přírodovědec Tadeáš Haenke a počátky českého vystěhovalectví do Latinské Ameriky (Naturalist Tadeáš Haenke and the beginnings of Czech emigration to Latin America), Češi v cizině 1 (1986), pp. 165-178.

Jan Nepomuk Kubíček (1801-1880)

"Jan Nepomuk Kubíček," in: Wikipedia. See: http://en.wikipedia.org/wiki/Jan_Nepomuk_Kub%C3%AD%C4%8Dek

Johann Emanuel Pohl (1784-1834)

"Pohl, Johann Emanuel," in: Appletons' Cyclopaedia of American Biography. 1900.

III. Specific Countries

A. Argentina

Jetmar, J., "Hrst úvah o Argentině a české emigraci" (Reflections on Argentina and Czech Emigration), in: Do Argentiny a do Brazilie. Dopisy dvou krajanů. Praha, 1906, pp. 52-53.

Haloda, Antonín and F. G. Skamenov, Informační spis pro vystěhovalce do Jižní Ameriky, hlavně do Argentiny (Information for emigrants to South America, especially to Argentina). Buenos Aires: Sdružení Slovanů, 1926-27. 52p.

Čvančarová, Boža, Na tvrdem úhoru . . . vzpomíná na dobu prožitou v Argentině a na začátky a vznik první Československé školy v Berisso, F.C.S. (On a rough fallow . . . recalls the times spent in Argentina and the beginnings and the origin of the first Czechoslovak school in Berisso, F.C.S.). Praha: Author, 1931. 102p.

Kazimour, Karel, Památník československé kolonie v argentinském Čaku, 1912-1937 (Souvenir of Czechoslovak Colony in Argentina's Chaco).Chaco, 1937. 280p.

T.J. Sokol Buenos Aires 1908-1938. Buenos Aires, 1938. 28p.

Hajda, Vladimír, Spolek Komenský, jeho vznik a práce. 1928-1938 (Komenský club, its origin and activities, 1928-1938). Buenos Aires: Spolek Komenský, 1938. 28p.

Kodytková, Anna, 21 let v Argentině (21 years in Argentina). Praha: Práce, 1951. 213p.

Míšek, Rudolf. Československé vystěhovalectví do Argentiny od roku 1922 do počátku třicátých let (Czechoslovak emigration to Argentina since 1922 to the beginnings of the thirties). Ph.Dr. Dissertation, Charles University, 1965. 150p.

Míšek, R., Poznámky o československém vystěhovalectví do Argentiny ve dvacátých letech (Commentary on Czechoslovak emigration to Argentina in the twenties), Bulletin Komise pro dějiny krajanů, Čechů a Slováků v zahraničí, 4 (1966), pp. 39-49.

Baďura, Bohumil, K historii prvních spolků českých a slovenských vystěhovalců v Argentině" (History of first orgranizations of Czech and Slovak emigrants in Argentina), in: Sborník k problematice dějin imperialismu. Praha: Ústav československých a světových dějin ČSAV, 1981, pp. 279-332.

Dubovický, Ivan, "Krajanská kolonie Presidencia Roque Saenz Pena—Příspěvek k počátkům českého vystěhovalectví do Argentiny" (The Czech Colony Presidencia Roque Saenz Pena—The beginnings of Czech emigration to Argentina), Češi v cizině, 2 (1987), pp. 139-181.

Dubovický, Ivan, "Kolonizační pokusy v Argentine a meziválečná Československá republika (Colonization attempts in Argentina and the inter-war Czechoslovak Republic), Češi v cizině, 3 (1989), pp. 193-236.

Dubovický, Ivan, Formování českého a slovenského etnika v Argentině" (The Formation of the Czech and Slovak ethnic groups in Argentina), Češi v cizině, 4 (1988), pp. 130-161.

Botik, J., "The Czechs and the Slovaks in the Argentinian Chaco", in: Ethnologia Europae Centralis 3, The Journal of Ethnology of Central Europe. Brno, 1996.

Spěvák, Přemysl, Z Břeclavska do Argentiny. Vystěhovalectví v letech 1913-1938. Bakalářská diplomová práce (From Břeclav Region to Argentina. Emigration during 1913-1938. A Bachelor's Thesis. Masarykova univerzita, Brno, 2008.

B. Brazil

Kybal, Vlastimil, "Kolik je nás Čechoslováku v Brazilii?" (How many are we Czechoslovaks in Brazil?), in: Jižní Amerika a Československo. Praha, 1928, pp. 142-145.

Vesely, Janand Lorenz Franciso Vladimiro, Pequena Anthologia Tcheca. Sao Laurenco J. Vesely, 1928. 88p.

Kresta, Václav, Brazilie. Poučení pro československé vystěhovalce (Brazil. Guidance for the Czechoslovak emigrants). Praha, 1929.

Krejčí, Alois, Práce a život kolonisty v jihobrasilském pralese (Work and life of a colonist in the South Brazilian forest). Praha, 1930. 120p.

Barteček, I., "Československá kolonizace v Brazilii" (Czechoslovak colonization in Brazil), Češi v cizině, 3 (1988), pp. 237-251.

Barteček, I., "České a slovenské vystěhovalectví do Brazilie před druhou světovou válkou" (Czech and Slovak emigration to Brazil before World War II), in: Latinska Amerika—Dějiny a současnost. Praha, 1989, vol. 2, pp. 161-180.

Baďurová, M. and B. Baďura, "Vystěhovalectví z českých zemí do Brazilie před vznikem ČSR" (Emigration from the Czech Lands to Brazil before the establishment of the Czechoslovak Republic), Český lid, 82 (1995), pp. 323-335.

Štěpánek, Pavel, Historické a kulturní svazky mezi Brazílií a Českou republikou (Historical and cultural relations between Brazil and the Czech Republic). Brno: L. Marek, 2008. 300p.

C. Chile

Krajané v Chile (Our Compatriots in Chile). A Website of the Ministry of Foreign Affairs of C.R. http://www.mzv.cz/jnp/cz/zahranicni_vztahy/kultura_a_krajane/krajane/krajane_ve_svete/chile/index.html

D. Cuba

Nálevka, Vladimír, "La Colonia chechoslovaca en Cuba durante y la secunda guerra mundial," in: Ibero-Americana Pragensia, 4 (1970), pp. 231-236.

E. Mexico

Nykl, A. R., "Česká kolonie v Mexiku" (Czech Colony in Mexico), Amerikán, Národní kalendář, 49 (1926), pp. 298-311.
Odložilík, Otakar, "Hrst dojmů z Mexika" (A Handful of impressions from Mexico), in: S druhého břehu. 1943.
Barteček, Ivo, Československý antifašistický exil německého jazyka v Mexiku (Czechoslovak antifascist exile of German language in Mexico). Olomouc: Studie a dokumenty, 1999.
Krajané v Mexiku (Our countrymen in Mexico). A Website of Czech Ministry of Foreign Affairs. http://www.mzv.cz/jnp/cz/zahranicni_vztahy/kultura_a_krajane/krajane/krajane_ve_svete/mexiko/index.html

F. Paraguay

Dubovický, Ivan, "K otázce evropského přistěhovalectví do Paraguaye" (European immigration to Paraguay), Acta Universitatis Carolinae—Philosophica et Historica 3, Studia Ethnographica 7 (1991), pp. 77-98.
Kázecký, Stanislav, "Češi a Paraguay" (Czechs and Paraguay), Češi v cizině, 12 (2004), pp. 69-133.

G. Venezuela

Stohr, Carlos, Los Checos en Venezeula. Caracas, 1998.
Barteček, Ivo, "Češi v Caracasu, Venezuela" (Czechs in Caracas, Venezuela), Facultas Philosophica Historica 31 (2002), pp. 423-425.

IV. Cultural and Other Contributions

A. General Surveys

Kybal, Milič, "Czechs and Slovaks in Latin America," in: The Czechoslovak Contribution to World Culture. Ed. By Miloslav Rechcigl, Jr. The Hague-London-Paris: Mouton & Co., 1964, pp. 516-522.

Samuel Fritz: České stopy na březích Amazonky (Czech footprints on the shores of Amazon River) Text: Kamila Šimková Broulová, Photo: Vladimír Šimek. Příbram: Kent, 2002. 128p.

B. Individuals

Samuel Siegfried Karl von Basch (1837-1905)

Singer, Isidor, "Samuel Siegfried Karl von Basch," in: Jewish Encyclopedia, 1901-1906.

Jan Antonin Baťa (1872-1957)

Baťa, Jan Antonín," in: Český biografický slovník XX. století. Praha: Paseka, 1999, p. 56.

Vilém Flusser (1920-1991)

Finger, Anke et al., Vilém Flusser. An Introduction. Minneapolis: University of Minnesota Press, 2011.

Juscelino Kubitschek (1902-1976)

Alexander, Robert J., Juscelino Kubitschek and the Development of Brazil. Athens, Ohio: Ohio University Center for International Studies, 1991.

Jiří Pelikán(1906-1984)

"Jiri Pelikan," in: Wikipedia. See: http://en.wikipedia.org/wiki/Ji%C5%99%C3%AD_Pelik%C3%A1n_(chess_player)

Miroslava Stern (1926-1955)

Bouza, Alejandra Espasande, "Remembering Miroslava Stern Becka (1926-1955)," in: LatinoLA, February 22, 2006.

V. Organizations

Hajda, Vladimír, "Spolek Komenský, jeho vznik a práce 1928-1938 (Komenský Club, its origin and activities 1928-1938). Buenos Aires: Komenský Club, 1938. 28p.

Baďura, Bohumil, "K historii prvních spolků českých a slovenských vystěhovalců v Argentině" (From the history of the first organizations of Czech and Slovak emigrants in Argentina), in: Sborník k problematice dějin imperialism, 11 (1981), pp. 279-332.

Nálevka, Vladimír, "Krajanské hnutí v Latinské Americe v letech druhé světové války" (Compatriot movement in Latin America during the World War II), Češi v cizině, 5 (1995), pp. 36-44.

VI. Relations with Czechoslovakia

Kašpar, Oldřich, Eva Mánková, Pavel Štěpán and Miloš Tomandl, Kapitoly z dějin vztahů knižní kultury českých zemí, Španělska a španělského zámoří v 15.—18. stol. (Chapters from the history of literary culture of the Czech Lands, Spain and the Spanish overseas in the 15th—18th centuries). 2006, Dvojjazyčná česko-španělská edice. Praha: Univerzita Karlova v Praze—Filozofická fakulta, Ústav etnologie, 2006. 126p.

Nálevka, Vladimír, "Krajanské hnuti v Latinské Americe v letech druhé světové války" (Compatriot movement in Latin America during World War II), Češi v cizině 8 (1995), pp. 36-43.

Index

Abbott, Edith — *author* 119, 129
Acrelius, Israel — *author* 58
Adler, David — *subj.* 131
Advising farmers: Czechs in US — 35-37
Advising homes and households: Czechs in US — 37-39
Advising new settlers: Czechs in US — 35
Alabama, Czechs in — 74
Albieri, Pavel — *author* 24, 62, 101
Albright, Madeleine — *author* 16, 136; *subj.* 11, 16, 136
Albieri, Pavel — *subj.* 154
Alexander, Robert J. — *author* 245
Alzo, Lisa — *author* 84
Andelman, Bob — *author* 162
Anderle, Josef — *author* 26
Anderson, Nels — *author* 89, 130
Anderson, Robert — *author* 132
Anderson, Timothy — *author* 104
Andic, Vojtech — *author* 127
Anthropology: Czechs in US — 92
Aras, John J. — *author* 186
Archival material: Czechs in Canada — 222
Archival material: Czechs in US — 4-6
Archives: Czechs in US
general surveys — 44
specific institutions — 44-45
Archives of Czechs and Slovaks Abroad
see University of Chicago
Argentina, Czechs in — 241-243
Arnstein, Karl — *subj.* 182
Arvey, Verna — *author* 158
Ash, E. — *author* 226
Assimilation and acculturation: Czechs in US — 115-117
Astaire, Fred — *subj.* 165
Attitude-behavior-communication: Czechs in US — 124-125
Auerhan, Jan — *author* 46, 62, 63, 93, 201
Augier, Mie — *author* 176
Babcock, C. Merton — *author* 98, 99
Babička, Václav — *author* 4
Baca, Leo — *author* 207
Bader, Gershom — *author* 110
Baďura, Bohumil — *author* 233, 242, 243, 246
Baďurová, M. — *author* 243
Baist, Stanley — *author* 90
Bakanic, Laddie — *subj.* 167
Balch, Emily Green — *author* 46, 62, 115, 119, 126, 129, 184
Banfield, Stephen — *author* 159
Banking & finance: Czechs in US — 134-135
Baptists: Czechs in US — 109

Barber, M. — *author* 176
Barborová, Eva — *author* 49
Barler, Beatrice Ripple — *author* 214
Barnhart, William — *author* 139
Barteček, Ivo — *author* 233, 234, 236, 238, 243, 244; *subj.* x
Bartell, Frank W. — *author* 82
Barton, Elsie — *author* 186
Barton, Josef J. — *author* 103, 130
Barton, Rev. Josef — *author* 211
Barvínek, V. K. — *author* 94
Basch, Samuel Siegfried Karl von — *subj.* 245
Bašta, F. X. — *author* 36
Baťa, Jan Antonín — *author* 238, 245; *subj.* 245
Baťa, Thomas J. — *author* 227; *subj.* 133, 227
Battles, Ford Lo — *author* 173
Baxter, Angus — *author* 203
Bažil, T. — *author* 79
Beck, Abraham Reinke — *author* 214
Beck, Herbert Huebener — *author* 147
Beck, Martin — *subj.* 165
Beckerman, Michael B. — *author* 158
Behaim, Martin — *subj.* 55
Bender, George H. — *subj.* 138
Beneš, A. E. — *author* 75
Beneš, Anton — *author* 147
Beneš, Bohuš — *author* 198, 199
Beneš, Eduard — *author* 190
Beneš, Frank — *author* 91
Beneš, Vojta — *author* 34, 130, 142, 145, 148, 187, 190, 192, 193, 196, 200; *subj.* 148, 196
Benesh, Anton — *author* 78
Benjamin, Richard Spiers — *author* 136
Berger, John N. — *author* 105
Berger, Meyer — *subj.* 151
Berger, Oscar — *author* 161; *subj.* 161
Bergmann, Joseph Ernst — *subj.* 106
Bernard, H. K. — *author* 136
Bernays, Edward — *author* 174; *subj.* 174
Bibliographies: Czechs in Canada — 221
Bibliographies: Czechs in US
guide to bibliographies — 2
selected bibliographies — 2-3
Bibliographies: Czechs in Latin America — 233
Bičík, M. — *author* 127
Bielik, František — *author* 195, 237
Biga, Leo Adam — *author* 131
Bicha, Karel — *author* 9, 85, 91, 113, 114, 125, 135
Billman, Larry — *author* 165
Binková, Simona — *author* 239, 240
Biographies: Czechs in Canada — 221
Biographies: Czechs in Latin America — 235
Biographies: Czechs in US — 10-12
Biological & medical sciences: Czechs in US — 177-180
Biroczi, David — *author* 115
Bittmman, Ladislav — *author* 202
Bittner, Bartoš — *author* 83, 111
Blaha, Albert J. — *author* 106, 203, 206, 207, 208, 209, 211
Blanda, George — *subj.* 167
Blatzell, W. J. — *author* 225
Blau, Dick — *author* 157
Blewitt, Paul — *author* 45
Block, Geoffrey Holden — *author* 159
Bloch, Claude C. — *subj.* 142
Bloch, Edward — *subj.* 151

Bloch, Felix — *subj.* 180
Bloch, Henry W. — *subj.* 134
Bloch, Thomas M. — *author* 134
Blood, Thomas — *author* 136
Bloomfield, Maxwell — *author* 151
Blue, Adrianne — *author* 169
Boas, Max — *author* 132
Bočánková, M. — *author* 125
Bodnar, John — *author* 146
Bogardus, Emory Stephen — *author* 116
Boháč, Antonín — *author* 52, 93
Bohemian Brethren: Czechs in US — 106-107
Bohemian Catholic Central Union of Texas — 186
Bohemian Jesuit missionaries: Czechs in Latin America — 237-241
Bohemian Roman Catholic Central Union of Women — 186
see also Czech Catholic Union
Bohemian Slavonian Benevolent Society — 185
Bondi, August — *author* 14, 142; *subj.* 14, 142, 143
Bonner, Thomas Neville — *author* 148
Bordman, Gerald — *author* 159
Boreaunaz, David — *subj.* 11
Borecký, Jan — *author* 62
Bořkovec, Věra — *author* 165
Bosley, E. M. — *author* 230
Botik, J. — *author* 242
Bouza, Alejandra Espasande — *author* 245
Bowmer, Martha — *author* 87
Boxerman, Barton Alan — *author* 132, 139
Boyer, G. Bruce — *author* 165
Brackin, Dennis — *author* 168
Brager, Bruce L. — *author* 138
Brandeis, Frederika Dembitz — *author* 15; *subj.* 15
Brandeis, Jonas — *subj.* 131
Brandeis, Louis Dembitz — *subj.* 139
Brandejs, Stanislav — *author* 52
Brázda, Dominik — *author* 81
Brazil, Czechs in — 243
Breuer, Hynek — *author* 129
Breuer, Karel — *author* 78
Breuer, Karel Hugo — *author* 36, 41
Breuer, Louis — *author* 79
Březáček, Josef — *author* 36, 57
Brody, Seymour — *author* 143, 149
Brouček, Stanislav — *author* 13, 47, 48, 50, 53, 69, 201, 202; *subj.* x
Brown, Barbara Illingworth — *author* 177
Brown, Melvin L. — *author* 85
Brown, Peter H. — *author* 166
Brož, Ivan — *author* 195, 198
Bruce, William George — *author* 131
Bubeníček, Rudolf — *author* 75
Bucco, Martin — *author* 173
Budín, Stanislav — *author* 199
Bujarková, F. L. — *author* 141
Bujnoch, Dorothy — *author* 209, 210
Bulova, Arde — *subj.* 133
Buňata, Josef — *author* 84, 128, 193
Bunža, Bohumír — *author* 187
Burger, Jariszen — *subj.* 60
Burnett, David W. — *author* 120
Bush, Solomon — *subj.* 143
Bušek, Vratislav — *author* 83, 94
Business, *see* Commerce

Butler, Elizabeth Beardsley — *author* 119
Buttlar, Lois — *author* 44
Buzek, Karel — *author* 222
Cabela, Richard N. — *subj.* 131
Čada, Joseph (*see also* Chada, Joseph) — *author* 75, 104, 121, 122, 186
Calda, Miloš — *author* 191, 192
California, Czechs in 74
Campbell, Thomas, F. — *author* 137
Canada, Czechs in
general references — 221-222
history — 222-225
society — 226
cultural life — 226-230
organizations — 230
Čapek, Jan Vratislav — *author* 82
Čapek, Thomas — *author* 2, 3, 11, 15, 20, 44, 48, 57, 59, 60, 63, 65, 67, 68, 83, 91, 93, 96, 103, 107, 112, 113, 114, 115, 116, 121, 122, 123, 125, 126, 128, 129, 130, 131, 132, 134, 138, 140, 144, 147, 148, 149, 150, 153, 184, 185, 192, 193; *subj.* 15, 20, 171
Čapek, Thomas, Jr. — *author* 134
Čapková, Kateřina — *author* 71
Capron, Seth — *author* 191
Carrington, James Beebee — *author* 162
Carroll, R. G. — *author* 89, 129
Casanovas, J. Keenan — *author* 241
Cassidy, David C. — *author* 181
Cather, Willa — *author* 25, 124, 125
Catholic Central Union — 186
Catholic Union of Texas (KJT) — 186
Catlos, Edward — *author* 103
Čech, J. — *author* 48
Cech, Thomas — *subj.* 180
Cekota, Antonín — *author* 226
Čelovský, Bořivoj (Boris) — *author* 13, 16, 72, 187, 222, 230; *subj.* 13
Census records: Czechs in US — 209-210
Čepička, K. — *author* 149
Čermák, Anton Joseph — *subj.* 11, 136, 137
Čermák, Emil — *author* 37, 41
Čermák, Josef — *author* 141, 221, 223, 227
Čermák, Z. — *author* 54
Čermáková, D. — *author* 54
Cernosek, Donald — *author* 214
Červený, Jaroslav — *author* 198
Červinka, Vincenc — *author* 20
Chada, Joseph (*see also* Čada, Joseph) — *author* 64, 66, 70, 104, 106, 113, 122, 125, 150, 194, 199
Chain, Steve — *author* 132
Chalupný, Emanuel — *author* 124
Character: Czechs in US — 124-125
Charbonneau, Louis — *author* 168
Charvát, Otakar — *author* 24
Chasins, Abrams — *author* 160
Chile, Czechs in — 243
Chladek, F. F. — *author* 86
Chládek, Vojta — *author* 36
Chlumský, Adolf — *author* 106, 186; *subj.* 107
Chmelar, Hans — *author* 53
Chmelar, Johann — *author* 48
Chotek, Hugo — *author* 84, 88, 185
Chotrpenning, Joseph F. — *author* 105
Chrislock, C. Winston — *author* 65, 80, 136

Christmann, Wenceslao — *subj.* 239
Chroust, Daniel — *author* 28
Chroust, David — *author* 8, 89, 106, 150, 156, 171; *subj.* x
Church membership records: Czechs in US — 211
Church register records — 211-214
Churches: Czechs in US — 103
Chyle, Faith — *author* 163
Cink, Kenneth — *author* 27, 121
Činoveský, J.F. — *author* 23
Cironisová, Eva — *author* 49, 50
Civil register records: Czechs in US — 214
Clapham, John — *author* 160
Clark, E. B. — *author* 179
Clifford, Roy A. — *author* 117
Clowe, Grace Campbell — *author* 209, 210, 214
Cole, A. — *author* 177
Coleman, James S. — *author* 175
Colorado, Czechs in — 74
Commerce & trade: Czechs in US — 131-132
Communism, refugees from: Czechs in US — 71-73
Community leadership: Czechs in US — 144
Conard, Henry S. — *author* 179
Connelley, William E. — *author* 142
Constantine, Mildred — *author* 164
Cookbooks: Czechs in US — 100-101
Cooperation: Czechs in US — 125
Cope, Lída (*see also* Dutková-Cope) — *author* 96, 97
Cori, Carl F. — *subj.* 177
Cori, Gerty R. — *subj.* 177
Corzine, Jay — *author* 81, 114
Costello, R. M. de — *author* 106
Council of Free Czechoslovakia — 187
Council of Higher Education — 188
Cox, Archibald — *author* 175
Creswell, Barbara — *author* 152
Crisler, William Neville — *author* 60
Cross, Hardy — *author* 183
Cuba, Czechs in — 244
Cultural contributions: Czechs in Canada — 226-230
Cultural contributions: Czechs in Latin America — 245
Cultural contributions: Czech in US
- drama & dance — 164-167
- education — 145-149
- general surveys — 144-145
- journalism & publishing — 149-152
- literature — 153-156
- music — 156-161
- sports — 167-169
- visual art — 161-164

Curley, Michael Joseph — *author* 105
Currey, Josiah Seymour — *author* 131
Čvančarová, Boža — *author* 241
Czech-Americans
- aid in founding Czechoslovakia — 192-198
- aid in liberating Czechoslovakia from Nazism — 198-200
- aid in liberating Czechoslovakia from Communists — 200
- attitude – behavior – communication of — 124-125
- character of — 123-124
- community, future of — 66-67
- heritage, preservation of — 66-67

image of — 125-126
see also: United States, Czechs in
Czech Catholic Union of Texas
see Catholic Union of Texas (KJT)
Czech Center Museum Houston — 45
Czech Heritage Society of Texas — 187
Czech National Alliance — 187, 198
Czechoslovak Foreign Institute, Prague — 201
Czechoslovak National Council of America — 187
Czechoslovak Society of America (ČSA) — 185
Czechoslovak Society of Arts and Sciences (SVU) — 29, 188
Czechoslovakia (later Czech Republic)
contacts and attitude toward Czech-Americans — 201-202
founding of — 192-198
relations and contacts with the US — 189-192
relations with Latin America — 246
role of Czech-Americans in the founding of — 192-198
Czechs in Canada
see Canada, Czechs in
Czechs in Latin America
see Latin America, Czechs in
Czechs in US
see United States, Czechs in
Dabrowski, Irene — *author* 81, 114
Daniels, John — *author* 63
Daniels, Roger — *author* 64
David, Zdeněk — *subj.* x
Davis, Jeff — *author* 168
Demetz, Peter — *author* 17, 173; *subj.* 17
Demography: Czechs in US — 92-94
Demuth, Charles — *subj.* 161
Den, Petr (Ladislav Radimský's pseud.) — *author* 153
Dérer, Ivan — *author* 194
Deutsch, Karl W. — *subj.* 174
Diamant, H. — *author* 178
Diamant, J. — *author* 117
Diamond, Edwin — *author* 152
Dictionaries: Czechs in US — 30
Dignowity, Anthony Michael — *author* 14; *subj.* 14
Dillia, Irving — *author* 151
Dinnerstein, Leonard — *author* 110
Directories: Czechs in US — 28-29
Dissertations: Czechs in US — 26-28
Dluhošová, Helena — *author* 12, 102
Dočekalová — *author* 112
Doležal, Karel — *author* 39, 119
Donato, A. Z. — *author* 19; *subj.* 19
Dongres, L. W. — *author* 86
Dostál, Hynek — *author* 116, 146
Dostalík, M. — *author* 122, 129
Doubrava, Ferdinand F. — *author* 130
Downer, Alan S. — *author* 165
Drama & dance: Czechs in US 164-167
Drbohlav, Dušan — *author* 54
Drnec, Gustav — *author* 137
Droba, Daniel D. — *author* 10, 196, 198
Drtina, František — *author* 201
Dryden, Hugh L. — *author* 183
Duben, Vojtěch — *author* 3, 150, 199
Dubovický, Ivan — *author* 53, 65, 115, 117, 124, 242, 244; *subj.* x
Dubská, Irena — *author* 22
Dudek, J. B. — *author* 94

Dufek, George — *author* 22; *subj.* 22
Duncan, H. G. — *author* 116
Ďurovič, Michal — *author* 6
Dusatko, Tomas — *subj.* 227
Dushek, Camille — *author* 91
Dutková-Cope, Lída (*see also* Cope, Lída) — *author* 28, 96, 97, 99
Duzbábová, Lucie — *author* 76
Dvořák, Antonín — *subj.* 158
Dvořák, Josef A. — *author* 86
Dvořák, Ladislav — *author* 20
Dvořáková, Jarmila — *author* 161
Dvořáková, Zora — *author* 72, 113
Dvornik, Francis — *author* 64, 68, 127, 141, 145; *subj.* 171, 172
Dwyer, Joseph — *author* 4
Dybala, Barbara — *author* 99
Dzúrová, D. — *author* 54
Early perceptions of and **early contacts with the New World** — 56
Early pioneers: Czechs in Canada — 224-225
Early pioneers: Czechs in Latin America — 237-241
Early pioneers: Czechs in US — 57-61
Ebestein, William — *author* 175
Eckert, Eva — *author* 88, 89, 95, 97, 117, 150
Economy: Czechs in US
  banking & finance — 134-135
  commerce & trade — 131-132
  corporate executives — 135
  farming — 129-131
  general surveys — 126-127
  industry — 132-134
  labor — 128-129
  living conditions — 127-128
  occupations — 128
Edson, L. — *author* 183
Education: Czechs in US — 145-149
Eichler, Jiří — *author* 221, 247; *subj.* x
Eidlitz, Leopold — *subj.* 162
Eisner, Michael — *subj.* 135
Eisner, Sigmund — *subj.* 133
Eisner, Will — *author* 162; *subj.* 162
Eliot, Chip — *author* 168
Ellenson, David — *author* 110
Ellis Island — 61
Elznic, William — *author* 83
Emigration from Czech Lands
  causes of — 48-49
  Ellis Island — 61
  from specific areas — 49-52
  general surveys — 46-47
  policy — 52-53
  prospects for future — 54
  reemigration — 53-54
  up to the ocean and across — 61
Emigration policy — 52-53
Engineering: Czechs in US — 182-183
Englund, T. B. — *author* 124
Enz, Charles P. — *author* 181
Epstein, Joseph — *author* 165
Ethnic identity: Czechs in US — 114-115
Ethnography: Czechs in Latin America — 235
Ethnography: Czechs in US — 101-102
Etiquette: Czechs in US — 42
Evangelic Union of Bohemian-Moravian Brethren — 186
Everett, William — *author* 158

Evjen, John Oluf — *author* 58, 59, 60
Ewen, David — *author* 158, 159, 161
Exner, Petr — *author* 184
Faber, Marion — *author* 161
Fabritius, Jacobus — *subj.* 58
Family organization: Czechs in US — 118
Farek, Florence Hertel — *author* 142
Farmers Mutual Protective Association of Texas (RVOS) — 185, 186
Farming: Czechs in US — 129-131
Farnham, Emily — *author* 161
Farris, June Pachuta — *author* 6, 45
Farský, Oldřich — *author* 78
Fast, Jane — *author* 203
Faust, Albert Bernhardt — *author* 151
Fechtnerová, Anna — *author* 57, 233, 235, 237, 240
Federation of Moravian Societies — 185
Fedor, Helen — *author* 5
Feigl, Herbert — *subj.* 172
Feminism: Czechs in US — 119-121
Fermi, Laura — *author* 71
Fiala, Anthony — *author* 19, 224; *subj.* 19, 224
Ficová, Klára — *author* 125
Fiction: Czechs in US — 23-26
Figarová, Alena — *author* 6
Filípek, Jan — *author* 16; *subj.* 16
Finger, Anke — *author* 245
Firkušný, Rudolf — *subj.* 158
Fischer, Edward — *author* 40
Fischler, Stan — *author* 228
Fišer, Benjamin — *author* 79
Fisher, Harrison — *author* 162; *subj.* 162
Fisher, J. — *author* 181
Fleischmann, Charles Louis — *subj.* 133
Fleischmann, Julius — *subj.* 137
Fleischner, Col. Louis — *subj.* 132
Flexner, Abraham — *author* 15, 174; *subj.* 15, 148, 174, 175
Flexner, James Thomas — *author* 155, 177; *subj.* 154
Flexner, Simon — *subj.* 177
Fligl, L. J. — *author* 75
Flint, Martha Bockée — *author* 60
Flint, Peter B. — *author* 172
Florida, Czechs in — 74
Flusser, Vilém — *subj.* 245
Folda, Folgin — *author* 24
Folkins, Gail — *author* 99, 157
Folklore: Czechs in US — 98-101
Folprecht, Josef — *author* 63, 124
Fordin, Hugh — *author* 159
Forejt-Alan, Vladimír — *author* 21
Forman, Miloš — *author* 16, 165; *subj.* 11, 16, 165
Forman, Václav B. — *author* 123
Fornůsková, Jana — *author* 48
Fořt, Josef — *author* 46
Foustková-Wattersonová — *author* 20
Food & Cuisine: Czechs in US — 99-101
Forty-Eighters (1848s) — 15
Fox, W. H. — *author* 156
Foxlee, Ludmila Kuchařová — *author* 83
Fradel, Jurian — *subj.* 58
Francl, Joseph — *subj.* 22
Francis, Sam — *author* 136
Francl, F. — *author* 32

Francl, Joseph — *author* 22
Freeland, Michael — *author* 165
Freethinkers: Czechs in US — 111-113
Freeze, Karen Johnson — *author* 64
Frenštát pod Radhoštěm Museum — 6
Freund, J. L. — *author* 117
Freund, Paul A. — *subj.* 175
Fried, Charles — *subj.* 11
Friemel, Nollie — *author* 210
Fries, Adelaide Lisetta — *author* 156
Friml, Rudolf — *subj.* 158
Fritch, Charles, E. — *author* 166
Fritz, Samuel — *author* 245; *subj.* 239
Fuchs, Jan — *author* 80
Furth, Jacob — *subj.* 134
Gág, Wanda — *author* 15, 162; *subj.* 162
Galandauer, Jan — *author* 195
Gallup, Sean — *author* 88, 99, 208
Gans, Joachim — *subj.* 58, 59
Garcia, Angel — *author* 141
Garofalo, Alessandra — *author* 165
Garver, Bruce M. — *author* 106, 113, 195
Gaston, Joseph — *author* 132
Gazarik, Rita Mae — *author* 118
Gazetteers: Czechs in US — 204-205
Geboire, Clive — *author* 121
Gellner, John — *author* 223
Genealogy: Czechs in US
archival materials — 204
cemetery records — 214-215
census records — 209-210
church membership records — 211
church register records — 211-214
civil register records — 214
gazetteers — 204-205
general references — 203-206
guides — 203
insurance claims — 217
naturalization records — 210-211
newspaper abstracts — 215-217
passenger lists — 206-207
periodicals — 204
settler lists — 207-209
societies — 205-206
sources of vital data — 206-217
surname records — 217
General references aids: Czechs in Canada
archival material — 222
bibliographies — 221
biographies — 221
periodicals — 221
General reference aids: Czechs in Latin America
bibliographies — 233
biographies — 235
ethnography — 235
historiography — 233-235
General references aids: Czechs in US
archival materials and library holdings — 4-8
bibliographies — 2-3
biographical compendia — 10-12
fiction — 23-26
genealogy — 203-206
dictionaries & textbooks — 30-35
directories — 28-29
dissertations — 26-28
handbooks – manuals – guides — 35-44
historiography — 8-10
libraries – museums – archives — 44-45

memoirs and oral history — 12-17
periodicals — 3-4
travels through America — 17-23
Gentry, James R. — *author* 74
Gerber, Michael A. — *author* 179
Geringer, Vladimír August — *author* 39
Geringer, August — *subj.* 151
Geršic, Miroslav — *author* 49
Getting, Milan — *author* 193
Gieser, Suzanne — *author* 181
Gilg, Adam — *subj.* 239
Glenn, Thomas Allen — *author* 59
Gloeckner, Annie Mae — *author* 209
Gődel, Kurt Frederick — *subj.* 180
Goldmark, Josephine — *author* 15, 68
Good, Rachel Applegate — *author* 85
Goodman, Grethe — *author* 108
Goodman, Richard E. — *author* 183
Gottfried, Alex — *author* 136
Gottfried, Kurt — *author* 182
Grassi, Gary C. — *author* 58, 59
Green, Stanley — *author* 158
Greene, Victor — *author* 98, 121, 157
Greenfield, John — *author* 145
Greenstein, Jesse L. — *author* 182
Gregorovich, Andrew — *author* 221
Griffith, Martha Eleanor — *author* 76
Gruen, Victor — *subj.* 162
Grulich, Tomáš — *author* 202
Grund, Francis Joseph — *author* 17, 151; *subj.* 151
Guides: Czechs in US — 35-44
genealogical — 203
Guinzburg, Harold Kleinert — *subj.* 151
Guth, Jiří — *author* 19
Haas, Arthur — *subj.* 181
Haasová, A. — *author* 222
Habenicht, Jan — *author* 14, 62, 113, 122, 148; *subj.* 14
Haberman, Gustav — *author* 14; *subj.* 14
Haenke, Thaddeus (Tadeáš) — *subj.* 23, 224, 236, 241
Hahn, Fred — *author* 109
Hachová, Veronika — *author* 48
Haidušek, Augustin — *subj.* 139
Hajda, Vladimír — *author* 242, 246
Hájek, J. (Oklahoma) — *author* 84
Hájek, J. (Canada) — *author* 222
Hájek, Josef J. — *author* 43
Hájek, J. S. — *author* 190
Hájková, Dagmar — *author* 196
Halas, George — *author* 168; *subj.* 168
Haloda, Antonín — *author* 241
Haman, Aleš — *author* 155
Hamanová, J. — *author* 124
Hamata, M. — *author* 230
Hamilton, John Taylor — *author* 107
Hamilton, Kenneth — *author* 4
Hampl, Patricia — *author* 16; *subj.* 16
Hanáková, Markéta — *author* 239
Handbooks – manuals – guides:
Czechs in US
advising farmers — 35-37
advising homes and households — 37-39
advising new settlers — 35
etiquette — 42
legal matters — 39-40
letter writing — 42-43
medical matters — 40-41
speeches — 43-44
Hannan, Kevin — *author* 95, 97, 115, 186
Hanzlík, František — *author* 196

Harden, Willam — *author* 145
Hardwick, M. Jeffrey — *author* 162
Harling, Frederick — *author* 140
Harris, Eileen Nini — *author* 104, 115
Harris, Othello — *author* 167, 168
Harris, Seymour C. — *author* 176
Hašek, Dominik — *subj.* 168
Haskell, Barbara — *author* 161
Hašková-Coolidge, Eliška — *author* 16; *subj.* 16
Haubelt, J. — *author* 236
Haurowitz, Felix — *subj.* 178
Havel, Nelson — 77
Havlasa, Jan — *author* 19, 25, 149; *subj.* 19
Havlicek, John — *subj.* 168
Heck, Earl L. — *author* 59
Heckewelder, John — *author* 13, 22; *subj.* 13, 22, 108, 224
Health & welfare: Czechs in US — 118-119
Hegar, Joseph — *author* 186
Heidelberger, Michael — *author* 178
Heineman, Bret — *author* 132
Heinrich, Antony Philip — *subj.* 158
Hejhal, John Stanley — *author* 117
Hejl, Edmond — *author* 205, 206, 210, 211, 214
Hejl, Edward — *author* 87
Hejl, James L. — *author* 212
Hejret, Jan — *author* 52
Heller, Erich — *subj.* 172
Heller, James G. — *author* 111
Heller, Max — *subj.* 110
Heller, Richard — *author* 36
Heller, Steve — *author* 164
Hellwald, Fr. — *author* 61
Henzl (Henzlová), Věra M. — *author* 27, 95
Herben, Ivan — *author* 155
Herben, Jan — *author* 196
Herites, František — *author* 19
Heřman, Augustine — *subj.* 59
Heroldová, Iva — *author* 102
Herrnhut Moravian Brethren Archives — 45
Hessoun, Joseph — *subj.* 105
Hewitt, William P. — *author* 27, 28, 114, 134
Hikl, Mario — *author* 222
Hill, Robert L. — *author* 179
Hines, Thomas — *author* 163
Historic places: Czechs in US — 91-92
Historiography: Czechs in Latin America — 233-235
Historiography: Czechs in US — 8-10
History: Czechs in Canada
early pioneers — 224-225
general surveys — 222-224
History: Czechs in Latin America
Bohemian Jesuits — 237-241
early pioneers — 237-241
general surveys — 235-236
History: Czechs in US
causes of emigration from Czech Lands — 48-49
early pioneers — 57-61
emigration from specific areas — 49-52
immigration to US — 61-65, 67-73
periods of immigration — 67-73
reemigration — 53-54
settlement in US — 61-65
Hlavac, James — *author* 77

Hlaváček, F. J. — *author* 121
Hlaváček, František — *subj.* 122
Hlavatý, Václav — *subj.* 181
Hlavinka, Paul T. — *author* 89
Hlubůček, T. B. — *author* 76
Hodges, LeRoy — *author* 130
Hoffman, Edward — *author* 174
Hoffman, Martinus Hermanzen — *subj.* 59, 60
Hoffman, Max E. — *author* 59
Hoffmann, Banesh — *author* 181
Hoffmann, Rudolf Stephan — *author* 159
Hoffmanová, J. — *author* 49
Holeček, Josef V. — *author* 81
Holick, Robert — *author* 27, 97
Holliday, Kathryn E. — *author* 161
Holmes, Frederick Lionel — *author* 91
Holub, Miroslav — *author* 22
Holzberg, James — *author* 78
Holzner, Burkart — *author* 175
Homolka, Oscar — *subj.* 165
Honan, William — *author* 138
Hoover Institution — 5
Hora, Václav — *author* 153
Horak, Jacob — *author* 27, 70
Horak, Joseph — *author* 115
Horčáková, Václava — *author* 11
Horna, Jarmila — *author* 73, 223, 226
Horner, Henry — *subj.* 132
Horner, Henry (Governor) — *subj.* 137
Hostovský, Egon — *author* 15, 154; *subj.* 15, 154, 155
Houdek, František — *author* 11
Houšť, Antonín — *author* 103
Howard, John Tasker — *author* 158
Howard, Johnette — *author* 169
Hoyle, Karen Nelson — *author* 162
Hrachovsky, Frank — *author* 188
Hranicky, Roy — *author* 87
Hrbek, Kent — *subj.* 168
Hrbek (Hrbková), Šárka B. — *author* 63, 76, 81, 116
Hrdlička, Aleš — *author* 21, 92; *subj.* 21, 178
Hřebík, Antonín — *author* 188, 189
Hribal, C. J. — *author* 153
Hrncir, Marilyn McGehearty — *author* 212
Hroch, Maximilián — *author* 96
Hromádka, Josef Lukl — *author* 20; *subj.* 20
Hron, Madelaine — *author* 54
Hruban, Zdeněk — *author* 4
Hrubeš, Jiří — *author* 55
Hrubý, Jiří — *author* 222
Hrubý, Karel — *author* 47, 69, 202
Hrubý, M. Karel — *subj.* 148
Hruska, John H. — *author* 188
Hruska, Roman Lee — *subj.* 138
Hubenák, Ladislav — *author* 195
Hudson, Estelle — *author* 87
Humanities: Czechs in US — 171-173
Hummel, William W. — *author* 147
Humpal-Zeman, Josefa — *author* 62; *subj.* 120
Hunter, Mark Stoffer — *author* 77
Hunter, Stanley Armstrong — *author* 117
Husa, Karel — *subj.* 28
Hutchinson, Jack — *author* 60
Hutton, J.E. — *author* 224
Idaho, Czechs in — 74
Illichman, S. J. — *author* 91
Illinois, Czechs in — 11, 27, 28, 40, 74-76
Illowy, Bernard — *subj.* 110
Image, of Czech Americans — 125-126

Immigration History Research Center (IHRC)
see University of Minnesota
Immigration to Latin America
Argentina — 241-243
Brazil — 243
Chile — 243
Cuba — 244
Mexico — 244
Paraguay — 244
Venezuela — 244
Immigration to US before and through World War I — 70
between World War I and World War II — 70
chronology of — 67
in 17th Century — 67
in 18th Century — 68
in 19th Century — 68-69
in 20th Century — 69-73
Industry: Czechs in US — 132-134
Ingham, John N. — *author* 133
Innes, John H. — *author* 60
Iowa, Czechs in — 76-77, 207
Irwin, Inez Haynes — *author* 121
Irwin, William H. — *author* 15, 198
Ispa-Landa, Simone — *author* 73
Israel, Lee — *author* 133
Iška, František — *author* 14, 38, 118; *subj.* 14
Ivanov, Miroslav — *author* 158, 223
Jackson, J. David — *author* 182
Jaffe, Bernard — *author* 178
Jágr, Jaromír — *author* 168; *subj.* 168
Jahelka, Joseph — *author* 194
Jaklová, Alena — *author* 4, 47, 61, 96, 150
Jakobson, Svatava Pírková — *author* 98
Janacek, John E. — *author* 208
Janák, Jan — *author* 35, 36, 37, 129
Janak, Robert — *author* 9, 89, 92, 106, 187, 205, 209, 212, 213, 214, 215
Janauschek, Franziska Magdalena — *subj.* 165
Janda, Alois — *author* 43
Janda, Rudolf — *author* 185
Jandáček, Antonín — *author* 22
Jandáčková, Marie — *author* 101
Janecka, Edward F. — *author* 147
Janská, E. — *author* 54
Jansky, Karl — *subj.* 182
Jarmush, Jim — *subj.* 11
Jedlička, Václav František — *subj.* 196
Jelínek, Jarka — *author* 167, 188
Jelinek, Otto — *subj.* 227
Jerabek, Esther — *author* 2, 79, 80, 116, 147, 148
Jerabek, Milan Woodrow — *author* 27, 80
Jeritza, Maria — *author* 14, 159; *subj.* 14, 159
Jermář, Jaromír — *author* 50
Jeřábek, Vojtěch — *author* 72, 189
Ješina, Čestmír — *author* 194
Jesuits from Bohemia: Czechs in Latin America — 237-241
Jetmar, J. — *author* 241
Jews: Czechs in US — 109-111
Ježek, Jan P. — *author* 41
Jícha, František — *author* 80
Jičinský, J. R. — *author* 167
Jirásek, Zdeněk — *author* 3, 71, 72, 200
Jirečková, Olga — *author* 233
Jirouch, Frank — *subj.* 162
Johansen, J. O. — *author* 117
Johnson, Christopher — *author* 28, 103
Johnston, Jesse — *author* 99, 157

Jochec, Jesse — *author* 139
Jonáš, (Karel) Charles — *author* 30, 31, 32, 33, 35, 39, 46, 75, 119, 129; *subj.* 135
Jones, Alex S. — *author* 152
Jones, Patricia L. — *author* 81
Jordan, E. L. — *author* 155
Jordan, John W. — *author* 206, 211
Journalism & publishing: Czechs in US — 149-152
Jovanovich, Marek J. — *author* 223
Jožák, Jiří — *author* 189, 199, 200
Julien, David A. — *author* 228
Jung, Leo — *author* 110; *subj.* 110, 111
Jung, Václav Alois — *author* 24
Jungk, Peter Stephan — *author* 156
Juránek, Tomáš — *author* 35
Juren, Henry — *subj.* 107
Juricek, Vlasta — *author* 208
Jurka, Anton (Antonín) — *author* 43; *subj.* 148
Kabala, Mirek — *author* 117
Kaessmann, Beta — *author* 78
Kafka, Franz — *author* 26
Kahler, Erich von — *subj.* 172
Kahuda, Jan — *author* 44
Kalda, Josef — *author* 43
Kalina, Alois — *author* 85
Kalista, Zdeněk — *author* 237
Kallus, Bohdan — *author* 186
Kalvoda, Josef — *author* 194
Kana, Sharon — *author* 208
Kansas, Czechs in — 77
Kaplan, K. — *author* 73
Kaplický, Jan — *subj.* 11, 12
Kapr, V. — *author* 41
Kaptainis, Arthur — *author* 228, 229
Karas, Joža — *author* 157
Kármán, Theodore von — *author* 183; *subj.* 183
Kárník, Jan — *author* 25, 32, 112
Karpeles, Leopold — *subj.* 143
Karták, Michael — *author* 79
Kašpar, Anton — *author* 36
Kašpar, Oldřich — *author* 9, 12, 23, 56, 57, 69, 102, 201, 233, 235, 236, 237, 238, 241, 246
Kaufman, Martin — *author* 140
Kavalířová, Marie — *author* 76
Kázecký, Stanislav — *author* 244
Kazimour, Karel — *author* 242
Kedro, M. James — *author* 74
Keil, Angeliki V. — *author* 157
Keil, Charles — *author* 157
Kejř, Václav — *author* 106
Keller, Ignaz Xaver — *subj.* 239
Kelsen, Hans — *subj.* 175
Kennedy, Alice — *author* 60
Kern, Jerome David — *subj.* 159
Kerner, Otto — *subj.* 139
Kerner, Robert Joseph — *subj.* 172
Kernmeter, Donald L. — *author* 134
Kerry, John Forbes — *subj.* 138
King, D. — *author* 177
King, Rebecca — *author* 77
Kirchman, Max — *author* 85
Kirsch, George B. — *author* 167, 168
Kisch, Guido — *author* 8, 48, 55, 57, 68, 109, 126, 140, 146, 190, 194
Kissner, J. G. — *author* 103
Kittler, Pamela Goyan — *author* 100
Klácel, Ladimír — *author* 37, 38; *subj.* 113
Klácel, Ladislav — *author* 119
Klášterský, Milan — *author* 233
Klein, Alois J. — *subj.* 105

Kleinschmidt, John R. — *author* 135
Klicperová-Baker, Martina — *author* 192
Klieger, P. Christian — *author* 133
Klíma, Stanislav — *author* 63, 93, 102, 125, 128, 147, 201
Klimesh, Cyril — *author* 77
Klimesh, Michael — *author* 77, 148
Klimesh, Steven — *author* 104
Klučka, Jiří — *author* 51
Kluge, Edw. T. — *author* 214
Klumpp, Dorothy — *author* 106
Klutschak, Heinrich — *author* 18, 23, 225; *subj.* 18, 23, 225
Kneidl, P. — *author* 55
Kneipp, Šebestián — *author* 40
Knopp, František — *author* 153
Knorr — *author* 175
Kochman, Leopold — *subj.* 122
Kocourek, R. — *author* 48
Kodytková, Anna — *author* 242
Koerner, Leon J. — *subj.* 228
Kohlbeck, Valentine — *author* 62, 103
Kohler, Fred — *subj.* 137
Kohn, Hans — *subj.* 172
Kohn, Samuel — *subj.* 134
Kohn, Walter — *author* 181; *subj.* 181
Kohnová, Marie J. — *author* 116
Kohout, Alois Lecoque — *subj.* 162
Kochis, Bruce — *author* 96
Kolaja, Jiří — *author* 71
Kolář, Petr — *subj.* x
Kolář, W. — *author* 90
Koller, Carl — *subj.* 178
Kolodin, I. — *author* 160
Kolowrat-Krakovský, Jindřich — *author* 20
Konecny, Lawrence — *author* 61, 88
Konečná, Elvira — *author* 21, 22
Konvitz, Milton R. — *author* 111
Kopperl, Moritz — *subj.* 134
Korbel, Francis — *subj.* 133
Korbel, Mario — *subj.* 162
Korčák, Jaromír — *author* 49
Korytová-Magstadt, Štěpánka — *author* 47, 48, 69, 91, 92, 115, 120, 128, 130
Kořalka, Jiří — *author* 47, 53
Kořalková, Květa — *author* 47, 53
Kořenský, Josef — *author* 18, 19, 20; *subj.* 18, 20
Korngold, Erich Wolfgang — *subj.* 159
Kosta, J. — *author* 173
Kostlán, Antonín — *author* 12, 73, 170
Koubská, Libuše — *author* 11
Koudelka, Jaroslav — *author* 21, 26
Koudelka, Josef Maria — *author* 33, 34; *subj.* 105
Koukal, Pavel — *author* 122
Kovacs, Sandor Bodonsky — *author* 27
Kovacs, Sandra A. — *author* 90
Kovář, Frantšek — *author* 79
Kovtun, George — *author* 3, 7, 67, 153, 191, 195, 197
Kraglund, John — *author* 229
Krajina, Vladimír Joseph — *subj.* 228
Král, Josef Jiří — *author* 26, 39
Kramerius, Václav Matěj — *author* 55
Kratochvíl, Antonín — *author* 2
Kratochvíl, Jan — *author* 70
Kraus, Adolf — *author* 14; *subj.* 14
Kreisel, C. — *author* 180
Kreisler, Matthais — *subj.* 60
Krejčí, Alois — *author* 243
Krejčí, František Václav — *author* 20
Křen, Jan — *author* 71, 199

Krenek, Ernst — *author* 159; *subj.* 159
Kresge, Nicole — *author* 179
Kresta, Václav — *author* 243
Křesťan, Jiří — *author* 6, 44, 45
Krestan, Jo-Ann — *author* 118, 119
Kříž, Frank — *subj.* 168
Kříža, John — *subj.* 166
Křížek, Čeněk — *author* 41
Křížová, Markéta — *author* 108, 238
Kroc, Ray — *author* 132; *subj.* 132
Kroupa, Bohuslav — *author* 18, 225; *subj.* 18, 225
Kroupa, Jan — *author* 36, 37
Krupař, A. C. — *author* 89
Kubálek, Antonín — *subj.* 228
Kubicek, Clarence John — *author* 82
Kubíček, Doug — *author* 204
Kubíček, Jan Nepomuk — *subj.* 241
Kubitschek, Juscelino — *subj.* 245
Kučera, Henry — *author* 171
Kučera, K. — *author* 95
Kučera, Vladimír — *author* 82, 103, 157, 164
Kuděj, Zdenek — *author* 20, 25
Kugler, John — *author* 146
Kukral, Michael — *author* 84
Kuksa, Milan — *author* 192
Kulhánek, Jiří — *author* 238
Kún, Francis — *subj.* 109
Kundera, Milan — *subj.* 11
Kurfürst, Jaroslav — *author* 192
Kurland, Philip B. — *author* 175
Kutac, Margaret May — *author* 96
Kutak, Robert — *author* 27, 114, 116, 118, 130
Kutes, A. — *author* 74
Kutnar, František — *author* 9, 12, 46, 68
Kybal, Milič — *author* 245
Kybal, Vlastimil — *author* 235, 243
Kyle, R. A. — *author* 180
Kymlička, Milan — *subj.* 228
Kysilka, Karel — *author* 50
Labaj, Stacy Mikulencak — *author* 216
LaBaume, F. H. — *author* 89
Labitsky, Wilhelm — *subj.* 225
Labor: Czechs in US — 128-129
movement of — 121-123
Lachmanová-Medová, L. — *author* 54
LaMartin, William — *author* 61
Lamprecht, Barbara — *author* 163
Landsteiner, Karl — *subj.* 178
Langer, Edward G. — *author* 49
Langer, William — *subj.* 138
Language: Czechs in US
Americanization and corruption of — 96-97
general surveys — 94-96
maintenance a and perspective for future — 97-98
Lasak, Francis W. — *subj.* 132
Láska, Věra — *author* 64, 67, 71, 135
Lathem, Edward Connery — *author* 164
Latin America, Czechs in
cultural life and contributions of — 245
general references — 233-235
history — 235-241
organizations — 246
relations with Czechoslovakia — 246
specific countries — 241-244
LaTrobe, Benjamin — *author* 224
Lauder, Estée — *author* 133; *subj.* 133

Lauer, Gerhard — *author* 172
Lavin, Sylvia — *author* 163
Lawton, Mary — *author* 160
Layman, Helen — *author* 210
Lazarsfeld, Patricia Kendall — *author* 175
Lazarsfeld, Paul Felix — *subj.* 175
Leary, James — *author* 98, 157
Ledbetter, Eleanor — *author* 84
Lees, Frederic — *author* 163
Legal Matters: Czechs in US
civics — 39-40
general laws — 39
naturalization & citizenship — 39
parliamentary rules — 40
Lehman, Stephen — *author* 160
Leland, Anthony DeWitt — *author* 211
Lendl, Ivan — *subj.* 168
LeRoy, Hodges — *author* 89
Lewis, M. — *author* 142
Lewis, Lloyd — *author* 137
Lexa, Antonin — *author* 76
Lifka, Bohumír — *author* 44
Limmer, E. A., Jr. — *author* 208
Linck, Wenceslaus — *author* 22, 239, 240
Lindenthal, Gustav — *subj.* 183
Lindorff, David — *author* 181
Link, Václav — *subj.* 22, 239, 240
Linková, Marcela — *author* 7
Letter writing: Czechs in US — 42-43
Libraries: Czechs in US — 44-45
Library holdings: Czechs in America — 6-8
Library of Congress — 5, 7
Literature: Czechs in US — 153-156
Littlewood, Thomas B. — *author* 137
Lochwing, Walter F. — *author* 179
Locker, Ann — *author* 146
Löher, Franz — *author* 55
Lojda, Václav — *author* 185
Long, Edmond R. — *author* 178
Losa, Václav — *author* 62
Louis, Carol — *author* 101
Louisiana, Czechs in — 27, 77-78
Löwenbach, Jan — *author* 55, 156
Lubek, Sister M. — *author* 191
Luebke, Frederick — *author* 10
Luk, Vincent — *author* 76
Lukeš, Igor — *author* 72, 200
Lundák, J. F. — *author* 81
Lustig, Arnošt — *subj.* 155
Lutz, Frank — *author* 14
Luža, Radomír V. — *author* 171
Lynch, Russell — *author* 27, 130
Lysacek, Evan — *subj.* 11
Mácha, Helen — *author* 87
Mácha, Z. — *author* 141
Machala, Lubomír — *author* 154
Machalek, Richard — *author* 114
Machann, Clinton — *author* 12, 61, 87, 98, 139, 145, 154, 157; *subj.* x
Machek, A. — *author* 33, 147
Machotka, Otakar — *author* 26
Machovsky, Anna — *author* 185
Macy, Harry, Jr. — *author* 60
Mádl, Jan — *author* 21
Majdová, Hana — *author* 196
Majerová, Marie — *author* 20
Makon, K. — *author* 222
Malik, Joseph — *author* 87, 97
Malina, Frank J. — *author* 183; *subj.* 183
Mallery, Charles Payson — *author* 59
Malone, Barbara S. — *author* 110

Malý, Jakub — *author* 61
Malý, Jindřich — *author* 177
Malý, Jiří — *author* 92
Mamatey, Victor S. — *author* 190, 191, 194
Mandeličková, Monika — *author* 54, 73, 170, 171
Mannheimer, Louise — *subj.* 148
March, James G. — *author* 176
Marek, Daniel J. — *author* 107
Mares, Claire — *author* 206
Maresh, Henry R. — *author* 87
Maretzek, Max — *author* 14, 16, 159; *subj.* 14, 16, 159
Marhefka, Blanche — *author* 77
Marik, Helen — *author* 100
Marley, W. — *author* 84
Marsh, James H. — *author* 227, 228, 229
Martin, Douglas — *author* 154
Martin, Pat — *author* 100, 101
Martin, William Earl — *author* 116
Martínek, Josef — *author* 118, 121, 153, 185, 187, 194
Martinů, Bohuslav — *subj.* 11, 160
Maryland, Czechs in — 78
Masaryk, Alice Garrigue — *author* 15, 75, 157, 158; *subj.* 15
Masaryk, Thomas Garrigue — *author* 112; *subj.* 189, 190, 191, 192, 195, 196, 197
Mašek, Josef — *author* 34, 187
Mašek, Matěj — *author* 141
Mashek, Nan — *author* 129
Mason, Alpheus Thomas — *author* 139
Mason, E. S. — *author* 177
Masters, Charles — *author* 137
Mastný, V. — *author* 94
Matocha, B. F. — *author* 144
Matulka, Jan — *subj.* 11
Matz, Mary Jane — *author* 160
May, Joseph — *author* 138
May, Max B. — *author* 111
Mayer, Alfred — *author* 48
McBrewster, John — *author* 168
McCabe, Lida Rose — *author* 98
McCardell, Lee — *author* 78
McCarthy, E. R. — *author* 184
McCaskey, Patrick — *author* 168
McClure, Archibald — *author* 144
McKay, Frederick E. — *author* 165
McLaurin, Donald — *author* 28
Medical matters: Czechs in US — 40-41
Meilbeck, Leo — *subj.* 123
Meinhold, Stephen S. — *author* 140
Memoirs: Czechs in US — 12-17
Mendl, James W. — *author* 12, 87, 94, 95
Meredith, Joan — *author* 228
Merrill, Pauline Skorunka — *author* 76
Merritt, Richard I. — *author* 174
Merton, Robert K. — *author* 175
Mesecke, Anjanette — *author* 208
Meserve, Walter J. — *author* 167
Mexico, Czechs in — 244
Mézl, F. — *author* 52
Míček, Eduard — *author* 87, 146
Michigan, Czechs in — 78
Mikeska, Jan — *author* 49, 51
Mikita, Stan — *subj.* 228
Mikšička, A. V. — *author* 80
Mikula, Bohumil — *author* 33
Milberger, Olivia — *author* 203
Military: Czech in US

general surveys — 140
in American Revolution — 140
in Civil War — 141
in Mexican War — 140
in Spanish-American War — 141-142
in World War I — 142
in World War II — 142
Miller, Frederic P. — *author* 168
Miller, Herbert Adolphus — *author* 92
Miller, June Eick — *author* 119
Miller, Kenneth Dexter — 17, 46, 63, 86, 92, 93, 102, 116, 117, 118, 125, 126, 127, 128, 144, 147, 149; *subj.* 17
Miller, Olga K. — *author* 203
Miller, Wayne Charles — *author* 2
Miniberger, Václav — *author* 24, 25, 26
Minnesota, Czechs in — 27, 78-80, 207
Míšek, Rudolf — *author* 234, 242
Missouri, Czechs in — 80-81, 207
Mitchell, Broadus — *author* 175
Mohelská, Jana — *author* 102
Mohr, John McGuire — *author* 86
Mokotoff, Gary — *author* 58, 110
Molinari, C. — *author* 64
Moody, Suzanna — *author* 4
Moravian Brethren: Czechs in US — 4, 10, 45, 57, 107-108, 216
Moravský zemský archiv, Brno — 4
Morawetz, Oskar — *subj.* 11, 12, 228, 229
Morgan, Christopher — *author* 58
Morgenbesser, Sydney — *author* 172
Morkovsky, Alois — *author* 11
Morris, Nick — *author* 185
Motlíček, Tomáš — *author* 6
Motycka, Anton — *author* 211
Mrázek, Jaroslav — *author* 190
Mucha, Alphonse — *subj.* 163
Mucha, Jiří — *author* 163
Muhlena, David — *author* 5, 8, 13, 45
Muller, K. — *author* 46
Murphy, David — *author* 164
Museums: Czechs in US — 44-45
Musial, Stanley Frank — *subj.* 169
Music: Czechs in US — 156-161
Musil, Ferdinand — *author* 37, 63, 184, 230
Nagel, Ernest — *subj.* 172
Nálevka, Vladimír — *author* 244, 246
Náprstek, Vojta — *subj.* 12, 23, 151, 201
Náprstek Museum, Prague — 7, 8, 13, 45
Naramore, Ronald — *author* 85, 114
National Archives, Prague — 4, 6, 45
National Czech & Slovak Museum & Library, Cedar Rapids — 5, 8, 13, 45
Natonek, Hans — *author* 15; *subj.* 15
Naturalizations records: Czechs in US — 210-211
Navara, Luděk — *author* 155
Navrátil, Michael — *author* 177
Navrátilová, Martina — *author* 16; *subj.* 11, 16, 169
Nazism, refugees from — 71
Nebraska, Czechs in — 81-82, 207
Nebraska Historical Society — 8
Nečas, Daniel — *author* 5, 45
Neill, C. A. — *author* 179
Neisser, George — *author* 207, 208
Nekola, E. — *author* 226
Nekola, Rudolf — *author* 21

Nelson, Vernon H. — *author* 203
Nemcova, Bozena — *author* 77
Němec, Ludvík — *author* 173
Nemecek, Paul — *author* 45
Němeček, Zdeněk — *author* 26; *subj.* 155
Nerada, Zdeněk — *author* 167
Nešpor, Zdeněk — *author* 10, 54
Nesvadbík, Lumír — *author* 136
Nettl, Paul — *author* 156
Neubauer, David W. — *author* 140
Neumann, J. N. — *author* 105
Neumann, Jan — *subj.* 240
Neumann, John Nepomucene — *subj.* 105
Neutra, Richard Joseph — *subj.* 163
New Bohemia — 65
New Jersey, Czechs in — 82
New World
early contacts with — 56
early perceptions of — 56
early pioneers in — 57-61
news of its discovery — 55-56
New York, Czechs in — 29, 82-83
New York Public Library — 8
Newman, Peter Charles — *subj.* 229
Newspaper abstracts: Czech in — US 215-217
Nigrin, Jaroslav Victor — *author* 32, 34, 147
Nicholas, Sinclair — *author* 124
Nitschmann, Anna — *subj.* 108
Nitschmann, David — *subj.* 108
Noblitt, Julie A. — *author* 120
Nolte, Claire E. — *author* 167, 168
North Dakota, Czechs in — 83
Nosková, Helena — *author* 202
Nováček, Alfred — *author* 82
Novák, Antonín — *author* 38, 90
Novak, Frank — *author* 75
Novák, Jan — *author* 13, 16; *subj.* 155
Novak, John A. — *author* 99
Novak, Kim — *subj.* 166
Novák, Vladimír — *author* 19
Novotná, Eva — *author* 238
Novotná, J. — *author* 226
Novotná, Jarmila — *subj.* 160
Novotný, Antonín "Tony" — *subj.* 123
Novotný, Jan — *author* 187
Novy, Fredrick George — *subj.* 178, 179
Nygrin, Rudy — *author* 130
Nykl, A. R. — *author* 244
O'Donnell, Lida — *author* 85
Obsta, Doris — *author* 203
Ocenasek, Mildred — *subj.* 136
Occupations: Czechs in US — 128
Odložilík, Otakar — *author* 16, 135, 237, 244; *subj.* 16, 71, 173
Ohio, Czechs in — 28, 84
Oklahoma, Czechs in — 27, 84-85
Oliverius, J.A. — *author* 123
Opatrný, Josef — *author* 10, 22, 56, 141, 142, 234, 236, 240
Opie, Redveras — *author* 176
Oral histories: Czechs in US — 12-17
Oregon, Czechs in — 85
Orel (organization) — 189
Orel, Vítězslav — *author* 113
Organizations: Czechs in Canada — 230
Organizations: Czechs in Latin America — 246
Organizations: Czechs in US
charitable & relief — 189

cultural – scholarly
– scientific — 188
fraternal &
benevolent — 184-185
genealogical — 205-206
general surveys — 184
heritage — 186-187
physical education — 188-189
public affairs & political — 187
religious — 186
Osten, Margaret E. — *author* 6
Ottendorfer, Oswald — *subj.* 152
Owen, Marie Bankhead — *author* 135
Owen, Thomas McAdory — *author* 135
Pacák, Louis — *author* 40
Pace, Eric — *author* 175
Paclt, Čeněk (Vincenc) — *author* 18, 21; *subj.* 18, 21, 23
Pacner, Karel — *author* 11, 170
Palacký University, Olomouc — 6
Palda, Leo (L. J.) — *author* 112, 121, 123; *subj.* 123
Pánek, Jaroslav — *author* 11; *subj.* x
Pap, Michael — *author* 84
Papánek, Ján — *author* 199
Paper, Lewis J. — *author* 139
Papoušek, Vladimír — *author* 153, 154, 155; *subj.* x
Paraguay, Czechs in — 244
Parenton, V. J. — *author* 118
Paris, Leonard Allen — *author* 158
Parker, Franklin — *author* 174
Parshall, Ardis E. — *author* 143
Partl, Václav — *author* 190
Pasternak, Blanka — *author* 5
Pastor, Josef — *author* 18, 30, 61, 91; *subj.* 18
Pastorek, John B. — *author* 105
Passenger Lists: Czechs in US — 206-207
Paterson, T. W. — *author* 225
Paukertová, Libuše — *author* 72
Pauli, Wolfgang — *subj.* 181
Paulson, Robert — *author* 64
Pavelka, Jan — *author* 79
Payer, Julius — *author* 18; *subj.* 18
Pazdral, Olga — *author* 27, 98
Pazourek, Vladimír — *author* 190
Peaslee, Margaret Heřmánek — *author* 113
Pecka, Josef Boleslav — *author* 185; *subj.* 123
Pecinovsky, Gerald — *author* 77
Pecival, Josef P. — *author* 114
Pečírka, Josef — *author* 40
Pehotsky, Bessie Olga — *author* 119
Pejskar, Jožka — *author* 11, 71, 217
Peklo, Jaroslav — *author* 21
Pelant, Karel — *author* 20
Pelikán, Jiří — *subj.* 245
Pelikánová, Jitka — *author* 73, 120
Pennsylvania, Czechs in — 85-86, 207-208
People: Czechs in US
anthropology — 92
demography — 92-94
ethnography — 101-102
folklore — 98-101
language — 94-98
Peprnik, Jaroslav — *author* 221
Pergler, Karel (Charles) — *author* 39, 190, 193, 197; *subj.* 136, 197
Periodicals: Czechs in Canada — 221
Periodicals: Czechs in US — 3-4
genealogical — 204
Perk, Ralph J. — *subj.* 137

Perkins, Sharon — *author* 103
Perkowski, Jan — *author* 96, 97
Peroutka, Ferdinand — *author* 16; *subj.* 11, 16
Peroutka, Michael — *subj.* 136
Peterka, Petr — *author* 76
Peterková, J. — *author* 223
Petrák, Anton — *author* 86
Petrik, Robert — *author* 74
Petrik, Vlasta — *author* 85
Petura, J. L. — *author* 90
Peuker, Paul — *author* 45
Pflanzer, Vilém — *author* 21; *subj.* 23
Philipson, David — *author* 14
Phillips, A. — *author* 159
Phillips, Howard — *author* 136
Philipse, Frederick — *subj.* 60
Phillipus, Karen — *author* 208
Physical sciences: Czechs in US — 180-182
Pichlík, Karel — *author* 194, 195
Pimper, Antonín — *author* 52
Pírková-Jakobson, Svatava — *author* 98
Piskač, Antonín — *author* 36
Plach, Maryrose — *author* 146
Placzek, George — *subj.* 182
Podlipny, Julius — *subj.* 11
Pohl, Johann Emanuel — *subj.* 241
Pokorný, Ondřej — *author* 238
Polák, Josef — *author* 22
Polansky, Mary Ann — *author* 208
Polášek, Albin — *subj.* 163
Polasek, Emily 163
Polišenský, Josef — *author* 9, 10, 12, 22, 47, 55, 56, 61, 64, 66, 69, 70, 71, 121, 122, 131, 136, 191, 195, 233, 234, 236, 240
Politics: Czechs in US — 135-136
Pollak, Simon — *author* 14, 179; *subj.* 14, 179
Pollitzer, Anita — *subj.* 121
Popper, Frank — *author* 183
Popper, Hans — *subj.* 179
Porter, Jack Nusan — *author* 152
Pospíšil, F. — *author* 78
Pousta, Zdeněk — *author* 13, 73
Povolný, Mojmír — *author* 16; *subj.* 16
Prantner, Emil F. — *author* 10, 112, 126, 162
Preiss, Eduard — *author* 18; *subj.* 18
Preissig, Vojtěch — *subj.* 163
Presbyterians: Czechs in — US 109
Prchal, Tim — *author* 124, 126
Pricher, Jerry — *author* 61
Přístupa, G. — *author* 230
Pritchard, Joyce M. — *author* 90
Probasco, Juriaen — *subj.* 60
Probst, Vojtěch — *author* 162
Prochaska, Alvin J. — *author* 88
Procházka, Matěj — *author* 240
Prokeš, Josef — *author* 41
Prokosch, Frederick — *subj.* 155
Protestants: Czechs in US
  Baptists — 109
  Bohemian Brethren — 106-107
  general surveys — 105-106
  Moravian Brethren — 107-108
  Presbyterians — 109
Průcha, Václav — *author* 106
Pšenka, Rudolf Jaromír — *author* 25, 75
Public Life: Czech in US
  community leadership — 144
  government executive branch — 136-138

government judiciary branch — 139-140
government legislative branch — 138-139
military service — 140-144
politics — 135-136
Putnam, Frank W. — *author* 178
Rabstejnek, Hermina — *author* 84
Rabušic, L. — *author* 124
Radetsky, Peter — *author* 180
Raková, Svatava — *author* 11
Rankin, Peggy Holland — *author* 89
Raška, Francis D. — *author* 187, 200
Raška, Karel, Jr. — *author* vii
Rasponi, Lanfranco — *author* 160
Ratkoš, Peter — *author* 55
Rau, John E. — *author* 86
Ray, Randy — *author* 230
Readers & primers: Czechs in US — 33-35
Reagan, Patrick D. — *author* 176
Rechcígl, Eva — *author* 29, 221; *subj.* x
Rechcígl, Miloslav, Jr. — *author* 2, 3, 5, 6, 10, 11, 17, 29, 44, 56, 57, 58, 59, 60, 64, 65, 67, 69, 73, 75, 78, 83, 85, 89, 91, 92, 105, 107, 108, 109, 110, 120, 124, 131, 134, 138, 140, 145, 146, 148, 151, 152, 159, 161, 165, 166, 167, 169, 170, 171, 172, 173, 174, 175, 176, 177, 178, 179, 180, 181, 182, 183, 188, 195, 203, 207, 221; *subj.* 11, 17, 188
Rechcígl, Miloslav, Sr. — *subj.* 11, 12
Reemigration — 53-54
Refugees from the Czech Lands
from Communism – after February 1948 — 71-73
from Communism – after Soviet Invasion in 1968 — 73
from Nazism — 71
Regional and local history: Czechs in America
Alabama — 74
California — 74
Colorado — 74
Florida — 74
Idaho — 74
Illinois — 10, 11, 27, 28, 74-76
Iowa — 76-77, 207
Kansas — 77
Louisiana — 27, 77
Maryland — 78
Michigan — 78
Minnesota — 27, 78-80, 207
Missouri — 80-81, 207
Nebraska — 81-82, 207
New Jersey — 82
New York — 29, 82-83
North Dakota — 83
Ohio — 28, 84
Oklahoma — 27, 84-85
Oregon — 85
Pennsylvania — 85-86, 207-208
South Dakota — 86
Texas — 9, 11, 12, 27, 28, 86-89, 208-209
Virginia — 27, 89-90
Wisconsin — 27, 90-91
Reichel, William — *author* 10
Reichman, John — *author* 11, 75
Reincke, Abraham — *author* 211
Relations with the old Homeland: Czechs in Latin America — 246

Relations with the old Homeland: Czechs in US
Contacts and attitudes of the Homeland to Czech-Americans and vice versa — 201-202
Czech-US and US-Czech relations and contacts — 189-192
Czech-American aid — 192-200
Religion: Czechs in US
Freethinkers — 111-113
General surveys — 102-103
Jews — 109-111, 186
Protestants — 105-109, 186
Roman Catholics — 11, 103-105, 186
Reynish, Timothy — *author* 98
Reynolds, Paul — *author* 137
Reynolds, Simon — *author* 45
Rezek, Jan — *author* 90
Rhodes, Anne — *author* 209
Richards, Marilee — *author* 86
Richardson, James F. — *author* 137
Richman, Julia — *subj.* 149
Richter, Frank Xavier — *subj.* 225
Richter, Václav — *subj.* 240
Riis, Jacob A. — *author* 128, 129
Rippley, La Vern — *author* 64
Roberts, John G. — *subj.* 11, 140
Robbins, Jane — *author* 119
Robek, Antonín — *author* 9, 102
Rodríguez, Luis Gonzales — *author* 240
Roedl, Bohumír — *author* 240
Rogow, Faith — *author* 148
Roldan, Roman E. — *author* 233
Rollerová, V. — *author* 226
Roman Catholics: Czechs in US — 11, 103-105, 186
Rondthaler, Edward — *author* 108
Rosen, Charles — *author* 160
Rosenbaum, S. E. — *author* 21, 109; *subj.* 21
Rosene, Effie — *author* 45
Rosewater, Edward — *subj.* 152
Rosická (Rosicky), Marie — *author* 100
Rosická, P. — *author* 202, 223
Rosická, Růžena (*see also* Rosicky, Rose) — *author* 37, 101
Rosicky, John (Jan) — *author* 35, 184; *subj.* 152
Rosicky, Rose (*see also* Rosická, Růžena) — *author* 81, 104, 106, 112, 135, 147, 152
Rossi, Peter H. — *author* 175
Rostinský, Josef — *author* 99, 150
Rottenberg, Dan — *author* 203
Roucek, Joseph — *author* 2, 63, 64, 94, 114, 116, 126, 142, 144, 145, 146, 194
Rovenský, Joseph Charles — *subj.* 134
Rubeš, Jan — *subj.* 229
Rucker, Della G. — *author* 91
Ruda, V. — *author* 222
Rudiš-Jičinský, Jan — *author* 76, 112, 188
Ruml, Beardsley — *subj.* 175
Russett, Bruce M. — *author* 174
Růžička, Rudolph — *subj.* 163, 164
Ryan, Lawrence — *author* 98
Rychlík, Jan — *author* 53
Rychlík, Martin — *author* 238
Ryneš, Václav — *author* 237
Sabath, Adolph J. — *author* 189,

197; *subj.* 139, 197
Sabatos, Charles — *author* 154
Sabol, John T. — *author* 84
Sadílek, Frank J. — *author* 14; *subj.* 14
Safertal, Frank — *author* 226
Šafránek, Miloš — *author* 160
Sandrolini, Mike — *author* 168
Santilli, Evelyn Hornak — *author* 74
Sarris, K. E. Zwolanek — *author* 107
Šašková-Pierce, Míla — *author* 97
Šatava, Leoš — *author* 46, 47, 69, 102, 116, 150
Savage, C. Wade — *author* 172
Saxon-Ford, Stephanie — *author* 64
Schabas, Ezra — *author* 229
Schacter, Jacob J. — *author* 110
Schattschneider, David A. — *author* 107
Schermerhorn, R. A. — *author* 64
Schlyter, Daniel M. — *author* 203, 204
Schmelzer, Janet L. — *author* 120
Schmid, Rudi — *author* 179
Schmirler, A. — *author* 83
Schnabel, Artur — *author* 16, 160; *subj.* 16, 160
Schneider, Erich — *author* 176
Schneider, Joseph — *author* 15
Schneirov, Richard Samuel — *author* 113, 122
Schoenberg, Arnold — *subj.* 160
Scholarship – science – technology: Czechs in US
biological & medical sciences — 177-180
engineering — 182-183
general surveys — 169-170
humanities — 171-173
physical sciences — 180-182
social sciences — 173-177
Schonberg, Harold C. — *author* 159
Schools: Czechs in US — 146-148
Schovajsa, Henry J. — *author* 139
Schuchalter, Jerry — *author* 155
Schulman, Michael — *author* 228
Schultz, Adolph — *author* 178
Schultze, Augustus — *author* 214
Schumann- Heink, Ernestine — *subj.* 160
Schumpeter, Joseph Alois — *author* 176; *subj.* 176
Schuyler, Montgomery — *author* 161
Schűtz, Alfred — *subj.* 176
Schweinitz, Edmund de — *author* 108
Scott, Alma Olivia — *author* 162
Screws, Raymond D. — *author* 115, 117
Sealsfield, Charles (Karl Postl's pseud) — *author* 17, 23; *subj.* 155
Searchinger, Cesar — *author* 160
Sears, Charles Hatch — *author* 63
Sebesta, Stephen — *author* 142
Secká, Milena — *author* 8, 10, 13, 44, 45, 65, 151, 222; *subj.* x
Šedivý, Josef Pavel — *author* 81
Seifert, Augustin — *author* 133
Šejnoha, Jaroslav — *author* 161
Sekanina, František — *author* 10, 196, 197, 198
Sekyrková, Milada — *author* 71
Selsam, J. Paul — *author* 190
Šembera, Alois Vojtěch — *author* 92
Semrad, Elizabeth M. Zvolanek — *author* 107
Serkin, Rudolf — *subj.* 160
Sersen, Fred — *subj.* 12
Settlement: Czechs in US — 61-65
Settler lists: Czech in US — 207-209

Severa, Václav E. — *subj.* 133
Shampo, M. A. — *author* 180
Shawn, Allen — *author* 160
Sheldon, Addison E. — *author* 126
Sheldon, Carol L. — *author* 124
Shepard, Karleen Chott — *author* 207
Sheridan, Frank J. — *author* 128
Sherwood, Ruth — *author* 163
Shimek (Šimek), Bohumil — *author* 76; *subj.* 179
Shimmick, Lillian — *author* 77
Shintay, Jan — *author* 83
Shultz, Randy — *author* 168
Siemaszkiewicz, Wojciech — *author* 8
Šilar, František — *author* 49
Šiler, Josef — *author* 86
Šilhan, F. — *author* 239
Šiller, Vilém — *author* 105
Simak, Clifford D. — *subj.* 11
Šimek, Vladimír — *author* 78, 239
Simoni, Robert D. — *author* 179
Šimíček, Josef — *author* 50, 51
Šimková, Kamila Broulová — *author* 239
Simon, Herbert A. — *subj.* 176
Sinclair, Sonja — *author* 227
Šindelář, Bedřich — *author* 46, 48
Šindelář, František — *author* 193
Singer, Isidor — *author* 245
Singerman, Robert — *author* 151
Sinkula, P. — *author* 140
Šír, L. — *author* 48
Šisler, Stanislav — *author* 4
Skála, Josef — *author* 227
Skalský, Gustav Adolf — *author* 68
Škaloud, František — *author* 24
Skamenov, F. G. — *author* 241
Škarda, František — *subj.* 123
Skrabanek, Robert — *author* 27, 115, 118, 124, 125, 130
Skrivanek, John — *author* 27, 87, 146
Škvor, J. G. — *author* 221
Škvorecký, Josef — *author* 23, 26, 229; *subj.* 229
Sládek, Josef Václav — *author* 25, 153; *subj.* 22, 27, 156
Slater, Thomas J. — *author* 165
Slavonic Benevolent Order of the State of Texas (SPJST) — 185
Slezak, Eva — *author* 78
Slezak, Walter — *subj.* 166
Slouka, Zdeněk — *author* 17; *subj.* 17
Slovacek, Marvin — *author* 185
Slovak-Americans — 194, 195
Šmaha, Josef — *author* 18, 62
Smekal, Ferdinand G. — *author* 178
Šmeral, Jiří — *author* 6
Smerek, John — *author* 223
Smetánka, Jaroslav — *author* 63, 144, 146, 147, 197; *subj.* 197
Šmíd, Jan — *author* 168
Smith, C. S. — *author* 96
Smith, E. F. — *author* 214, 216
Šnajdr, Václav — *author* 19, 84
Sobota, Emil — *author* 21
Sobotka, Margie — *author* 140, 206, 207, 214, 215, 216, 217
Sobotka, Rudie — *author* 203
Social organization: Czechs in US — 117-118
Social sciences: Czechs in US — 173-177
Society: Czechs in Canada — 226
Society: Czechs in US attitude – behavior – communication — 124-125

assimilation and acculturation — 115-117
character — 123-124
cooperation — 125
ethnic identity — 114-115
family organization — 118
health & welfare — 118-119
image among Americans — 125-126
labor movement — 121-123
social organization — 117-118
women – feminism — 119-121
Society for the History of Czechoslovak Jews — 186
Sokol (organization) — 188, 189
Sokol-Tůma, František — *author* 19, 20
Šolle, Zdeněk — *author* 12, 23, 69, 145, 151, 201
Sommer, June — *author* 81, 207
Sonneschein, Rosa — *subj.* 152
Soucek, Apollo — *subj.* 143
Soukup, Antonín — *author* 30, 32, 118
Soulard — *author* 80, 81, 114
South Dakota, Czechs in — 86
Sovík, Thomas — *author* 157
Spacek, Sissy — *subj.* 166
Špaček, Stanislav — *author* 20, 130
Španihel, Jaroslav — *author* 29
Speeches: Czechs in US — 43-44
Speidel, Bill — *author* 134
Speiser, Paul — *author* 178
Spěvák, Přemysl — *author* 52, 243
Spinka, Matthew — *author* 109
Spinka, Matthew — *subj.* 173
Splawn, Vlasta Margaret — *author* 27, 87, 118
Sports: Czechs in US — 167-169
Spurná, J. — *author* 83
Squires, Radcliffe — *author* 155
Srba, Bořivoj — *author* 164
Sršeň, Karel — *author* 79
Stalmach, Hilda Schiller — *author* 109
Staněk, Jan — *author* 9
Stange, Maren — *author* 164
Stansel, Valentin — *subj.* 241
Starý, Václav — *author* 105
Stasa, David — *author* 28
Stassen, Harold E. — *subj.* 137
Stastney, Mollie Emma — *author* 87
Stastny, Matthew — *author* 85
Stavařová, Ivana — *author* 65
Štědronský, František — *author* 2, 3, 9
Štefánik, Milan — *author* 190
Steiner, Burghard — *subj.* 135
Steiner, E. A. — *author* 62, 124
Štěpánek, Orin — *author* 32, 33
Štěpánek, Pavel — *author* 243
Stěpina, James F. — *subj.* 197
Štěrba, F. C. — *author* 235
Stern, Miroslava — *subj.* 245
Sternstein, Malynne — *author* 76
Stewart, Wayne — *author* 169
Stickgold, Emma — *author* 180
Stillman, Yanki — *author* 143
Stockbauer, Bette — *author* 89
Stohr, Carlos — *author* 244
Stolarik, Mark — *author* 194
Štolba, Josef — *author* 17, 24
Stone, Gregory Martin — *author* 28, 135
Stoppard, Tom — *subj.* 11
Strand, Paul — *author* 164; *subj.* 164
Strasser — *author* 175
Štrbáňová, Soňa — *author* 12, 73
Strnadel, Drahomír — *author* 49,

50, 51
Strobach, Augustin — *subj.* 240
Střížová, E. — *author* 222
Šturm, Rudolf — *author* 27, 153, 156
Styer, Henry Delp — *subj.* 143
Styer, Wilhelm D. — *subj.* 143
Sucher, Kathryn — *author* 100
Sullenger, T. Earl — *author* 81
Sullivan, Margaret LaPiccolo — *author* 80
Sullivan, W. T. — *author* 182
Šulz, Joseph — *author* 80
Sulzberger, Arthur Ochs — *subj.* 152
Sum, A. — *author* 52
Susskind, Walter — *subj.* 229
Sutnar, Ladislav — *author* 164; *subj.* 164
Svátek, Josef — *author* 237
Švejda, George — *author* 104
Svejkovský, František — *author* 56
Sviták, Ivan — *author* 57
Svoboda, George Josef — *author* 191
Svoboda, Joseph — *author* 82
Swehla, Francis — *author* 77
Sychrava, Lev — *author* 193
Szegedy-Maszak, Andrew — *author* 164
Táborský, Edward — *author* 199
Taggart, Glen — *author* 27, 118
Taussig, Edward David — *subj.* 144
Taussig, Helen Brooke — *subj.* 179
Taussig, Joseph Knefler — *subj.* 144
Taussig, Louis — *subj.* 132
Taussig, William Frank — *subj.* 176
Terzaghi, Karl — *author* 183; *subj.* 183
Tesař, František — *author* 37, 118
Tesařová, Lucie — *author* 65
Těsnohlídek, Rudolf — *author* 225
Texas, Czechs in — 9, 11, 12, 27, 28, 86-89, 184, 186, 208-209
Texas A&M University — 8
Textbooks: Czechs in US — 31-33
Thomas — *author* 136
Thompson-Raymová, Veronika — *author* 70
Thung, Swan N. — *author* 179
Tibbets, John C. — *author* 158
Tifft, Susan E. — *author* 153
Tigrid, Pavel — *author* 71
Tise, Sammy — *author* 215
Tlapák, Václav — *author* 48, 226
'Tlumače' (Czech interpreting guides) — 30-31
Tomek, Prokop — *author* 200
Tomeš, Josef — *author* 227, 228, 229
Trapl, Miloš — *author* 71, 72, 200
Traub, Otto — *author* 193
Travels through America: Czechs in US — 17-23
Trenský, Paul I. — *author* 229
Trnka, Jaroslav — *author* 162
Trojacek, Mary Betik — *author* 61
Trousil, František — *author* 90
Tucker, Spencer C. — *author* 144
Tůma, Emil — *author* 86, 193
Tůma, Josef — *author* 82, 83
Tůma, Oldřich — *subj.* x
Tůma, Vojtěch — *author* 25
Turčín, R. — *author* 63, 94
Tvaroh, Přemysl — *author* 86
Tvrzický, Joseph — *author* 189, 192
Twombly, Wells — *author* 167
Tye, Larry — *author* 174
Udell, Emily — *author* 191
Uherek, Zdeněk — *subj.* x
Uhlendorf, Bernhard Alexander —

author 155
Ulč, Otto — *author* 47
Ulčík, J. — *author* 36
United States, Czechs in
genealogy of — 203-217
general references — 2-45
cultural life and contributions — 144-169
economy — 126-135
history — 46-92
organizations — 184-189
people — 92-102
public life — 135-144
relations with the old Homeland — 189-202
religion — 102-113
scholarship – science – technology — 169-183
society — 114-126
United States Government
Czechs in Executive Branch — 136-138
Czechs in Judiciary Branch — 139-140
Czechs in Legislative Branch — 138-139
Czechs in military — 140-144
Unity of Bohemian Ladies in the US — 185
University of Chicago — 6, 8, 10, 45
University of Minnesota — 4, 5, 45
University of Nebraska — 8
Unterberger, Betty Miller — *author* 191
Updyke, E. B. — *author* 163
Upton, William Treat — *author* 158
Urban, Joseph Jaroslav — *author* 17
Urofsky, Melvin — *author* 139
Vaculík, Jaroslav — *author* 53
Vaculík, V. — *author* 53
Valášek, Hubert — *author* 4
Valášková, Naďa — *author* 53
Valchar, Jerry E. — *author* 185
Van Hoff, Joseph John — *author* 82
Van Hove, Leon — *author* 181
Van Meter, Sandy — *author* 77
Vandome, Agnes F. — *author* 168
Venezuela, Czechs in — 244
Vaněk, Pavel — *author* 23
Vanorny-Barcus, LaVina — *author* 101
Varlez, L. — *author* 93
Varn, Jacob — *subj.* 61
Vasilijev, I. — *author* 53, 65, 236
Vašků, Bedřich O. — *author* 34, 40, 112
Vecsey, George — *author* 16
Veleminský, Karel — *author* 146
Vesely, Janand — *author* 243
Veverka, František — *author* 34
Vičár, Jan — *author* 157
Vintrová, Magdalena — *author* 100
Virginia, Czechs in — 27, 89-90
Visual Art: Czechs in US — 161-164
Vita, Sister M. — *author* 35
Vital data, sources of: Czechs in US — 206-217
Vitula, M. — *author* 223
Vlach, J. J. — *author* 90, 124
Vlček, Tomáš — *author* 163
Vlchek (Vlček), Frank J. — *author* 15, 133; *subj.* 15, 133
Vlha, Marek — *author* 6, 13, 141, 192
Vojan, Jaroslav Egon Salaba — *author* 39, 62, 66, 75, 83, 93, 112, 198; *subj.* 198
Vojta, Václav — *author* 109
Vondracek, Paul — *author* 86

Vondrášek, Václav — *author* 195
Vongreyová, Jana — *author* 238
Voska, Emanuel Viktor — *author* 15, 119, 193, 198; *subj.* 15, 198
Voskovec, George — *subj.* 166
Voss, Carl H. — *author* 111
Vrana, William — *author* 210
Vránová, Martina — *author* 99
Vraz, E. Stanko — *subj.* 20
Vrázová, Vlasta — *author* 20, 150
Vrhel, František — *author* 102, 235
Wagner, H. R. — *author* 176
Wagner, Jan — *author* 18, 19, 62
Waldauf, Jan — *author* 230
Walker, Rosie — *author* 28, 146, 147
Wall, Alex — *author* 162
Wallace, Paul — *author* 22, 108, 224
Walter, Katherine — *author* 8
Warta, J. J. — *author* 41
Watkins, Albert — *author* 131
Watson, Robert — *author* 176
Wauthierová, L. — *author* 222
Wechsberg, Joseph — *author* 15, 156, 190; *subj.* 15, 156
Weinberger, Caspar Willard — *subj.* 137, 138
Weinberger, Jaromír — *subj.* 161
Weinlick, John R. — *author* 140
Weiskopf, Franz — *subj.* 156
Weiskopf, Victor F. — *subj.* 182
Welcl, J. V. — *author* 137
Wellauer, Marylyn A. — *author* 203
Wellek, René — *author* 173; *subj.* 173
Wells, John E. — *author* 90
Welzl, Jan E. — *author* 15, 21, 225; *subj.* 15, 21, 225
Wenzbauer, A. K. — *author* 230
Werfel, Franz — *subj.* 156
Werstadt, Jaroslav — *author* 193
Wertheimer, Max — *subj.* 176, 177
Wertheimer, Michael — *author* 177
Wertheimer, Valentin — *subj.* 123
West, Theresie M. — *author* 108
Western Bohemian Fraternal Association (ZČBJ) — 185
Wheatley, S. C. — *author* 148
White, James T. — *author* 166
White, Lewis, M. — *author* 142
White, Michael — *author* 209
Wiggs, Augusta Chalabal — *author* 100
Wilkinson, Andy — *author* 99
Williams, Jennifer D. — *author* 94
Williams, Marjorie L. — *author* 209
Wilson, Laurie J. — *author* 89
Wilson, Woodrow — *subj.* 135, 190, 191, 194
Wilt, Vera A. — *author* 75
Wingfield, Nancy M. — *author* 109
Wisconsin, Czechs in — 27, 90-91
Wise, Isaac Mayer — *author* 14, 111; *subj.* 14, 111
Wise, Stephen S. — *author* 111; *subj.* 111
Wittke, Carl — *author* 68
Wohl, David Philip — *subj.* 132
Wojta, Joseph Frank — *author* 91
Wolf, Ken — *author* 172
Wolf, Lucien — *author* 134
Wolf, Simon — *author* 143
Wolff, Konrad — *author* 160
Wood, David — *author* 80
Woods, Robert — *author* 128
Women: Czechs in US — 119-121
Working, Win V. — *author* 79
Wurl, Joel — *author* 4

Wychopen, L.C. — *author* 87
Wymetal, Wilhelm — *author* 159
Wynar, Lubomyr — *author* 4, 44
Yurka, Blanche — *author* 15, 167; *subj.* 15, 167
Zahradníček, Vladimír — *author* 7
Zach — *author* 153
Zamecnik, Paul C. — *subj.* 179, 180
Zaoral, Roman — *author* 221, 222, 223, 224, 230
Zárasová, Alena — *author* 120
Zaruba, Jerry, Jr. — *author* 207
Zatočil, A. — *author* 90
Zátopek, Jiří — *author* 88
Zdrůbek, František (Frank) — *author* 30, 31, 32, 33, 34, 39, 40, 43, 74, 75, 82, 111, 113, 146, 149; *subj.* 113
Zecker, Robert — *author* 142
Zeisberger, David — *author* 14, 16, 108, 225; *subj.* 14, 16, 108, 225
Žekulín, Nikolai — *author* 221
Zeman, Josefa Humpal — *author* 75
Zemánek, Dita J. — *author* 223
Zemek, Bedřich — *author* 64
Zenkl, Petr — *author* 16; *subj.* 16
Zentos, N.J. — *author* 84
Zerzan, John — *subj.* 11
Zibit, Benjamin — *author* 183
Zíbrt, Čeněk — *author* 62
Zima, Otakar — *author* 41
Zink, Lubor J. — *subj.* 229
Žižka, Arnošt — *author* 117
Zlámal, Oldřich — *author* 15, 198; *subj.* 15, 198
Zmrhal, Jaroslav J. — *author* 32, 35, 40, 167; *subj.* 149
Zumpfe, Joseph — *author* 85
Zwart, Ann Townsend — *author* 160

www.ingramcontent.com/pod-product-compliance
Lightning Source LLC
Chambersburg PA
CBHW061338280526
45784CB00001B/53